FEAR IS THE MIND KILLER

WHY LEARNING TO LEARN DESERVES LESSON TIME – AND HOW TO MAKE IT WORK FOR YOUR PUPILS

Dr JAMES MANNION
& KATE MCALLISTER

First published 2020

by John Catt Educational Ltd,
15 Riduna Park, Station Road,
Melton, Woodbridge IP12 1QT
Tel: +44 (0) 1394 389850
Fax: +44 (0) 1394 386893
Email: enquiries@johncatt.com
Website: www.johncatt.com

ISBN: 978 1 911382 77 5

Set and designed by John Catt Educational Limited

PRAISE FOR
FEAR IS THE MIND KILLER...

'As school systems around the world recognise that they are preparing their students for a world that no one can imagine, attention has, perhaps unsurprisingly, turned to whether it is possible to teach learners how to learn, and this has led to a rather polarised debate. On one side are those who argue that our traditional curriculum is unfit for the needs of today's learners, and that we should instead focus on the so-called 21st century skills. At the other are those who provide mountains of evidence that such skills tend to be highly specific to particular subjects and that learners rarely transfer what they have learned in one subject area to another. The truth is that both sides are right about some things. Some of what we need our students to learn is highly specific to a subject, but there are also ideas that go across the whole curriculum. The challenge is to discover what those are and how they can be effectively incorporated into the curriculum.

This is why *Fear Is the Mind Killer* by James Mannion and Kate McAllister is so welcome. The book tells the story of the implementation of a Learning to Learn curriculum in an English secondary school, and how that approach increased student achievement while at the same time closing the gap in achievement between students from more affluent and less affluent homes. More importantly, the story is told in sufficient detail that it provides a clear plan for how to implement such a curriculum elsewhere, with honest discussions of the challenges and difficulties encountered. I don't know of any other book that provides such clear guidance on how to harness the common elements of learning across the curriculum, bringing greater coherence to pupils' experiences in school while at the same time respecting the real differences between school subjects. Highly recommended.'

Professor Dylan Wiliam (Education researcher, author of
***Leadership for Teacher Learning* and *Embedded Formative Assessment*)**

'I really enjoyed *Fear Is the Mind Killer*. One of the most original pieces I've encountered in a long time, it elegantly sets out the case for Learning to Learn in a way that is both robust and fair. The Sea View study is handled very carefully and the impressive results make a comprehensive case for taking Learning to Learn seriously. The measured balance of the arguments actually makes the case stronger. *Fear Is the Mind Killer* reclaims those important aspects of provision which bring learning alive, deepen understanding and support pupils to become learners in the deepest sense of the word. Highly recommended for everyone in education.'

Mary Myatt (Author of *The Curriculum: Gallimaufry to Coherence* and *Back on Track: Fewer things, greater depth*)

'Mannion and McAllister thoughtfully thread the needle between two prevailing camps – the advocates of transdisciplinary Learning to Learn and thinking skills, taught explicitly and applied via project-based learning contrasted with those who declare that substantive content knowledge is paramount and that teaching generic skills is fruitless. As is the case with most educational matters, the optimal approach lies somewhere in the middle, and the achievement results their students attained affirm the value of the balanced approach they advocate.'

Jay McTighe (Educational author, consultant, and co-author of the *Understanding by Design®* series)

'As someone who has always been somewhat sceptical about the potential for Learning to Learn, I found this book an eye-opening and refreshing read. It clearly acknowledges the criticisms of previous attempts to implement the teaching of learning skills, whilst also showing how it could be implemented successfully in the future. As interest in metacognition and self-regulation grows, this will be the handbook we'll turn to.'

Mark Enser (Head of Geography and Research Lead, Heathfield Community College, author of *Teach like Nobody's Watching*)

'The field of Learning to Learn, or the development of "learning character", has come on in leaps and bounds in the last 20 years – and Mannion and McAllister's book makes a new and significant contribution: it extends still further the state of the art. It is accessible, witty and grounded in well-conducted research and a broad and deep understanding of the scientific literature. I can't recommend it too highly.'

Professor Guy Claxton (King's College London, author of *The Learning Power Approach*)

'Engagingly written and stylistically seamless... I found it not only informative, but it filled me with hope.'

Sue Gerrard (Education researcher and blogger)

'*Fear Is the Mind Killer* is an excellent, accessible, first-hand account of how teachers can successfully carry out an educational intervention in their own school which, while based firmly on available evidence from educational research, also takes into account the specific context and needs of their students. It should be an inspiration to all teachers who wish to do the same, and it makes an important contribution to our understanding of school-based research more generally.'

Professor Neil Mercer (Emeritus Professor of Education, University of Cambridge; Director, Oracy Cambridge; author of *Words and Minds: How we use language to think together*)

'Steeped in evidence, delightfully balanced and highly accessible – a much needed grand *tour de force* of the theory and practice around Learning to Learn.'

Peps McCrea (Dean of Learning Design, Ambition Institute, author of *Memorable Teaching*)

'A fascinating read that examines the controversy and draws exciting conclusions about the purpose and future of education. Its brutally honest analysis of the story of Learning to Learn and implementation of a *Learning Skills* curriculum in one school is told in a pragmatic and extremely readable style. This book reflects my own experience of the transformative influence of a curriculum that embraces the Learning to Learn philosophy.

But it offers much more than that. There is a thoroughly researched and extremely comprehensive story of a *Learning Skills* curriculum and its effect on outcomes. The authors show how students, especially the disadvantaged, learn more effectively if they experience a powerful Learning to Learn input delivered by a committed team of enthusiastic teachers. The GCSE results for the *Learning Skills* cohort demonstrate a closing of the gap for disadvantaged students and better results for all.

The book isn't just a convincing argument for the power of teaching metacognition, self-regulation and oracy; it offers a useful checklist for schools to create their own bespoke *Learning Skills* curriculum. Perhaps the most important conclusion is that schools improve when their primary focus is on the "how" of learning rather than just performance. Transferring *Learning Skills* across the whole curriculum creates just such a learning culture. The journey outlined at Sea View demonstrates that a laser-sharp focus on Learning to Learn develops better teaching, better outcomes and more emotionally resilient future citizens. And, as the title suggests, it might just help our kids become the fearless learners we want them to be!'

Jackie Beere OBE (Former head teacher, author of
The Complete Learner's Toolkit: Metacognition, mindset and beyond)

'A focused, ambitious and intelligent attempt to answer one of the more interesting questions of our educational era: is Learning to Learn of any use? Its authors, who have spent the small matter of 15 years (count them) researching and implementing highly developed and academically trialled programmes, argue, quite convincingly, that it is. Whilst its tone is light – on occasions it is very funny indeed – its intent is highly serious: the desire here is to find a way to make our students more independent learners. For those with an interest in this area, it will become a compulsory text.'

Phil Beadle (English teacher, author of *How to Teach*)

'As someone who is very critical of educational books, I was very pleased to see how James and Kate captured the great challenges of education – the personal and professional journey that is involved with engaging with deep and fundamental issues of learning. They open-mindedly explore their own claims with rigorous analysis and reference to a wide diversity of research. Their own stories and the level of commitment to a broad humanistic concept of education are still guiding many of my thoughts about my own future practice. A book to read, re-read and keep coming back to for advice.'

Alex Black (Teacher, educational consultant and teacher trainer)

'James and Kate's work on the topic of *Learning Skills*, as laid out in this excellent book, is the initiative that I'm most excited about in education at present. I see nothing more powerful, promising or impressive than providing students with the tools and freedom to take charge of their own learning.'

Ollie Lovell (Maths teacher, host of *The Education Research Reading Room* podcast, author of *Cognitive Load Theory in Action*)

'A quite remarkable book, which describes findings that everybody in education should sit up and take notice of. Written with clarity, humour and commendable honesty, *Fear Is the Mind Killer* builds a compelling case for the *Learning Skills* curriculum. The book leaves the reader with just one question: why isn't everyone doing this?'

Martyn Steiner (Environmental science teacher, Halcyon London International School)

'This book is a fascinating and rich account of the creation of a *Learning Skills* curriculum, and will be invaluable to any teacher who believes that we can help our students to become more confident, curious, proactive learners.'

Roo Stenning (Head of High School, St Andrews International School, Bangkok)

'This important book dives deeply into what many of us know instinctively as teachers – that children learn better when they connect with their peers and are given tools to reflect on and understand the process of learning. This thorough and well-documented study sheds light on why Learning to Learn has had such a rocky journey to date; looking carefully at the nuances of the classroom and learning that have so far made it difficult to implement and replicate Learning to Learn strategies. It is also a book that builds empathy and understanding across the plurality of views in the educational landscape and thus not only invites us to find ways forward to develop more confident, articulate, reflective and tolerant learners, but encourages us to uphold these qualities as well.'

Becky Carlzon (Early years teacher, co-author of *Powering up children*)

'What a fantastic read! *Fear Is the Mind Killer* brilliantly balances its grounding in research with clear practical advice. Above all else, it tells an inspiring human story of improving learning in schools to better prepare children for life. I want to buy a copy for every teacher I know.'

Andrew Threadgould (Head of Upper School, Dulwich College)

'A very thoughtful and thought-provoking book about the processes of learning that will stimulate dialogue among colleagues. The act of dialogue will, in itself, clarify thinking. The quantity and quality of references, academic books, papers, articles and blogs from a range of authors show the breadth and depth of research that underpins this book. It's a book that questions itself and its own premise through a fascinating discussion of the pros and cons of the Learning to Learn approach.

The book manages to be both academic and practical. It recognises that the central core of teaching is telling children things but extends this through the idea of children becoming more successful independent partners in their learning. I was struck by the resonances with other books in my career, most notably the two by John Holt that I had to read before starting my initial teacher training: *How Children Learn* and *How Children Fail*. *Fear Is the Mind Killer* sits very comfortably as an update to those books. It will support any teacher from beginning through to experienced colleagues.'

Chris Chivers (Former head teacher, university tutor and advisor)

'I had my highlighter all over this book as I was reading it... so many ideas... I just wanted to keep reading more. It made me feel like I was being invited into an exciting place where discourse is welcomed. How the book is written models exactly how we should work with children. It self-regulates! It's human. It's why I came into teaching. It's what, for many, will provide a lightbulb moment. It may reinvigorate knowledge-swamped teachers. And it makes a strong case for the teaching of *Learning Skills* in any curriculum.'

**Joanne Gurvidi (Assistant Principal,
Trumpington Community College, Cambridge)**

'This book is both visionary and realistic, rooted in classroom-based experiences that have been carefully researched and deeply examined by both scholars and practitioners. A pleasure to read, too.'

**Dr Scherto Gill (Senior Research Fellow,
Guerrand-Hermès Foundation for Peace)**

'*Fear Is the Mind Killer* is a welcome addition to education's literary canon.' It has a contemporary feel and situates itself firmly in current educational debates about the role of *Learning Skills*. It may come as a surprise, but some feel that education should concern itself primarily with the storage of knowledge in long-term memory. In fact, Ofsted's current definition of learning endorses that view. The book deals with the problems of such a view before outlining the authors' experience of introducing a *Learning Skills* intervention into a school.

As such, it provides a useful antidote to an overly mechanistic view of educational practice. Additionally, it offers a detailed view on what constitutes *Learning Skills* – structural elements, oracy, metacognition and self-regulated learning – before considering avenues for future thinking. *Fear Is the Mind Killer* is a research-evidenced view of *Learning Skills* that would be a worthwhile addition to any educator's bookshelf.'

**Dr Peter Ford (Advanced Digital Education and Professional Training
Programme Manager, University of Salford)**

'I found this book incredibly refreshing. The introduction really draws you in – I found myself nodding along. Mannion and McAllister are thorough in their use of evidence to back up claims, allowing the research to speak for itself. They present their research findings in a way that is easy to read and understand for teachers who may have limited experience of education research, without ever patronising the reader. They write as if they were talking to their peers, sharing their experiences in a frank and honest way. They tell the story of *Learning Skills* warts and all, leaving it up to the reader to make up their own mind. This is an important read for anyone with an interest in education.'

Amy Cooper (Director of Teaching and Learning, Trinity School)

'Power to the pupils! This inspiring, thoughtful and amusing book is jam-packed with stories, insights and practical steps and sets out an important manifesto for how the education system can be reformed to better serve the next generation of learners.'

**Simon Lancaster (Speech-writer,
author of *You are not human: How words kill*)**

ABOUT THE AUTHORS

DR JAMES MANNION, FCCT (@RETHINKINGJAMES)

James worked as a science teacher for 12 years. He has an MA in Person-Centred Education from the University of Sussex and a PhD in Learning to Learn from the University of Cambridge. James's doctoral thesis is an 8-year evaluation of the *Learning Skills* curriculum, the focus of this book. He is also a passionate advocate of practitioner inquiry as an approach to professional development, and implementation science as a framework for school improvement. James works as a Bespoke Programmes Leader at the Centre for Educational Leadership in the UCL Institute of Education. He is an Associate of Oracy Cambridge, an organisation dedicated to promoting effective speaking and listening skills in schools and the wider society, and a Founding Fellow of the Chartered College of Teaching. He lives in Sussex with his wife, son and dog, but not necessarily in that order.

KATE MCALLISTER, FRSA (@RETHINKING_KATE)

Kate worked as a French teacher for 14 years. She first started work on a year 7 'junior model' curriculum in 2005, with the aim of helping students develop the knowledge and skills they need to navigate the often difficult transition from primary to secondary school. She then spent the next 15 years refining the approach and improving the outcomes. In 2015, Kate took *Learning Skills* to new frontiers when she set up the School Bus Project, a charity providing mobile education for refugees. Following the closure of the refugee camps in Calais, Kate set up the Human Hive, a global community of organisations and individuals working together to create a more welcoming and inclusive world. Kate is an Associate of the Centre for Educational Leadership in the UCL Institute of Education, a Fellow of the Chartered College of Teachers and a Fellow of the Royal Society of Arts. In 2020, Kate set up the first Hive School in the Dominican Republic. The *Learning Skills* journey continues...

CONTENTS

INTRODUCTION

WHAT'S THE ONE THING YOU WOULD CHANGE?

If you had a magic wand, what's the one thing you would change about your pupils? We ask teachers this question a lot. Sometimes, they say things like this:

'I wish they would read for pleasure.'

'I wish they would behave better.'

'I wish they would respond to my feedback. They make the same mistakes week in, week out!'

These are perfectly sensible things to wish for and to work towards, and there are many excellent books that can help you achieve these goals. This book is about something different. Because whenever we ask this question, by far the most common response we hear is a variation on the following theme:

'I want my pupils to be more independent.'

'I want them to be less apathetic/needy/helpless.'

'I wish I didn't have to spoon-feed them all the time.'

Let's be clear: education is a truly wonderful thing. It's humanity's best hope for a brighter future. To paraphrase Dylan Wiliam: if education were a pill, you'd neck the bottle. But there is a problem with the way in which we educate young people, and it goes something like this. Children don't know what they don't know, and so teachers set the agenda for what needs to be learned, and how, and by when. This makes for an efficient use of time, but it has an unfortunate side effect. Many children become dependent on their teachers, and often they come to depend on them so much that they can't do very much... well, independently.

This problem takes many forms, and it can reach ludicrous extremes. For example, in primary and even in secondary schools, it is quite common for a pupil to approach their teacher to inform them that they have reached the bottom of the page. These young people have become so dependent on an adult telling them what to do that they feel they need permission to turn the page in their own exercise book! And it goes way deeper than *end-of-page-itis*. In researching this book, we posed the following question to the wonderful world of EduTwitter:

'What's the most helpless question a pupil has asked you?'

We don't typically get much reaction to our tweets, but this one attracted over 150 responses. The responses make for alarming reading. Here are some examples, grouped together into loose themes:

NON-PROBLEMS, POSED AS A STATEMENT RATHER THAN A QUESTION:

- 'My pen's on the floor.'
- 'My pencil broke' (while holding the pencil out to me – it needed sharpening).
- 'I don't have a chair' is one of my favourites. There's usually a stack quite obviously in the room.
- Student: 'I haven't got my book.' Me: 'Where is it?' Student: 'I think it's in my bag.' Me: 'Well then...'
- It's the questions they don't ask. Like, five minutes into a task and you ask why they haven't started and they say, 'I haven't got a pen.' And they're not the kind to be deliberately avoiding the work... Oh God, this is making my blood boil.

STATIONERY-BASED FUN:

- 'Should I sharpen my (very blunt) pencil?'
- 'Can I use blue pen instead of black?'
- 'Should I use a ruler to underline the date and title?'
- 'Shall I stick this in my book?' (which they then don't)

LAZY-ITIS:

- 'Why do we have to use the index? Can't you just tell us the page?'
- 'Can you fold this piece of paper for me?'
- 'Can I get him to draw this part for me? I can't draw.' (Year 6 art lesson)
- In the middle of my lesson: 'What lesson do we have next?'
  1. What has that got to do with my lesson?
  2. Why would I have your timetable memorised?
  3. Why don't YOU know your timetable, or at least have a copy to hand?

NOT LISTENING/FOLLOWING INSTRUCTIONS

- Five mins into task I've explained, had another student explain, AND is on the board, 'Miss, what do we have to do?'
- Me: (writes p. 54 on board) 'Turn to page 54... guys, we're starting on page 54...' Two sentences into reading... 'Miss, what page are we on?'
- 'Do we have to write in full sentences?' (after I've specifically told them to and it's written on the board)
- Me: 'Let's discuss the lesson objective. Don't copy it.' Student: 'Miss, go back. I didn't finish copying the objective.'

QUESTIONS THEY REALLY OUGHT TO KNOW THE ANSWER TO:

- 'How do you spell DNA/TV/GCSE/PSHE/ICT/KFC?' *[There were a lot of these!]*
- 'Do I have to put my name on this?'
- 'How do you fold in half again?'
- Student: 'Where's the water?' Me: 'In the tap.'
- When doing any form of assessment: 'Is this a real test?'
- 'Do I need to answer in French?' (Day before mock speaking exam)
- 'What lesson are we in?' (Twenty minutes into it)
- 'I've done question 1. What should I do now?'
- 'Where shall I put the rubbish?'

Now, you might object that holding the words of children up to scrutiny in this way is a bit uncharitable, and you would have a point – to a point. For example, at first glance, 'How do you spell TV?' is a funny question. But a child might never have seen it written down, or been told that TV is short for television, or they might have thought it was spelt 'teevee' or something. Also, some schools have strict protocols around how children set out their work, and so asking whether they should use a ruler to underline the title might be a reasonable question to ask. Fair enough. Asking questions in order to find out about the world is the cornerstone of child development. We often say to children, 'There's no such thing as a silly question' (even though there definitely is), but the sentiment is well intentioned: in schools, it's important that children feel comfortable to ask questions without fear of ridicule or the dreaded sarcastic retort.

But it would be an impressive feat of intellectual acrobatics to write off this entire list as a normal part of growing up – something that we as teachers can do nothing about. Every teacher will be familiar with questions and comments such as these, and the sense of exasperation that runs through the list is palpable. Indeed, many of the teachers we have worked with over the years have described a sense of feeling weighed down by the constant need to deal with questions that their pupils really should not need to ask.

It is also quite common to see these behaviours persist into late adolescence, and even into adulthood. Witness this recent account, relayed by a university professor:

> Recently, I received an email from a student asking me the name of a writer – a writer whose book we'd been reading for two weeks. (And discussing in class. And writing about in class.) It was not a textbook, anthology or unusual digital source. It was an old-fashioned printed book containing one play by one writer. I knew that the student owned the book, because I had seen her with it in class, and in fact, she had told me she was enjoying the reading. However, when it was time for her to do an assignment on the playwright... well, she was stumped. She just didn't know his name. I had to explain to her, carefully, and with what I hope was compassion, that if she hadn't picked up his name in the class discussions so far (or, I was thinking, in the course syllabus and calendar), then she could always try looking on the **front cover of the book**.[1]

Note that in all of these examples, the questions are almost always focused on mundane procedure, and not on learning. Just imagine how much more learning could be achieved if we could teach children in such a way that they become more confident, proactive, independent learners! Here, we arrive at the first of several burning questions that compelled us to write this book: *Is it possible to teach children to become more confident, proactive, independent learners?*

At first glance, this may appear to be a non-starter. How can you teach someone to teach themselves? It's like asking how you can feed someone to feed themselves – it's a logical absurdity, a snake that eats its own tail. And yet it remains a question worth asking. After all, we do feed children until they learn to feed themselves. At first, they make a mess of it and just mash stuff in the general direction of their face, but they get the hang of it eventually. And the messy phase is important, developmentally; the caterpillar must turn to mush before it can take flight on brightly coloured wing.

> **BURNING QUESTION**
>
> Is it possible to teach children to become more confident, proactive, independent learners?

What if, as well as teaching children *what* to learn, we could also teach them *how* to become confident, proactive, independent learners? Would this not be the most incredible gift we could bestow upon every young person before they head out into the world beyond the school gates, where there isn't always (or really ever) a teacher to tell you what to learn, and how, and by when? In fact, should this not be the central aim of our education system – to equip young people with the confidence, the curiosity and the skills they need for a life where learning never ends? In this 'post-truth' age of fake news and 'alternative facts', the need to teach young people how to learn, how to think for themselves, and how to evaluate the reliability of sources, for example, has never been more pressing. Is it possible to teach children in such a way that they become more discerning, more curious, more critically engaged with the world around them? And if so, why aren't we already doing it?

Before we address these questions, there is another common answer that we often hear when we ask, 'What's the one thing you would change?' This was expressed memorably by a teacher we worked with recently:

> *'The resident evil of fear of failure.'*

As teachers and as parents, we knew immediately what he meant. Among young people, fear of failure is all too common and can take many forms: fear of getting a bad grade, fear of public speaking, fear of putting their hand up to ask or answer a question, fear of letting people down, fear of what their peers will say if they do anything outside of accepted social norms. If they misspell a word, some young people will tear the entire page out of their exercise book and write it out again rather than have a single word crossed out. Some children's exercise books become extremely thin because they do this so frequently.

Fear of failure really is endemic in our schools, and it's really problematic. It causes many students to experience anxiety around exams. It contributes to any number of adolescent mental health conditions – especially in private schools, where students often feel an additional pressure to perform.[2] And in an education system where all young people are required to sit exams that around a third will fail (by design), fear of failure can ultimately stop some students from trying, in a last-ditch attempt to preserve a sense of self-worth: if they don't try, then they can't really fail, because they 'don't care about school anyway'. When we have arrived at the point where a young person has literally stopped trying to learn stuff, we can only conclude that something has gone very badly wrong.

Notice how, in each of these cases, fear *stops people from doing things*. Fear can stop young people in their tracks as they go to raise their hand, *even when they're confident they know the answer*. Fear can stop young people from volunteering to speak publicly, *even when a part of them really wants to give it a go*. Fear can stop young people from succeeding in exams, because they're so worked up *they can't even begin to access the contents of their long-term memory*. Fear keeps you in your lane and makes you afraid even there. In a literal sense, fear really is the mind Killer. It prevents young minds from growing and developing and trying new things as young minds should.

Here we arrive at our second burning question: *Is it possible to teach children in such a way that they become more courageous, fearless learners?* Is it possible to help them become more willing to take risks, more willing to step outside their comfort zone, and more willing to recognise failure for what it is – feedback in wolf's clothing – rather than something to be avoided at all costs?

> **BURNING QUESTION**
>
> Is it possible to teach children in such a way that they become more courageous, fearless learners?

INTRODUCING THE
LEARNING SKILLS CURRICULUM

We are not the first people to ask such questions. Around 40 years ago, a field of educational theory and practice known as 'Learning to Learn' emerged in an attempt to answer questions like these – with mixed results to date, a fascinating puzzle that we will unpack in Part I of this book. For the last 15 years or so, we have been on a mission to rethink Learning to Learn from first principles – to examine previous initiatives in close detail, to pull them apart and see whether we might be able to salvage the best bits, ditch one or two dodgy ingredients, add a few sprinkles of our own – and stick it all back together again to create a new approach that is greater than the sum of its parts. This 15-year mission has culminated in the *Learning Skills* curriculum, a new approach to Learning to Learn that we developed at Sea View, a secondary school in the south of England.

We believe (and have evidence to suggest) that *Learning Skills* advances the field in three important ways. First, it is a *complex intervention*, meaning that it has several moving parts. In this way, the 'marginal gains' to arise from each individual component stack up and interact, resulting in a larger effect size overall. We'll examine each of these moving parts in detail in Part II. However, the *Learning Skills* approach really boils down to a combination of three key ideas:

Metacognition: Monitoring and controlling your thought processes

Self-regulation: Monitoring and controlling your feelings and behaviours

Oracy: The ability to speak and listen effectively across a range of contexts

Metacognition and self-regulation have long been associated with Learning to Learn, as ways of helping children become more independent in their learning. Previously, oracy has not generally been viewed as a critical part of this process. However, we believe that developing children's speaking and listening skills is fundamental to helping them become more confident, proactive, independent learners. As well as learning how to listen and therefore learn more effectively from those around them, oracy helps young people find their voice – literally and metaphorically – and learn how to use spoken language as a tool for getting things done.

Second, we adopted a combined, *taught *and* embedded* approach. Throughout the last 40 years or so, there has been an ongoing debate about whether you can teach Learning to Learn through a discrete course or whether it should be embedded throughout the curriculum. There are pros and cons to each approach, and for some reason, previous Learning to Learn initiatives have almost always taken one or other of these positions. Adopting a pragmatic stance, we realised that if you really want to make this thing fly, you need to do both. You need to have timetabled *Learning Skills* lessons *and* to try as far as possible to have metacognition, self-regulation and oracy embedded in subject learning throughout the school. And third – crucially – it is necessary to put in place strategies to facilitate the *transfer* of knowledge, skills, habits and dispositions *out* of the *Learning Skills* classroom and *into* subject learning across the curriculum.

The *Learning Skills* study at Sea View

The intervention:

Taught *Learning Skills* lessons:

- Year 7: 5 lessons/week
- Year 8: 3 lessons/week
- Year 9: 2.5 lessons/week

A whole-school approach to teaching and learning

- Shared language of learning
- Joined up approach to CPD
- Strategies for transfer

Who was involved?

- 5 *Learning Skills* teachers (initially)
- 3 *Learning Skills* cohorts
- 1 control cohort
- Teachers & support staff
- Parents & carers

How was it studied?

- An 8-year study, following four cohorts from year 7 to GCSE

Outcome measures:

- Subject attainment at 3 years
- Subject attainment at GCSE
- A range of qualitative measures

Outcomes:

Significant gains in subject learning at 3 & 5 years:

Disadvantage gap at GCSE closed by over 65%:

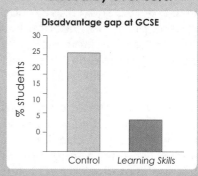

'I thought about everything that I have learned and how I can use that in other lessons. And it kind of sticks with you, and then it becomes part of you and your routine.' – Olivia, Year 8

To cut to the chase: we are convinced that the answer to these two burning questions is a resounding YES! It is absolutely possible to teach children how to become more confident, proactive, independent, courageous, fearless, effective learners. We know this because the *Learning Skills* curriculum was subjected to a rigorous, eight-year evaluation as the focus of James's PhD.[3] This evaluation found that *Learning Skills* led to significant gains in subject learning across the curriculum, with accelerated gains among children from disadvantaged backgrounds.[4, 5] We will explore this evidence in detail in Part II, but the essential ingredients of the *Learning Skills* curriculum – and the key findings from the Sea View study – are summarised in the infographic on the left.

Learning Skills was developed in a secondary school, but it's really a universal set of ideas and practices that can help anyone – adult, teen or toddler – become a more effective learner. The approach is already taking root and bearing fruit across a range of contexts: from reception classes to universities, from schools in deprived areas to elite international colleges, from workplaces to refugee camps. Although we adapt the methods we use when working with different age groups and in different settings, the underlying approach – the combination of metacognition, self-regulation and oracy – is fundamentally the same. It is still early days, but the evidence we have collected to date suggests that we might just be on to something here – and there is good reason to believe that *Learning Skills* will go from strength to strength in the years to come.

We have so much to tell you, it's difficult to know where to begin. So, we'll start at the beginning... our beginning, at least.

KATE'S STORY

When I began this project, I had no idea that it would prove to be so life changing. Stuart McLaughlin, the head teacher I had worked with for a few years, phoned me up and invited me to join his new school, to help him set up a Learning to Learn curriculum. I had worked on a similar initiative at our previous school for a number of years.

When we met, Stuart explained that we would have five hours each week with the entire year 7 cohort to deliver a bespoke curriculum. What's more, I could build my own team to design and teach it with me. I didn't have to think for long. From that point on, all I can really remember is Stuart waving his hand and saying, 'Just do that thing you do – and have it ready to go in September'. Or something along those lines – I was already imagining how amazing it would be and had stopped listening properly!

We set out to create a curriculum that would help all young people, especially the vulnerable ones, feel safe, welcome, connected to one another and able to flourish as confident, effective, courageous learners.

Never in my wildest dreams did I think that it would lead to all that it has, or that it would have such a profound impact – especially on me.

JAMES'S STORY

Even now, looking back, it's hard to believe it happened. The first I heard of it was an email from our head teacher, Stuart, to all staff: 'Who wants to get involved in designing and teaching a year 7 Learning to Learn curriculum?' I had recently completed a Masters in person-centred education – the best professional development I'd ever had by a country mile – and I was keen to take my teacher-research journey to the next level.

I was looking for a topic for a PhD; I knew in a heartbeat that this was it. I wasn't the only one to jump at the opportunity. There was a competitive selection process to decide who should be on the team. Kate had been brought in by Stuart to lead the initiative, although – in the best possible sense – she did an amazing impression of not being the boss. This was going to be owned by the team. The early team meetings were incredibly liberating, and utterly unlike anything we had experienced before. Our brief was as follows:

- We would have the whole of year 7 for five lessons a week, in mixed ability groups.
- The team would have the autonomy to do with this time as we saw fit.
- We had three months to pull something together.

It was clear that this was a once-in-a-career opportunity to do something bold and different. But it was incredibly daunting as well. What on earth would we do with five lessons a week?

OUR STORY

As it turned out, five lessons a week was just the beginning. When the first *Learning Skills* cohort moved into year 8, the curriculum time expanded with them. When they progressed into year 9, it expanded again. All told, the first cohort had more than four hundred lessons of *Learning Skills* over a three-year period. By this time, *Learning Skills* had essentially become a whole-school approach to teaching and learning.

When we left Sea View for pastures new, *Learning Skills* continued to evolve and adapt to new and diverse contexts. Throughout the last 15 years, we have faced countless challenges, learned from some whopping great mistakes, and made some purposeful strides in the right direction. But really, we are still at the beginning of this journey, which is a life's work at the very least. This book is an account of the story so far, and an invitation for you to get involved in the next chapter.

In Part I, we'll provide a brief history of Learning to Learn, to establish the context and the tradition in which the *Learning Skills* curriculum is situated – and a fascinating story it is too. As we will see in *Chapter 2: A brief history of Learning to Learn*, the literature on Learning to Learn has grown steadily throughout the last 50 years. Internationally, an interest in Learning to Learn remains in robust health. In the UK, the practice of Learning to Learn in secondary schools reached its peak around 2010. However, for the last ten years or so, it has been in a state of steep decline. We aren't aware of any published data on the prevalence of Learning to Learn in the UK in recent years. So, we recently conducted a poll on Twitter, which received over 1700 responses in total:

1. For secondary teachers who were teaching in the 2000s: Did you ever work in a school where there were timetabled 'Learning to Learn' lessons in year 7?

64% yes, 36% no

2. For secondary teachers teaching currently: In the school where you work, are there timetabled 'Learning to Learn' lessons in year 7?

13% yes, 87% no

This is a remarkable decrease – from 64% to 13% in around ten years. The results of this poll confirmed what we suspected regarding the recent collapse in taught Learning to Learn courses in the UK. In Part I, we will explore the reasons behind this collapse. In particular, we will attempt to resolve what we refer to as the 'Learning to Learn paradox' – the fact that the field is rooted in apparently contradictory research findings. On the one hand, we will discover that Learning to Learn provides 'high impact for very low cost, based on extensive evidence'.[6] On the other, we will find that whenever Learning to Learn initiatives have been implemented and evaluated on a large scale, the benefits tend to fall away, leading some to conclude that Learning to Learn is 'bad education'.

Unpacking the research, we will conclude that reports of the death of Learning to Learn have been greatly exaggerated. Looking beyond the evidence, we will round off Part I by putting Learning to Learn on trial, to examine a number of arguments for and against teaching children *how*, as well as *what*, to learn.

We think it's important to understand the history of Learning to Learn, because this allows us to stand on the shoulders of giants and avoid repeating the mistakes of the past. We also believe it's important to understand the theory of Learning to Learn, because it's only when you grasp the 'why' of something that you can really get to grips with the 'what' and the 'how'.[7] However, if you're a time-pressed teacher and you're thinking, *this is all well and good, but what does it look like in the classroom?*, you might want to turn straight to Part II.

Often, we describe educational research using quite scientific language: research questions, data analysis, effect sizes and so on. And indeed, all that stuff features in this book. But in our experience, when you're a teacher, you don't feel much like a scientist. You feel like a really busy person with an endless to-do list, trying your best to do something that is at once important and mundane, elating and frustrating. So, we begin Part II with the story of *Learning Skills* as we experienced it as teachers – what happened, what it felt like and what we learned along the way.

In *Chapter 5: Components of a complex intervention*, we set out in detail what the *Learning Skills* curriculum is, and how it differs from previous Learning to Learn initiatives. Primarily, this will focus on the way in which we reconceptualised Learning to Learn as a complex intervention – an intervention with several moving parts. For each moving part, we will provide a rationale for its inclusion in the programme and consider what it looks like in practice. This is by far the longest chapter, because we really want this book to be of practical use to teachers and school leaders.

In *Chapter 6: The evidence for Learning Skills*, we outline the key findings from the Sea View study, which followed four cohorts of students from year 7 through to year 11 (one control cohort and three *Learning Skills* cohorts). In *Chapter 7: The case for Learning Skills*, we pull all the evidence together and explain why and how we think it works. And we round off Part II with a checklist that we hope will serve two purposes. First, implementation: to set out five simple, practical steps you can take to maximise the chance that *Learning Skills* will bring about the changes you want to see in your pupils, in your setting, at this particular point in time. And second, evaluation: to serve as a set of criteria for deciding which schools to include in future evaluations of the approach, should *Learning Skills* become as widely implemented as we hope it will.

Finally, in the *Conclusion*, we will return to the 'resident evil of fear of failure'. We will find that even though fear can be an incredibly powerful force, it is remarkably fragile when you expose it to the light. We will identify a number of antidotes to fear – practical steps we can take to overcome, minimise and dissipate the endemic fear of failure that permeates our schools – and explain how these antidotes can be enacted by implementing a *Learning Skills* curriculum. And we will suggest that the question of how teachers and school leaders can help young people become more confident, independent, fearless learners really boils down to our understanding of what education is for.

This book is about a whole-school approach to teaching and learning that improves children's ability to learn subject knowledge and pass exams, and closes the disadvantage gap – at least, it did in the Sea View study. Whether these findings can be replicated elsewhere remains to be seen. That, we hope, is where you come in, reader, and we will get to that in good time. But when we set out on this journey 15 years ago, we were not motivated by a desire to turn Ds into Cs, As into A*s or 8s into 9s.

What gets us out of bed in the morning is the desire to help every young person find their feet, find their voice, get better at learning stuff, develop a strong sense of identity – and, in so doing, a streak of resilience – and become a more confident, independent, critically, socially and politically engaged citizen of the world. In short, we want to help every young person find their 'on switch'. We strongly suspected that if we set out to achieve this, we would see exam results improve and the disadvantage gap close – and indeed, that's what we did see. Exam results are important – but in this case, they weren't the motivating factor, because there is more to human development than passing exams. At heart, the *Learning Skills* curriculum is rooted in a vision of education as a process of self-actualisation – helping every young person grow into themselves, become more fully themselves, and develop into the best version of themselves they can possibly be.

One more thing before we get started. In recent years, there has been a groundswell of interest in the concept of metacognition, which is often referred to as 'thinking about thinking', but a better definition is 'monitoring and controlling your thought processes', as we will explain in *Chapter 2: A brief history of Learning to Learn*. One way to promote metacognition might be to create a rule that each pupil can only ask the teacher one question in a given lesson. This kind of practice helps pupils monitor their internal dialogue and realise that 'Where shall I put the rubbish?' might not be the best use of their question.

We'll explore metacognition in detail throughout this book, but we would like to make an important point at the outset. Often, we find that metacognition is discussed in quite narrow terms – as a strategy for helping a student improve their performance on a weekly spelling test, for example.[8] However, when the developmental psychologist John Flavell coined the term in the 1970s, he envisaged something altogether bolder and more far-reaching:

> It is at least conceivable that the ideas currently brewing in this area could some day be parlayed into a method of teaching children (and adults) to make wise and thoughtful life decisions as well as to comprehend and learn better in formal educational settings.[9]

This is very much in line with our understanding of metacognition and our vision for education – that as well as teaching children how to read, write and add up, we might also teach them in such a way that they develop into confident, proactive, independent learners – and maybe even make some 'wise and thoughtful life decisions' along the way. A glance at the average news bulletin suggests that we could do with a bit more wisdom and thoughtfulness on this planet of ours.

If we are going to realise this bold vision of education as a process of self-actualisation (with improved attainment and a closing of the disadvantage gap as happy consequences), we are going to have to face, embrace and overcome our fears – teachers and students alike. The good news is that when we do so, it makes us stronger – individually and collectively. Confronting fear may be daunting, but it is also the very thing that makes us develop and grow into the best version of ourselves that we can become. This is why we are so drawn to the 'litany against fear' that features on the inside cover of this book, and from which the book takes its title: 'Where the fear has gone, there will be nothing. Only I will remain'.

YOUR STORY

We think the ideas and practices in this book have the power and the potential to produce generations of confident, articulate, curious, effective, proactive, switched-on, courageous learners. At present, whether the positive findings from the Sea View pilot study can be replicated elsewhere remains to be seen. We strongly suspect that they can not only be replicated, but significantly improved upon. But we are still at the start of this journey, and that part of the story lies ahead of us.

This, we hope, is where you come in, reader. Because one thing is for sure: we can't do this alone. So, whoever you are, whatever you think of the ideas in this book, and wherever you live and work: we want to hear from you. We invite you to dive in, discuss it with your colleagues, and let us know what you think using one or more of the many available channels:

Contact:	rethinking-ed.org/contact
Twitter:	twitter.com/rethinking_ed
Instagram:	instagram.com/rethinking.education
Facebook:	facebook.com/groups/rethinkinged
Mighty Networks:	rethinking-education.mn.co

Fancy an adventure?

PART I
THE LEARNING TO
LEARN PARADOX

CHAPTER 1

HIGH IMPACT FOR LOW COST, OR SNAKE OIL FOR HIPSTERS?

'Those who cannot remember the past are condemned to repeat it.'

George Santayana (1905)[1]

In 2010, the UK's newly formed coalition government announced the establishment of a new body, the Education Endowment Foundation (EEF), on a wave of uncompromising rhetoric about 'turning around our weakest schools' by 'trailblazing innovative, bold and rigorous approaches to school improvement'[2]. The EEF's mission statement explains that the organisation is 'dedicated to breaking the link between family income and educational achievement. We aim to raise the achievement of [3- to 18-year-olds], particularly those facing disadvantage; develop their essential life skills; and prepare young people for the world of work and further study'.[3]

In 2011, the EEF published the *Teaching and Learning Toolkit*, which aims to help schools figure out how best to spend the Pupil Premium (additional government money paid directly to schools with the aim of improving outcomes for disadvantaged children). This essentially involved carrying out a wide-ranging review of the educational research literature and comparing the effect sizes of various practices in a kind of league table, ranging from the highly impactful to the highly counterproductive.[4] It proved influential; by 2016, according to EEF chairman Sir Peter Lampl, 'a staggering two-thirds of UK schools' were using the Toolkit to inform decision-making.[5] At the time of writing, this figure is likely to have staggered even higher.

Figure 1.1. The twelve most impactful practices in the EEF Teaching and Learning Toolkit[6]

Teaching and Learning Toolkit

An accessible summary of the international evidence on teaching 5-16 year-olds

Toolkit strand	Cost	Evidence strength	Impact (months)
Feedback High impact for very low cost, based on moderate evidence.	£	🔒🔒🔒	+8
Metacognition and self-regulation High impact for very low cost, based on extensive evidence.	£	🔒🔒🔒🔒	+7
Reading comprehension strategies High impact for very low cost, based on extensive evidence.	£	🔒🔒🔒🔒	+6
Homework (Secondary) Moderate impact for very low cost, based on limited evidence.	£	🔒🔒	+5
Mastery learning Moderate impact for very low cost, based on moderate evidence.	£	🔒🔒🔒	+5
Collaborative learning Moderate impact for very low cost, based on extensive evidence.	£	🔒🔒🔒🔒	+5
Early years interventions Moderate impact for very high cost, based on extensive evidence.	£££££	🔒🔒🔒🔒	+5
One to one tuition Moderate impact for high cost, based on extensive evidence.	££££	🔒🔒🔒🔒	+5
Oral language interventions Moderate impact for very low cost, based on extensive evidence.	£	🔒🔒🔒🔒	+5
Peer tutoring Moderate impact for very low cost, based on extensive evidence.	£	🔒🔒🔒🔒	+5
Phonics Moderate impact for very low cost, based on very extensive evidence.	£	🔒🔒🔒🔒🔒	+4
Outdoor adventure learning Moderate impact for moderate cost, based on moderate evidence.	£££	🔒🔒🔒	+4

As we can see in Figure 1.1, perched atop this league table of educational effectiveness – which is actually quite a problematic idea because it compares apples and oranges, but let's park that for now[7] – we find 'feedback', which we are told provides 'high impact for very low cost'. That sounds absolutely amazing, doesn't it? High impact? Very low cost? What's not to like? Well, quite a lot as it turns out. Because when you dig into the research that sits behind this headline, you find that if you implement a feedback intervention in your school, there's around a one in three chance that you'll be making things worse.[8, 9]

> **TEACHER TAKEAWAYS**
> Even when we implement education's 'best bets' (e.g. a feedback intervention), there is a surprisingly high chance that we can make things worse.

This is rather an astonishing fact, don't you think? Remember, this is 'feedback', which sits at the top of the toolkit – education's best bet, you might say. Imagine if a head teacher stood at the front of the school hall on a training day and said, 'Good morning, colleagues. The senior team and I have consulted the research, and we're all going to do this new thing. There's just one thing – there is around a one in three chance that we'll be making things worse. WHO'S WITH ME?' They would be unlikely to garner much support for their initiative. However, this is *precisely* what school leaders risk when rolling out any new research-informed policy. The moral of the story is clear: when seeking to implement findings from the research literature in new and diverse contexts, we need to tread with extreme caution.

METACOGNITION AND SELF-REGULATION: THE DYNAMIC DUO

In second place, bobbing in feedback's turbulent wake, we find 'metacognition and self-regulation'. Now, before we go any further, we should probably address the fact that the phrase 'metacognition and self-regulation' tends to induce a range of emotions in people, not all of them positive. This is not language you often hear at the bus stop or down the pub. Who are these impactful imposters, and what do they want? Well, that's more or less what this book is about, so let's get cracking.

The EEF toolkit suggests that metacognition and self-regulation provide 'high impact for very low cost, based on extensive evidence', which is even more impressive than the entry for feedback, whose claims to glory are rooted merely in 'moderate' evidence. To get to grips with this dynamic duo, we will begin by quoting at length the toolkit entry for 'metacognition and self-regulation'. This is not the best definition in our view – we'll explain why in *Chapter 2: A brief history of Learning to Learn* – but it will serve our purposes for now:

> *Metacognition and self-regulation approaches aim to help pupils think about their own learning more explicitly, often by teaching them specific strategies for planning, monitoring and evaluating their learning. Interventions are usually designed to give pupils a repertoire of strategies to choose from and the skills to select the most suitable strategy for a given learning task.*
>
> *Self-regulated learning can be broken into three essential components:*
>
> - *Cognition: the mental process involved in knowing, understanding, and learning;*
> - *Metacognition: often defined as 'learning to learn'; and*
> - *Motivation: willingness to engage our metacognitive and cognitive skills.*[10]

According to the EEF, then, self-regulated learning is a broad umbrella term comprising cognition (thinking), metacognition (thinking about thinking) and motivation (the desire to learn). And all of this can be further broken down into a number of processes, including knowing and understanding; planning, monitoring and evaluating learning; thinking about learning; learning how to get better at all of the above; and being willing and able to do so. So, it should be clear at the outset that we aren't talking about something simple here. Metacognition and self-regulation are inherently multifaceted concepts that consist of, and are intertwined with, many other aspects of cognitive, social and emotional development. To put it another way: Learning to Learn is *complex*.

It is also worth mentioning that Learning to Learn is *popular*. Perhaps unsurprisingly, there is no shortage of people on the planet who want to get better at learning stuff. For example, an online course called *Learning How to Learn* has been taken by over 2 million people in around 200 countries, and was described by the *New York Times* as 'the most popular course of all time'.[11]

Here, however, we encounter the first indication that there may be more to Learning to Learn than meets the eye. The creator of *Learning How to Learn*, Professor Barbara Oakley, recently co-authored a book of the same name,[12] which was described in glowing terms by one reviewer as 'rescuing the idea of "learning how to learn"'.[13] But hang on a minute. According to the EEF, metacognition and self-regulation – widely viewed as synonymous with Learning to Learn – are among the most impactful practices teachers can use. Why on earth might something so impactful need 'rescuing'?

DISSENTING VOICES

Despite the EEF's glowing report for metacognition and self-regulation, not everybody is equally enthusiastic about Learning to Learn. There are a number of reasons for this, which we will explore in detail in *Chapter 3: Learning to Learn on trial.* Here, we will briefly consider a few common objections, beginning with the fact that Learning to Learn often involves children working in groups. Here's the EEF toolkit again:

> *These strategies are usually more effective when taught in collaborative groups so that learners can support each other and make their thinking explicit through discussion.*[14]

The idea of children learning through collaboration and discussion may not strike you as particularly controversial, but not everybody is on board with it. Presumably, Michael Gove, the former Secretary of State for Education in England who set up the EEF, did not familiarise himself with the key recommendations of the organisation he founded, because in 2013, he said:

> *All too often, we've seen an over-emphasis on group work – in practice, children chatting to each other – in the belief that is a more productive way to acquire knowledge than attending to an expert.*[15]

To be fair to Mr Gove, who would later famously declare that people have had enough of attending to experts,[16] he is not alone in his dislike of group work. For example, if you type 'group work meme' into an image search engine, you will find plenty of evidence for the unpopularity of group work, with reference made to different types of group member, some of whom say they will help but don't, disappear at the start and don't reappear until the work is done, don't know what's going on, or end up doing 99% of the work. Others imply that while the aim of group work may be to teach communication, responsibility, collaboration and teamwork, what a person may actually learn from group work is to trust no one.

Whenever we share such memes in our workshops, they tend to raise the laughter of recognition. But don't you think they're also a bit tragic? If people's experience of working with others leaves them feeling that they can trust no one, we have a serious problem. Human beings are amazing – we made the internet out of bits of metal we found in the ground, for goodness' sake – but it is fair to say we could do with a few pointers on how to get along with one another a bit better, as anyone who has spent more than five minutes on the internet will attest.

We understand why this anti-group-work feeling exists. If you get children working in groups without first teaching them how to do so successfully, it can easily go pear-shaped. As Littleton and Mercer (2013) point out, group work is a bit like the little girl in Longfellow's poem: when it is good, it is very good indeed – and when it is bad, it is horrid.[17] Happily, it's surprisingly easy to teach children how to talk and work productively in groups. By agreeing a simple set of ground rules for how to talk together, we can transform the quality of group work. We'll explain how to do this in *Chapter 5: Components of a complex intervention*. We'll also explore some powerful arguments for 'children chatting', otherwise known as oracy education.

But the challenges of implementing 'metacognition and self-regulation' successfully go beyond group work. Here's another extract from the EEF toolkit:

> The potential impact of [metacognition and self-regulation] is high, but can be difficult to achieve in practice as they require pupils to take greater responsibility for their learning and develop their understanding of what is required to succeed.[18]

Again, the notion of students taking greater responsibility for their learning might seem reasonable enough – desirable, even. However, some people – typically, those on the traditional (as opposed to the progressive) side of the aisle – are unconvinced. Children, the argument goes, are novices – they don't know what they don't know. It is therefore more efficient if the curriculum is designed and taught by an expert, rather than letting the children call the shots. Traditionalists often cite a study – the unfortunately named *Project Follow Through* – which found that Direct Instruction, a highly structured, scripted approach to teaching, was more effective than other approaches.[19] Such concerns are perhaps what prompted Tom Bennett (2013) to write: 'Learning to Learn: It isn't even a thing. We've been hoaxed... the hipsters are selling snake oil on this one, whether they know it or not.'[20]

Elsewhere, we find educational researchers and commentators objecting to Learning to Learn on the basis that 'teaching generic skills does not work',[21] or that the idea we can teach transferrable skills is a 'myth'.[22] Essentially, the argument here is that attempting to teach generic skills such as critical thinking in the absence of subject knowledge is misguided

– that in order to think critically about a particular historical event, say, the most important thing is that you are knowledgeable about that period of history.[23] Knowledge is foundational, and our ability to think critically emerges from a rich knowledge base. Therefore, instead of teaching generic 'learning skills', schools should focus primarily on teaching subject knowledge – the stuff that critical thinking is made of. This understanding of the primacy of knowledge draws on ideas from evolutionary psychology and cognitive science, and it presents a serious challenge to advocates of Learning to Learn. We will explore these arguments in detail in *Chapter 3: Learning to Learn on trial*.

We also find articles by people like Professor Dennis Hayes, who has written that 'Education is bad for you when it is about the process of "Learning to Learn", rather than learning'.[24] In their book *The Dangerous Rise of Therapeutic Education*, Ecclestone and Hayes (2008) suggest that an 'interest in personalised learning and learner voice, learning to learn and assessing soft skills erodes [the] belief that young people need subject knowledge'.[25] Elsewhere, Hayes has warned against the 'damaging claim that it is important for children and young people to engage in "Learning to Learn"... What all the supposedly exciting and innovative techniques amount to is the idea that children and young people need to learn to learn before they can, er, learn'.[26]

EDUCATIONAL MARMITE

Hopefully you can see by now that the literature on Learning to Learn paints a rather puzzling, polarised picture. Either Learning to Learn is one of the most effective games in town, offering 'high impact for very low cost, based on extensive evidence' – or it's bad education that overlooks the importance of subject knowledge; a snake oil hoax peddled by unwitting hipsters. There is not a great deal of grey in this picture.

This unsatisfactory state of affairs – or this fascinating mess, depending on your attitude toward complexity – is the Learning to Learn paradox, and this is the overarching theme that runs through Part I of this book. Learning to Learn, it seems, is educational Marmite. Either it leads to the palace of wisdom, or it's the road to hell. Which, of course, begs the question: which is it? Or might the truth be something more nuanced; something more interesting; something in between?

As with all the best stories, if you really want to understand what's going on, you need to start at the very beginning...

CHAPTER 2

A BRIEF HISTORY OF LEARNING TO LEARN

'Let the beginning and the end of our didactics be: seek and find the methods where the teacher teaches less, but they who sit in the desks learn more. Let schools have less rush, less antipathy and less vain effort, but more wellbeing, convenience and permanent gain.'

John Amos Comenius (1632)[1]

At heart, the idea is a simple one. Learning to Learn is a field of educational theory and practice that aims to help people – children and adults alike – get better at learning stuff. The whole enterprise is based on the observation that some people are better at learning stuff than others, and on the assumption that it is possible for anyone to get better at learning stuff, given the right opportunities, instruction and guidance. Typically, such guidance involves drawing attention to the processes of learning, as well as the content (the 'how' as well as the 'what').

The processes of learning are often implicit, tacit, unspoken; in Learning to Learn, we draw them out into the light and make them explicit, tangible – and therefore learnable. Learning to Learn also involves people taking more ownership (and therefore control) over their own learning through things like goal setting, trying out different approaches, monitoring and evaluating their progress toward those goals, and deciding on next steps.

> **TEACHER TAKEAWAYS**
>
> The processes of learning are often implicit, or invisible. In Learning to Learn, we draw them out into the light and make them explicit, visible – and therefore learnable.

LEARNING, PERFORMANCE AND MARGINAL GAINS

On a deeper level, Learning to Learn is rooted in an understanding of the difference between *learning* and *performance*. Consider a sprinter. They might try to improve their performance by simply doing lots of sprinting. Over time, they will likely see some small improvements in their performance, reinforcing their belief in the idea that 'practice makes perfect' and deepening their resolve to practise sprinting even more. However, in recent years we have discovered that if you really want to get better at something, rather than focusing on performance, it is often more effective to focus on improving *the processes that underpin* high performance.[2, 3]

Thus, rather than simply gritting their teeth and doing more sprinting, the best athletes and coaches spend their time thinking about things like diet, sleep, their training regime, how they breathe, how they come out of the blocks, sports psychology, race tactics and so on. This is the central idea of *marginal gains theory*, the wisdom of which can be seen in the astonishing success of the British cycling team in recent years.[4] As described by Sir David Brailsford, the team's former Performance Director:

> The whole principle came from the idea that if you broke down everything you could think of that goes into riding a bike, and then improved it by 1%, you would get a significant increase when you put them all together... There's fitness and conditioning, of course, but there are other things that might seem on the periphery, like sleeping in the right position, having the same pillow when you are away and training in different places. Do you really know how to clean your hands? Without leaving the bits between your fingers? If you do things like that properly, you will get ill a little bit less. They're tiny things, but if you clump them together it makes a big difference.[5]

The sprinter who tries to improve their performance by doing lots of sprinting is analogous to the student who prepares for an exam by doing lots of practice exam papers. In each case, one's preparations should of course *include* practice sprints and past papers. But such things should really be seen as checkpoints along the way, rather than as a strategy for success.

MARGINAL GAINS THEORY

The idea that many small incremental changes can combine to bring about significant improvements in overall performance.

CHARACTERISTICS OF SUCCESSFUL STUDENTS

High-performing students take many forms. Occasionally, a teacher will encounter one of those infuriating individuals who barely puts pen to paper, rarely hands in their homework and routinely achieves top marks. But such individuals are rare – and even these students often find that such a *laissez-faire* approach doesn't work so well at A level, by which time it's not so easy to change your stripes.

Over the years, we have asked many of our most successful students about how they approach learning. Typically, they describe a range of ways in which they embody the principles of metacognition and self-regulation. In particular, successful students often:

- have a process for identifying what they know and what they don't, and focus on systematically filling in the gaps in their knowledge.
- make lists of short-term, achievable goals and tick them off when they've been met, creating a 'virtuous cycle' of getting things done alongside a rewarding sense of achievement and progress.
- experiment with a range of strategies for learning and revising, so that they come to know what works for them.
- pay attention to how they feel, physically and emotionally, and act accordingly – stretching, taking short breaks, and giving themselves tasks suited to their mood.
- monitor their own progress toward medium and long-term goals, adapting their approach by trialling new strategies and behaviours as necessary.
- are motivated to do the above:
  - in the short term, by treating themselves to simple rewards in exchange for progress (e.g. 'I'll finish making flash cards on this topic and then I'll have a biscuit').
  - in the medium to long term, by having a clear idea about what all this hard work is in aid of (e.g. by having clearly defined career or educational goals).

Like athletes, successful students concern themselves with the micro-processes that underpin high performance; the performance takes care of itself. When you see the recipe for successful independent learning written down like this, it can seem deceptively simple. This brings us to the next of our burning questions: *Are the habits of effective learners themselves learnable?*

> **BURNING QUESTION**
> Are the habits of effective learners learnable?

FEAR IS THE MIND KILLER

This is the question that drives the Learning to Learn movement, which is effectively an ever-growing number of people who respond to this question by asking, 'Well, why wouldn't they be?'

THIS STUFF IS NOT NEW

The quote (at the start of this chapter) from Comenius – the 17th century teacher and philosopher often described as the 'father of modern education' – suggests that the desire for 'methods where the teacher teaches less, but they who sit in the desks learn more' is not exactly new.

Nobody is saying we should do away with teachers. However, there is clearly a balance to be struck somewhere between the situation where the teacher works far harder than their pupils, who in turn expect to be spoon-fed what they need to know, when they need to know it (exhausting in practice and all too common), and an idealised, romantic vision of education based entirely on open-ended inquiry and unguided 'discovery learning' (appealing in theory; in practice... not without its challenges).

Psychologists first started paying attention to metacognition in the late 19th century, although they used slightly different language. For example, the psychologist William James wrote in 1890 that 'a mind which has become conscious of its own cognitive function plays what we have called "the psychologist" upon itself. It not only knows the things that appear before it; it knows that it knows them.'[6]

This central insight – that people can become aware of their own cognitive processes, and that this can be a good thing – was developed throughout the early 20th century, with theorists such as James, Piaget and Vygotsky illuminating different parts of the whole.[7] By the mid 20th century, people were starting to apply the idea of 'thinking about thinking' to education. One of the earliest explicit references to Learning to Learn in the literature is by the American educator Alice Miel (1959):

> Curriculum workers must be alert to... the points where many people or certain individuals seem to stop short of the maturity they might achieve. They must be guided... by changes in process – developments which call for new dimensions of understanding and skill and human sympathy. In short, it appears that learning more about learning is a primary, continuing responsibility of the teacher and of all other educators with more or less direct

46

influence on the learning opportunities being offered in any one school or college. Indeed, learning about learning is a key to curriculum development.[8]

Here we can see some of the themes of later thinking around Learning to Learn beginning to emerge – notably, the idea that young people can be helped to greater maturity than they otherwise might achieve, and that doing so requires a multi-pronged approach involving curriculum design, understanding, skill and sympathy. However, it is also clear that 'learning about learning' is seen here as a concern for teachers rather than for the students themselves.

The shaping of the field can also be seen in the 1966 publication *Learning about Learning*, edited by the influential American psychologist Jerome Bruner.[9] This report was pioneering in identifying the big ideas that would shape the field in the years to come, including social and emotional learning, character education and thinking and reasoning skills.

The literature on Learning to Learn has grown exponentially throughout the last 50 years (Figure 2.1).[10] According to the Education Resources Information Center (ERIC) database, there were no articles published on Learning to Learn prior to 1967. In the period 2016–2020, which was still not complete when this analysis was carried out, there have been over 5000 articles published – and this trend does not show any sign of slowing down any time soon. In Figure 2.1, we can also see how the literature on Learning to Learn really got going in the 1970s, following foundational work into metacognition by John Flavell, Ann Brown and others.[11, 12, 13] As with so many things, the Learning to Learn movement began in that remarkable, creative decade that was the midwife to *Star Wars*, glam rock, email – and both the authors of this book.

Figure 2.1. Published literature on Learning to Learn

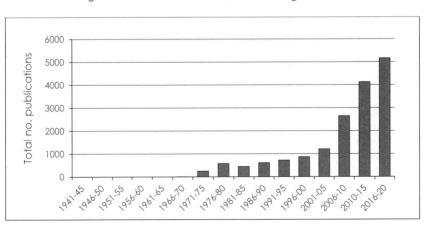

FOUR GENERATIONS OF LEARNING TO LEARN

Looking back over the 40 or so years since the word 'metacognition' entered the lexicon, it is safe to say that Learning to Learn has been on a journey. There have been highs; there have been lows; and, as we will see, this journey has some distance left to run. In a really useful publication, Claxton (2006) suggested that the theory and practice of Learning to Learn can be seen as having evolved through four distinct, if overlapping, generations of theory and practice:

> There have, over the last twenty years or so, been three generations of response, each more powerful than the last... [We] are now ready to make a step change into a Fourth-Generation approach to helping young people become better learners. Each of these generations is still with us: they overlap and linger, rather than replacing each other in a series of neat revolutions. But there are strong signs that the third generation is rapidly metamorphosing into the fourth.[14]

The characteristics of Claxton's four generations of Learning to Learn are summarised in Table 2.1.

Table 2.1. Four generations of Learning to Learn[15]

Generation	Characteristics
1	Focus on raising attainment, the outcomes of schooling Concerned with subject content and knowledge acquisition
2	Focus on study skills – hints and tips for organising time and resources, revision, exam technique Study skills seen as something teachers should teach alongside subject knowledge
3	Focus on social and emotional factors (e.g. self-esteem) Focus on particular ways of learning (e.g. learning styles, multiple intelligences) Concerned with the 'how' of teaching (e.g. differentiation, personalisation)
4	Focus on how students can be helped to help themselves (e.g. resilience, collaboration, 'habits of mind') Focus on the processes of learning and the idea of 'learnable intelligence' Concerned with the 'how' of learning (e.g. setting goals, discussing ideas, reflecting on learning)

The first generation – where learning was viewed in terms of outcomes and 'good teaching' that focused on things like subject knowledge, literacy and numeracy – can be seen in the 1959 quote by Alice Miel we saw above, where 'learning about how learning happens' was seen primarily as a concern for teachers.

Second generation approaches were characterised by an emphasis on study skills and a desire to help students perform better in exams. This was based on the idea that as well as learning knowledge, students can learn a range of practical strategies to help them get better at organising information, time and resources, to revise more effectively, to make the best use of their time in an exam and so on. In the second generation, then, we begin to see the emergence of meta-learning strategies – learning about how learning happens. As might be expected, some of these efforts were more effective than others. A 2006 meta-analysis conducted by Hattie et al. concluded that the extent to which study skills interventions are successful depends on the context within which they are taught and, in particular, whether the process engages metacognitive strategies such as monitoring and reviewing.[16]

And so to the troublesome thirdborn. The third generation of Learning to Learn was a wave of theory and practice that took root around the turn of the millennium. It placed an emphasis on things like personalisation, 'active learning' and the social and emotional aspects of learning. Third generation approaches represent a marked shift from generations one and two in that teachers began to pay more attention to the needs of individual students in their classes, differentiating their practice accordingly.

One practice that was widespread around this time – in the UK, at least – involved administering a survey to determine whether students are predominantly visual, auditory or kinaesthetic (hands-on) learners – the so-called VAK model. Teachers were then expected to differentiate their lesson activities to cater to the preferred learning style of different groups of students. Other third generation approaches to Learning to Learn included the theory of multiple intelligences,[17] emotional intelligence,[18] personalised learning,[19] Social and Emotional Aspects of Learning (SEAL)[20] and Personal Learning and Thinking Skills (PLTS).[21] As Claxton (2006) explained, a concern for students' self-esteem became particularly prominent during this period:

> It became widely believed that children couldn't learn (as well, or at all) if they were stressed, and so 'good teaching' came to include the modulation of the emotional climate of the classroom. Self-esteem, it was thought, could be undermined by the experience of failure, so a 'good' teacher might try to do her best to protect her students from this distress by concealing her (inevitable) judgements of (relative or absolute) failure as much as possible, and by creating gentle gradients of difficulty in the tasks she set, so that children could proceed smoothly upwards without ever getting frustrated or confused – and therefore upset.[22]

This emphasis on the emotional aspects of learning has been described as a 'therapeutic turn' in educational policy and practice,[23] and this has been the subject of heated debate among philosophers of education. Here we find essentially two camps, with some scholars expressing concern at the way in which 'professional and popular support for these ideas... [has] become a new social and educational orthodoxy',[24] while others suggested that a concern for self-esteem is appropriate in some circumstances.[25, 26, 27]

It is understandable that the therapeutic turn triggered such unease. Third generation approaches to Learning to Learn were accompanied by a proliferation of branded teaching materials, often marketed using pseudo-scientific language. The dubious practice of Brain Gym became commonplace, which saw classrooms full of children vigorously rubbing their clavicle 'brain buttons' so as to increase the flow of oxygenated blood to their brain. In another exercise, children were required:

> ... to take a swig of water and hold it in their mouths for a few seconds until the teacher [told] them they [could] swallow... [T]he teacher, who had been sent on a Brain Gym course by the school, informed me that the water was partially absorbed through the roof of the children's mouths and [into] the brain, improving learning.[28]

With the benefit of hindsight, it is easy to mock the naïve quackery of practices such as these, and many have expressed indignation at the snake-oil opportunism of the profiteers.[29] However, Claxton offers a more forgiving analysis:

> The fact that [third generation] approaches to Learning to Learn have sometimes been guilty of exaggeration or naivety does not mean that the whole project of trying to help young people become better learners is doomed: far from it. Such lapses and excesses are part of the growing pains – the adolescence, if you like – of any worthwhile educational innovation.[30]

In this view, the third generation of Learning to Learn can be seen as analogous to retrospectively risible ideas from the history of science, such as the four humours, or alchemy, or the belief that consciousness was located in the heart. Looking back, it's hard to believe that anyone took these ideas seriously, let alone the most respected thinkers of the day. But they did, and they did so in good faith. So perhaps third-generation approaches to Learning to Learn were a necessary, painful stage of development that we just kind of had to work through – an adolescent haircut that seemed like a good idea at the time, but which is best not repeated. But it is certainly true that many third-generation practices fell short of the hype that trumpeted their arrival. In particular, the practice of learning styles – the idea that you can reliably diagnose a person's innate learning preferences and then use this information to prescribe certain educational activities – has now been widely discredited.[31, 32]

If third-generation approaches were concerned with the 'how' of teaching, Claxton describes the fourth generation of Learning to Learn as being increasingly focused on the 'how' of learning:

> *In fourth-generation approaches... transparency and student participation are becoming more common. Instead of simply dishing out good advice to students as consumers, classrooms are becoming places of day-by-day knowledge generation about learning, with students being involved, in all kinds of ways, in discovering for themselves, both individually and collectively, what the ingredients of 'good learning' are, and how best they can help themselves develop.*[33]

As might be expected, the Learning to Learn field has continued to develop since Claxton published *Learning to Learn: The Fourth Generation* in 2006. Claxton's 2018 book *The Learning Power Approach* is 'an attempt to synthesise and synergise a variety of approaches that are already well developed and increasingly well evidenced'.[34] Here, Claxton helpfully assembles a 'nuclear family' of approaches from around the world that exemplify best practice in the field, including:

- Project Zero (USA).[35] This spawned a number of related initiatives, including:
  - Intellectual Character/Visible Thinking[36, 37]
  - Studio Thinking[38]
  - Expeditionary Learning[39, 40]
- The Habits of Mind (USA)[41]
- Chris Watkins' 'elegant work on the powerful effect of getting students to tell their own stories of learning, and the implications of narrative approaches for the development of the learner-centred classroom',[42] which doesn't have a snappy title (UK)[43]
- Cognitive Acceleration in Science and Maths Education (CASE/CAME) (UK)[44]
- Project for the Enhancement of Effective Learning (PEEL) (Australia)[45]
- The Hundred Languages of Children (Italy)[46]
- The Round Square Schools network (an international chain of schools in over 50 countries)[47]
- The International Baccalaureate Learner Profile (international, obviously, but based in Switzerland)[48]

Drawing together insights from decades of theory and practice around the world, Claxton presents a powerful case that character traits and dispositions – the non-cognitive motivations, habits of mind and dispositions that drive the learning process – are absolutely teachable and learnable:

> Schools should be preparing kids to flourish in a complicated and demanding world. Just trying to squeeze better test scores out of them is not enough. We know that, in the long run, character counts for more than examination results. To prosper – to live good lives – today's students will need curiosity, determination, concentration, imagination, camaraderie, thoughtfulness and self-discipline as well as literacy, numeracy, general knowledge, and the best possible grades. These attributes contribute hugely to people's success and fulfilment in life. And we also know that they are capable of being intentionally developed – or unintentionally stifled. The desire to cultivate them has to be at the heart of every school's endeavour.[49]

Claxton suggests that the question of how to develop these character traits is cultural rather than curricular:

> Such dispositions cannot be 'taught' directly. Of course they can be made explicit and talked about, and that helps, but merely understanding the concept of 'resilience', say, and even being able to write an A-grade essay about it, does not by itself make you any more resilient. Character is a constellation of habits, and habits are tendencies that are built up over time. If you regularly find yourself in a culture – a family, for example – where the people you look up to continually model, value and expect politeness, honesty or curiosity, you are likely to grow towards those qualities, as a plant grows toward the sun. Such habits begin to become part of your natural way of being.[50]

As we look back over the last 40 or so years, we can see that Learning to Learn is a dynamic field of theory and practice that is continually evolving and adapting, experimenting with new ideas and keeping some while discarding others. The field is now in a state of far greater maturity than it was even 15 years ago, and there is good reason to believe that this process of maturation will continue into the future. Later in this chapter, we will examine the evidence base relating to the practice of Learning to Learn in schools, and in Part II we will explain why we think the *Learning Skills* approach advances the field in several important ways – in terms of theory and practice, and in terms of adding to that evidence base.

Before we go any further, however, we need to grasp the nettle of definitions.

METACOGNITION, SELF-REGULATION AND SELF-REGULATED LEARNING: WHAT'S THE DIFFERENCE?[51]

As we mentioned in *Chapter 1: High impact for low cost, or snake oil for hipsters?*, there has been considerable interest in metacognition and self-regulation since the EEF declared in 2011 that these practices provide 'high impact for very low cost, based on extensive evidence'.[52] However, teachers are not always clear about what 'metacognition and self-regulation' means, or what it looks like in the classroom. This is not surprising, because educational researchers aren't always clear about what it means, either.

Dinsmore et al. (2008) reviewed over 250 studies in an attempt to determine the 'core meaning of metacognition, self-regulation and self-regulated learning, as well as where these constructs converge and diverge'.[53] This review found that only 49% of the studies provided explicit definitions, and that where this did happen, there was considerable overlap between the three constructs. As Schunk (2008) lamented:

> These definitions have become diluted to the point where today we ask such questions as: Is metacognition part of self-regulation? Is self-regulated learning part of self-regulation? Is self-regulation more environmentally sensitive than metacognition, which is more of a personal factor?[54]

In 2018, the EEF published a guidance document entitled *Metacognition and Self-regulated Learning*, in an attempt to simplify this complex field for busy teachers.[55] The guidance outlines seven key recommendations for schools; these are great, and we would urge all teachers and school leaders to read, digest and implement them forthwith.

However – and bear with us if this seems pedantic, but we really do think it's important – there are a number of problems with the way in which the EEF defines its terms. If we are going to get to grips with how to teach children to become confident, independent learners, we need to understand the theory (the 'why') as well as the practice (the 'what'). In this way, teachers can adapt their practice from first principles rather than taking recommendations off the shelf without a clear understanding of the underlying concepts.

As we saw in Chapter 1, the EEF defines self-regulated learning as a broad umbrella concept comprising three components – cognition, metacognition and motivation (Figure 2.2). The EEF defines these terms as follows:

Cognition is the mental process involved in knowing, understanding, and learning... Metacognition is about the ways learners monitor and purposefully direct their learning... Motivation is about our willingness to engage our metacognitive and cognitive skills and apply them to learning.[56]

Figure 2.2. The EEF model of self-regulation/self-regulated learning[57]

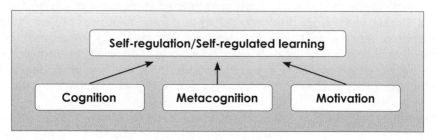

However, we believe there are three fairly significant problems with the EEF's definition. First, as we will see, this is not how metacognition and self-regulation are usually defined in the research literature. This definition therefore introduces confusion into an already complex arena.[58]

Second, the EEF model is primarily concerned with cognition, and overlooks the self-regulation of emotions and behaviours. As we will argue in *Chapter 5: Components of a complex intervention*, developing the ability to monitor and control our feelings (physical and emotional) – and therefore our behaviours – is really the bedrock of self-regulated learning. This goes way beyond motivation, important though motivation undoubtedly is.

And third, the EEF uses the terms self-regulation and self-regulated learning interchangeably. In the guidance document, there are 42 references to self-regulated learning and 19 references to self-regulation, and no attempt is made to differentiate between the two. This is a problem, because understanding how these concepts help define one another is actually quite illuminating. As Alexander (2008) put it: 'How better to comprehend the nature of metacognition... than to ponder its associations with self-regulation or self-regulated learning?'[59]

How indeed? Let's consider each in turn.

METACOGNITION

As we mentioned in the *Introduction*, metacognition is often referred to simply as 'thinking about thinking', which often prompts hilarious gags about 'thinking about thinking about thinking'.[60] However, when John Flavell devised the word in 1976, he defined it as a complex, dynamic process that goes beyond merely 'thinking about thinking'.To be precise, Flavell defined metacognition as 'the active monitoring and consequent regulation and orchestration of [thought] processes... usually in the service of some concrete goal or objective'.[61] In 1979, Flavell developed his thinking further in a short paper called 'Metacognition and cognitive monitoring', which remains the best model we have (Figure 2.3).[62]

Figure 2.3. Flavell's model of metacognition and cognitive modelling

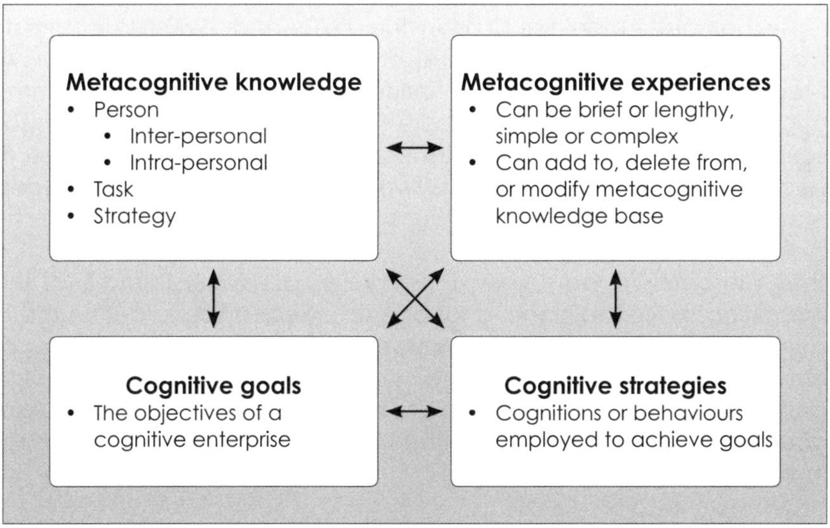

To break this down: Flavell, a developmental psychologist, suggested that we learn to control our thinking by monitoring what we know about people (self and others), tasks and strategies. He proposed that this metacognitive knowledge grows through experience, setting goals and identifying and using strategies to achieve these goals. All of these components interact with one another, and through these interactions we develop metacognitive skills and further our knowledge, improving our ability to independently achieve our goals in the future.

You can see why the EEF wanted to simplify things: Flavell's model has great explanatory power, but it is too complex to be easily called to mind in the context of a busy classroom. However, metacognition can be simplified without distorting the message too badly. For example, Chris Watkins – a giant of the Learning to Learn movement[63] – defined metacognition succinctly as 'awareness of thinking processes, and "executive control" of such processes'.[64] Here, we propose an even simpler definition:

> **Metacognition: monitoring and controlling your thought processes**

SELF-REGULATION

Our understanding of self-regulation is largely based on the work of the psychologist Albert Bandura in the 1970s and 1980s. In contrast to the cognitive, thought-based world of metacognition, Bandura viewed self-regulation as the process of influencing the external environment through our feelings and behaviours.[65] However, the language used to describe self-regulation is often strikingly similar to that used to describe metacognition, and in a sense the two can be seen as mirror images of one another.

In their aforementioned review, Dinsmore et al. (2008) found that there was significant overlap in the language researchers use to define the two terms, with two words cropping up far more than any others: *monitor* and *control*. Echoing Bandura, Dinsmore et al. concluded that there is 'a clear cognitive orientation for metacognition, while self-regulation is as much concerned with human action as the thinking that engendered it'.[66] Here we propose the following definition:

> **Self-regulation: monitoring and controlling your feelings and behaviours**

The importance of monitoring and control is also emphasised by van Merriënboer and Kirschner (2018):

> *Monitoring is the term used to refer to the – metacognitive – thoughts learners have about their own learning. For example, learners who are reading a study text should monitor their level of comprehension of the text. Control refers to how learners respond to the environment or adapt their behaviour based on their thoughts. Thus, if comprehension monitoring leads a learner*

to the thought that a text is not yet well understood, (s)he may decide to restudy one or more parts of this text. Monitoring and control are closely linked to each other in one and the same learning cycle: One is of no use without the other.[67]

Here, van Merriënboer and Kirschner suggest that monitoring is primarily a metacognitive concern, while control relates to an individual's behaviours. However, we take a slightly different view: we can monitor and control our thoughts, feelings (physical and emotional) and behaviours. We can visualise this as follows:

	Thoughts	Feelings	Behaviours
Monitoring	Metacognition	Self-regulation	
Control			

SELF-REGULATED LEARNING

Thought processes, feelings, behaviours... clearly, metacognition and self-regulation are broad concepts that extend far beyond academic learning. As Fox and Riconscente (2008) put it: 'understanding metacognition and self-regulation... requires situating them within the broad context of all activities for humans of all ages and points of development'.[68]

Following the publication of Bandura's classic 1986 work *Social Foundations of Thought and Action*, the concept of self-regulation was increasingly applied to the process of learning.[69] This led to the development of a new term, 'self-regulated learning'. Schunk (2008) describes self-regulated learning as 'the process whereby students activate and sustain cognitions and behaviours systematically oriented toward the attainment of their learning goals'.[70] Here, we propose the following definition:

> **Self-regulated learning: the application of metacognition and self-regulation to learning**

To recap: metacognition is monitoring and controlling your thought processes; self-regulation is monitoring and controlling your feelings and behaviours; and self-regulated learning is the application of metacognition and self-regulation to learning (Figure 2.4).

Figure 2.4. Metacognition, self-regulation and self-regulated learning

Metacognition
Monitoring and controlling your thought processes

Self-regulation
Monitoring and controlling your feelings and behaviours

Self-regulated learning
The application of metacognition and self-regulation to learning

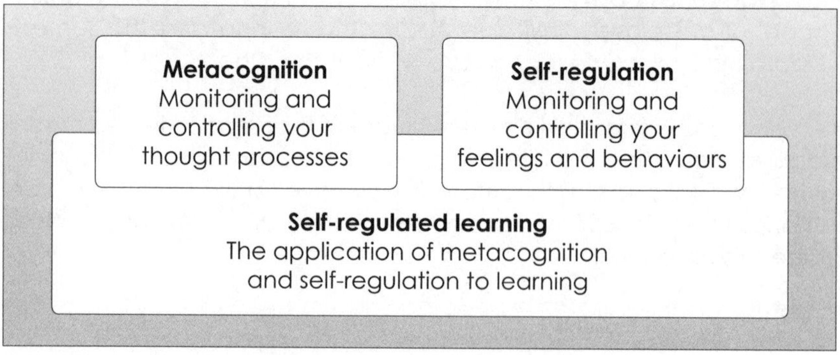

As with all models, this is a simplified version of reality. For example, there are a number of additional factors that influence the extent to which a student is able or willing to regulate their own learning. As the EEF's model recognises, this includes things like motivation (to what extent are students motivated to learn, and is this intrinsic or extrinsic?). However, there are additional factors to consider, such as autonomy (do the students have any choice about whether or how to engage in their learning, or are the expectations being imposed by the teacher or a looming deadline?), self-efficacy (to what extent do they believe they can learn effectively within this domain?) and so on. As ever, context is king. However, we believe that the model of self-regulated learning outlined above is more helpful than that proposed by the EEF, for three reasons.

First, our model does not introduce new concepts or definitions into an already overcrowded field. Rather, it simplifies established definitions of metacognition, self-regulation and self-regulated learning, and explains how they relate to one another.

Second, it makes clear that metacognition and self-regulation are essentially mirror images of one another – the former relating to the monitoring and control of thoughts, the latter relating to the monitoring and control of feelings and behaviours. As we will see in Part II, this key insight that both metacognition and self-regulation essentially comprise two processes – monitoring and control – is of great practical use when thinking about how these ideas play out in the classroom.

And third, it makes clear the difference between self-regulation and self-regulated learning. In so doing, it recognises the importance of emotional and physical self-regulation as prerequisites to self-regulated learning, which are critical even in early childhood.[71] We will explore self-regulation in detail at the end of *Chapter 5: Components of a complex intervention.*

THIS IS ALL WELL AND GOOD, BUT WHAT DOES IT LOOK LIKE IN PRACTICE?

The boundaries between thoughts, feelings and behaviours are often blurry. Where does a thought end and a feeling begin? Are our behaviours really separate from our thoughts, or are they simply extensions or manifestations of them? In reality, the three overlap and interact to a significant degree. However, it is important to tease them apart as far as we can, because each has different consequences for the classroom.

In schools, teachers set the agenda for what needs to be learned, and how, and by when. We set deadlines for the pupils to meet; we remind them of those deadlines regularly; and, if it looks like a pupil is not going to meet that deadline, we swoop in and 'intervene' – especially as they approach GCSE. We organise after-school catch-up sessions, we phone their parents and carers, we send reminders via their tutor... we do whatever it takes to get them over the line.[72] All of this is done with the best of intentions, mindful of the need to use our time efficiently and to maximise the students' chances of success. But the question almost asks itself: how can we expect children to learn how to self-regulate in such a top-down, micro-managed environment?

The answer, in our view, is obvious: in order for children to learn how to regulate their thoughts, feelings and learning behaviours, teachers need to occasionally take a step back to find out (and to allow the children to discover) what they can and cannot do by themselves. This process of stepping back can be done in a measured way, for just a part of a lesson – or, we can really 'throw them in at the deep end' and set them a task that lasts for several weeks. To extend the metaphor: clearly, we do not want them to drown or to flail around fruitlessly for lesson after lesson. But nor should we provide them with a lifeboat at the first sign of struggle. Instead, we might toss them a branch – something to help them keep their head above water until they can survey their surroundings and build a raft of their own. OK, we've definitely taken the metaphor too far now. But you get the idea.

In practical terms, there are three parts to this process. First, we set them a challenging task. Something they have never done before; something they may feel is currently beyond them; something that requires them to stretch out into new territory – just beyond the edge of their comfort zone. Next, we provide them with the support and guidance they need to get started or to nudge them back on track when they get stuck. And finally, we withdraw that support over time until they are able to achieve success without constant supervision.

This is closely related to Jerome Bruner's notion of *instructional scaffolding*, the idea that teachers should provide children with the guidance and support they need to learn something, and then gradually withdraw that support as the child grows in confidence or proficiency.[73] Scaffolding is a good framework for most forms of instruction, but when the aim is self-regulated learning, we need to take the

> **SCAFFOLDING**
>
> The idea that teachers should provide students with the guidance and support they need to learn something, and then gradually withdraw that support as the student grows in confidence or proficiency.

scaffolding idea even further, because if we provide that guidance and support too readily – at the first sign of difficulty or in response to the first request for help – we can breed dependence. When the goal is self-regulated learning, therefore, the question becomes: What is the *minimum* scaffolding we need to have in place? When we 'step back', should we remain one step behind the child, or ten?

This process of stepping back needs to be done judiciously – choosing carefully when to do so, and why, and for how long. It's probably not a good idea to trial this a few weeks before the GCSE exam. In our view, Key Stages 2 and 3 are the best time to do this work, when children are aged roughly between 8 and 14.

The need to step back is one of the reasons why Learning to Learn requires discrete lessons as well as being embedded throughout the curriculum. A child cannot expect to become a stronger swimmer without practising swimming repeatedly. Similarly, if we want children to become self-regulated learners, we have to provide them with the time and space in which to develop and practise the knowledge, skills, habits and dispositions that underpin self-regulated learning. We will outline the arguments for discrete lessons in more detail in *Chapter 5: Components of a complex intervention*.

To be clear, 'stepping back' does not mean indulging in some uber-permissive, child-centred experiment in unguided discovery learning, hoping that they will figure out for themselves how to manage their feelings and behaviours. We can teach children how to self-regulate using the tried and tested, traditional methods that we use to teach anything else. We explain it, we model what it looks like, we deconstruct it and make sure they understand all the moving parts, we co-construct it with them (co-regulating in this case), we provide feedback and give them time to respond to it and act on it, and we gradually withdraw our support over time. Progressive ends through traditional means, you might say. A useful end goal to have in mind when teaching children how to self-regulate is to get them to the point where they 'know what to do when they don't know what to do'. Claxton, another giant of the Learning to Learn movement, describes this rather excellently as a process of helping them learn how to 'flounder intelligently'.[74]

PROMOTING SELF-REGULATED LEARNING THROUGH QUESTIONING

Zimmerman (2002) offers the following guide for how to spot a self-regulated learner, should you encounter an example of this rare species in the wild:

> *These learners are proactive in their efforts to learn because they are aware of their strengths and limitations and because they are guided by personally set goals and task-related strategies... These learners monitor their behaviour in terms of their goals and self-reflect on their increasing effectiveness. This enhances their self-satisfaction and motivation to continue to improve their methods of learning.*[75]

If children are to learn how to become such proactive, self-assured, self-regulated learners, we need to provide them with regular opportunities to monitor and control their *thoughts, feelings and behaviours*, such as through weekly and termly goal setting and review sessions, long-term project-based learning, or the use of learning journals. We will explore these practices in detail in *Chapter 5: Components of a complex intervention*. It is also important to establish a classroom culture where pupils are encouraged to take ownership over aspects of their own learning, and where failure is framed as invaluable feedback rather than something to be avoided at all costs.

Such a classroom culture is perhaps most powerfully established and reinforced through the kinds of questions teachers ask. The questions we can ask about metacognition, self-regulation and self-regulated learning are almost limitless. However, the overarching aim is to help students generalise from the particular, moving their thinking from domain-specific insights (relating to the task) to domain-general insights (relating to learning in general). In this way, students can learn to monitor and control their learning in ways that can transfer to new learning contexts.[76] Here are a few examples:

Metacognition
(monitoring and controlling thought processes)

- What beliefs do you have about yourself and your abilities?
- Do you ever hear yourself thinking things like the following?
    - I can't do X.
    - I am usually quite good at X, but I find I really struggle with Y.
    - I am useless at X.
    - I don't know how to do X yet – what do I need in order to move forward?
    - I can do X if I set my mind to it.
- What do you think when you are set a task that you find too easy?
- What do you think when you are set a task that you find too difficult?
- What do you think when you are set a task that is 'just right' in terms of difficulty?
- What tools or strategies can help people organise their thinking when they are working on a complex or challenging task? Do you ever use any of these?
- Would you say you have a good memory or a poor memory? Why do you think this?
- When someone feels their thoughts racing, what can they do to slow down or control their thinking? Do you ever use any of these strategies?
- What is the difference between concentrating and becoming absorbed?
- Is it possible to force yourself to concentrate?

Self-regulation
(monitoring and controlling feelings and behaviours)

Feelings

- What does it feel like when you achieve something that you initially found difficult, challenging or confusing?
    - What does it feel like in your mind?
    - What does it feel like in your body?
- Do you feel your emotions as ideas/words or as physical sensations?
- What does it feel like when you find it difficult to learn something, despite trying really hard?
- What does it feel like to 'lose control' of your behaviour?
    - What does it feel like in your mind?
    - What does it feel like in your body?
- Would you say you are an emotional person? What does this mean?

- Are people able to control their feelings, or do feelings just happen to us?
- Are people able to control how they respond to their feelings? Can you think of any examples?

Behaviour

- Would you say you are an impulsive person or are you good at controlling how you behave? Why do you think this?
- Can you think of an example of when you have acted impulsively?
- Can you think of an example of when you have been able to override your impulses?
- To what extent are people able to control their behaviour, would you say?
- Have you ever felt like your behaviour has been 'out of control'? What happened? Is there anything you could have done to prevent this from happening?
- Do you think you have 'free will'? What does this mean to you?
- How good are you at managing distractions in the classroom or at home?
- What strategies can people use to help them manage distractions? Do you ever use any of these?
- Outside school, do you set goals and work toward them or do you tend to drift from one thing to the next?

Self-regulated learning (applying metacognition and self-regulation to learning)

- What have you learned today/this week/this term?
- What were you *doing* when you learned X?
  - Was it when you asked someone a question and they answered it?
  - Did you ask a question and the answer 'came to you' as you were asking it?
  - Was it through listening to the teacher or a classmate?
  - Did you look it up in a book, or online?
  - Were you thinking about something else and suddenly something 'clicked'?
  - Through which sense or senses did you receive the information? Did you read it? Overhear it? Was it by 'thinking out loud'?
- What does it feel like when you know you have learned something difficult?
- How long did it take you to learn X? Did it take more or less time than you anticipated?
- How can you tell whether you can trust a source of information you find online?

- What do really good short-, medium- and long-term goals look like? Why do you think this?
- What do really bad short-, medium- and long-term goals look like? Why do you think this?
- Is it possible for anyone to get better at learning? Is it possible to get worse at learning?
- What are the characteristics of an effective learner?
  - How would you describe their personality?
  - What strategies do they use?
  - What beliefs do they have?
- Some students always seem to learn what they need to learn from every lesson. What are they doing in their heads, or in their books, when they are learning stuff? It's not magic – they will have some kind of a process. Maybe we should ask them...?
- What is the difference between learning something and memorising it?
- What tools or strategies do people use to help them remember things better? Do you ever use any of these?
- What steps could you take to help you learn more effectively in [insert subject] in the future?
- When you learned X, was there a period of confusion or discomfort beforehand? What did that feel like?
- Is it possible to feel comfortable with feeling uncomfortable? What does this mean?

As Flavell's model suggests, the focus of such questioning can be applied at the level of the person, task, strategy, experiences or goals; all of these are represented in the list above. A useful rule of thumb is simply to reflect regularly on the 'how' of learning as well as the 'what'. The overarching aim is to enable young people firstly to describe and then to increasingly control their inner and outer worlds.

TEACHER TAKEAWAYS
A useful rule of thumb is to ask your pupils to reflect regularly on the 'how' of learning as well as the 'what'.

Such work is not limited to questioning. Talking points (provocative statements) and ground rules to promote exploratory talk are also powerful tools for stimulating metacognitive discussions in the classroom.[77, 78] In these ways, pupils learn to ask such questions of one another, and ultimately of themselves. When they're asking these questions of themselves: that's when you know you've cracked it.

TEACHER TAKEAWAYS
As an alternative to questioning, the use of talking points (provocative statements) is a powerful method for stimulating classroom discussions.

This understanding of what metacognition, self-regulation and self-regulated learning really mean – and what they can look like in practice – will be useful to bear in mind as we turn now to consider the evidence that underpins all this 'high impact for very low cost' business.

LEARNING TO LEARN: THE EVIDENCE BASE

EVIDENCE FOR...

The value of helping children develop metacognition and self-regulated learning is supported by a large number of studies that report significant benefits across a range of outcomes, including cognitive function, study skills and academic achievement.

In the last 30 years or so, there have been a number of meta-analyses of controlled studies focusing on metacognition and self-regulation. Table 2.2 compares the effect sizes of several such studies. As you can see, for each of these studies, the average effect size falls in the 0.5 to 0.7 range. To explain what this means in real-world terms, according to Professor Rob Coe:

META-ANALYSIS
When researchers combine the findings from several studies on the same topic and carry out statistical analyses to look for overall trends.

> An improvement of one GCSE grade represents an effect size of 0.5–0.7. In the context of secondary schools therefore, introducing a change in practice whose effect size was known to be 0.6 would result in an improvement of about a GCSE grade for each pupil in each subject. For a school in which 50% of pupils were previously gaining five or more A*–C grades, this percentage (other things being equal, and assuming that the effect applied equally across the whole curriculum) would rise to 73%. Even [a] 'small' effect of 0.2 would produce an increase from 50% to 58% – a difference that most schools would probably categorise as quite substantial.[79]

These data therefore strongly suggest that efforts to improve metacognitive and self-regulatory processing reliably lead to significant, measurable gains in student learning outcomes.

Table 2.2. Meta-analyses of Learning to Learn programmes: a summary of effect sizes[80]

Focus of meta-analysis	No. effect sizes	Average effect size
Metacognitive reading programmes[80(a)]	123	0.67
Self-regulated learning interventions[80(b)]	357	0.61 (primary) 0.54 (secondary)
Strategies to improve self-regulated learning[80(c)]	180	0.66
Self-regulated learning interventions[80(d)]	263	0.69
Metacognitive instruction on reading comprehension[80(e)]	115	0.71
Learning skills interventions[80(f)]	270	0.57
Thinking skills approaches[80(g)]	122	0.74
Inductive reasoning training[80(h)]	74	0.69

Many other studies have also reported the positive impact of metacognition and self-regulation on academic outcomes. For example, a 2012 study of self-regulatory interventions on reading, writing and maths reported that all effect sizes exceeded the 'large effect' threshold, and concluded that 'self-regulatory interventions have promise as an effective approach that is both minimally invasive and involves minimal resources'.[81] Similarly, a 2014 Randomised Controlled Trial (RCT) found that a self-regulation-focused approach to helping struggling writers led to a 'large positive impact on writing outcomes', and that 'participating pupils made approximately nine months' additional progress compared to similar pupils who did not participate in the intervention.' This study also reported that the effect was far higher for pupils eligible for Free School Meals (FSM), who made an estimated 18 months' additional progress compared with pupils in control schools.[82]

This finding that the development of metacognition and self-regulation is particularly beneficial for students from disadvantaged backgrounds was also reflected in the findings of a Randomised Controlled Trial looking at an approach known as Thinking, Doing, Talking Science (TDTS). This study found that TDTS had a significant positive impact on the attainment of pupils in science, with year 5 pupils making an additional three months' progress compared with pupils in control schools. And the approach was particularly beneficial for pupils eligible for FSM, who made an average five months' progress.[83]

Metacognition and self-regulated learning also form a significant component of the Embedded Formative Assessment (EFA) approach developed by Dylan Wiliam and colleagues.[84] Wiliam outlines five strategies that support the effective implementation of formative assessment:

1. Clarifying, understanding and sharing learning intentions
2. Engineering effective classroom discussions, tasks and activities that elicit evidence of learning
3. Providing feedback that moves learners forward
4. Activating students as learning resources for one another
5. Activating students as owners of their own learning

In strategies 2, 4 and 5, we can see clear parallels with metacognition and self-regulation, with pupils discussing evidence of learning (making the implicit processes of learning explicit), collaborating with and supporting one another, and taking ownership over their own learning. Through these five strategies, the EFA approach promotes metacognitive processing among teachers as well as students.

The efficacy of EFA was evaluated in a recent RCT involving 140 secondary schools, with 70 schools implementing EFA and 70 in the control condition (doing 'business as usual'). This three-year study found that students in the EFA schools achieved statistically significant gains in subject learning compared with control schools, making 'the equivalent of two additional months' progress in their Attainment 8 GCSE score'.[85] Furthermore, 'the additional progress made by children in the lowest third for prior attainment was greater than that made by children in the highest third', suggesting that implementing EFA was especially beneficial for students from disadvantaged backgrounds.[86]

To successfully develop self-regulatory processing in students, teachers need to be able to reliably monitor their pupils' ability to self-regulate over time.[87] A number of instruments have been devised to help monitor self-regulatory processes in real-world settings.[88] Such instruments have found self-regulation to be associated with positive outcomes across a range of age groups, including enhanced academic performance, improved motivational beliefs, and students making more effective use of peers and teachers.[89, 90] In one study, student self-regulation was found to be 'very similar across the three subject areas examined', suggesting that self-regulatory skills may be highly transferable across domains.[91]

Finally, there is evidence that metacognition contributes to learning outcomes over and above an individual's intellectual ability. According to Veenman et al. (2006), on average:

Intellectual ability uniquely accounts for 10 percent of variance in learning, metacognitive skills uniquely account for 17 percent of variance in learning, [and] both predictors share another 20 percent of variance in learning for students of different ages and background, for different types of tasks, and for different domains.[92]

This suggests that metacognitive skills can both compensate for, and boost, an individual's intellectual ability.

In sum, there is a compelling body of evidence from the research literature to suggest that teaching pupils using methods that develop metacognitive and self-regulatory processing leads to demonstrable, statistically significant gains across a range of pupil outcomes, with accelerated gains among young people from disadvantaged backgrounds.

'MIXED' EVIDENCE

Based on the findings summarised above, you would be forgiven for thinking that there is a consensus among educational researchers that Learning to Learn is a *very good thing indeed*. But that word 'consensus' should set alarm bells ringing; there's hardly *anything* on which educational researchers universally agree. So much so that Professor Sir Chris Husbands suggests there are three rules of educational research:

1. If something seems too good to be true, it is too good to be true.
2. Things are always more complicated than they appear.
3. There is always evidence to the contrary.[93]

These rules are useful to bear in mind – but like all rules, there are exceptions. In the case of Learning to Learn, there isn't *evidence to the contrary*, as such; there is no research that we know of to suggest that Learning to Learn can *negatively* affect student outcomes in the way that feedback interventions can, for example. However, in the last 20 years or so, there have been several evaluations of large-scale Learning to Learn initiatives where the findings have been mixed, with no clear evidence of impact (either positive or negative) on academic outcomes. Of these, there are four in particular that have been implemented on a fairly large scale in the UK: *Opening Minds*,[94] *Learning to Learn in Schools*,[95] *Building Learning Power*,[96] and *Learning How to Learn*.[97] We will now briefly consider each in turn.

Opening Minds

The *Opening Minds* programme is a competency-based approach to Learning to Learn, whereby schools create an 'integrated curriculum' based around five key ideas: citizenship, learning, managing information, relating to people, and managing situations. *Opening Minds* was first trialled in 2000 and has subsequently been implemented in over 200 schools throughout the UK.[98] Despite such widespread implementation, however, there is no clear evidence that the *Opening Minds* programme was able to replicate or scale up the positive research findings in the literature on metacognition and self-regulated learning.[99, 100]

Learning to Learn in Schools

The *Learning to Learn in Schools* study ran from 2000 to 2010, and involved 41 primary and secondary schools across four local authorities.[101] In this study, groups of teachers carried out a series of action research projects over four phases of implementation and evaluation, developing various aspects of learning-centred (as opposed to performance-centred) practice. The evaluation report points out that 'for an intervention to be seriously considered, it would be desirable to have a demonstrable impact on school attainment'.[102] However, the project had no clear impact on school attainment:

> Over the three years, there is no clear evidence for Learning to Learn having a general effect, either negative or positive, on the GCSE results of the secondary schools involved... Similarly... there is no clear evidence of Learning to Learn having a significant impact on national test results at the end of Key Stage 2.[103]

Building Learning Power

Building Learning Power (BLP) is a whole-school approach to teaching and learning centred around 17 'learning capacities', organised into four domains of learning:

- Reflectiveness (planning, revising, distilling meta-learning)
- Reciprocity (interdependence, collaboration, listening/empathy, imitation)
- Resilience (absorption, managing distraction, noticing, perseverance)
- Resourcefulness (questioning, making links, imagining, reasoning, capitalising)[104]

Following the publication of *Building Learning Power* in 2002,[105] 'thousands of schools and classrooms around the planet... experimented with BLP'.[106] Nine years later, evidence from a range of sources was published in a follow-up publication, *The Learning Powered School* (2011). Although there was evidence of impact from a range of qualitative sources, including Ofsted inspection reports, student self-perceptions and teacher interviews, analysis of student attainment in eight primary schools and nine secondary schools revealed a 'mixed picture'.[107] To date, no independent evaluations of BLP have reported a clear impact, either positive or negative, on academic outcomes.

Learning How to Learn

The *Learning How to Learn* (LHTL) project ran from 2001 to 2005, and involved 43 primary and secondary schools across five local authorities.[108] The LHTL researchers were dismissive of the idea that it is possible to teach Learning to Learn through a taught course:

> LHTL capabilities would involve the development of dispositions and skills, but these were unlikely to be sufficiently generic to allow them to be fostered in specific study skills or 'learning to learn' courses... we came to the conclusion that LHTL cannot be separated from learning itself: i.e., learning something. Rather, it is an activity involving a family of learning practices (tools) that enable learning to happen. This explains our preference for 'learning how to learn' over 'learning to learn' – the how word is important.[109]

Instead, the LHTL project 'took a narrower view of learning within the curriculum and the development of students' understanding of their academic learning through a focus on formative assessment and feedback in lessons'.[110] An evaluation of the LHTL project reported pockets of effective practice. Overall, however, the impact of the LHTL project on academic learning was once again mixed: 'Has the project observed improvements in pupils' measured attainments? As might be expected, the answer was "Yes and No"'.[111]

MAKING SENSE OF A MIXED PICTURE

To recap: there is a wealth of evidence that teaching children in such a way as to develop their metacognitive and self-regulatory abilities is associated with significant gains in student learning. However, it is important to understand that many of the studies outlined in the 'evidence for' section above are meta-analyses of smaller studies.

For various reasons, it's a lot easier to achieve a large effect size in a small study than it is to do so in a large study. For example, small studies (involving one school, for example) often involve a small number of highly motivated teachers who really believe in what they're doing and are strongly motivated to make it work. It is also relatively easy to make sure each of those teachers understands precisely what the initiative involves, to monitor and evaluate their practice over time, and to provide top-up support as needed.

When we scale up an initiative across dozens of schools, involving hundreds of teachers, all of these things are much harder to do. No two schools are alike: catchment areas can vary widely; some schools have high levels of staff turnover while others have high levels of teacher retention; and schools can vary enormously in size, from one-form-entry primary schools to secondary schools with thousands of students.

For all of these reasons and many more besides, implementing an initiative across dozens of schools is incredibly challenging; you tend to get pockets of good practice, but the signal gets lost in the noise and the benefits of the approach appear to fall away. There are other reasons for this – not least the wider challenge of effective change management – but the essential point here is that educational research has another troubling rule: the bigger the study, the smaller the effect size.[112]

When people have tried to translate the compelling research findings relating to metacognition and self-regulation into large-scale approaches to Learning to Learn, implemented and evaluated across dozens of schools, the impact on academic learning has been decidedly mixed. Indeed, some scholars have suggested that Learning to Learn isn't really about improving exam results at all:

> The point... is not to raise conventional results; it is to expand the range of valued outcomes to include the development of the confidence and capacity to learn all kinds of things, out of school as well as in. Expanding young people's capacity to learn, and their appetite for learning, is seen as a valuable end

of education in its own right; not just as a way of improving scores on existing indicators.[113]

Although we would agree that Learning to Learn (and, indeed, education more widely) should be about more than passing exams, we believe there are two problems with this idea. First, if an initiative that seeks to expand children's capacity to learn does not lead to improved exam results, then we might reasonably question the extent to which it has been effective in achieving its goals. Improving exam results is clearly a desirable end in its own right, but it is also valuable in a technical sense, as an indicator of the extent to which the Learning to Learn programme is doing what it says on the tin – namely, to help people get better at learning stuff.

Second, it's important to measure the impact of Learning to Learn using existing indicators (i.e. teacher assessments and exam results), because the alternative is to create new indicators, and this just creates a whole new set of problems. In recent years, there have been several attempts to develop instruments that measure Learning to Learn in some way, with limited success to date.[114, 115, 116] And even if a perfect measure of Learning to Learn could be achieved, in the absence of a clear understanding as to the impact of Learning to Learn on academic attainment, its practical utility to school leaders and policymakers would remain unclear.

Here we find ourselves at a crossroads. On the one hand, we could conclude that Learning to Learn is a busted flush – a once-promising avenue of theory and practice that turned out to be a dead end. As we saw in *Chapter 1: High impact for low cost, or snake oil for hipsters?*, some people have already vocally adopted this position. However, there is an alternative interpretation of the 'mixed evidence' outlined above – a far more plausible explanation, in our view.

First, we need to reflect on the fact that the word 'mixed' suggests that there was at least *some* evidence of a positive impact in these studies. Under what conditions did schools achieve success? As it turns out, if you read the evaluation reports in detail, an interesting pattern emerges:

> *The highest-performing secondary school... achieved significant increases in their practice of 'making learning explicit' and 'promoting learning autonomy', and significant decreases in their practice of 'performance orientation'.*[117]

> *Where either whole-school or the majority of classes have been involved in Learning to Learn... results... were fairly consistently above those expected.*[118]

[Learning to Learn] really takes root in a school when the whole community supports the vision and finds ways of helping to make it real.[119]

Three of the four schools with the highest value added [i.e. impact] had high levels of engagement with the project and explicit organisational strategies to support teachers' professional development and networking.[120]

It seems that where Learning to Learn was implemented effectively – when there was whole school buy-in and teachers were supported in developing their practice – there was some evidence of improved learning outcomes. It is therefore likely that the mixed results of these evaluations were caused by two related factors.

First, some of the schools may not have implemented the approach as it was described in the research literature – either because the project used a different approach or because teachers interpreted the approach in different ways. Faithful implementation, or fidelity, is a well-documented problem in educational research, and that may have been a live issue here. If you look at what was happening in terms of classroom practice in these four studies, you find it isn't always closely related to the practices described in the research literature on metacognition and self-regulated learning.

And second, it appears that the researchers threw the net too wide and didn't use stringent enough criteria to decide which schools to include in their sample. Each of the 'mixed findings' studies included dozens of schools across multiple local authorities, with patchy implementation *within* the schools sampled let alone *across* schools. In a sample of 30 or 40 schools, if some schools implemented Learning to Learn in a whole-school way and others just had a handful of teachers running metacognition-themed action research projects, then it's not surprising that the net finding was one of 'no clear evidence of impact'. The signal would have been lost in the noise.

Translating insights from research into practice in such a way as to reliably improve student outcomes across a large number of schools is a complex undertaking. That doesn't mean it can't be done: as we saw above, the evidence is abundant and compelling that teaching in such a way as to develop metacognition and self-regulation improves student outcomes.

In our view, there are two possible reasons for the 'mixed results' outlined above. First, there is room for improvement on the 'classroom practice' side of the equation – in the way that Learning to Learn was conceived, developed and practised in those studies. Second, there is room for improvement on the 'implementation' side of the equation – in the way the change process was managed in those schools. We think there is some truth in both of these reasons, as we will explain in the next chapter.

Of course, we aren't approaching this problem from an ivory tower. As we mentioned in the introduction, ten years ago we set out to rethink Learning to Learn from first principles. This involved scouring the research literature for ideas and practices known to be effective, and combining them into a 'complex intervention' that is greater than the sum of its parts.

This resulted in the *Learning Skills* curriculum – a whole-school approach to Learning to Learn with three key elements: taught lessons, shared whole-school practices, and policies in place to promote the transfer of knowledge, skills, habits and dispositions from *Learning Skills* lessons into subject learning across the curriculum. We believe – and have evidence to suggest – that the *Learning Skills* approach advances the field on both sides of the equation: in terms of classroom practice and also in terms of implementation.

But before we get into the detail of how *Learning Skills* is different from what has gone before, and the impact that it has had so far – all that is in Part II – we firstly need to address the fact that some people object to Learning to Learn, not on the basis of 'mixed evidence', but because they don't believe it is possible to teaching children how to get better at learning in an abstract or 'generic' way.

We need to put Learning to Learn on trial.

CHAPTER 3

LEARNING TO LEARN ON TRIAL

'If you have a theory, you must try to explain what's good and what's bad about it equally.'

Richard Feynman (2007)[1]

In *Chapter 2: A brief history of Learning to Learn*, we saw that the research on Learning to Learn presents us with an apparent paradox. On the one hand, there is a compelling body of research literature to suggest that teaching children in such a way as to develop metacognition and self-regulation – the key components of Learning to Learn – leads to significant gains in student learning. On the other, when Learning to Learn initiatives have been evaluated on a large scale, the results have been rather more mixed. In Silicon Valley parlance, Learning to Learn *doesn't scale* – or, at least, it hasn't been proven to be scalable *yet*.

There are two ways in which we might interpret this observation. First, it is possible that there is something about Learning to Learn *itself* that makes it hard to scale. We might be able to harness the power of metacognition and self-regulation with a small number of highly motivated teachers, but it doesn't lend itself to being implemented at a system level. A second interpretation would be to say that scaling up *itself* is hard to do. We think it's likely that there is some truth in both of these interpretations.

However, there is good news on both fronts. First, there is good reason to believe that the *Learning Skills* curriculum is easier to implement, and therefore to scale up, than previous initiatives. We will explain why in Part 2, and especially in *Chapter 8: An implementation (and evaluation) checklist*. And second, in recent years, a new field of study has emerged – implementation science – which we believe holds the answers to the problem of how to scale up promising initiatives in such a way that the benefits can be replicated at a system level. We'll discuss implementation science in more detail later in this chapter, and again in *Chapter 8*.

However, some people – typically, those who would describe themselves as traditionalist – don't think this is a scaling up problem at all. Instead, they object to Learning to Learn because they don't believe it is possible to teach people how to get better at learning in an abstract or 'generic' way. There is a fascinating discussion to be had here. So, in this chapter – in the spirit of Feynman's excellent suggestion in the quote above – we will explore a number of arguments for and against teaching children how, as well as what, to learn. To do this, we will put Learning to Learn in the dock. Its alleged crime? Well, as we saw in *Chapter 1*, Learning to Learn stands accused of being 'bad education'; a 'snake oil hoax'; a mistaken attempt to teach the unteachable.

The trial will run as follows:

- The prosecution: arguments against Learning to Learn
- The prosecution, cross-examined
- The defence: arguments in favour of Learning to Learn
- The defence, cross-examined

Court is in session: let battle commence!

THE PROSECUTION: ARGUMENTS AGAINST LEARNING TO LEARN

Ladies and gentlemen of the jury. For as long as schools have existed, people have argued that we should do education differently – that instead of having a curriculum designed and taught by experts, we should teach children to teach themselves. In this way, it is believed, we will better prepare them for a life of learning beyond the school gates. As well as teaching subject content, therefore, schools should help children 'learn how to learn'.

At face value, this is an attractive proposition. However, we are here to persuade you that any attempt to teach children how to learn is misguided – a mirage that rests on the false belief that it is possible to get better at learning in an abstract or 'generic' way. To do this, we will draw on three lines of argument: knowledge is foundational; children are novices; and generic skills can't be taught/don't transfer. Let's consider each in turn.

ARGUMENT 1: KNOWLEDGE IS FOUNDATIONAL

In this country, we are winning the argument in favour of a knowledge-rich curriculum.

Nick Gibb MP, Minister of State for School Standards (2017)[2]

In the 2000s, under the UK's New Labour government, educational policy and practice were strongly guided by two big ideas: personalisation and skills. Schools were encouraged to personalise learning to suit the particular preferences and needs of individual pupils, through practices such as learning styles, differentiation and student voice.[3] And there was a strong emphasis on skills throughout this period, with the publication of frameworks such as the Personal Learning and Thinking Skills (PLTS)[4] and the Social and Emotional Aspects of Learning (SEAL).[5] The centrality of skills to educational policy during this period can even be seen in the fact that in 2001 the Department for Education and Employment was renamed the Department for Education and Skills.

Under the more recent coalition and Conservative governments, there has been a marked shift away from the personalisation/skills agenda and towards a 'knowledge-rich curriculum'. However, support for this idea comes from across the political spectrum, and it should not be seen as a party-political concern. For example, E.D. Hirsch, an influential advocate of a 'core knowledge' curriculum, considers himself 'practically a socialist'.[6] Hirsch's work centres around the idea of 'cultural literacy', which he defines as:

> ...the network of information that all competent readers possess. It is the background information, stored in their minds, that enables them to take up a newspaper and read it with an adequate level of comprehension, getting the point, grasping the implications, relating what they read to the unstated context which alone gives meaning to what they read.[7]

In his 1987 book *Cultural Literacy*, Hirsch included an appendix with a list of 5000 names, phrases and historical dates under the heading *What Literate Americans Know*.[8] For Hirsch, a knowledge-rich curriculum is needed to provide young people with the minimum background information required to join what the philosopher Michael Oakeshott referred to as the great 'conversation of mankind'.[9] In his 2007 book *The Knowledge Deficit*, Hirsch suggests that teaching children 'a coherent, knowledge-based curriculum' is the best way to close 'the needlessly wide achievement gaps between ethnic and racial groups', as well as between children from different socio-economic backgrounds.[10]

Alongside Hirsch, advocates of a knowledge-rich curriculum often cite the work of the cognitive scientist Daniel Willingham. In his book *Why don't students like school?*, Willingham makes a powerful case that knowledge is foundational – it is the stuff that supposedly 'higher order' skills such as synthesis, analysis and critique are made of:

> *Trying to teach students skills such as analysis or synthesis in the absence of factual knowledge is impossible. Research from cognitive science has shown that the sorts of skills teachers want for their students – such as the ability to analyse and to think critically – require extensive factual knowledge. The cognitive principle that guides this chapter is: 'Factual knowledge must precede skill'.*[11]

To explain Willingham's key insight in a little more detail: the most powerful determinant of whether an individual is able to think creatively or critically about a particular subject is how knowledgeable they are within that domain. By way of a thought experiment, try thinking creatively or critically about a difficult problem – how to get large multinational companies to pay more tax, say. It is unlikely that you will get very far without knowing a considerable amount about systems of taxation, 'creative accountancy' practices and how to write watertight legislation and regulations. Similarly, when your car breaks down, who would you rather call – a mechanic or a university professor? University professors are often extremely knowledgeable, but it's not usually the kind of knowledge that can help you diagnose and fix a faulty alternator.

In recent years, Willingham's work – in particular this idea that knowledge is foundational – has been widely embraced by teachers, researchers and politicians alike. For example, in 2012, Michael Gove – then Secretary of State for Education (in England) – said:

> *One of the biggest influences on my thinking about education reform has been the American cognitive scientist Daniel T. Willingham... [who] demonstrates brilliantly in his book, memorisation is a necessary precondition of understanding.*[12]

Similarly, Nick Gibb, the current Minister for Schools Standards in England, twice invoked Willingham in a recent debate in which he argued in favour of the proposition that 'Learners' heads should be filled with facts':

> *Daniel Willingham talks about [how] an educated person has vast amounts of knowledge in his or her long-term memory which you can retrieve instantly... As Daniel Willingham has said, education is about... ensuring that we have facts and knowledge securely embedded in long-term memory.*[13]

In recent years, some people have suggested that we don't need to teach knowledge in the internet age, because when they need to know something, children can just 'look it up on their smartphone'. However, this is mistaken – you need knowledge in order to look something up in an accurate way. As Hirsch (2000) explains:

> There is a consensus in cognitive psychology that it takes knowledge to gain knowledge. Those who repudiate a fact-filled curriculum on the grounds that kids can always look things up miss the paradox that de-emphasizing factual knowledge actually disables children from looking things up effectively. To stress process at the expense of factual knowledge actually hinders children from learning to learn. Yes, the internet has placed a wealth of information at our fingertips. But to be able to use that information – to absorb it, to add it to our knowledge – we must already possess a storehouse of knowledge. That is the paradox disclosed by cognitive research.[14]

As Hirsch argues powerfully, when it comes to thinking critically or creatively about something, it is vastly preferable to have the relevant knowledge stored in your long-term memory rather than in your smartphone. Indeed, it is having relevant knowledge stored in your long-term memory that allows you to both comprehend and critique the search results that appear on your screen. The implications for Learning to Learn are clear: teach them knowledge instead. This brings us to our second argument...

ARGUMENT 2: CHILDREN ARE NOVICES

Children, it will not surprise you to learn, tend to be relatively young and inexperienced. This means that, by definition, children are usually novices rather than experts – especially in the school context, where much of what they learn they are encountering for the first time. As we will see, this has important consequences for how we educate young people. To understand why, we need to acquaint ourselves with cognitive load theory, described by Dylan Wiliam as 'the single most important thing for teachers to know'.[15]

Cognitive load theory is based on the 'multistore model of memory' first proposed by Atkinson and Shiffrin (1968).[16] A simplified version of this model – described by Willingham as 'just about the simplest model of the mind possible'[17] – can be seen in Figure 3.1.

Figure 3.1. The working memory model of the mind[18]

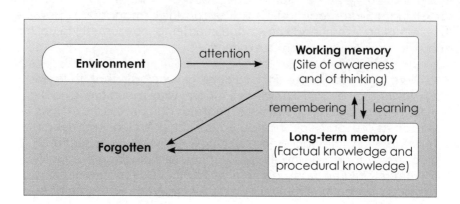

In this scheme, working memory is defined as the 'site of awareness and thinking'. This is often thought of as the window of mental space we 'live in' or through which we attend to the world. There are two ways in which information can enter your working memory: by paying attention to something in your immediate environment (e.g. teacher, book, screen) or by recalling information stored in your long-term memory.

In a seminal 1956 paper, George Miller proposed what would become known as Miller's Law – that the number of 'bits' of information that can be held in the working memory is limited to 'the magical number seven, plus or minus two'.[19] While the precise value has been contested over the years (others have suggested the limit is more like four, plus or minus one[20]), the central idea of Miller's Law is widely accepted. Working memory – the window of human consciousness through which we attend to the world and manipulate mental objects – operates within a fairly narrow bandwidth. It's easy to demonstrate this by asking someone to hold a novel string of random numbers in their head for, say, 20 seconds, without rehearsal: 2473 is pretty doable; 24739638194… not so much.

Building on Miller's Law, cognitive load theory states that because working memory has a limited capacity, if a student is presented with too much information or an overly complex task, their working memory becomes overloaded and they can't learn effectively.

John Sweller, the founder of cognitive load theory, highlights a crucial point about the limited capacity of working memory. That is, the limit on the number of 'bits' of information that can be held in working memory applies 'when dealing with novel information, and only when dealing with novel information'.[21]

In other words, the limitations of working memory are especially pertinent to the education of children – novices who are almost always dealing with novel information. In experts, information stored in the long-term memory is organised into schemata – dynamic networks of knowledge and

> **SCHEMA (PLURAL: SCHEMATA)**
> Dynamic networks of knowledge and understanding, stored in long-term memory, which guide our beliefs and behaviours. Networks of schemata serve as a kind of index for searching, recalling and retrieving information.

understanding that guide our beliefs and behaviours. Together, networks of schemata act as a kind of 'index' that allows knowledgeable experts to recall and retrieve relevant information instantly from long-term memory without burdening the working memory.[22]

To place this in a classroom context, suppose a student is working on a complex maths problem. As part of the solution, they need to work out 7 × 6. If they have to stop what they're doing to find a calculator or count it out on their fingers, this will take up valuable working memory capacity. In contrast, had the student memorised their times tables, they would have known in an instant that the answer is 42, and this would have allowed them to think about the wider problem. Thus, by storing and automating information in the long-term memory, we can bypass the limits of Miller's Law and free up our working memory to attend to the problem in hand. So when people say, 'There's no point teaching knowledge any more. People can just look stuff up on their smartphone,' they would do well to look up cognitive load theory on their smartphone and then reflect a little longer.

Cognitive load theory suggests that if we want people to be able to think creatively and critically – and everyone seems to agree that this is a desired goal of education – we need to view creativity and critical thinking as the endpoint and not as the method by which we get there. The way to get there is to teach a knowledge-rich curriculum. If you aren't persuaded by the cognitive science, you can arrive at the same conclusion using common sense. If you want a student to think creatively about something – to write a song for a musical, say – it stands to reason that they'll write a better song if they know a lot about music theory and have seen lots of musicals than if they just thrash away on a detuned ukulele in a state of blissful ignorance. Likewise, if you want your students to think critically about why a science experiment produced unexpected results, they'll stand a better chance if they know their dependent variable from their control variable.

Here we can see how cognitive load theory connects the fact that children are novices with our first argument, that knowledge is foundational. Working memory acts as a kind of 'bottleneck' – a narrow passage through which information passes into an individual's mind. When we try to force too much information through this bottleneck, it can become overloaded and this can prevent the individual from learning effectively. However, the bottleneck can be bypassed by having knowledge stored in the long-term memory, freeing up working memory to attend to the task in hand. The difference between a novice and an expert on a given topic is the amount of relevant information stored in the long-term memory. And storing knowledge and building schemata in long-term memory is precisely how novices become experts.

When we are dealing with the education of novices – and that, by definition, is what schools exist to do – we need to think carefully about how to teach in such a way that the learning is remembered over the long term. In schools, time is finite, and every decision we make about how to spend that time comes with an opportunity cost: what else might we have achieved, had we spent that time differently? Which is likely to be the most efficient use of time if we want to furnish children's minds with 'the best of what has been thought and said': to have a knowledge-rich curriculum, designed and taught by experts, or to teach novice children to 'learn how to learn' in the hope that they will learn it by themselves?

ARGUMENT 3: GENERIC SKILLS CAN'T BE TAUGHT/DON'T TRANSFER

There are two related arguments here. First, so-called 'generic skills' such as creativity and critical thinking are not really generic at all – they are highly domain-specific – and therefore they cannot be taught in a generic way. And second, learning is *situated*, which is to say, knowledge and skills tend to remain rooted in the context in which they were developed. Therefore, even if we could teach such skills, it is unlikely that they would meaningfully transfer to other lessons. We will now consider these arguments in turn.

Perhaps the best-known example of the argument that generic skills such as creativity and critical thinking cannot be taught is an article by Tricot and Sweller (2014).[23] Following the evolutionary psychologist David Geary,[24,][25] Tricot and Sweller draw a distinction between 'biologically primary' and 'biologically secondary' knowledge.[26] They define biologically primary knowledge as that which 'we have evolved to acquire over many generations'; this includes things like 'learning to listen and speak, learning to recognise faces, engage in social relations, basic number sense or learning to use a problem-solving strategy'.[27] In contrast, biologically secondary knowledge has no evolutionary precedent; this is defined as things like 'reading, writing and arguably, all other content taught in modern educational establishments'.[28]

According to Tricot and Sweller, biologically primary knowledge 'is acquired easily, unconsciously and without explicit tuition. Barring learning deficits such as those associated with autism, it will be acquired automatically simply as a consequence of membership of a normal society'.[29] Tricot and Sweller consider biologically primary knowledge to be synonymous with 'generic skills', and because biologically primary knowledge is 'acquired easily' and 'without explicit tuition', this is presented as 'an alternative to the perspective that teaching generic skills is important'.[30]

Elsewhere, Sweller has written: 'If children are not explicitly taught to read and write in school, most of them will not learn to read and write. In contrast, they will learn to listen and speak without ever going to school'.[31] This idea that written literacy needs to be taught, while people usually learn to speak and listen even in the absence of schooling, is supported by historical literacy rates. In 1820, only 12% of the world could read and write. Following the invention of schools, this pattern was swiftly reversed: in 2015, the global literacy rate was around 86%.[32] In contrast, one assumes at least, the proportion of people capable of holding a conversation in 1820 was very much the same as it is today.

We will now turn to the second part of the argument – that even when people do develop so-called higher-order skills such as creativity and critical thinking, they tend to be quite specialised to particular situations and do not transfer easily from one context to another. There is a considerable body of research literature on *situated learning*, 'the idea that much of what is learned is specific to the situation in which it is learned'.[33] To return to our car mechanic: though they may be good at solving problems to do with alternators, that doesn't mean they will be equally good at solving chess problems or the problem of tax avoidance by multinational corporations.

Similarly, skills like creativity are highly context-specific, and do not transfer easily from one domain to another. Kaufman and Baer (2002) made this argument forcefully when they asked, 'Could Stephen Spielberg manage the New York Yankees?' and concluded, having considered the cognitive science, that the answer 'appears to be no. Just as Joe Torre [*the Yankees coach at the time*] should probably restrict his camera activity to birthday parties, Spielberg should probably only enter Yankee Stadium as a fan.'[34]

Learning to Learn is based on two assumptions: first, that it is possible to teach generic skills; and second, that skills transfer easily from one context to another. If both of these assumptions are false – and we hope to have persuaded you that they are – then the foundations upon which Learning to Learn is built begin to look decidedly shaky.

Summing up, the prosecution declares: Ladies and gentlemen of the jury. This is an open and shut case. We have seen that knowledge is foundational. We have seen that children are novices. And we have seen that generic skills cannot be taught and do not transfer easily from one context to another. Our opponents will try to persuade you that all of this is blindingly obvious – that "of course knowledge is important, nobody ever said it wasn't". But in recent years, those on the progressive side of the aisle have claimed precisely this. They say things like 'You can just Google it', and 'We are preparing children for jobs that don't exist yet, so what's the point in teaching knowledge?'

You may very well shake your head, sir, but I kid you not! Thank goodness the teaching profession has come to its senses. The whole idea of Learning to Learn rests on the assumption that learning skills are generic – that once you become an effective learner, you are able to learn anything, in any context. But as we have just heard from our key witnesses, generic skills can't be taught! It's a misunderstanding, based on an ignorance of the cognitive architecture of the human mind. To be perfectly honest, I'm not really sure what Learning to Learn is; I doubt very much that proponents of Learning to Learn really understand it either. But I do know one thing: it doesn't sound very much like teaching knowledge. And as we have heard: teaching knowledge is the thing! Members of the jury: let us not step back into the dark ages. It is incumbent upon you to lock up Learning to Learn – whatever it may be – and throw away the key!

THE PROSECUTION, CROSS-EXAMINED

Well. That was quite the finish, prosecution! You obviously know a thing or two about rhetorical devices: anaphora (repetition of key phrases); tricolon (the rule of three); apostrophe (addressing a single person); metaphor ('the dark ages'); counter-argument ('our opponents will argue'); rhyme-as-reason ('whatever it may be – throw away the key')... Wouldn't you agree that such a knowledge of rhetorical devices could be applied across a range of contexts, independent of the subject matter being discussed?

And there is more than mere knowledge of rhetoric on display here. You also show an impressive ability to apply this knowledge to skilfully persuade the jury of the truth of your position. How might we describe the ability to effectively deploy one's knowledge of rhetoric in a novel situation? As a transferable skill? A *generic skill*, perhaps? Please, there is no need to answer: this is a rhetorical question in more ways than one. We will allow the jury to reach their own conclusions while we turn to address the substance of your arguments.

1. KNOWLEDGE IS FOUNDATIONAL

We agree. The problem with this argument is not that it's wrong; it is that it is only half right. This point is perhaps best illustrated by comparing what people *say* about the work of Daniel Willingham with what Willingham says himself. Let's remind ourselves of what the two UK politicians who have most influenced education policy in the last ten years have said about his work:

> One of the biggest influences on my thinking about education reform has been the American cognitive scientist Daniel T. Willingham... [who] demonstrates brilliantly in his book, memorisation is a necessary precondition of understanding. (Gove, 2012)[35]

> Daniel Willingham talks about [how] an educated person has vast amounts of knowledge in his or her long-term memory which you can retrieve instantly... As Daniel Willingham has said, education is about... ensuring that we have facts and knowledge securely embedded in long-term memory. (Gibb, 2017)[36]

Now let's examine Willingham's own words. The following excerpts are from the same chapter as the line about how 'factual knowledge must precede skill' that was quoted by the prosecution:

> The implication is that facts must be taught, **ideally in the context of skills**.

> **We want our students to think, not simply to memorise.** When someone shows evidence of thinking critically, we consider her smart and well-educated. When someone spouts facts without context, we consider her boring and a show-off.

> The conclusion from this work in cognitive science is straightforward: we must ensure that students acquire background knowledge **in parallel with practising critical thinking skills**.

> *In this chapter I describe how cognitive scientists know that* **thinking skills and knowledge are bound together**.
>
> **Our goal is not simply to have students know a lot of stuff** – *it's to have them know stuff in service of being able to think effectively.*[37]

He even includes the following quote by J.D. Everett (1873):

> *There is a great danger in the present day lest science teaching should degenerate into the accumulation of disconnected facts and unexplained formulae, which burden the memory without cultivating the understanding.*[38]

Clearly, a closer reading of Willingham's work reveals a more sophisticated understanding of the relationship between knowledge and skills than these politicians acknowledge. In short, knowledge may be *necessary* for critical thinking, but it is not *sufficient*. It is abundantly clear that Willingham's central message is one of balance, and he could not sum up the twin insights of cognitive science more clearly:

> *It is certainly true that facts without the skills to use them are of little value. It is equally true that one cannot deploy thinking skills effectively without factual knowledge.*[39]

If our aim is to create a knowledge-rich curriculum, it is important to be clear about what we mean by knowledge, what we mean by skill, and how the two connect. Epistemology – the branch of philosophy concerned with the theory of knowledge – is enormously complex, and we have no intention of disappearing down *that* rabbit hole. However, it is useful to consider the distinction that is often drawn between declarative knowledge – knowing *that* – and procedural knowledge – knowing *how*. The Merriam-Webster dictionary defines 'knowledge' as:

1. *the fact or condition of knowing something with familiarity gained through experience or association;*

2. *acquaintance with or understanding of a science, art, or technique.*[40]

Here we can see both declarative knowledge ('knowing something') and procedural knowledge ('acquaintance with a technique'). We can also see that there is more to skill than procedural knowledge. An individual might be 'acquainted with a technique' – they might understand the principle of juggling, say, and could maybe even juggle three balls for a few seconds – but that doesn't mean they could join the circus. The

Merriam-Webster dictionary defines 'skill' as:

1. a) *the ability to use one's knowledge effectively and readily in execution or performance;*
   b) *dexterity or coordination especially in the execution of learned physical tasks;*

2. *a learned power of doing something competently: a developed aptitude or ability.*[41]

We can therefore view skill as the ability to use either declarative or procedural knowledge for a purpose and to a high standard, through repeated practice.

Learning a subject often requires a combination of declarative knowledge, procedural knowledge and skill. As we will see in *Chapter 5: Components of a complex intervention*, Learning to Learn is no different in this regard. Teaching children how to work together productively in groups; how to build powerful arguments, identify questionable assumptions and recognise logical fallacies; how to independently plan, execute, monitor and evaluate a project over a period of weeks; how to write and deliver a knockout speech using a range of rhetorical techniques... all of these things involve a combination of declarative knowledge, procedural knowledge and practised skills.

In addition, as we will see in Part II, in Learning to Learn lessons pupils accumulate a wealth of knowledge, skills, habits and dispositions that they would not otherwise learn through a purely subject-based curriculum. So to argue that knowledge is foundational is correct, but it is also to push at an open door. It does nothing to undermine the case for Learning to Learn – indeed, it strengthens it considerably.

Finally, we must ask: how do we determine the extent to which a school is successful in helping pupils store knowledge in their long-term memories? Obviously, it is not possible to look inside children's heads and inspect their schemata, and so we use other methods as proxies – methods like teacher assessments and exam results. The higher the grade, the more knowledge we can assume the child has accumulated. If there is strong evidence that other approaches significantly improve exam results – approaches that involve the development of metacognition, self-regulation and oracy, say – then clearly, anyone who thinks knowledge is foundationally important should give those approaches serious consideration.

2. CHILDREN ARE NOVICES

Clearly, it would be unwise to argue against the proposition that children are young and inexperienced. We also agree that, as novices, children are more hamstrung than experts are by the limited capacity of working memory. By definition, novices, unlike experts, are unable to bypass the limitations of working memory by accessing knowledge stored in their long-term memory. There is therefore a strong case for teaching children in such a way as to ensure that their working memory is not overwhelmed or overloaded with irrelevant, extraneous information.

Where, then, do we part company with the prosecution's argument? Well, with a characteristic flourish, the prosecution presented their argument with a sleight of hand when they asked the rhetorical question: 'Which is likely to be the most efficient use of time... to have a knowledge-rich curriculum, designed and taught by experts, or to teach novices to 'learn how to learn' in the hope that they will learn it by themselves?' This, of course, is a straw man argument. Perhaps in the past it has been proposed that Learning to Learn is somehow an argument for abolishing subject-based learning altogether, but this is not a position that we would take. Instead, Learning to Learn is something that should run alongside – and be intertwined with – a knowledge-rich, subject-based curriculum.

At this point, the question arises: why do we need timetabled lessons? Should Learning to Learn not be embedded throughout the curriculum? This is an excellent question, to which the answer is: 'Yes, but not exclusively. We need timetabled lessons as well.'

In his 2017 book *The Learning Rainforest*, Tom Sherrington suggests that there are essentially two types of teaching: Mode A and Mode B. Mode A teaching is about 'building knowledge... this is the teacher-led instruction mode where you lead the learning from the front, deploying the full range of instruction and feedback techniques',[42] while Mode B teaching includes things like project-based learning, 'deep end' learning, going off-piste, allowing greater student autonomy, developing presentational talk and debating skills and so on. Essentially – we're paraphrasing here – Mode A is traditional, subject-based teaching, and Mode B is Learning to Learn type stuff. As a rule of thumb, Sherrington proposes a roughly 80:20 split of Mode A to Mode B teaching, although he acknowledges that he would expect 'vigorous debate about the 80:20 split... as different values and contexts come into play'.[43]

The problem with an embedded-only approach to Learning to Learn is that not all teachers are equally on board with the Mode B stuff. Some teachers don't see it as part of their job, or they don't feel they have the time to do it in the context of a packed curriculum, or they don't have the knowledge, skills or experience to do it well even if they wanted to.

In one study, researchers identified two distinct interpretations of Learning to Learn among secondary school teachers: a 'narrow' conception, described as being 'limited to mere tips and advice in order to prepare [for] examinations or tests',[44] and a 'broad' conception, in which the aim is to 'develop attitudes and skills which are important outside the school and classroom context'.[45] This study found that only 28% of the teachers surveyed had a broad conception of Learning to Learn, and most of the remaining 72% of teachers reported that they did not have enough time to pursue it with their classes. The researchers concluded that for the majority of teachers, 'teaching how to learn seems of minor importance. They do not consider it an essential part of their task'.[46] In contrast, for teachers with a broad conception of Learning to Learn, it was 'not a problem to find time to teach students how to learn. These teachers make time for it.'[47]

In schools, we need teachers who are really passionate about teaching their subject. And we also need teachers who are really passionate about the Mode B stuff. Some teachers can do Mode B teaching brilliantly, but the quality and quantity varies hugely throughout the profession as a whole. An embedded-only approach to Learning to Learn therefore means that many students miss out on receiving the best we have to offer with regard to Mode B teaching.

With timetabled Learning to Learn lessons, we can outsource most of the heavy lifting with regard to Mode B teaching to a dedicated team of teachers who are as enthusiastic about project-based learning and developing oracy skills as subject-based teachers often are about inspiring the next generation to learn about geography, maths or drama. It is also more efficient that way, and less confusing for the children, who get to learn the skills of metacognition, self-regulation and oracy from enthusiastic teachers in dedicated lessons rather than having it taught in ten different ways by ten different teachers.

As Bjork et al. (2013) point out, most students aren't naturally very good at regulating their learning,[48] which is to say: children are novices at Learning to Learn as well. Teaching novice children to become effective self-regulated learners requires the same level of painstaking, time-consuming instruction that subject-based learning requires: modelling, explaining, practising, questioning, providing plenty of rich feedback, and then scaffolding and withdrawing that support once the children have built up a rich network of schemata, habits and dispositions relating to self-regulated learning itself.

Indeed, some of the most fascinating work taking place in the field of cognitive load theory at the moment relates to the implications of the theory for self-regulated learning and collaborative learning.[49, 50, 51, 52] How much better would children be at regulating their own learning if they themselves had a sophisticated understanding of working memory, long-term memory and cognitive load theory, and played a proactive role in developing and tending a vibrant mental garden of knowledge-rich schemata? As with the argument that knowledge is foundational, the existence of cognitive load theory does nothing to undermine the case for Learning to Learn; rather, it opens up promising new avenues of research and practice where these two theories collide. As Sweller, van Merriënboer and Paas (2019) suggest:

> Both cognitive load theory and models of self-regulated learning, which deal with learners' monitoring and control of their learning processes, may be seen as particularly important perspectives for supporting lifelong learners in an information-rich, complex and fast-changing society.[53]

This recognition that monitoring and control are common to both cognitive load theory and self-regulated learning theory provides a powerful case for standalone Learning to Learn lessons. As van Merriënboer and Kirschner (2018) suggest:

> Because monitoring and control are closely linked to each other in the same learning cycle, it makes no sense asking learners to monitor their own learning (e.g., assess their own learning, reflect on their own learning processes) if they have no opportunity to control it. To illustrate this: Suppose you are in the passenger seat of a car and required to monitor the traffic in the rear view mirror. This would feel like a pointless exercise because it does not help the car be driven more safely, and you would probably ignore the request. Looking in the rear view mirror only makes sense when you are in the driver seat, that is, when you are in control and can use the information on the traffic behind you to drive more safely. The same is true in education: It only makes sense to ask learners to monitor or reflect on their own performance when they are in a position to use their thoughts to control or plan future actions.[54]

Only by providing children with the space and time in the curriculum to practise monitoring and controlling their thoughts, feelings and learning behaviours can we expect them to develop expertise in the arena of self-regulated learning. In this book, we argue and have evidence to suggest that the best way to provide that time and space is a) to have timetabled Learning to Learn lessons, and b) to have aspects of Learning to Learn embedded throughout the curriculum, so that students get to practise using their knowledge, skills, habits and dispositions in the context of subject-based learning.

3. GENERIC SKILLS CANNOT BE TAUGHT/ SKILLS DON'T TRANSFER

The trends in historical literacy rates suggest that there is some truth to Sweller's assertion that people 'learn to listen and speak without ever going to school',[55] whereas reading and writing require formal instruction. The question is: Do all people speak and listen to the same standard – and if not, why not? Throughout human history, a small number of people have given sensational, world-changing speeches, while many others – incredibly – rank their fear of public speaking higher than their fear of death.[56]

Why is it that some people relish public speaking, while many others would literally rather the earth swallowed them whole? Is a propensity for public speaking simply a genetic or familial lottery, or might it be influenced by the education a child receives?

To help us answer this question, we might reflect on the fact that Eton College – a school that has produced no fewer than 20 prime ministers – recently spent £18 million on a new debating chamber.[57] Could the fact that Eton puts so much resource into the teaching of debating skills possibly be linked to the fact that it produces so many 'gifted' orators? Or should we more accurately consider them 'practised' orators?

BURNING QUESTION

Do all people speak and listen to the same standard, and if not, why not?

We do not suggest that the teaching of debating alone accounts for the surplus of Old Etonian prime ministers. However, it is clear that schools like Eton do not leave the development of speaking and listening skills to chance. Instead, they give their students time, expert tuition and plenty of practice. Elsewhere, there is an extensive body of research literature to suggest that an individual's experience of conversational turn-taking in childhood[58] – and the extent to which they receive explicit oracy education in school – are powerful predictors of their future cognitive, social and emotional and life outcomes.[59] We'll explore this in more detail in *Chapter 5: Components of a complex intervention*.

Tricot and Sweller (2014) argue that biologically primary cognitive abilities are synonymous with 'generic skills', and that generic skills cannot and should not be taught. But the assertion that speaking and listening skills are 'acquired easily, unconsciously and without explicit tuition'[60] – and that therefore schools need not concern themselves with teaching them – is just not supported by the available evidence.

Why, for example, do some children arrive at school in a 'preverbal' state, while others can speak in full sentences? And why is it that such a high proportion of children diagnosed with Speech, Language and Communication Needs come from disadvantaged areas?[61] Is this simply a *coincidence*? While it may be true that humans have an innate *capacity* for spoken language, there is also overwhelming evidence that speaking and listening skills are influenced by environmental factors – both inside and outside of school – to a significant degree.

The evidence that generic skills *can* be taught to a significant degree is not limited to speaking and listening, either. In the research literature on critical thinking, there is a consensus that the ability to think critically about something is partly domain-specific (i.e. it depends on your knowledge of a given topic) and partly domain general (i.e. it requires an understanding of what it means to think critically that is transferable across domains).

For example, a wide-ranging meta-analysis carried out by Abrami et al. (2015) concluded that 'a variety of critical thinking skills (both generic and content-specific) and dispositions can develop in students through instruction at all educational levels and across all disciplinary areas using a number of effective strategies'.[62]

Many other studies have found that critical thinking training leads to better performance in critical thinking, regardless of domain.[63, 64, 65, 66] Indeed, Tricot and Sweller themselves acknowledge that there is a 'nearly universal consensual view that... knowledge imparted during instruction includes some mixture of domain-general and domain-specific information'.[67] So, while domain-specific content knowledge is undoubtedly important, it is also clear that generic aspects of critical thinking exist – and that they can be taught to a significant degree.

If we accept that speaking and listening and critical thinking skills can be taught and do transfer – and there is abundant evidence that they can – then the claim that 'generic skills cannot be taught' starts to look pretty tenuous. Indeed, van Merriënboer and Kirschner (2018) provide us with some fairly specific guidance on how to teach generic skills.[68] They point out that teaching domain-general skills *in isolation* does not work, and that the development of domain-general and domain-specific knowledge and skills should be intertwined – a proposition we agree with wholeheartedly.

The second part of the argument was that skills tend to be quite specific to the context in which they were developed, and that they do not transfer easily. Unfortunately for the prosecution, there is abundant evidence that this is not the case. A helpful summary of the research literature on transfer is provided by Anderson et al. (1996):

> A large body of empirical research on transfer in psychology... demonstrates that there can be either large amounts of transfer, a modest amount of transfer, no transfer at all, or even negative transfer. How much there is and whether transfer is positive depends in reliable ways on the experimental situation and the relation of the material originally learned to the transfer material.[69]

In short, the answer to whether knowledge and skills can transfer from one domain to another is: it depends. Transfer does not always happen automatically, but that does not mean it is a lost cause. It simply means that we have to manage transfer carefully, at both ends of the process – transfer *out* of the *Learning Skills* classroom and transfer *in* to subject learning across the curriculum. We will consider what this looks like in practice in *Chapter 5*. For now, we will conclude with another short excerpt from the paper by Anderson et al., which encapsulates the research literature admirably:

> While cognition is partly context-dependent, it is also partly context-independent; while there are dramatic failures of transfer, there are also dramatic successes; while concrete instruction helps, abstract instruction also helps.[70]

Ladies and gentlemen of the jury. The prosecution's arguments, though insightful and fascinating to consider, do nothing to undermine the case for Learning to Learn; indeed, they strengthen it considerably. The argument that knowledge is foundational is of course correct – and there is abundant evidence that the development of metacognition, self-regulation and oracy skills help children become significantly more knowledgeable. The argument that children are novices is undeniably true – but this only lends weight to the idea that we should provide children with expert guidance in the arena of self-regulated learning, too. And the claims that generic skills cannot be taught and that skills do not transfer from one context to another are simply not supported by the available evidence.

Members of the jury: in responding to the arguments advanced by the prosecution, we do not expect to have converted you to the merits of Learning to Learn just yet. However, perhaps we have succeeded in allaying one or two concerns. All we ask is that you maintain an open mind as we turn our attention to some positive arguments for giving Learning to Learn curriculum time alongside traditional, subject-based learning.

THE DEFENCE: ARGUMENTS IN FAVOUR OF LEARNING TO LEARN

'Martin Luther King didn't say "I have a nightmare."'

Rutger Bregman (2017)[71]

So far in this chapter, we have focused on arguments against Learning to Learn. But – as the above quote captures so brilliantly – in this life, you also need to be *for something*. This book is very much for something – it is an argument for Learning to Learn to be given lesson time in schools, and for that time to be used to implement a *Learning Skills* curriculum. In Part II, we will explore what this looks like in practice, as well as outlining the evidence from the Sea View study. But first, in order to persuade the jury that Learning to Learn is worthy of further consideration, we will present three lines of argument: 1) The field has evolved since it was last evaluated; 2) Scaling up is hard to do, but implementation science is a thing now; and 3) The death of Learning to Learn has been greatly exaggerated. Let's consider each in turn.

ARGUMENT 1: THE FIELD HAS EVOLVED SINCE IT WAS LAST EVALUATED

If it is possible to teach children (and indeed adults) how to get better at learning stuff, then it is self-evidently a good idea to do so. However, it is important to recognise the scale of the task before us. As we have mentioned, translating insights from research into practice in such a way as to reliably improve student outcomes across a large number of schools is no mean feat. That doesn't mean it's impossible. However, it is reasonable to expect that it may take some time until we are able to do so reliably, on a large scale and across a diverse range of school contexts.

As we saw in *Chapter 2*, Learning to Learn is a dynamic field of theory and practice that has developed and grown significantly throughout the last 40 years. There is no reason to believe that this process of evolution will cease any time soon. In this book, we present an approach that we believe advances the field in several important ways, and we can already think of a dozen ways in which we will do things differently in the future. As the field continues to evolve, and as new ways of conceptualising and practising Learning to Learn emerge, it is important that we should continue to evaluate the latest state of the art.

We also saw in *Chapter 2* that the last large-scale evaluations of Learning to Learn in the UK were carried out between 2000 and 2010, when questionable third-generation approaches to Learning to Learn were all the rage. By way of confirmation, Professor Steve Higgins, the lead investigator on the *Learning to Learn in Schools* study, reflected that this project 'mainly investigated the third generation of Learning to Learn, with teachers in primary and secondary schools researching ideas such as emotional intelligence, brain-based learning and learning styles'.[72] It is therefore clear that the *Learning to Learn in Schools* study – by far the largest study of Learning to Learn conducted in the UK to date – evaluated practices that were very much of their time, including several that have since been discredited.

We understand why the prosecution are jumpy about generic skills. The problem is not really that generic skills cannot be taught. The real concern is with the idea that generic skills can be taught or developed *in the absence of subject knowledge*, and these concerns are well justified. During the late 2000s, as we have seen, there was a strong focus on skills and personalisation promoted by the government of the day. In particular, the Personal Learning and Thinking Skills (PLTS) framework promoted the idea that 'generic skills' such as creativity and teamwork could be taught or developed in the abstract – in the absence of subject knowledge.[73] This led to some decidedly dubious teaching practices, as Sherrington (2017) captures well:

> For a time during the late 2000s... a lot of teachers and school leaders warmed to the idea that we should be trying to develop students' dispositions as well as teaching them knowledge... The problem I found with this approach was that in some schools the dispositions were presented in abstract, removed from any learning content... I've been to a school where they had off-timetable... days, including 'resilience workshops' which had no knowledge base at all. I once observed a history lesson where a teacher started by holding up his Resilience poster, announcing that 'today we will be building up our resilience'. There was some

*discussion about the idea of resilience but nothing in the content
of the lesson required students to actually be resilient.*[74]

By weighing the merits of Learning to Learn on the basis of evaluations
that were carried out during the third-generation era – an era when
questionable ideas about teaching and learning abounded, driven by
the government policy of the day – we are in danger of throwing out the
baby with the bathwater. Instead, we should continue to evaluate latest
practice as the field continues to develop and grow in confidence.

By way of analogy, think of the ludicrous contraptions early flight pioneers
smashed around in just a hundred or so years ago, before the Wright
brothers finally took to the skies in glorious flight.[75] Many of the schemes
were clearly hare-brained, and at the time there was no shortage of
Doubting Thomases who loudly proclaimed that the whole business of
aviation was a reckless waste of time, resources and human lives. But the
same conviction underpinned every attempt: we can fly, we just can't fly
yet! With the benefit of hindsight, we can see the wisdom in what once
seemed like reckless abandon: at any given point in time in recent years,
there have been more than half a million people zooming around the
upper atmosphere.[76]

We should not judge Learning to Learn on the basis of a small number
of evaluations that were carried out at a particular point in time. In the
last ten years or so, facilitated to a significant degree by the internet,
the teaching profession has made huge strides toward becoming a far
more evidence-informed, research-literate, sure-footed profession. As our
understanding of learning develops, so should our ideas about teaching
children how to get better at learning. We should continue to evaluate
the latest thinking and whatever we deem to be best practice at every
step along the way. It is surely worth the effort. If it does transpire that it is
possible to reliably teach young people how to become more confident,
proactive and self-regulated learners on a large scale, and across a wide
range of contexts...well, that would be quite something, wouldn't it? Let's
continue to innovate and evaluate until we get this baby off the ground.

ARGUMENT 2: SCALING UP IS HARD TO DO, BUT IMPLEMENTATION SCIENCE IS A THING NOW

This line of argument has the same starting point as the last one – the belief that teaching children how to get better at learning stuff is self-evidently a good idea. After all, this belief is rooted in 'extensive evidence' that teaching which develops metacognitive and self-regulatory processing leads to significant, measurable gains across a range of pupil outcomes. The challenge is to figure out how to replicate these findings reliably, on a large scale and across a diverse range of contexts – which is no surprise, given the scale of the task. It's not so much that Learning to Learn doesn't scale – it's more that we haven't quite got the hang of scaling up itself. Yet. At least, not in education.

Scaling up in other fields is relatively easy. Take technology. All you need is for a few people to become interested in your shiny new gizmo, and when you reach a certain proportion of population – as little as 10 to 25%, surprisingly[77] – it 'tips' and suddenly achieves market saturation. Home computers, smartphones, social media platforms – there are loads of examples of this. And it's not just tech: every household brand and high street chain you can think of is an example of an idea that has scaled up successfully. There are also many examples of excellent ideas and products that didn't scale; usually, this is due to suboptimal marketing and messaging. But you get the idea: in the world of commerce, things scale all the time.

Scaling up in education, however, is far harder to do – so much so, in fact, that it's actually quite difficult to think of examples of promising educational initiatives that scaled up and maintained their efficacy at scale. One of the key problems – a question we will return to in *Chapter 8: An implementation (and evaluation) checklist* – is how to avoid 'lethal mutations'.

When you scale up a promising educational initiative, it's important to understand that no two schools are alike. If you're too rigid in how you implement the initiative – if you provide people with a 'recipe for success' or a ring binder full of lesson plans that they are supposed to teach straight from the shelf – you may very well find that it doesn't work because it doesn't take account of the local context or harness the autonomy and agency of the teachers involved. So, you might introduce some flexibility in how you implement your initiative. However, if you give people too much freedom over how (or how frequently) an idea is implemented, you may find that it becomes riddled with 'lethal mutations'. People skip a step here and add something else there, time wears on, and, before you know it, what is being implemented bears little resemblance to the original idea.

A good example of an idea that struggled to scale is Assessment for Learning (AfL, also known as formative assessment) – an idea that overlaps significantly with metacognition and self-regulation, as we saw in *Chapter 2: A brief history of Learning to Learn*. AfL became popular following the publication of the seminal publication *Inside the Black Box* by Black and Wiliam (1998). Black and Wiliam

> **LETHAL MUTATION**
>
> When an educational initiative is changed in such a way as to render it ineffective. Adapted from biology, where it describes a genetic copying error that causes the death, or reduces the lifespan, of the organism.

carried out a systematic review of the research literature and concluded that formative assessment, which they defined simply as assessment that is 'used to adapt the teaching to meet student needs',[78] is education's best bet for improving academic attainment. Indeed, they went so far as to say that 'we know of no other way of raising standards for which such a strong *prima facie* case can be made'.[79]

Following the publication of *Inside the Black Box*, AfL scaled up in a big way. It had everything going for it – a compelling research base, the support of both government and teachers, and a wealth of resources. However, scaling up this simple, common-sense idea in such a way as to replicate the results at scale proved far more difficult than anyone anticipated. As described by Professor Rob Coe (2013):

> *[AfL] became the focus of national policy, widely endorsed by teachers and supported by extensive government training... It is now a rare thing, in my experience, to meet any teacher in any school in England who would not claim to be doing Assessment for Learning. And yet... during the fifteen years of this intensive intervention to promote AfL, despite its near universal adoption and strong research evidence of substantial impact on attainment, there has been no (or at best limited) effect on learning outcomes nationally.*[80]

So, what went wrong? The problem isn't that formative assessment is a bad idea – clearly, teachers adapting their practice in response to assessment data is preferable to them ploughing on regardless. Perhaps the root of the problem lies in the final paragraphs of *Inside the Black Box*, where Black and Wiliam wrote: 'it is the responsibility of governments to take the lead... Our plea is that national and state policy makers will grasp this opportunity and take the lead in this direction.'[81] This appeal for government to take the lead in implementing AfL may well have been the kiss of death. As Daisy Christodoulou (2016) suggested:

Government support for [AfL] was, in fact, counterproductive... the minute the government get their hands on anything that has the word assessment in it, beware. Because they'll turn it into something that is about high stakes tracking and monitoring, and it won't be about that low stakes improvement of teaching and learning, of diagnosing what the problem is and trying to fix it.[82]

Wiliam later suggested that:

In hindsight, it would have been better to introduce what we are doing as 'responsive teaching' and then, later, to expand the frame to include the learner's role. By starting out with formative assessment as a label, it allowed people to relabel what they were already doing as formative assessment. The concept hasn't changed, but the strategy was wrong.[83]

As we mentioned in *Chapter 2*, a recent large-scale RCT found that the Embedding Formative Assessment (EFA) approach led to statistically significant gains in subject learning compared with control schools.[84] So the story has a happy ending. But almost 20 years after the publication of *Inside the Black Box*, Wiliam wrote: 'Looking back at the subsequent development of this work... if we had realised how long it would take, I doubt that either of us would have had the courage to begin.'[85] The message is clear: implementing educational innovations at scale – even really good ideas, rooted in a strong evidence base – is no picnic.

Perhaps the biggest problem with scaling up is that it so often involves top-down implementation, with a heavy emphasis on compliance and that dreaded phrase, 'holding people to account'. The problem with top-down implementation is that people don't like being told what to do when they don't get a say in the process – even when what they're being told to do is a good idea – and so they find ways of paying lip service to the innovation without really doing anything different.

> **FORMATIVE ASSESSMENT**
>
> Assessment that is used to adapt the teaching to meet student needs.

This is a really big problem because, in the UK at least, the whole education system is based on top-down implementation. At least it has been since 1988, when the Education Reform Act ushered in the era of the National Curriculum. Top-down is our go-to model for getting things done, and it means that we live in an endless loop where people in leadership positions, whether they are politicians or school leaders, announce their latest wheeze – some scheme that promises to make everything better – and almost regardless of whether the idea is brilliant or bonkers, the end result is that it often fizzles out within a matter of months.

But we're in luck. In recent years, a new field of study has emerged – implementation science – which has been described as 'a new area of scientific, academic and practitioner interest focused on exploring and explaining what makes interventions work in real-world contexts'.[86] In short, implementation science is a systematic

> **IMPLEMENTATION SCIENCE**
> A new field of theory and practice focused on exploring and explaining what makes interventions work (and not work) in real-world contexts.

attempt to answer the burning question school leaders and policymakers have wrestled with, often in vain, for decades: *How can we translate what we know about 'what works' into policies and practices that reliably replicate (or improve on) those positive outcomes when implemented in new and diverse contexts?*

We will present some relevant insights from implementation science in *Chapter 8: An implementation (and evaluation) checklist*, although it really deserves a book all of its own – watch this space![87] Over the last two years, we have been trialling a new implementation programme for schools in the UK and internationally, and the feedback has been incredible. But the short version is that implementation science provides us with a set of powerful, tried-and-tested tools for answering this burning question, and there is good reason to believe that scaling up the *Learning Skills* approach will be a lot more straightforward as a consequence.[88]

> **BURNING QUESTION**
> How can we translate what we know about 'what works' into policies and practices that reliably replicate (or improve on) those positive outcomes when implemented in new and diverse contexts?

ARGUMENT 3: THE DEATH OF LEARNING TO LEARN HAS BEEN GREATLY EXAGGERATED

A good example of how the death of Learning to Learn has been greatly exaggerated can be seen in a speech the School Standards Minister Nick Gibb gave at the 2015 researchED conference, entitled *The Importance of the Teaching Profession*. In his speech, Mr Gibb lent his vocal support to the EEF *Teaching and Learning Toolkit*:

> *The work of teachers has allowed the EEF to make great strides since we founded the organisation in 2011… The thirst for quality education research, which is so evident at this conference today, has begun to change how decisions are made within schools… But there is still a long way to go. We created the EEF*

due to a belief that high-quality, robust research could empower classroom teachers, and I firmly believe it can.[89]

In the same speech, Mr Gibb decried a 2006 report published under the preceding New Labour government:

It remains important to ask why so many poor ideas were sustained for so long within schools. To answer such a question, we must not forget the role played by central government. To give just one example, in 2006 the Department for Children, Schools and Families formed the 'Teaching and Learning in 2020 Review Group'. Their subsequent report, entitled 2020 Vision, threw its weight behind 'personalised learning', explained as:

> *'Learners are active and curious: they create their own hypotheses, ask their own questions, coach one another, set goals for themselves, monitor their progress and experiment with ideas for taking risks'.*

2020 vision suggested that the school of 2020 should pursue: 'learning how to learn'; 'themed project work'; and 'using ICT to enhance collaboration and creative learning'. Lots of talk about learners learning, but almost nothing about teachers teaching.[90]

The remarkable thing here is that the passage Mr Gibb holds up as an example of a 'poor idea' – students setting goals, experimenting with different ideas, monitoring their own progress – is strikingly similar to the EEF's definition of self-regulation. As we saw in *Chapter 1: High impact for low cost, or snake oil for hipsters?*, the EEF *Teaching and Learning Toolkit* ranks metacognition and self-regulation – which it describes as being synonymous with 'Learning to Learn' – as being among the most impactful practices teachers can use, providing 'high impact for very low cost, based on extensive evidence'. Here's a reminder of how the EEF toolkit describes these practices:

Metacognition and self-regulation approaches aim to help pupils think about their own learning more explicitly, often by teaching them specific strategies for planning, monitoring and evaluating their learning. Interventions are usually designed to give pupils a repertoire of strategies to choose from and the skills to select the most suitable strategy for a given learning task.[91]

Here, then, we have a Schools Minister who proclaims the golden age of the EEF toolkit while decrying the very practices the EEF toolkit says are the most effective – in the same speech! It is difficult to know how to interpret this. One could be forgiven for thinking that politicians cherry-pick research evidence that suits their ideological position and wilfully ignore any counter-evidence. We subscribe to the more charitable view that this is unknowing rather than wilful – but either way, such a mis-reading of the research literature by those who shape education policy should be robustly challenged.

In *Chapter 2*, we reviewed the research evidence relating to Learning to Learn. On the one hand, we found overwhelming evidence relating to the significant impact of metacognition and self-regulation on improving student outcomes. On the other, we saw that four large-scale evaluations of Learning to Learn in the UK had 'mixed results'. These mixed results are important to understand, and we have suggested that they were likely due to a combination of factors, namely: patchy implementation; being a product of their time; researchers throwing the net too wide when evaluating findings across dozens of schools; and the difficulties associated with scaling up. None of these problems are insurmountable, and in this book we propose a number of practical ways in which we might avoid such problems in the future.

To recap: the evidence in favour of Learning to Learn – conceived in the *Learning Skills* approach as a combination of metacognition, self-regulation and oracy education – is abundant and compelling. In the 'mixed evidence' column, we have four studies that we have already discussed at length. And in the 'evidence against' column, we have... tumbleweed. On balance, it would be fair to say that the weight of evidence remains overwhelmingly in favour of Learning to Learn – and we add to that weight of evidence in this book.

We saw earlier that Learning to Learn has been described by various commentators as 'bad education'[92] and a 'snake oil hoax'.[93] Having reviewed the literature and explored the surrounding issues, these claims now look rather overblown. Indeed, these claims seem to have been based solely on the basis of the 'mixed results' of the four studies we examined above. Bennett's critique of Learning to Learn focused primarily on two of those four studies, while Hayes' concerns focused mainly on just one of them.[94] We have done a more thorough job of critiquing the field in this book. But we also recognise what we believe to be the glaring truth of the matter – that there is far more evidence in the 'for' column.

The conclusion is clear: the death of Learning to Learn has been greatly exaggerated – in the literature and in political speeches, at least. As we saw in the *Introduction*, the demise of taught Learning to Learn courses in UK secondary schools in the last ten years is very real.

It's time to redress the balance.

Ladies and gentlemen of the jury. We have seen – and we will continue to see throughout Part II of this book – that the field of Learning to Learn has evolved significantly since it was last evaluated on a large scale. We have seen that the 'mixed results' of previous large-scale evaluations of Learning to Learn were due to a combination of factors – not least the challenge of scaling up effective practices – and there is good reason to believe that we can overcome these challenges in the future. And we have seen that claims relating to the death of Learning to Learn look rather ill-founded in the face of the overwhelming research evidence we see when teachers and school leaders take the teaching of self-regulated learning seriously.

In seeking to unravel the Learning to Learn paradox throughout Part I of this book, we have considered three questions:

1. Is it possible to teach children to become more confident, curious, independent learners?
2. Is it possible to improve how Learning to Learn is implemented in new and diverse contexts?
3. Is it possible to improve how Learning to Learn is evaluated?

We believe that the answer to each of these questions is a resounding YES! We should not casually dismiss Learning to Learn on the basis of a small number of studies carried out over ten years ago or a selective reading of the research literature. Instead, we should ask: why have the positive research findings relating to metacognition and self-regulation not been replicated when these practices have been scaled up into whole-school approaches? Is it because it cannot be done – or just that it has not successfully scaled up yet? Is it the metacognition and self-regulation that's the problem, or might it be something to do with the complex task of scaling up and evaluating impact across a large number of schools? And, perhaps most importantly: have all lines of inquiry been thoroughly exhausted, or might there still be ways to learn from and build on previous work in this area – both in terms of implementation and evaluation? Might there be a fifth generation of theory and practice that could develop the field further still?

We hope that by now we have succeeded in opening your mind to the possibility that Learning to Learn is currently undervalued and underrepresented in the way schools are organised. We hope that your mind will open further as you discover what the *Learning Skills* curriculum looks like in practice in Part II. And we hope that it will open further still as you and others begin to trial and evaluate these ideas and practices in the

FEAR IS THE MIND KILLER

months and years to come, and when further evidence of their efficacy comes to light. First, though, it is only fair that we conclude this chapter by allowing the defence to be cross-examined...

THE DEFENCE, CROSS-EXAMINED

Prosecution: You claim that the theory and practice of Learning to Learn is still evolving – that it is in a state of *adolescence*, if you will. But the field is more than 40 years old! How much longer will it take to reach maturity? Is this not simply a case of *arrested development*?

Defence: It isn't the case that there hasn't been any evidence of impact in that 40-year period. As we saw in *Chapter 2*, there is abundant evidence of impact relating to metacognition and self-regulation. In many ways, maturity has already been achieved, although there is always room for improvement. The challenge is firstly to improve the way in which Learning to Learn is conceived and practised in schools, and then to scale up those practices in such a way that the positive results are replicated or even improved upon when implemented in new and diverse contexts. We believe – and have evidence to suggest – that with the *Learning Skills* curriculum we have made some purposeful strides in achieving both of these aims. We'll explain how in Part II.

Prosecution: Very well, very well... *shuffles papers*. Next, you argued that the failure of Learning to Learn to produce positive outcomes on a large scale is because it is difficult to scale up good ideas. But is it really? A good idea is a good idea, and effective practice is effective practice. Aren't you just trying to resurrect an edu-myth that has had its day? For how much longer must we flog this dead donkey?

Defence: Scaling up in education is incredibly challenging, as we saw in the case of Assessment for Learning. But thanks to the emerging field of implementation science, we now know much more than we used to about how to scale up educational interventions successfully. We'll get into this in more detail in *Chapter 8: An implementation (and evaluation) checklist*. But really, we don't need to implement *Learning Skills* at a system level, or even at the level of a local authority or multi-academy trust. We just need to do it one school at a time – and this book contains all you need to know to get started.

Prosecution: Speaking of implementation, it strikes me that as a 'complex intervention' *Learning Skills* might be quite hard to implement. And if an educational initiative is hard to implement, it's probably not a very good idea. How sure are you that *Learning Skills* is scalable?

Defence: This is an excellent point. *Learning Skills* is a complex intervention. However, that doesn't mean it's complicated to implement. After all, we made it work at Sea View – and we didn't have this book to guide us! From a whole-school perspective, it only requires teachers to do a few simple things – the *Learning Skills* teachers, and the students themselves, do most of the heavy lifting. As to whether it is possible to replicate the results of the Sea View study at scale, it is too soon to say at present. Firstly, it depends on whether other schools decide to implement the approach – we certainly hope so. If that happens, we've given the question of scalability a lot of thought and we think it stands a really good chance – much more so than in the past. But it is an important point – thank you for raising it – and we will return to it at the end of *Chapter 5*.

Prosecution: *Time will tell*. How convenient. The prosecution rests. For now...

PART II
THE *LEARNING SKILLS* CURRICULUM

CHAPTER 4

THE STORY OF
LEARNING SKILLS

'If you always do what you've always done,
you'll always get what you've always got.'

Stuart McLaughlin (n.d.)[1]

We (the authors of this book) are very different people and very different teachers, and although we share firmly in the belief that it's a good idea to teach children how to learn as well as what to learn, we arrived at this shared understanding in very different ways. For this reason, the first part of this chapter is written from each of our individual perspectives.

KATE'S STORY
THE KETTLING

When I first started teaching, I found that I was drawn to working with pupils who displayed 'challenging behaviour'. I suppose, with the clarity of hindsight, I wanted to be the kind of teacher I needed when I was twelve. Today, I would be described as a 'school refuser'. I found school to be a confusing and unwelcoming place, and so I avoided it as much as I could. It was only when I left school and got a job that I realised I could teach myself the things I needed to learn. I became fluent in French, worked abroad, became a parent and got a degree. Ten years after I'd left with two GCSEs, I returned to my old school as a very proud and slightly terrified trainee teacher.

As a newly qualified teacher (NQT) of French, I didn't think much about the learning side of things. My focus was on teaching. I wanted to do a good job, to make a difference, all that stuff. My NQT year was going well – my mentor was very supportive and encouraging about my developing practice.

However, I couldn't shake the feeling that I was missing something. Had I missed an important lecture during my teacher training, perhaps? My problem was this: no matter how diligently I planned my lessons, some of my students – not many, but a significant minority – seemed all but incapable of learning stuff and retaining it from one lesson to the next. I began to wonder whether there might be more to this teaching lark than designing lesson plans and wall displays. I became increasingly concerned with the question of how learning happens, and whether it might be possible for children to learn how to get better at learning stuff. Slowly but surely, this interest grew into an obsession that I'm still in the grip of almost 20 years later.

One incident really shaped my thinking about how teaching should and shouldn't be done. It came halfway through my NQT year. I was drawn to my door by a kerfuffle in the corridor. Raised voices, scurrying feet, doors slamming. A year 10 boy was being what I can only describe as 'kettled' by some of my colleagues. He reminded me of a fox cornered by hounds. He didn't want to do what they wanted (to go back into the class), and they weren't going to let him escape. I felt his fear. I wanted to intervene. I felt protective of him. But who was I? I was just an NQT. He wasn't my student.

It ended badly and the boy was excluded. The incident marked me. I couldn't help but wonder if there was a better way to deal with children who sometimes find it difficult to stay in the room. I wanted to find a way of teaching that renders that kind of conflict-based behaviour management obsolete; to create a culture and an environment where children are not just forced to learn through the threat of unpleasant consequences, but where they feel safe enough to willingly engage in learning, to be nourished by it and to grow stronger from the experience.

THE 'SO WHAT' MOMENT

I moved to a new school – let's call it City High – where the proportion of students eligible for Free School Meals (FSM) was well above the national average, and around 50% were on the Special Educational Needs and

Disabilities (SEND) register. At City High, many students found it difficult to stay in the room for a full lesson without pushing the boundaries and getting into trouble. Many wouldn't put pen to paper willingly. If a mistake was made, their exercise book would literally go sailing out of the second-floor window and onto the grass below. Suddenly, the question of how to engage students in learning had become fundamental to my ability to teach.

One day, it occurred to me that I needed to stop focusing on how to teach *French* and start thinking about how to teach *them*. Who were these young people? Why did so many of them find it so difficult to stay in the room? Why were they so frightened of making mistakes? I thought that if I could answer these questions, it might become easier to teach them the content I was being paid to deliver. Perhaps then they would be able to engage with the curriculum and make progress. Perhaps they might even enjoy the experience!

So, as well as burning the midnight oil making colourful OHP slides to engage my students,[2] and as well as drilling behaviour routines to create a positive climate for learning, I fed the hungry ones and I kept a store of clothes for the underprepared ones. I had spare books, food, shoes, pens, pencils, bags and time. Time to listen; time to watch; time to learn who they were, what they liked, why they were tired, frightened, lacking in confidence. After a while, the books stopped flying out of the window, the students stayed in the room and I could begin to teach some French.

Building relationships with my students in this way was making teaching possible. They were calm enough most of the time, they were listening, they were trying their best to absorb the information and pass the tests. There were other signs that gave me confidence I was on the right track, too. The 'Star of the Week' display in the corridor had students stopping and smiling as they moved through the school. The displays of key grammar no longer had comedy penises drawn on them. I gave out fewer sanctions and more rewards. With my amazing colleagues, we made it department policy to be 'emotionally literate' (early 2000s!). We would start lessons by asking, in the target language, how students were feeling and we would to listen to their responses, look for any outward signs that they weren't 'ça va bien', and respond accordingly. The impact was profound; we doubled our uptake at GCSE and had to expand the teaching team.

So, when a school inspector was invited in to support the school, I practically skipped to his office, clutching my ring binders, eager to gush about our bilingual breakfast club, our emotionally literate behaviour policy and our nurturing systems. As I recounted each initiative, the inspector responded with the same question: 'So what?'

We'd reduced the number of exclusions from lessons to almost zero. We rarely set detentions. Students kept their exercise books for a whole year. We'd doubled our uptake at GCSE. 'So what?' came the question, again and again.

I was crushed. I was lost for words. *'So what?'* I wanted to spit back. *'Are you kidding me?'*

I went home and I cried. Hot, angry tears of frustration. I was exhausted, but I knew deep down that the inspector had a point. I'd given it my all and yet I'd missed the mark. I felt sure that our actions had made a difference. I'd have bet my house on it. I can still picture the children whose lives those actions impacted. The children for whom I wrote letters to philanthropists so they could go on school trips. The children who wore my kids' hand-me-downs. The children I visited in hospital and at home. The ones I let sleep in my cupboard when they'd been up all night hiding from an abusive home life. The ones I know I kept a little longer from slipping through the cracks.

I thought that what we had done was enough, but suddenly it was clear to me that we had sacrificed measuring student progress on the altar of student wellbeing. I wasn't able to point to any evidence that any of it had had a positive impact on learning.

'So what' indeed! For every child I'd helped to feel included, there were probably ten more whom I hadn't been able to give enough of my attention to. It simply wasn't a sustainable model. One teacher cannot maintain that level of input – not in a school that had so many students with additional learning needs. I was on the right track, but my thinking wasn't quite there yet. It wasn't a question of whether my job as a teacher was to keep the vulnerable ones safe and build them up as individuals, or to teach all students the knowledge and skills they needed to pass exams. The education system has to do both. I needed to figure out how to have my cake and eat it – and to be able to spend time with my own family, enjoy my work and not be a wrung-out tearful wreck.

FIRST FORAYS INTO LEARNING TO LEARN

A question began to form in my mind: what if it were possible to teach the children how to get *themselves* ready to learn instead of relying on adults to do it for them? If we could teach them how to help themselves and each other, they would be able to maintain that learning trajectory over time, and I would be able to focus on teaching and assessment, tracking progress and evaluating the impact of what we were doing.

The first step was to focus on language for learning. For the first half-term of year 7, we followed a curriculum designed by my colleague to encourage a deep understanding of language and culture. This not only helped us to isolate specific skills, it also created a context within which learning the target vocabulary made sense. We focused on developing oracy skills, the rationale being that the more confident they were about speaking and listening in English, the easier it would be to transfer those skills across to learning French and Spanish.

Around this time, the school's leadership team was wrestling with the question of how to help our year 7 students overcome the often difficult transition from primary to secondary school. Essentially, the problem with transition is that the children go from having one teacher in one classroom to many teachers in many classrooms.

This has several consequences. It can be unsettling for pupils – their physical environment changes several times a day, whenever a bell rings. And it is challenging for secondary school teachers, who often have as many as 200-300 pupils pass through their classroom each week. It is therefore not possible to get to know your pupils to anywhere near the extent that is possible in a primary school. So we decided to implement a 'junior model' curriculum where the students had just one teacher for most of their lessons. We still had timetabled lessons – geography, English, art and so on – but it all took place in the same classroom and was taught by the same teacher.

I suspect that at this point some readers will be recoiling in horror. 'So you had teachers teaching outside of their subject specialism... across multiple subjects... through choice?!!' Well, yes, we did, and if we had our time again, we wouldn't go down that route. It did have some advantages, though. We got to know the students really well, which meant that we had far fewer problems with behaviour than with previous year groups. It also meant we could identify very quickly who had the literacy skills to access the curriculum and who didn't, who had social and emotional needs that were affecting their learning, what the circumstances were that sat behind these difficulties, and so on. It also meant we were able to form much stronger relationships with parents and carers. So, from a getting-to-know-the-students perspective, the junior model was really, really powerful.

From a workload perspective, however, it was a tough gig. As teachers, we had to work constantly to gen up on our knowledge of geography, history, art, drama, ICT and so on. And because we were teaching outside of our subject specialism for much of the time, the quality of teaching and learning was inconsistent across the piece. Looking back, it's clear that the junior model was very much a developmental phase – something we had to try in order to realise that the answers must lie elsewhere.

The following year, instead of having timetabled subject lessons, we carved up the curriculum and arranged it into cross-curricular topics. For example, when we created the topic of 'Italy', we taught mountains and volcanoes in geography and the Renaissance in history, made 3-D models of Italy in art and learnt Italian in modern foreign languages. The next term, the topic was the Battle of Hastings, and everything was lined up around that: in English we read Beowulf, in art we created tapestries...

From the pupils' perspective, this approach helped them make sense of their learning. It was much more joined up, and it enabled them to make links between different subjects and to transfer their knowledge and understanding from one subject to another. Each term, instead of being all over the place, they were anchored in time, space and topic. It was also a fantastic opportunity for teachers to gain knowledge and skills through collaborating with teachers from other departments.

From a teaching perspective, colleagues who were comfortable and happy to teach in this collaborative, joined-up way flourished. But some were more 'old school'. They wanted to teach in the manner to which they had become accustomed, and they did not enthusiastically embrace this new way of working. The problem was that we didn't have a team of teachers who could fully embrace all that Learning to Learn requires. We were taking some teachers too far out of their comfort zone, so the students didn't feel as safe as they needed to be to feel courageous and take risks in their own learning. The main lesson we learned was that for Learning to Learn to work, you really need a small team of dedicated teachers who are up for working in a different way.

The previous year, Stuart, our head teacher, had moved to a local school, Sea View, where he encountered a familiar picture – year 7s struggling with the transition from primary school, struggling to organise their time and resources, and struggling to make meaningful progress in lessons. One day he phoned me and invited me to join him, to lead on a new year 7 Learning to Learn curriculum. I didn't have to think long – Stuart is the most inspirational head teacher I've ever worked for.

SAFETY: AN ANTIDOTE TO FEAR

Although I knew we hadn't quite cracked it at City High, we had made huge strides and I was buzzing with ideas about how to make it even better this time around. I had made three key observations. First, students can only learn effectively and make good progress when they feel safe. This might seem obvious, but it takes time and effort to build the relationships and the trust that create a safe climate for learning. We needed to find a way to build those relationships that didn't rely upon the teacher doing all the work. What I wanted was to get the students themselves to create that climate by weaving their own relationships into a supportive web that could hold them all. It isn't sustainable to expect one adult to hold the responsibility for forming all those positive relationships. We needed to develop an approach to classroom practice that allowed the students to really get to know one another, and to create that climate of safety and security for themselves.

Second, you can't leave that to chance, because fear is everywhere in schools. It's not always obviously recognisable, but it's there. Fear of being rejected by peers, fear of being ridiculed, fear of standing out and becoming vulnerable. In the most extreme cases, this fear of failure can stop some students from trying altogether.

I had noticed that my students' behaviour was completely different during school trips. They were nicer to one another and polite to strangers; they were more relaxed and open and more inclined to give things a go. It was as if there was a set of behaviours and attitudes woven into their school uniform that came off when you took them out of the school environment. The fear subsided somehow. Although I didn't yet know why they acted so differently outside of school, I knew that I wanted to recreate that relationship to learning in the classroom – the curious, collaborative, playful attitudes to learning that I had seen. And I knew it had something to do with safety being the antidote to fear.

When a student has reached the point where they're actively trying not to learn stuff, we can only conclude that the education system has failed them. If we were going to help all our students get better at learning, we had to figure out a way to disrupt this vicious cycle and replace it with a virtuous cycle where learning becomes its own reward.

I imagined a classroom where students would ask questions and share answers without fear of ridicule... a classroom where students collaborate effectively, even with students they aren't close friends with... a classroom where children are able to regulate their learning, their feelings and their behaviour... a classroom where thinking and questioning is commonplace and where failure is not only tolerated, but accepted, normalised and embraced as a fundamental part of what it means to be a successful learner.

Instead of being the only person in the room exercising these skills on behalf of the students, I imagined a community where we were all actively engaged in achieving our learning goals together, each sharing our strengths and working on our weak spots. In such a classroom, there is every possibility that students who lack confidence can begin to trust themselves and get that virtuous cycle in motion.

The third insight was that an initiative such as this needs to be designed and delivered by a team of teachers who really believe in what they are doing and who are willing to inject their own strengths and talents into the mix. In the same way that I wanted the students to weave a supportive web of trust that would hold them when they felt nervous, I wanted the same thing for my colleagues. We had to trust one another if we were going to make this work. We had to overcome our own fears around making mistakes, over-stretching or underachieving in order to truly transform the way teaching and learning happened in our classrooms.

We held a competitive selection process to appoint a team of teachers dedicated to the cause. In the interviews, it was immediately apparent to me that at Sea View there was an abundance of talent and experience on which to draw. It was a bit of a dream ticket, really. Stuart had given us five lessons a week to do with as we wished. At our first team meeting, which, as I recall, took place in the local, the excitement was palpable. We couldn't wait to get started.

JAMES'S STORY

THE PROBATION OFFICE

When I was at 6th form college, you had to do something called 'complementary studies' alongside your A levels. I chose 'keyboard skills', picturing myself noodling around on synthesizers in the music room. As it turned out, I found myself in a room with no teacher, an electric typewriter, a book of typing exercises and a tea towel to cover my hands with. So I didn't become a pop star, but I did learn how to type really fast. Years later, I found myself looking for temping work, and because you get slightly better pay if you can type fast, I found myself working as a typist at the local probation office, which was absolutely fascinating.

When someone has been convicted of a crime, a probation officer interviews them to find out about their life and what led them to do what they did. They then write a pre-sentence report, which is sent to the judge to inform sentencing. It was my job to transcribe the probation officers' dictated notes into pre-sentence reports. Over a period of a few months, I had an incredible insight into the life stories of hundreds of people whose lives had gone off the rails – most often, in the cases I was dealing with anyway, habitual shoplifting in order to feed an addiction to drugs and/ or alcohol. In the database, there were literally thousands of people in my town whose lives had gone down this path.

Perhaps it's the way probation officers write pre-sentence reports, but after a few weeks I started to notice a pattern. Typically, the story would begin with the normal good stuff that fills people's lives – a job, a partner, a place to live, some kids perhaps. Then, almost without fail, something bad would happen – a redundancy, a sudden illness or death in the family, an infidelity perhaps. Next came the bit I found the most puzzling: a complete inability to cope with whatever hand it was that life had dealt them. Almost without exception, they would start self-medicating, which in turn led to addiction and debt. Over a period of weeks or months, they would lose their job, their partner, their friends, their accommodation, access to their children. Finally, they would 'hit rock bottom' and find themselves homeless or living in sheltered accommodation, stealing stuff from shops to feed their addiction.

Now, you might think that this is an extremely shallow and generalised account of a complex social phenomenon, and no doubt you would have a point. I'm not holding this up as a robust sociological theory, but at the time it really influenced my thinking and my decision to become a teacher. Some children are born into unbelievably difficult circumstances, and it's obviously a lot harder for those children to make 'good choices' as they grow into adulthood. Fixing this problem is really difficult, because it takes place in millions of homes around the country and it never ends. But every one of these people passes through the education system – a 12-year, almost daily window into every young life. I began to wonder: to what extent do schools prepare young people for how to deal with life's knocks – which come to us all, sooner or later – without falling apart and losing everything they hold dear? And is there more we could do in this regard?

STUDENTS RIGHT IN FRONT OF ME, BUT BEYOND REACH

When I became a teacher, I soon found that I was more interested in helping children develop non-cognitive characteristics (defined as the 'attitudes, behaviours and strategies that are thought to underpin success in school and at work, such as motivation, perseverance, and self-control'[3]) than I was in teaching science. No matter how hard I tried to engage certain students in a conversation about electromagnets, or respiration, or the reactivity of alkali metals – whatever we were doing that day – they would just stare at me blankly in a way that made it clear that they wanted me to leave them alone.

These students were right in front of me, but somehow they were beyond my reach. I don't think it's that they were incapable of understanding the work – they just didn't see the relevance to their lives, and they didn't feel it was something at which they could succeed. I found that this was especially true of students in the lower sets – those who are branded a failure every time there's a graded assessment (several times a year, year in, year out), or whenever they hear their class being referred to as the 'bottom set'.

One day, there had been some issues with bullying at the school, and I asked my year 8 class if we could talk about it if they got their work done with 20 minutes to go. I had prepared some fictional scenarios for them to discuss, firstly in pairs and then as a class. All of a sudden, students that I hadn't been able to squeeze two words out of all year came to life, constructing persuasive arguments as to why so-and-so was out of order, demonstrating their ability to consider a complex situation from multiple perspectives, and changing their minds in real time as new evidence came to light. The transformation was really quite astonishing.

In order to develop students' learning skills, dispositions and attitudes – speaking and listening, interpersonal skills, critical thinking and reasoning, organising their time and resources, being proactive rather than reactive, and so on – you need something for them to think and reason *about*.

Maybe it's a reflection of my lack of skill as a science teacher, but I found that topics like electromagnets and respiration and the reactivity of alkali metals are of limited use in this regard. It's a lot easier if the subject matter has a creative, moral or mysterious dimension. Animal rights, crime and punishment, do ghosts exist, can we imagine a world without money, is the world a computer simulation – that sort of thing. Such topics do crop up in science, from time to time – the ethics of designer babies, for example – but they are the exception rather than the rule.

To err on the side of clarity, I am not maligning the teaching of science in any way. I firmly believe that the solutions to the biggest problems facing humanity are in the hands of scientists rather than politicians, and I know many science teachers who do a brilliant job of it. It's just that as a teacher my interests lay elsewhere.

Whenever an opportunity arose to do something other than teaching science, I leapt at it. First, I became the school's Gifted and Talented (G&T) coordinator. It was at a G&T conference that I was introduced to Philosophy for Children (P4C). My mind was blown – I got trained up as soon as possible and used it in my teaching whenever possible.

In case you aren't familiar, P4C is a teaching method where the class sits in a circle and discusses a question of their choosing (and framing) at length. P4C is less concerned with teaching children a domain-specific curriculum and more concerned with helping them develop a range of domain-general linguistic, interpersonal and critical thinking and reasoning skills.

The better you get at running P4C sessions, the less the teacher has to say and do, because the students themselves learn how to scan the room and choose the next person to speak. Observing quietly as my students took turns to politely and articulately interrogate their own and others' ideas; looking on in awe as 11- and 12-year-olds deconstructed complex questions and arrived at new shared understandings; feeling a quiet swell of pride when a student spoke up for the first time in months and walked out of the room an inch taller... helping young people find their voice, literally and metaphorically... this was what I had come into teaching for!

A SIX-MONTH RESEARCH PROJECT THAT 'DIDN'T WORK' – AND WAS UTTERLY TRANSFORMATIVE

Next, I became the Head of Personal, Social, Health and Economic (PSHE) education, a wonderful subject that will thankfully (finally!) become compulsory in the UK in 2020. PSHE covers a wide range of topics – sex and drugs and proportional representation and everything in between – and I love teaching it because the subject matter so often hits that criterion of being inherently interesting to the children.

Around this time, I did an MA in person-centred education, where I combined my two newfound loves in a research project looking at the use of P4C as an approach to teaching PSHE. I recorded myself teaching six lessons and transcribed everything the pupils said. I then spent the next six months analysing the data and bashing away at a keyboard, only to discover that it hadn't had any discernible impact on what the children said or how they said it. The problem was that I was trying to run before I could walk – I was still very new to P4C – and I had been teaching someone else's class, so the relationships weren't there. Writing the dissertation almost broke me. One day, I dragged myself away from my darkened room to attend a friend's 30th birthday on the seafront. 'There's a homeless guy eating your buffet,' said one guest to the birthday girl. 'No, that's just James,' came the reply. 'He's doing a masters.'

By the end of the summer, I was spent. 'No more academia for me,' I resolved. 'I have scraped the bottom of the barrel, and I don't like the noise it makes.' I submitted my dissertation and went back to teaching. When I did, however, something was different. Not just something. Everything. I planned, taught and spoke differently. The children spoke and behaved differently, and I responded to them in ways that were different again. And most importantly – they seemed to be learning more effectively.

Even though my P4C intervention hadn't 'worked' on paper, the act of carrying out a research project and then writing 20,000 words on it – reading, thinking and reflecting deeply on the role of spoken language as a driver of thinking and reasoning and of learning itself – had been utterly transformative. Ideas that I had previously grasped only on an intellectual level I now felt in my bones. Without wishing to over-egg the pudding, I felt as though my professional identity had been taken apart, reconditioned and put back together by people who knew what they were doing.

Naturally, I was keen to take my teacher research journey to the next level, and started looking around for potential topics for a PhD. As luck would have it, this was the year that the *Learning Skills* curriculum began. It was an obvious choice. I suddenly found myself in a team of enthusiastic, dedicated teachers who had just been given the whole of year 7 for five lessons a week, to do with as we saw fit. This was an unprecedented opportunity to do something bold and different, and I was keen to capture what we were doing in the most rigorous way possible. But first, there was the small matter of deciding what should go into the programme itself!

In our first few meetings, we talked a lot about the students' fear of failure. By this time, I had come to understand that despite the best efforts of teachers the compulsory GCSE exam filter through which all must pass systematically brands a significant minority of young people – around one third[4] – as failures. I had studied self-esteem and ability grouping as part of my MA, and through this had come to understand that in order to shore up their sense of self-worth, many students simply stop trying: if they don't try, then they can't really fail, as Kate mentioned above. As a profession, this is something we have known for a long time – at least since Covington and Beery published their self-worth theory in 1976.[5]

How might we design a curriculum that would enable our students to take risks without fear of failure? How might we help them develop the levels of self-confidence and articulacy we often see among the alumni of expensive independent schools? And how might we empower them to take greater responsibility for their learning and unleash their potential as confident, curious, independent learners? One thing was clear: this was a complex, multifaceted problem that would require a complex, multifaceted solution.

RETHINKING LEARNING TO LEARN AS A COMPLEX INTERVENTION

Before I became a teacher, I worked in neuroscience research labs at University College London and Harvard Medical School, and also as a medical writer. Working with researchers as well as clinicians meant that I got to see the whole process – from the bench to the bedside, as the saying goes.

One idea that's popular in the field of pain management is something called multimodal analgesia, which is a lot less complicated than it sounds. When someone has an operation, the standard approach to pain relief is to give them lots of morphine. Morphine is a really effective pain killer – the best there is, by some margin – but it has lots of horrible side effects, like nausea and vomiting and drowsiness and constipation and dizziness and headaches and itchiness and... you get the idea. It can be pretty horrible.

Multimodal analgesia is simply when you give someone two or more painkillers with different mechanisms of action. So, if you have a toothache and you take paracetamol and ibuprofen, that's multimodal analgesia. In the postoperative setting, it might involve giving the patient pain relief before the surgery as well as after (so-called pre-emptive analgesia). It might also involve combining local anaesthetic with systemic (whole body) medications. There are many studies in the medical literature describing wide-ranging benefits associated with multimodal analgesia compared with a single treatment, including less pain, fewer unpleasant side effects and faster recovery times, freeing up valuable hospital beds and therefore saving money... it's what you might call a win-win-win.[6, 7, 8]

Multimodal analgesia is an example of something called a complex intervention, which is defined by the Medical Research Council as an 'intervention with several interacting components'.[9] The rationale for complex interventions can be found in the commonly understood notion that something can be 'greater than the sum of its parts'. It is also found in the theory of 'marginal gains', an economic term that has gained popularity in recent years, in part through the success of the British cycling team, as we discussed in *Chapter 2: A brief history of Learning to Learn*.[10] Put simply, the rationale for a complex intervention is that the 'marginal gains' arising from each individual component stack up and interact to produce a larger effect size overall.

Complex interventions aren't unique to the world of pain management – in fact, they are 'widely used in the health service, in public health practice, and in areas of social policy that have important health consequences'.[11]

> **COMPLEX INTERVENTION**
> An intervention with several interacting components.

However, they are almost unheard of in education. For my PhD, I did a literature review comparing the use of complex interventions in medicine and education. If you want to read more about this, my thesis is available online,[12] but the short version is that complex interventions are used commonly in medicine (thousands of articles) and barely at all in education (I could find only a handful). Instead, in education – as Becky Allen pointed out recently – there is an overwhelming emphasis on 'endless silver bullets... the new initiatives that appear each month from people who claim they know how to fix educational underachievement'.[13]

In the UK, this focus on silver bullets can be seen in the Education Endowment Foundation's R&D (Research and Development) programme, which is set to spend around £250 million over a 20-year period with a view to getting to the bottom of 'what works' in education. Almost all of the projects undertaken to date – around 200 at the time of writing – have sought to evaluate single-variable interventions as a method for improving attainment in English and maths. Examples of projects carried out to date include evaluations of daily singing, picture books, providing breakfasts, learning chess, texting parents, encouraging children to wear glasses, writing about values and short bursts of physical activity between lessons – to name just a few.[14] I'm not suggesting that any of these things is a bad idea – but what if it's a *combination* of things like this that makes the difference? It seems that we stand to gain a lot in education if we can learn to embrace the idea of the complex intervention.

When I joined the Learning to Learn team at Sea View, it felt natural to think of the *Learning Skills* curriculum as a complex intervention. We set out to combine a range of research-informed ideas and practices in the hope that the marginal gains associated with each component would stack up and interact, resulting in a large effect size overall. We also wanted to collect evidence along the way to determine the extent to which these practices were working for us, for our pupils, and in our school context – and to adjust our practice accordingly.

The first thing to go in was a weekly P4C lesson. If you've ever seen P4C in action, it's really a no-brainer – plus, there's a wealth of research evidence to suggest that P4C leads to a range of cognitive and non-cognitive benefits for young people. We'll explore this evidence in detail in *Chapter 5: Components of a complex intervention*.

Next came project-based learning. This is a bit more contentious, because the evidence isn't strong on the efficacy of project-based learning as a method for teaching children subject content. However, we weren't concerned with teaching subject content – at least not in *Learning Skills* lessons. We were concerned with helping our students learn how to regulate their thoughts, feelings and learning behaviours. In order to achieve this, we knew we would have to take a step back and allow them to find out for themselves what they can and can't do without assistance, and project-based learning seemed like the obvious way to do this. The connection between self-regulation and project-based learning has also often been made in the research literature.[15, 16]

The big advantage of project-based work is that for most of the time most of the students have something to be getting on with. This means that as a teacher you're able to have in-depth conversations with individual students in lessons. As with anything, you can do project-based learning badly and you can do it well.[17] It's really a question of finding the balance – giving the students enough freedom to be able to find out for themselves what they can and can't do without assistance, but not so much that by the end of the term they have little to show for their time.

As we write this book, almost 15 years after we embarked upon this journey, it's easy to point with hindsight to research evidence that supports what we did. However, it would be disingenuous to suggest that we were this well-informed and self-assured when we began. For example, despite having applied to be a part of a Learning to Learn initiative, nobody in the team was aware that Learning to Learn was a field of theory and practice stretching back 40 years, until we stumbled upon Claxton's 2006 essay *Learning to Learn: The Fourth Generation* about halfway through our first year.[18]

That said, we did try to go about things in an evidence-based way, and in our planning meetings we would refer to published research from time to time – notably, *Visible Learning* by John Hattie,[19] *Evidence Based Teaching* by Geoff Petty,[20] and research relating to P4C, classroom talk and collaborative learning.[21, 22, 23, 24]

So we didn't begin this journey because we had read all the research, which is probably just as well, because as we saw in *Chapter 2*, the research literature does not point to any single conclusion or recommended course of action. We began this journey because we each felt it was imperative to do so. Something wasn't working with the way things were. The transition to secondary school is bumpy and difficult and our students were not blossoming into confident, independent learners in the way we believed possible. So we combined all our different areas of expertise and experience and began to piece together a curriculum that the whole team could get behind.

In *Chapter 5: Components of a complex intervention*, we'll outline the *Learning Skills* curriculum as it existed after three years of research and development, providing a rationale for each component and considering what it looks like in the classroom. In the remainder of this chapter, we'll try to convey what it was like teaching *Learning Skills*, as we experienced it at the time.

OUR STORY

The first thing to say is that there was an unusual level of commitment to this project from the get-go. Over the summer, the teaching team visited one another's houses to kick ideas around and to get some planning in place for the coming term. We decided that we would each be responsible for planning one half-term. In this way, we would drastically reduce the amount of planning we each had to do throughout the year.

For some reason, we decided early on that there should be a focus on the environment – reducing waste, recycling where possible and not wasting money on anything we didn't need. In fact, because we raised money throughout the year, either in charitable donations or through enterprise projects, we ended up with more money in our budget at the end of the year than we had at the start. This is one of the best things about implementing a *Learning Skills* curriculum – once you know how to do it, it doesn't cost a bean. And everything you need to get started is in this book.

The early team meetings were energetic, creative – and incredibly daunting. We were acutely aware that we were stepping out of our comfort zones and into the unknown, and we felt uncertain about what a good *Learning Skills* lesson would look and feel like. We were used to a regime of tightly planned lessons, organised and led from the front of the room. We were used to things like:

- seating plans
- aims and objectives
- starters, mains and plenaries
- worksheets, exercise books and glue sticks
- folders containing schemes of work, with lesson plans meticulously linked to the National Curriculum
- ready-made assessments and clear marking policies.

We were charting a different course, and it felt pretty scary.

TENTATIVE FIRST STEPS

In terms of classroom practice... well, if we're honest, it felt a bit rough and ready for the first few weeks. Partly, this is because we were new to it and made some rookie mistakes. Partly, it was because there is something inherently messy about trying to do something in a fundamentally different way – as we pointed out in the Introduction, the caterpillar has to turn to mush before it can become a butterfly. Mainly, however, it's because we had taken the idea of what our students thought school was about and turned it on its head. Suddenly, they could choose how they captured or presented their learning with drawings, notes or videos. They could take a leading role in a P4C lesson, or they could sit and listen for a whole hour. Some children would sit in silence for well over half the lesson and then contribute something so thoughtful that it changed the entire course of the lesson.

Rarely, it seemed, had our students ever really had the space to think, to listen to one another for extended periods of time, and to have the option of adding their own thoughts into the mix, should they so choose. Suddenly, there were many more ways to be a 'good' student, depending on the task at hand.

This meant that students who struggled with written literacy had the chance to shine. When a lesson called for other characteristics – things like problem-solving, business sense or leadership – students who often found it difficult to get through a lesson without picking up a detention suddenly excelled. Whereas in other lessons they might have been considered too talkative, or unpopular, or 'all over the place', in *Learning Skills* lessons their boundless energy could be channelled to good use. They might not have been able to organise their torrent of ideas into anything vaguely resembling a coherent paragraph, but that didn't matter, because someone else in the group could.

Eventually, the more measured and well-organised children became braver at having a stab at creative innovation, and the 'all over the place' students learned some organisational skills from their peers. They freed themselves from the shackles of being 'high achieving' or 'rubbish at learning' and just got on with doing things together, learning from one another as they went.

As teachers, we were also finding our feet with this new way of working. Some of us took to P4C like ducks to water, finding the lessons liberating and delightful. Others really struggled with P4C at first. Likewise with project-based learning. In the first half-term, the 'project' element of the curriculum remained very teacher led. The focus was on transition, and we spent lots of time doing things like writing a class charter, coping with change, getting to know the school, strategies for calming down, learning to work together, where to go for support and so on.

It's a good idea to focus on such things at the start of year 7, but by making this the focus of the first several weeks, we probably overdid it a bit. Looking back, it's clear that we didn't all really trust in the process of project-based learning yet. If we were going to teach our students how to regulate their thoughts, feelings and learning behaviours, we knew we had to give them more freedom to work in ways of their choosing. But we weren't all comfortable with letting go of the reins – not yet, anyway.

We found that some of our students struggled to adapt to this new way of working. We had some tricky conversations with parents in the beginning, too. In particular, some of the students with high prior attainment were quite sceptical about what we were trying to achieve. They were 'good at school' – they listened to instructions and underlined the date and always handed in their homework on time – and they didn't see the point of Learning to Learn. In fact, they actively disliked it, because suddenly neat handwriting and being able to speak to adults were not the marks of an elite student; rather, they were just two skills they had mastered among many others that were valued equally. These students often expressed frustration in P4C lessons, where there is no 'right answer' and no obvious way to demonstrate, either to themselves or to the teacher, that they were doing it better than their classmates.

Those first few weeks shone a spotlight onto the skills that had been overlooked and underdeveloped up until that point: being able to listen and take turns, being able to negotiate and reach a consensus, combining ideas and co-creating effectively, problem-solving under pressure, or taking a subordinate role for the benefit of the group. It was hard to watch those students struggle, to not know what they were supposed to do to get back into the 'top spot', just as it is hard to watch a student struggle to read aloud or to always be picked last for a sports team.

IT'S NOT CALLED THE STRUGGLE FOR NOTHING

Watching students struggle is always difficult, but there is a sweet spot somewhere between the comfort zone and the panic zone where growth takes place. The prevailing model of how schools work allows high-achieving students to reside in their comfort zone for most of the time, occasionally stretched but rarely feeling the panic of not knowing what to do, or feeling hopelessly out of their depth. In this same system, there are some students who always feel at sea, on the brink of drowning, not knowing how to write the words they need to express their ideas accurately.

Learning Skills changes this linear system, where students at either extreme are either at a huge advantage or a huge disadvantage, and throws all students into the same midway state of feeling just on the edge of their comfort zone. It deliberately levels the playing field. Our students weren't all challenged by the same things, but they all shared that experience of having their norms turned upside down. All students regularly had to go through a process of self-reflection, identifying their own strengths and areas for development. By valuing a wide range of knowledge and skills as equally important, *Learning Skills* changed the way they looked at themselves and one another.

Some students struggled even with the small amounts of freedom we had granted them in that first half-term – letting them choose where to sit or how to present their learning, for example. One boy who had been diagnosed as having an autistic spectrum condition (ASC) – we'll call him Liam – would regularly become overwhelmed because he didn't understand what the 'correct' thing was to be doing.

Liam began the year with a Learning Support Assistant (LSA) who was there to help him manage his anxiety. It was expected that he would need to leave the class regularly, as he had always done in primary school. In the beginning, he occupied the seat nearest the door, so that he could make a quick getaway if he needed to. He was also offered the option to sit on the floor, out of view, if that made him feel more at ease. As long as he could listen to what was happening, he could join in at any point.

Initially, he was confused by the fact that he was encouraged to write notes on the back of a piece of recycled paper during class activities or that he was allowed to just sit and listen if he didn't want to write. If he felt the notes he'd made were worth keeping, he could stick them into his scrapbook. If they were of no further use to him, they could go into the recycling. He didn't have to contribute orally if he had nothing to say either.

Over a period of a few weeks, his anxiety about having to produce a pre-determined amount of written evidence of his learning in every lesson gradually evaporated. Shortly into the term, the LSA stopped taking him out of class. By Christmas, she had stopped coming at all. Liam had realised he was safe in this strange new environment, had found his voice and had made some friends.

As teachers, the fear of failure was very real to us also. We often rushed to each other's classrooms after a lesson to compare notes. Before long, each teacher had developed slightly different ways of working. Surely we couldn't *all* be doing it right? What if this whole thing was just a huge waste of everybody's time? The stakes were high, not least because we had been placed in 'special measures' the previous year – the school was crawling with inspectors and 'school improvement partners' talking about lesson objectives and marking, and here we were letting the students decide if they needed to keep their notes from lessons or not!

So a fear of failure was very much on our mental dashboards in that first term – until our first departmental 'mocksted' inspection, in fact, when every teacher who was observed got a 'good' rating. Graded lesson observations are notoriously unreliable,[25] and thank goodness they seem to be going out of fashion. But in all honesty, it was a huge boost to our collective confidence at the time. It felt like a validation and reassured us that the sky wasn't going to come crashing down around our ears at any moment.

We deliberately didn't prepare anything special for the observations. We wanted the inspector's opinion on the *Learning Skills* curriculum as it was delivered every day, in all its unpredictable glory! He wasn't too impressed at first, and there was an awkward exchange when Kate explained that we didn't have any lesson plans to share with him, because the students were midway through a project and they had their own lesson plans that they'd written themselves. We weren't about to stop what we were doing to put on a show of 'outstanding' teaching for his benefit.

Despite looking a tad affronted, the inspector agreed that everything he had seen was 'good' according to his criteria. When we asked him what would take us from 'good' to 'outstanding', he replied that he wasn't sure. He hadn't seen anything like it before and had no frame of reference. That was 'good' enough for us.

GREEN SHOOTS

Around this time, the school carried out its first 'data harvest' of the year. This was the first evidence that these year 7s were different from previous cohorts – different in a good way. It was too soon to tell if they were making more progress in their learning, but there were fewer detentions and behaviour points, and their 'attitude to learning' (ATL) scores (a score given to each student by each of their teachers, on a 6-point scale) were significantly better than those of previous cohorts.

Because the team came with varied subject knowledge, pedagogical know-how and experience, we were able to pool our expertise and learn from one another. Those of us with years of experience could share anecdotes from personal experience; others brought in contacts and passions from outside of school; and others still were more concerned with evidence from the research literature. This had the effect of building up our repertoire as teachers. Any shortcomings that we had as individuals were balanced by the breadth of experience across the team. We grew stronger as individuals, as learners and as a team working together. We each became better teachers as a result.

In the second half-term, we ran a group project to create and run a stall at a Christmas market to which the local community would be invited. This is when it started to get real, and when it really started to come together. The only criterion was that nothing new could be purchased for resale. No sweet stalls. They had to create an experience, a service or a product that would a) raise awareness about sustainability, and b) raise money for our chosen charity, *Moving Mountains*.[26]

We invited the founder of *Moving Mountains*, Gavin Bate, to come in to the school to talk to the students. Following this, the students spent a week or so researching the issues Gavin had highlighted affecting populations in Kenya, Nepal and Borneo. They then formed groups of shared interest and started to think about which social issues they wanted to raise awareness around, and how they might raise money at the same time.

The Christmas Market included stalls selling second-hand books, toys and board games, the inevitable tombola (which had to be built from recycled materials), and selling jewellery made from old Lego bricks and Scrabble pieces (an idea that developed into a surprisingly lucrative social enterprise that would feature at parents' evenings and coffee mornings for years to come). Some made Christmas cards and decorations out of recycled materials, while others set up physical challenges with leader boards. We invited local artists and craftspeople to set up stalls as well, and opened it up to parents and carers if they wanted to be involved.

The fact that the general public were going to be invited really focused minds and motivated our students to raise the bar. It was a fantastic success, and the students organised all of it – from making the stalls to sending out invitations to organising signage around the school.

If you plan on doing a student-led Christmas market at your school, our only advice would be this: teach your students how to spell the word 'stall' before you allow them to put signs up around the school saying 'This way to our Christmas…' Especially if you live in the south-east of England, where the vowel sounds for 'all' and 'ool' sound remarkably similar! But every mistake or red-faced moment was a lesson learned, and every success a small confidence boost.

ASSESSMENT (OF LEARNING TO LEARN) IS FUTILE

The *Learning Skills* team argued about assessment a lot in the first year. Some of us wanted to abandon it entirely, but others understandably felt nervous about doing that and so we settled on a compromise. At first, we had a system whereby the students had to collect evidence that they had met various success criteria. These had to be signed off by another student, stuck in a scrapbook and the running total logged with the teacher.

We dutifully collected in the data and entered it into rainbow-coloured spreadsheets. But the pretty colours painted a picture that we just didn't recognise. By Christmas, some students had collected hundreds of pieces of evidence, while others were still in single figures. It was obvious that the students' ability to collect evidence was more an indication of how motivated they were to collect evidence – or perhaps of how good they were at coming to reciprocal arrangements whereby they would sign off one another's evidence on an industrial scale – than an accurate reflection of their progress with regard to goal setting, independent learning, collaboration and so on. So, we ditched the rainbow-coloured spreadsheets.

We experimented with a few other approaches, like teacher assessments where we awarded each student a 'holistic grade' (exam board speak for plucking a number out of thin air), or giving them an oracy level based on observations of paired talk (which is really hard to do in a valid or reliable way, and is a logistical headache, and takes ages).

By Easter, we had arrived at the troubling conclusion that it isn't actually possible to assess Learning to Learn itself. Teachers have a saying – you don't fatten a pig by weighing it, meaning that we shouldn't over-assess children – which is pretty unpleasant because it equates children to farm animals and the curriculum to slop. We tended to think more in gardening metaphors, which on reflection isn't much better, although it does have more explanatory power. If you plant a tomato seed in fertile soil, stick it in a greenhouse where it gets plenty of direct sunlight, and water it regularly, you can be confident that it will soon yield an abundance of tasty tomatoes. You don't dig it up every other week to measure its progress, and if you do, you'll be in for a disappointing crop.

To extend the metaphor, the greenhouse containing the soil and the water and the sunlight was the *Learning Skills* curriculum, the plants were obviously the children, and the tomatoes were the grades they achieved in their subject learning across the curriculum. Eventually, we realised that in order to assess whether *Learning Skills* was working, we didn't need to assess *Learning Skills* itself. Instead, we needed to look at subject learning across the curriculum. We just had to hold our nerve and suppress the very real fear that we would be deemed negligent when someone with a clipboard came along and raised their eyebrows at our decision to alight the Spreadsheet Express.

To clarify, we did do *some* assessments in *Learning Skills*. Each half termly project was given a grade (Fail/Pass/Merit/Distinction), arrived at through a combination of peer-, self- and teacher-assessment. We also continued to assess oracy, albeit formatively (providing verbal and/or written feedback to help the students get better at speaking and listening) rather than summatively (no levels). And we wrote dialogic feedback in the students' learning journals once a fortnight. But we stopped trying to track progress within *Learning Skills* itself, simply because it didn't seem to be possible.

EXPANDING TIMETABLED LESSONS INTO YEARS 8 AND 9

Thankfully, it wasn't long before the fear subsided and we began to feel vindicated in our decision. Throughout the first year, year 7 progress and behaviour data across the curriculum drifted upward; in Key Stage 3, there is often a plateauing or even a decline in progress data, leading Ofsted to describe Key Stage 3 as 'the wasted years' in one recent report.[27]

By the summer term, it was clear that we were on to something – so much so, that when we asked the senior team whether we might extend timetabled lessons into year 8, the answer was not 'ARE YOU OUT OF YOUR MINDS?!!' A meeting was arranged with our fellow heads of department (HoDs) to negotiate more curriculum time. Expecting fierce resistance, we prepared ourselves for battle.

To our amazement, we found ourselves pushing at an open door. The HoDs were on board – they could see the difference *Learning Skills* was making in their classrooms and on their spreadsheets. Compared with previous cohorts, the year 7s had made more progress in fewer lessons. We were given three lessons a week in year 8. A year later, the curriculum time extended again into year 9, this time for five lessons a fortnight.

Over three years, then, the first *Learning Skills* cohort took part in over four hundred lessons. By the end of Key Stage 3, they had taken part in countless projects, including the building of a school allotment, replete with a greenhouse made of plastic bottles; given numerous speeches and presentations to audiences ranging from one teacher to entire year groups; raised loads of money for charity; been to primary schools to teach *Learning Skills* lessons to year 5 pupils; organised school trips (researching and deciding where to go, raising and collecting the money, booking the transport, writing letters to parents and carers and even completing risk assessments); completed a formal course in critical thinking and reasoning skills... and much more besides. In short, they had become a cohort of organised, collaborative, proactive, effective, critically engaged ninjas.

A FEW VIGNETTES

To give you a sense of how these students were different to previous cohorts, we will conclude this chapter with a few snapshots. Sometimes, people are dismissive of stories. They say things like, 'Ah, but that's just anecdotal data.' The really annoying ones say things like, 'The plural of anecdote is not data.' We disagree.

Without wishing to sound too folksy, life can be seen as a tapestry of narrative threads; we live our lives through stories, and in a sense our professional identities are characters in a story: 'as a teacher, I pass on the best of what has been thought and said to future generations/help children overcome disadvantage/provide for my family', and so on. So, without apology, here are a few anecdotes that we feel capture the essence of what it was like to teach *Learning Skills*. If hard data is your thing, you might prefer to skip ahead to *Chapter 6: The evidence for Learning Skills*.

'I DIDN'T EVEN HAVE TO BE THERE!' (CAROLINE)

The following is an excerpt from an interview James did for his PhD with Caroline, the Head of PE.

> 'I came to this school from a school where attainment was higher and kids were more independent. When I arrived here, I found that all the kids expected to be spoon-fed. There was no independence. Even now, with the year 11s, they still crave that spoon-feeding. Because they haven't had any Learning to Learn. They even struggle to start a piece of coursework off. I have to put a page up on the board where I put the title up for them, I show them how to lay out their work, I show them how to structure it with like an introduction, their research, findings, opinions, their conclusions... they just don't know how to structure their work. I even have to start their sentences off – like they don't even know how to start a sentence.'

How is your experience different at Key Stage 3?

> 'It's huge. The type of feedback that they give to each other is much more constructive, it has more meaning and it's clearly not made up. It's accurate and demonstrates that they've really thought about what they're saying. I've got sentence stems that I take with me to some of the lessons and I don't need them, or if I do they only need to use it once and then they can transfer it and use it again and again in some of the other practical activities.

'In Key Stage 4, when we're teaching teamwork and leadership skills, there's usually the same students who do most of the leadership, whereas in Key Stage 3... there is contribution from all students. And they don't seem as scared to get things wrong. They're much more forthcoming, they give it a go and they are more critical of each other. Because it's a practical subject, some of the dialogue is in very short bursts. So we do practical activities and then we call them in and fire say three questions at once, and then say discuss. That could be in twos or in groups of six sometimes. And they usually have a time limit of say 30 seconds to discuss it with each other. Sometimes with Key Stage 4 they just sit there and just talk about something else, or they just sit there, but in years 7, 8 and 9 they have good discussions, they stay on task... nearly all of the time, coming up with the appropriate answers.

'Thinking back to what Key Stage 3 was like before Learning Skills, it just doesn't compare. Like asking them to discuss and give feedback – the feedback would always be so basic. Say in gymnastics, they would just say, 'She didn't point her toes' – they'd just say what the person before them said. Whereas now, they all say different things and they all seem to want to say something different, they watch to say something different that they've observed.

'In terms of leadership, my year 7s – even leading a warm-up, they could do that a lot better than the year 11s. Working together to set up equipment as well. That was a major problem when I came to the school, to ask them to set up a 10 × 10 square, it would take them a long time to do that, but now they are much more doers. In one lesson... a few weeks ago, was the feeling I had where I just facilitated the lesson, I didn't have to even be there really! And another teacher came over, and it was year 7 girls, and they had to design a warm-up... they had to teach it, they had to organise themselves and agree on their own roles within it. They did this so quickly, they then led another group through the warm-up activity, and once they'd finished the other group, they had a big group discussion about what level each student achieved on their leadership skills and why they then each had to give that feedback back to each kid who did they warm-up activity.

'And the other teacher who came over couldn't believe the quality of the feedback. It included grades, and advice as to how to improve... Each session, I gave minimum instructions *to them. You know, I didn't give them much to go on at all. And they just exceeded my expectations, they were brilliant. I definitely think that Learning to Learn has been a big influence in that. I also think the way in which we deliver PE has been a big influence on that, which does focus more on them leading each other, and using the whole school INSETs and whole staff meetings about Learning to Learn, using that within PE and discussing within meetings how to do it in PE.'*

YEAR 7 PROJECTS THAT SOUND LIKE PHDS (JAMES)

In recent years, teachers and educational researchers have become very sceptical about the idea of 'discovery learning', and it is easy to understand why. It is certainly the case that if you want children to learn a chunk of subject knowledge that they will later be tested on, it is far more efficient to teach it to them rather than hoping that they will discover it. However, the next story is an example of how an open-ended project that some might dismiss as 'discovery learning' can lead to the development of powerful knowledge.

'The first time we ran an independent research project, we let the children choose their own topic. We soon realised our mistake: cue lots of presentations about footballers, fast cars and The Hunger Games, which was all the rage at the time. We put up with the choice of topics because the students were still developing the skills of data collection, sorting, prioritising, presenting and so on. 'But we learned our lesson. The following year, we ran another independent research project, this time in groups of three. We took our students to the school library and said: 'You can research any topic you like, but it has to be from these shelves here.' In so doing, we directed them toward topics that you can learn about at university level, but not so much in school: life in other countries, politics, architecture and so on. The only catch was that they had to agree on a topic as a group of three, and then work on it together for six weeks, culminating in a presentation to the class.

'One girl – let's call her Rose – picked out a dog-eared book from the 1970s called An Introduction to Feminism. *She hadn't ever heard of feminism before, and it immediately resonated with her. She was resolute: this was going to be her topic. Meanwhile, her group buddy Joe had selected a coffee-table book about*

South America, full of huge colour photos. He realised that he knew next to nothing about this entire continent, a situation he was keen to resolve. We returned to the classroom, where the students reviewed the books their group had collected, and agreed on a topic to investigate for the next six weeks, which they would then present to the class.

'Neither Rose nor Joe wanted to relinquish their topic, and they soon became mired in deadlock, each reading their own book in silence. They were sitting at the front of the room, and I happened to be in earshot when Joe turned to Rose and said: 'What if we do it about feminism in South America?' My eyebrows shot up and my heart rate shot even higher as I fought the urge to interrupt them: this was incredible! However, there was a third student, Martin, in that group, who was absent that day. Would they be able to persuade him to get on board?

'Martin didn't need to go to the library. For some reason, he was obsessed with China and already had several books on it at home. He was learning Mandarin in his own time, as well as Chinese calligraphy, which he doodled incessantly. There was no way he wasn't doing China. You can probably see where this is going. Over the next six weeks, this group of three 11-year-olds did an independent research project called 'The history of feminism in South America and China'.

'They needed a bit of help from the teaching assistant to understand the reading materials they discovered online – there were no websites 'for kids' that covered their chosen topic – but they ran with it. They soon discovered that communism linked the two regions, and they were quick to draw parallels between communism and feminism in that they are both concerned with ideas of fairness and equality.

'In South America, they focused on influential historical figures such as Eva Peron and Frida Kahlo, while in China they discovered things like the one-child policy, foot binding and recent changes to the law to bring about greater equality for women. It was jaw-dropping stuff, and serves as a useful reminder that once children can read to a reasonable standard, an open-ended 'discovery' approach to project-based learning can result in the learning of powerful knowledge that they might not otherwise learn at school.

'In the final lesson of the half term, I sat with bated breath as Rose and Joe went up to present their findings to the class

(Martin was absent again). Unfortunately, we hadn't done much work on presentation skills yet. Joe turned bright pink and read nervously from his notes, while Rose spoke so quietly that you literally couldn't hear a word she was saying. I realised that we needed to work on their presentation skills, and fast.'

This brings us neatly to our next story, about a project that was very much focused on public speaking...

HARRY'S ASSEMBLY (RAV)

The following is an excerpt from an interview James did with Rav, a teacher of *Learning Skills* cohorts 2 and 3. It concerns a research project year 8 did on endangered animals, which the students then presented to the whole school through a series of assemblies.

'Harry had a severe case of dyslexia and behaviour issues, and was a low achiever in all of his subjects and constantly getting into trouble. So that was his background. And I think he didn't have any confidence... in terms of his reflections, he was really insecure and had a very low sense of confidence, not just with his learning, but in life, with his parents, with himself as a person. Yeah, that was Harry.

'So on the very first day that we had our assembly presentations, I think it was to the rest of year 8... he showed up, but then he disappeared 10 or 15 minutes before they were due to start their presentation. Everybody had their own specific roles, and they had rehearsed this. And Harry hadn't shown any sign of not wanting to do it or nerves... if you met Harry, he was the type of person who wouldn't show that he was nervous, he was always quite well spoken and always had something to say. So you would think that he was quite confident, but... anyway, I was surprised.

'So he disappeared just as the assembly hall was filling up, and he was nowhere to be found. Some students and a couple of teachers went to look for him around the school building, and he hadn't turned up. A few minutes before we were due to start, another student, Mo, said that he would step up – his exact words – and take Harry's place.

'Just as they were about to start, Harry turned up, and he was bright pink and just really flustered and looked frustrated. I asked him, 'What's brought this on? You can do this. We've rehearsed this many times – this is your opportunity to stand in front of everybody and do something amazing!' I think he really wanted the time to talk it through, but we didn't have that time… So for that assembly, he refused to go up and speak. Somebody else had to speak on his behalf.

'The following day – we had a whole week of presenting to every year group – I think after seeing the first presentation and then overcoming his nerves, he agreed to go up. And it was great. I think he was a little bit nervous, but everybody was really supportive. I think he needed to do something like that just to prove to himself, and I think to everybody, that he was capable of speaking and memorising his words, and sharing his learning journey with everybody. And he spoke about his challenges and how he overcame those.

'That was a really big moment for him. I don't really know what happened for him to change his mind. I think he just needed time and to see everybody else stand up and to see the sense of achievement they had afterwards. Maybe he wanted a sense of that as well. But he did agree to do it in the following assemblies, and it was perfect. It was really perfect.'

AN ACCIDENTAL DISPLAY OF AWESOMENESS (KATE)

'This story doesn't exactly cover me in glory, but here goes. One day, while heavily pregnant and increasingly forgetful, I was late to my first lesson. I had overlooked the fact that on Wednesdays we didn't have tutor time and lessons started at 8.30. I didn't have a tutor group and thought I had 15 minutes to spare. When I got to my classroom, I found that the students had found a key and let themselves in. Not only that, but they'd got their folders out, arranged themselves into groups and were cracking on with their projects. I thanked them for being so amazing, apologised profusely for my lateness, and sat at my desk to take the weight off my feet.

'When I looked up, to my horror I saw six NQTs standing at the back of the room, scribbling furiously in their notebooks. As well as forgetting what time school started at, I had completely forgotten that I was hosting a group from the university who *had come to find out about Learning Skills, which by now people were starting to talk about across the city. Naturally, I was horrified, but they were blown away – they had never seen children organising themselves in this way, in the absence of adult supervision.*

'Obviously, I wouldn't have planned it that way. But I couldn't have wished for a better display of how Learning Skills had unleashed the students' potential to become proactive, independent learners.'

TEACHERS MODELLING FAILURE

Not everything we did went swimmingly – far from it, in fact. A theatre production about recycling, which involved every child in year 7 and was performed to parents and carers one painful afternoon... well, let's just say it gave us a newfound respect for drama teachers. And a campaign project fell flat because the whole point of a campaign is that you keep going until you achieve your goals and so our students mainly just felt disappointed at the end of that half-term that their work had been in vain. That didn't feel great, and we admitted as much to the students.

We tell students all the time that they need to learn from their mistakes. It's important that as teachers we afford ourselves the same luxury. In the culture of high-stakes accountability that the teaching profession is very much in the grip of currently, it's easy to forget that failure can be a healthy thing – as long as you don't allow it to stop you taking risks. Because if you never mess anything up, you're just doing things you already know how to do – and where's the fun in that? And more importantly – where's the *learning* in that?

So there are loads of things we would do differently if we had our time again – we'll share a few examples in the next chapter. However, in the stories above, we hope you can see how, through a combination of factors – extended independent learning projects, high expectations for all and a culture of stepping back and allowing the students to find their feet – the *Learning Skills* curriculum enabled our students to achieve things that they and others did not think they were capable of.

Removing the spectre of endless progress checking gave the students some breathing room. They had the time and space to take risks, make mistakes and learn from them, to try on new skills for size and to get to know one another's strengths and weaknesses. They all had a chance to be brilliant at some things and to realise they had a long way to go with others. This challenged their perceptions of themselves and enabled them to be more open-minded about what they might achieve in the future.

In the next chapter, we will provide a detailed account of what went into the complex *Learning Skills* intervention. But first, we need to address a minor but important question...

WHY CALL IT THE *LEARNING SKILLS* CURRICULUM?

In recent years, the word 'skills' has undergone a spectacular fall from grace – in the UK, at least. Just 12 short years ago, it could be found perched at the very top of the education system, on the sign outside the door of the Department for Education and Skills. Later, the department was renamed to become the Department for Children, Schools and Families, before shapeshifting once again into its current incarnation, the Department for Education. Similarly, in 2016, the Department for Business, Innovation & Skills was renamed the Department for Business, Energy and Industrial Strategy, presumably following a brainstorming meeting about how to make it sound much more rigorous.

To be fair, the word 'skills' never seemed quite at home in the name of the government department. So it probably did need bringing down a peg or two, although perhaps not quite to the Orwellian depths to which it has plunged: at the time of writing, there are reports that Nick Gibb, the current Minister for School Standards, has 'banned civil servants from using the word "skills" in his correspondence because "he doesn't believe they exist"'.[28]

We didn't set out to reclaim the word 'skills', however. In the first two years we ran the programme at Sea View, we called it *Learning to Learn*. We were never particularly happy with it, but we needed a name and this seemed like the least bad option at the time. In the third year of the programme, the Learning to Learn department merged with the PSHE department, and we decided to rebrand the whole thing *Learning for Life* in an attempt to make clear that these lessons were at least partly concerned with preparing students for the world beyond the school gates.

Around this time, we started to notice that for some reason many students referred to it simply as *Learning Skills* regardless of whether we called it *Learning to Learn* or *Learning for Life*. We weren't particularly taken with this name either. We wanted something with a bit more pizzazz. At one point, we referred to it as *The Praxis Curriculum*. Praxis is an ancient word that means something like 'a combination of reflection and action', and it is kind of a cool concept that comes close to capturing what we were trying to do. But unfortunately – as we can now see, with the clarity of hindsight – *The Praxis Curriculum* is a truly dreadful name.

Once it became apparent that what we were doing might be worth reproducing in other schools, we realised we needed a name that would look at home on a school timetable. Reflecting on the fact that whatever we called it our students often called it *Learning Skills*, finally the penny dropped: it doesn't matter what we think, it just has to be something that makes sense to the students. So we finally settled on the name *Learning Skills*.

The word 'curriculum' we use advisedly, because if there's one thing we are convinced of, it is that teaching children how to get better at learning stuff requires dedicated curriculum time. Metacognition, self-regulation and oracy can and should be developed through all subject areas, and we absolutely advocate that.

But it isn't enough. As we argued in Part I, with the best will in the world an 'embedded-only' approach just doesn't get you where you need to go. It's easy to see why: there just isn't time to do all of this within the context of subject learning, because there's so much to cover already. An embedded-only approach would also be inefficient, because you'd be duplicating if you had every subject area teaching the students how to set effective short-, medium- and long-term goals; how to plan, monitor and evaluate their own learning; how to speak and listen effectively across a range of contexts; how to organise their time and resources effectively, and so on. It would also be confusing for the students, because they would likely be getting different messages from different departments.

We are acutely aware that the need to carve out curriculum time is the main obstacle to the *Learning Skills* approach becoming more widespread. But by the end of this book, we hope to have persuaded at least some readers of a truth that we hold self-evident, because we have lived and breathed it for the last 15 years: if you really want your students to become effective, self-regulated learners, you need to provide them with dedicated lessons in which this work can take place.

Whether you need as much curriculum time as we had in the Sea View pilot study – more than four hundred lessons over three years – is another question. No doubt some people would say that sounds like too much, but the truth is, we just don't know because we don't have the data yet.

What we do know from the Sea View study is that over four hundred lessons doesn't seem to do any harm – quite the reverse, in fact. As we will see in *Chapter 6: The evidence for Learning Skills*, the *Learning Skills* cohorts at Sea View were able to do more with less, performing significantly better in measures of subject learning than the control cohort, who had a corresponding four hundred plus more lessons of subject-based learning.

By way of a final word on the matter, we don't think the name is particularly important. It's the mission to create generations of confident, curious, independent learners that's the thing. So if you want to take the ideas in the book and call it something completely different, you do so with our blessing. If anything, we'd prefer it that way; what we really want is for you to take these ideas, play around with them and make them your own.

CHAPTER 5

COMPONENTS OF A COMPLEX INTERVENTION

'It struck me that we should think small, not big, and adopt a philosophy of continuous improvement through the aggregation of marginal gains. Forget about perfection; focus on progression, and compound the improvements.'

Sir David Brailsford (2015)[1]

As we have mentioned, *Learning Skills* is a complex intervention – a whole-school approach to teaching and learning with several moving parts. From the outset, our aim was to assemble a programme comprising elements for which there is evidence of improved student outcomes, in the hope that the marginal gains associated with each element would stack up and interact, leading to a larger effect size overall.

THE *LEARNING SKILLS* THEORY OF ACTION

The infographic overleaf outlines the 'theory of action' of the *Learning Skills* curriculum, and enables us to see all the major 'active ingredients' at a glance. To break it down: in Learning to Learn, we are interested in helping children develop their knowledge, skills and understanding of subjects – the traditional concerns of education.

> **THEORY OF ACTION**
>
> A theory that seeks to explain the links between cause and effect. In education, a theory of action connects the actions of teachers with the learning and development of their students.

The *Learning Skills* 'theory of action'

Based on an observation: Some people are better at learning than others

And an assumption: Anyone can get better at learning

What is learning?

The acquisition and retention of knowledge, understanding, skills, habits, beliefs, values, attitudes, motivations...

What is Learning to Learn?

A field of educational research and practice that aims to help students become self-regulated learners

What is *Learning Skills*?

A **whole-school approach** to Learning to Learn with three structural elements:

1. A **taught course** for all students in KS3 (age 11 to 14), centred around 3 key concepts: metacognition, self-regulation and oracy

2. An **embedded** approach to promoting self-regulated learning in subject learning across the curriculum

3. A set of whole-school practices designed to facilitate the **transfer** of learning skills into subjects across the curriculum

Metacognition

Monitoring and controlling thought processes

Self-regulation

Monitoring and controlling feelings and behaviours

Oracy

The ability to speak and listen effectively across a range of contexts

Self-regulated learning

The application of metacognition and self-regulation to learning

However, we also recognise the value of other kinds of learning – learning that involves the formation of new habits, beliefs, values, attitudes, motivations and behaviours – what the psychotherapist Carl Rogers referred to as 'significant learning'.[2] This is why we define learning in quite an expansive way – to reflect the idea that as well as building subject knowledge, education is a process of self-actualisation – helping every young person find their feet, find their voice and work towards becoming the best version of themselves that they can be.

We can also see in the infographic that *Learning Skills* is a whole-school approach to Learning to Learn with three structural elements: a taught course, an embedded approach to developing self-regulated learning across the curriculum, and strategies designed to carefully manage the transfer of knowledge, skills, habits and dispositions out of the *Learning Skills* classroom and into subject learning across the curriculum.

While recognising the vital role subject teachers have to play, the aim of Learning to Learn is to help students get better at regulating their own learning – becoming proactive as well as reactive learners.

The *Learning Skills* curriculum has many moving parts, as we will outline in this chapter. However, it really boils down to three key ideas: metacognition, self-regulation and oracy. Together, these three ideas interact to help students become more effective, self-regulated learners. Metacognition helps children take control of their thought processes. Self-regulation helps them take control of their feelings and behaviours. Oracy helps them develop confidence in using spoken language as a tool for getting things done in a range of contexts. And self-regulated learning is the application of these processes to learning.

So the 'theory of action' is quite self-explanatory, really: if the *Learning Skills* curriculum is effective at helping students become more effective, self-regulated learners, then we should see measurable improvements in learning, defined as the acquisition and retention of knowledge, understanding, skills, habits, beliefs, values, attitudes, motivations...

In *Chapter 2: A brief history of Learning to Learn*, we spent some time digging into definitions and making clear the difference between self-regulation (a broad construct that involves monitoring and controlling our feelings – both physical and emotional – and our behaviours) and self-regulated learning (the application of metacognition and self-regulation to learning). However, when we started the Sea View pilot study ten years ago, we didn't know what we know now. Although we understood the importance of making sure our students felt safe, built healthy relationships and were able to 'check in' with and articulate their emotions, we didn't yet have the vocabulary to describe what we were doing as self-regulation. We will explore self-regulation – monitoring and controlling feelings and behaviours – toward the end of this chapter, as an example of something we would do differently (by making it much more explicit to the students) had we known ten years ago what we know now.

In this chapter, we will break down the component parts of the *Learning Skills* curriculum as it existed after three years of research and development. We will firstly explore the three structural elements – a taught course, an embedded approach, and transfer. However, we will use slightly different headings to organise this discussion. In particular, we will focus on a) why we advocate a taught *and* embedded approach, b) the importance of having a dedicated teaching team, and c) strategies for promoting transfer out of the *Learning Skills* classroom and into subject learning across the curriculum. Following this, we will explore the three key ideas – oracy, metacognition and self-regulated learning – each of which can be broken down further into component parts (Table 5.1). We will examine each component part on two levels. First, we will provide a rationale for its inclusion in the programme, drawing on theory, research evidence and/or the professional judgement of the *Learning Skills* team. And second, we will consider what each component looks like in practice.

Table 5.1. The Learning Skills curriculum: components of a complex intervention

COMPONENT	Component parts
Structural elements	Taught *and* embedded
	Dedicated teaching team
	Strategies for transfer
Oracy	Talk rules
	Collaboration and complexity
	Structured debates
	Presentational talk
	Philosophy for Children
Metacognition	Learning journals
	Meditation/guided visualisations
	Shared language of learning
	Thinking and reasoning skills
Self-regulated learning	Inclusive practice
	Project-based learning
	Curated autonomy
	Organisational skills

One thing before we dive in. This chapter is by far the longest in the book, because we mainly want this book to be of practical use to teachers and school leaders seeking to replicate or improve upon the findings of the Sea View study. However – and we really cannot emphasise this enough – we do not present the ideas in this chapter as a guaranteed recipe for success that can be implemented in a top-down, off-the-shelf way. Perhaps the most important factor in the success we achieved at Sea View was that the *Learning Skills* team had genuine ownership and autonomy over what went into the programme. As we will see, this buy-in is essential to the success of the programme.

This chapter is an account of what worked for us, for our particular students, at a particular point in time. However, our thinking is developing all the time. At the end of the chapter, we will outline a number of ideas that may be worth including in future iterations of the approach. However, implementing all the ideas in this chapter would not be advisable. In the constraints of a mainstream school, there simply would not be time. Instead, think of this chapter as a list of ingredients that you might use, in combination with others, for creating your own version of a complex *Learning Skills* intervention – the version that makes the most sense at your particular school, for your particular pupils, at this particular point in time. Most of all, take ownership over the process. Instead of asking, 'Will this work at my school?', ask, 'What will it take to make this work here?'

STRUCTURAL ELEMENTS

TAUGHT *AND* EMBEDDED

Rationale

Ever since the word 'metacognition' first entered the literature in the 1970s, there have essentially been two schools of thought about what Learning to Learn should look like in schools: either it should be taught explicitly through discrete, timetabled lessons, or it should be embedded throughout the curriculum. As you might expect, there are advantages and disadvantages to each approach. Here are the most salient points:

Discrete lessons:

- Advantage – you can dedicate time to developing the many facets of metacognition, self-regulation and oracy in ways that can't easily be achieved in the context of subject-based learning, where there is always pressure to 'cover the content'.
- Disadvantage – a person's ability to be metacognitive or to self-regulate is highly dependent on context (where they are) and content (what they're learning). Because of this, learning skills do not transfer easily from one classroom to another – or, at least, they don't always transfer *automatically*. More on that later.

Embedded throughout the curriculum:

- Advantage – the drive to teach children 'how' to learn is rooted in 'what' they are learning, reducing the need for transfer because it is already situated in context and content.
- Disadvantage – with the best will in the world, the Learning to Learn stuff tends to get sacrificed at the altar of covering the curriculum. Also, teaching learning skills in every subject area would be an incredibly inefficient use of time, because there would be lots of duplication. And as we saw in the discussion of 'Mode A vs Mode B' teaching in *Chapter 3*, not all teachers buy into Learning to Learn, or feel confident teaching it, so in an embedded-only approach, students receive patchy provision with regard to Mode B/Learning to Learn teaching.[3]

For some reason, previous Learning to Learn initiatives always seem to have taken either the 'discrete' or the 'embedded' approach. Adopting a pragmatic stance, we thought: if we really want this thing to work, why not do both? It seems kind of obvious, but as far as we are aware, *Learning Skills* is the first example of a Learning to Learn curriculum to adopt an explicit, taught *and* embedded approach. If you know of any others, we'd love to hear about them!

Learning Skills is a whole-school approach to teaching and learning that aims to teach children 'how' to learn as well as 'what' to learn. When we talk about the 'what' and the 'how', clearly there is a balance to be struck. We don't want our education system to produce young people who are incredibly knowledgeable but lacking in interpersonal skills. The pub bore is not the goal here – and nor are the heartbreaking graduates who featured in the recent BBC documentary 'How to Break into the Elite', who have impeccable academic credentials but can't find employment because they fall apart in interviews.[4] Equally, we don't want to be turning out confident, verbally dexterous types who bluff and bluster their way through life without ever really knowing what they're talking about; there are already more than enough people in public life who fit that bill.

In recent years, we've heard a lot about the importance of a knowledge-rich curriculum, and armed with insights from cognitive science, the teaching profession has made great strides toward treating subject knowledge with the respect it deserves. This is entirely welcome – for too long, we haven't given sufficient thought to how subject knowledge is sequenced, memorised and built upon as children progress through the system. But as well as being knowledgeable, we also want our young people to be confident, creative, resilient, verbally fluent, autodidactic, critical thinkers who are able and willing to take their place as socially and politically engaged citizens of planet Earth. So a balance must be struck between knowledge and skills, between the 'what' and the 'how'.

Within the taught *Learning Skills* course, the balance is very much tipped toward the 'how' of learning, although there is necessarily some 'what' in the mix. In subject areas, naturally the balance remains tipped in the direction of the 'what'. However, we believe that all teachers should pay at least some attention to the 'how' – otherwise, children find it hard to see the commonalities in how they learn across the various subject disciplines, and this makes it harder for them to transfer their understanding of how they learn and apply it successfully across all of their subjects.

While the 'what vs how' balance is different in *Learning Skills* lessons and subject learning, as far as possible it is necessary for all teachers across the school to be pulling in the same direction – paying some attention to both the what and the how. In this way, students experience a far more joined-up diet of learning, and transfer becomes a lot easier to achieve. So, although it started out life as a taught course to help smooth the transition from primary school into year 7, the *Learning Skills* curriculum is really a whole-school approach to teaching and learning that requires everyone – teachers and support staff – to play their part in a way that makes sense to them, for their particular students, and within the context of their subject discipline or role.

What does it look like in practice?[5]

A taught *and* embedded approach to Learning to Learn comprises three elements:

1. **Timetabled lessons**, taught by a dedicated team

   How much time you allocate to the taught course, and how you find the time, is a matter for internal discussion within the school. At Sea View, the first *Learning Skills* cohort had five lessons a week in year 7, three lessons a week in year 8 and five lessons a fortnight in year 9. Here's how the year 7 lessons broke down:

Lesson	Activity	
	Week 1	**Week 2**
1		
2	Project-based learning	
3		
4	Philosophy for children	
5	Oracy: pairs/small groups	Mindfulness/Learning journals

   We didn't make a note of it at the time, but as far as we can recall, the five lessons a week in year 7 came from PSHE, ICT, MFL, Art and Humanities. At this point, we expect that some readers' jaws may have just hit the floor – especially those of a subject-knowledge-is-king persuasion.

   If that includes you, reader, we simply invite you to reflect on the fact that these students went on to achieve the best set of results the school had ever seen, by some margin. If you invest the time in teaching pupils how to learn more effectively, you and they will be able to cover more ground in fewer lessons of subject-based learning. We don't know what the optimal amount of time to dedicate to the taught course is. We won't know until the approach has been implemented in many more schools, each doing it for different amounts of time – and even then it will be difficult to know for sure, because the success of a Learning to Learn initiative is determined by many factors, and time is only one of them. But we do know you need to give it a decent whack of time – at least three or four lessons a week in year 7, and then tapering off as they progress through Key Stage 3. In primary schools, it's a simpler equation because the teacher is able to shuffle things around and integrate aspects of Learning to Learn into the topics they are covering.

2. Ensure that, as far as possible, the principles and practices of metacognition, self-regulation and oracy are **embedded throughout the curriculum**. We'll discuss this later in this chapter, but it involves things like having a shared language of learning, using shared practices such as using talk rules to govern class discussions, and having a joined-up professional development programme so that the

lines of communication are kept open between the *Learning Skills* department and subject departments throughout the school.

3. Put in place a range of strategies to ensure that the knowledge, skills, habits and dispositions developed through taught *Learning Skills* lessons are able to meaningfully **transfer** into subject learning throughout the school.

Apart from the section on 'strategies for transfer', the remainder of this chapter is primarily concerned with what happens in the timetabled *Learning Skills* lessons. However, many of these ideas and practices are applicable to subject learning across the curriculum. The extent to which this happens will require individual teachers and middle leaders to judge where they feel the balance should lie between the 'what' and the 'how' of learning (or between 'Mode A' and 'Mode B' learning) within their subject discipline, complementing rather than compromising the learning of subject knowledge.

The three elements outlined above describe how *Learning Skills* is organised at the teacher level, but there is an important fourth element – the students themselves. As we saw in Caroline's story at the end of *Chapter 4: The story of Learning Skills* – and as we will see in more detail when we set out the evidence for *Learning Skills* in *Chapter 6* – when you teach children in this way, *they* become the agents of change who transform the nature of teaching and learning across the school. Through the *Learning Skills* taught course, pupils develop a stronger sense of who they are and how they learn best. They learn to monitor and control their feelings and their behaviours. And, crucially, they learn to find their voice – literally and metaphorically. In so doing, they develop the confidence to make more (and more sophisticated) contributions to discussions. After a while, this newfound confidence starts spilling over into their friendship groups, their home lives and their learning in other lessons.

DEDICATED TEACHING TEAM

Rationale

If you're planning to implement a *Learning Skills* curriculum, there is perhaps no more important factor to consider than the appointment of a dedicated teaching team. When secondary schools write their timetable, their first concern is usually to make sure that all the GCSE classes are taught by subject specialists – preferably those with a track record of getting good results. Then they staff their Key Stage 3 classes, and then – finally – they look at non-examined subjects like Learning to Learn and PSHE, and allocate them to whichever teachers still have space on their timetable. In the Learning to Learn literature, such teachers have been described as 'sceptical conscripts'.[6] In the world of HR, they call it 'backfilling'.[7]

Among teachers, subjects like PSHE and Learning to Learn are like Marmite. Some absolutely love them; many absolutely do not. Very few people become teachers in order to teach PSHE – it's just something that comes with the territory. When James took over as the Head of PSHE at Sea View, it was taught by around 35 form tutors. Each half-term, tutors would receive a foot-high stack of photocopied worksheets, most of which would end up in the recycling untouched. In lessons, the students mostly made posters, watched videos and had unstructured 'discussion lessons'… it was not a model of good practice. The following year, all lessons were taught by a dedicated team of seven teachers who received up-to-date training and were neither sceptical nor conscripted.

The need for an initiative to be delivered by people who are committed to the cause is not limited to PSHE. It's common sense, and it's also a common finding in the research literature. For example, a RAND corporation report on school-based interventions concluded that:

> Whether a particular program 'works' in a specific population may rest on whether sufficient background work has been done in that population and whether the population itself is invested in the implementation of the intervention.[8]

Elsewhere, researchers have found that metacognition and self-regulation interventions typically show the highest effect sizes when they are implemented by their designers.[9]

The same goes for Learning to Learn. It's the team that drives the thing. They must believe it will work, want it to work and be invested in making it work. They need to have 'skin in the game'. Education is, after all, a human endeavour. It is human beings that make or break a school – not the buildings, books or IT infrastructure. So, in that phrase so beloved of politicians, let us be clear: if you aren't going to staff your Learning Skills team with people who actually want to be there (and who are judged to be a good fit), don't bother. It is simply not worth doing.

What does it look like in practice?

Well, it's pretty simple, really: advertise the posts internally within the school, and then carry out a competitive selection process to decide who will be on the team. Ideally, you should aim to have appointed the team by Easter (if you're UK-based; for international readers, around 12 weeks before the end of the school year). This gives the team time to plan, and gives whoever organises the timetable sufficient time to piece everything together for the new school year.

With regard to recruiting teachers to the team, there are really two key criteria. First, the team should have diverse interests, hopes and ambitions for the *Learning Skills* curriculum. At Sea View, some members of the team were interested in philosophy for children and the development of critical thinking skills; one was interested in helping the pupils work together and collaborate efficiently; another was interested in the children becoming more creative. This meant that we would each have one passion project we could lead on, we could learn from one another, and the collective output of the team would be greater than the sum of its parts. The second criterion is that teachers of *Learning Skills* should have a high 'tolerance for chaos'. At Sea View, most *Learning Skills* lessons were dedicated to project-based learning. In these lessons, the teacher circulates more and spends less time controlling the class from the front of the room, and the pupils have more autonomy than is typical in subject-based learning.

Teaching *Learning Skills* is not everyone's cup of tea, but in a secondary school it's likely that there will be enough people with a penchant for 'Mode B' teaching to put a core team together. If there isn't sufficient interest to put a dedicated teaching team together, now is probably not the time to press ahead with a *Learning Skills* curriculum. You can always try again the following year, having appointed people with this in mind.

Once you've appointed your team, it's important that you give them departmental status, with timetabled meetings, a budget and so on. This can be tricky, because the teachers will probably still be teaching in other subject areas, with department meetings of their own. So you might need to be a bit creative to find a way for the *Learning Skills* team to have department meetings on a different day. But most of all, the *Learning Skills* team needs two things that you can't touch or see: autonomy and trust.

As we mentioned in the *Introduction*, we were given an incredible amount of autonomy with regard to what should go into the programme.

Stuart, our head teacher, was a big believer in distributed leadership. Leadership is not a limited resource. If you give people the freedom to take a lead on some aspect of school improvement – assuming they are ready, willing and able to take on such a challenge – they will often exceed your expectations.

We felt an enormous debt of gratitude to Stuart and the senior team for giving us this opportunity when it would have been far easier to give the curriculum time to English and maths. In granting us the freedom to create a new Learning to Learn curriculum from scratch, he had placed his trust in us, and we were keen to repay it ten times over.

But it's one thing talking about how education should be done in an 'if I ruled the world' conversation around the dinner table. It's quite another to actually be given free rein to get on and make it happen. Suddenly being in a position to put our money where our mouths were made them go very dry. We started with what we had, and we worked to our strengths. On paper, Kate was the boss, but every member of the team was equally responsible for dreaming it, designing it and making it a reality.[10] Being given the licence to create something so significant felt incredibly liberating, but it came with a heavy weight of responsibility. The school had recently been placed in 'special measures' – think supernatural levels of scrutiny – and here we were boldly marching into the unknown. All of our necks were on the line, together. We would either succeed and share in the success, or we would blow it and share in the failure.

Trust is not a one-way street; it needs to be built up on all sides. This isn't easy to achieve in a profession littered with phrases like 'capability measures', 'performance-related pay' and 'holding people to account'. Stuart trusted us to not drop the ball, and we in turn trusted him to not intervene at the first sign of difficulty. We tell children all the time that they need to take risks and learn from their mistakes; we had to grant ourselves the same luxury. We also had to learn to trust ourselves. Individually, we had to trust that our values, professional judgement and ability to teach in this new way were going to come to fruition. And as a team, we had to trust one another to contribute equally and to be brutally honest with one another as we translated our shared vision into reality.

To a significant degree, it is these two factors – autonomy and trust – that made Learning Skills work at Sea View. We couldn't risk any other outcome. As we said above, our outlook was not 'Will this work?', but 'What will it take to make this work?' The difference between these two attitudes is the difference between success and failure.

Finally, in designing and teaching a *Learning Skills* curriculum, autonomy and trust are not limited to the teachers. We knew that if we wanted our pupils to become proactive, independent learners, we needed to grant them the freedom to... well, do things independently. In practice, this means stepping back far more than is usual in an education system where you hear the word 'intervention' about 12 times a day.

We will return to the question of student autonomy later in this chapter – in particular, the notion of *curated autonomy*. For now, it is worth noting that as teachers we had to trust that when we granted freedom to the pupils to work and learn independently, they wouldn't run amok with it. That trust can't be rushed, and it can't be bestowed out of the blue. It must be grown through shared experience, openness and honesty. The seeds of trust begin to germinate and take root the moment the students realise that when you say you're giving them the freedom to choose what to learn, and how, and with whom – you actually mean it.

STRATEGIES FOR TRANSFER

Rationale

As we saw in Part 1, the success of a Learning to Learn initiative is largely determined by the extent to which it is embraced as a whole-school cultural shift rather than something that is taken on board by a few keen souls and roundly ignored by everyone else. The importance of whole-school implementation can be seen elsewhere in the research literature. For example, a review of the Social and Emotional Aspects of Learning (SEAL) programme rolled out by the New Labour government in the mid 2000s reported that:

> *Ratings indicative of a whole-school universal approach to SEAL were significantly associated with school ethos, which in turn mediated associations with pupils' social experiences, overall school attainment, and persistent absence.*[11]

A similar emphasis on the need for whole-school implementation of social and emotional learning initiatives was also reported in a meta-analysis from the US.[12] It therefore seems that the extent to which social and emotional learning initiatives are successful is largely determined by the extent to which they are embraced on a whole-school level.

In the context of Learning to Learn, perhaps the most important component of whole-school implementation is the thorny issue of transfer. The importance of transferring knowledge and skills from one context to another has long been recognised in the research literature. One important idea is the distinction between 'near' and 'far' transfer. Many people have observed that transfer tends only to occur when two tasks are similar or contain similar features. This idea, known as 'near transfer', was first proposed by the American psychologist Edward Thorndike as long ago as 1901,[13] and continues to the present day.[14, 15, 16] However, an alternative narrative exists within the literature to suggest that 'far transfer' – the application of knowledge and skills to new or unfamiliar situations, problems or domains – is achievable when certain conditions are met.[17, 18, 19]

> **TEACHER TAKEAWAY**
> Transfer doesn't happen automatically, but that doesn't mean it doesn't happen at all. Designing and planning for transfer is critical to the success of any Learning to Learn initiative.

According to Hipkins and Cowie (2014), 'the question of how teachers might design learning experiences with transfer in mind is essentially the same question as how to design for Learning to Learn'.[20] In other words: planning for the effective 'far transfer' of knowledge and skills is critical to the success (or otherwise) of a Learning Skills curriculum. Some key insights from the transfer literature which helped inform the Learning Skills programme at Sea View are summarised in Table 5.2.

Table 5.2. Key insights from the transfer literature, and their relevance to Learning Skills[21]

Key insights from the transfer literature	Relevance to Learning Skills
The importance of language: language attributes are not cognitively separate, but transfer readily and are interactive.[21 (a)]	• Whole-school language of learning, co-constructed with students • Whole-school emphasis: exploratory talk
Intercontextuality: framing different learning contexts so that students come to see both the similarities and differences between them.[21 (b)]	• Transfer plenaries • Learning journals
The importance of dispositions: the critical role of teachers asking regular questions, to prompt transfer thinking. [21 (c)]	• Whole-school language of learning • Transfer plenaries • Learning journals
'Emerging evidence indicates that cognitive, intrapersonal, and interpersonal competencies can be taught and learned in ways that promote transfer'.[21 (d)]	• Interpersonal: oracy; inclusive practice • Intrapersonal: meditation, learning journals • Cognitive: Philosophy for Children, exploratory talk, thinking and reasoning

Key insights from the transfer literature	Relevance to *Learning Skills*
The applicability of knowledge is neglected in schools. Identification of three themes: • The importance of the perspective/stance of the learner • The neglected role of motivation • The existence of specific, validated techniques: teaching for transfer.[21 (e)]	• Whole-school CPD programme • Transfer plenaries • Learning journals • Shared language of learning • Whole-school expectations enforced through observations, planning pro formas
The importance of 'expansive framing' in promoting transfer across time, place and people.[21 (f)]	• Transfer plenaries • Learning journals
Three bridges for transfer: detect, elect, connect. The importance of motivation and disposition.[21 (g)]	• Transfer plenaries • Learning journals
Promoting the transfer of learning by mapping across situations.[21 (h)]	• Curriculum mapping by middle leaders • Transfer plenaries • Learning journals
The importance of motivation and disposition in transfer – students need the 'will' as well as the 'skill'.[21 (i)]	• Transfer plenaries • Learning journals • Student autonomy
The importance of 'noticing' in promoting transfer.[21 (j)]	• Meditation • Learning journals • Transfer plenaries

What does it look like in practice?

At Sea View, the extent to which we were concerned with transfer increased as time went on. In the first year, we were almost exclusively focused on the taught course: getting to know our students, trying out new ideas and adapting to new ways of working as classroom practitioners.

In the second year, we started to think more about how what we were doing related to subject learning across the school. We developed a new language of learning called the Sea View Habits of Mind (inspired by the work of Art Costa and colleagues in the US) and rolled it out as a whole-school language of learning. We also commissioned some researchers from a local university to evaluate the extent to which students and teachers referred to the Habits of Mind in lessons throughout the school. We will discuss this in more detail in the section on a 'shared language of learning', but long story short, the answer was: 'barely at all'. This prompted us to take stock and think much more deeply about how we might go about transferring what we were doing out into subject learning across the school. We realised that there are two aspects to transfer – transfer *out* of *Learning Skills* lessons and transfer *in* to other subject areas – and that we had to pay attention to both. We will now briefly consider each in turn.

Transfer out

Once a fortnight, students in year 7 had one lesson dedicated to writing in their learning journals. We'll explain how this worked later in this chapter. The aim of these lessons was primarily to provide the time and space to allow students to think about how they learn (or struggle to learn) in different contexts, and to plan how they would transfer their self-regulated learning skills from *Learning Skills* lessons into subject learning across the school.

In addition, throughout the taught *Learning Skills* course in years 7, 8 and 9, there was an ongoing effort to encourage students (a) to reflect on their increasing knowledge and understanding of themselves as learners, and of learning itself; and (b) to apply this knowledge and understanding to other subject areas, or to aspects of their life beyond the school gates. Typically, these 'transfer plenaries' would simply take the form of a single question, followed by a think/pair/share discussion – e.g. 'How might [*what we're doing today*] help us learn better in [*insert subject*]?'

We soon found that students became adept at making such connections, even where the similarities between contexts were not at all obvious to us as teachers. The most important thing was that the connections were made by the students, not by us.

Transfer in

As time went on, we put a number of strategies in place in a systematic effort to facilitate the transfer of knowledge, skills, habits and dispositions from *Learning Skills* lessons into subject learning across the school. Having a shared language of learning – twinned with the expectation that all teachers would use this language in lessons as a basis for discussing the 'how' of

TRANSFER PLENARY
Short, regular discussion points designed to help students make links between what they are doing and how they learn in other subjects, or in life outside school.

learning – was instrumental in providing students with a more joined-up diet of learning across the curriculum. We ran a whole-staff meeting where each department created a subject-specific policy for how they would embed the shared language of learning in their subject area. This resulted in subject-specific classroom displays and policies to ensure that metacognitive reflection was embedded in lesson planning, feedback practices and the setting and marking of homework.

Another important factor in promoting transfer throughout the school was the school's Continuing Professional Development (CPD) programme. When the Learning Skills programme first began in 2010, CPD was centred around half-termly meetings of Teaching and Learning Communities (TLCs) based on the work of Dylan Wiliam. However, many teachers felt the TLC meetings were too infrequent to be useful (to be fair, Wiliam recommends that TLC meetings take place nine times a year rather than six).[22]

In the third year of the programme, the senior team agreed to disaggregate our INSET days (it's less painful than it sounds) and distribute the time across the year, meaning that we could have a one-hour CPD session every week. By this time, three members of the Learning Skills team had become Lead Practitioners for Teaching and Learning, and so we were centrally involved in the planning and delivery of the whole-school CPD programme. The weekly sessions consisted of three rotating strands: a) taught workshops, in which all teaching and support staff explored an aspect of learning-centred practice (e.g. exploratory talk, differentiation through questioning, formative assessment); b) team sessions, where teachers worked within their departments to plan how to embed these ideas into their practice; and c) an action research component, whereby all teachers and support staff undertook a systematic professional inquiry into an aspect of their practice.

As time went on, whole-school expectations became much clearer. All teachers were expected to reflect on the 'how' of learning within lessons, and received training in how to do so. (It doesn't need to gobble up lots of valuable lesson time, by the way: simply asking, 'Here's what we're learning today. How do you think we might go about this?' can be a really powerful way to get the students' minds whirring and making connections between how they learn in different subjects). This expectation was also reinforced through lesson planning and observation protocols.

But perhaps the most important factor in transferring knowledge, skills, habits and dispositions from Learning Skills lessons out into subject learning was the students themselves. We saw an example of this in Caroline's story at the end of Chapter 4: The story of Learning Skills, where year 7 students were taking responsibility for leading learning, providing one another with insightful feedback and generally blowing everybody's socks off. As teachers of science (James) and modern foreign languages (Kate), we also saw for ourselves how *Learning Skills* students behaved very differently across the school compared with the cohorts that had come before them. They were more proactive, more resilient and a lot less inclined to utter the kinds of helpless questions that we listed in the *Introduction*.

Transfer is not an easy nut to crack. It is multifaceted and requires careful management at both ends of the process (transfer out and transfer in). And it certainly doesn't tend to happen automatically. But as we will see in *Chapter 6: The evidence for Learning Skills*, there is good reason to believe that at Sea View we made some significant strides with regard to transfer. The more time we invested in helping our students develop their speaking and listening skills, their organisational skills and their project management skills, the more they became confident, proactive, self-regulated learners – and that couldn't help but spill over into their other lessons, as well as their lives beyond the school gates. We will now turn our attention to the three powerful ideas at the heart of the *Learning Skills* curriculum – oracy, metacognition and self-regulated learning.

ORACY

Rationale

In case you aren't familiar, the word oracy was coined in 1965 by the British educational researcher Andrew Wilkinson, who defined it simply as 'the ability to use the oral skills of speaking and listening'.[23] That same year, Wilkinson wrote a book that began: 'The spoken language in England has been shamefully neglected'.[24] It is therefore clear that Wilkinson's invention of the word oracy was a deliberate attempt to raise the profile of spoken language, and to recognise it as being of equal importance to reading and writing.

Oracy is such an important topic – so supercharged with the ability to unleash untold human potential, and so laden with a sense of burning injustice that its status has been diminished for so long – that it is difficult to know where to begin. So we should probably start at the beginning.

Spoken language is perhaps the defining characteristic of our species. Some animals have a rudimentary spoken language, of course, and some are even quite sophisticated – capuchin monkeys have been known to lie to one another, for example, raising the 'snake' alarm in order to steal their neighbours' food.[25] But by and large, animals make for poor dinner party guests. The ability to speak and listen is the main reason our species has been able to invent so much cool stuff, like medicine and technology and crumpets. We might, of course, have achieved these things had spoken language never evolved, but it does seem less likely.

Spoken communication is the key to much of our success, and for much of recorded history, the importance of spoken language was reflected in our education systems. Throughout the middle ages, rhetoric was one-third of the trivium (alongside logic and grammar), a core curriculum first established in ancient Greece. And the high status of spoken language persisted until relatively recently. As the speechwriter and author Simon Lancaster recently pointed out:

> In London, right the way through to the 19th century, it was possible to get a free education in rhetoric, but not in mathematics, reflecting the importance that was placed on the topic.[26]

Since Wilkinson's coining of the word 'oracy' in 1965, the perceived importance of speaking and listening has ebbed and flowed throughout our education system. In the 1970s, there was a wave of interest in the nature of classroom interactions and the potential value of spoken language as a driver or mediator of learning.[27, 28, 29] And in the late 1980s, speaking and listening were briefly recognised as having equal status with reading and writing in the National Curriculum for England and Wales. A 'National Oracy Project', designed to support teachers in developing students' talk in the classroom, ran from 1987 to 1992.[30] An oracy revival seemed to be on the way.

But then something happened. For various reasons, by the turn of the century, speaking and listening had slipped off the educational agenda. Although many teachers continued to see the value in encouraging students to talk as part of their learning, oracy as an explicit policy aim largely disappeared from view. This has been compounded by more recent developments, such as the government's bonfire of thousands of vocational qualifications in 2012[31] and the decision in 2013 to remove speaking and listening from the English GCSE assessment.[32] A 2016 report entitled *Oracy: The state of speaking in our schools* revealed that although teachers 'feel oracy is critically important... support for oracy across different lessons, classrooms and schools is currently patchy'.[33]

To be clear, we do not single out oracy as being any more important than reading or writing in helping children become effective, self-regulated learners. However, schools are already pretty good at developing reading and writing. In the history of Learning to Learn – and in the recent history of education more broadly – oracy education has often been overlooked or undervalued.

The short version of the rationale for placing oracy at the heart of the *Learning Skills* curriculum, then, is simply to restore it to its former glory and to recognise spoken language as being at least of equal importance to the so-called '3 Rs' of 'reading, writing and arithmetic'. At the most basic level, we spend a far greater proportion of our waking lives speaking and listening than we do reading and writing. According to one estimate, we humans typically 'spend 70 to 80 percent of our waking hours in some form of communication. Of that time, we spend about 9 percent writing, 16 percent reading, 30 percent speaking, and 45 percent listening.'[34] Perhaps, then, we should really speak of the '4 Rs', recognising oracy as a worthy fourth member of that elite band of educational priorities.

But the rationale for taking oracy education seriously goes much deeper than this. In recent decades, researchers in fields such as developmental psychology and linguistics as well as education have developed a detailed understanding of the vital role of spoken language in children's social and cognitive development.[35, 36] Famously, this idea was first expressed by the Russian psychologist Lev Vygotsky, who recognised the importance of social interactions in the cognitive development of individuals.[37, 38] Vygostsky's central insight was expressed succinctly by Vass and Littleton (2010): 'it is through speech and action with others that we learn to reason and gain individual consciousness'.[39]

We have known for years now that the quality and amount of spoken communication children experience in early childhood is a powerful predictor of educational attainment in later life[40, 41] We also know that educational outcomes can be significantly boosted by teaching children how to use talk to communicate more effectively with their peers.[42, 43] A recent study carried out at the Massachusetts Institute of Technology found that conversational turn-taking in early childhood leads to increased activation in the left inferior frontal lobe of the brain (known as Broca's area), which 'significantly explain(s) the relation between children's language exposure and verbal skill'.[44] Explaining the importance of this study, the lead investigator said 'it provides the first evidence that family conversation at home is associated with brain development in children. It's almost magical how parental conversation appears to influence the biological growth of the brain'.[45]

There is now an extensive body of research literature detailing the ways in which oracy in the home and school predicts educational and life outcomes. Recently, James co-authored a report for the Welsh government with Professor Neil Mercer, entitled *Oracy across the Welsh Curriculum*.[46] This involved carrying out an extensive review of the literature on oracy education, which revealed three broad areas of impact: cognitive outcomes, social and emotional outcomes and life outcomes. These are summarised in Table 5.3.

Table 5.3. The impact of oracy education: a summary of research findings[47]

Category	Area of impact
Cognitive outcomes	Improved attainment in subject learning[47 (a)]
	Improved literacy skills[47 (b)]
	Improved verbal, non-verbal, quantitative reasoning[47 (c)]
	Enhanced communication for pupils with SEND[47 (d)]
	Enhanced communication/cognition among bilingual students[47 (e)]
	Transfer of comprehension, reasoning skills to other subjects[47 (f)]
Social and emotional outcomes	Self-esteem/self-confidence[47 (g)]
	Engagement and on-task focus[47 (h)]
	Social development/peer interactions[47 (i)]
	Emotional intelligence[47 (j)]
	Historical empathy[47 (k)]
	Ability to handle stress[47 (l)]
Life outcomes	Overcoming social disadvantage[47 (m)]
	Fewer exclusions, less juvenile offending[47 (n)]
	Improved future earnings[47 (o)]

Of course, much of a young person's life trajectory is determined by socioeconomic factors that lie beyond the school gates. However, it is clear from the research that schools have an important role to play. Oracy education – or the lack of it – can be a significant determinant of a child's future life outcomes. Teachers cannot eradicate poverty; nor can we go into every home and change the way families interact. However, we are uniquely placed to alter those future trajectories by ensuring that all young people are given every possible opportunity to expand their vocabulary and their interpersonal skills and to gain the confidence that comes with the territory.

Taking oracy education seriously is perhaps the most powerful thing a teacher can do to positively impact the future life chances of their pupils. The good news is that while the consequences of oracy education are deadly serious, teaching children how to speak and listen effectively is absolutely fascinating and loads of fun. All we need to do is make our classrooms talk-rich environments where every child is encouraged, expected and supported to develop highly effective speaking and listening skills in a range of contexts.

What does it look like in practice?

Broadly speaking, there are two aspects to oracy, each equally important: *learning to talk* (oracy education) and *learning through talk* (dialogic approaches to teaching and learning). At Sea View, we pretty much threw the kitchen sink at both; you name it, we taught them how to do it and then got them talking about it. In this section, we'll outline five key ways in which we developed our pupils' speaking and listening skills through the *Learning Skills* curriculum:

- **Talk rules** – a simple, powerful approach to helping students learn how to interact productively in paired, group and whole-class discussions
- **Collaboration and complexity** – a systematic approach to nudging pupils out of their comfort zones to the point where they are able to interact productively with anyone, in any group size
- **Structured debates** – to help students sharpen their wits, argumentation skills and rhetorical flair – and to put rocket boosters under their confidence
- **Presentational talk** – to ensure that all students are able to achieve success in public speaking – another huge boon to their self-confidence
- **Philosophical inquiries** – a weekly forum for discussing big ideas in a more curious, exploratory, collaborative way than is possible in structured debates.

As with the broader themes in this chapter, for each of these, we will provide a brief rationale before outlining what it looks like in practice.

TALK RULES

Rationale

The importance of talk rules came to light through a study that took place in the early 1990s called SLANT (Spoken Language and New Technology).[48] At this time, computers were starting to appear in schools, but there weren't enough for the children to have one each, and so they tended to be used in small groups. For researchers wanting to investigate the use of computers in schools, this was quite handy: 'the observable model for computer use is not the creative engagement of individual and machine... but a pair or small group of children talking and interacting with each other as they share the machine'.[49]

As every teacher knows all too well, not all pupil talk is educationally desirable, and so the researchers wanted to explore whether 'there might be ways of using the computer to encourage certain kinds of talk which had particular educational value'.[50] They recorded many hours of extended group discussions by primary school children grouped at computers, transcribed the conversations and set about coding the data.

The researchers identified three broad categories of classroom talk: disputational, cumulative and exploratory. These have been described as 'social modes of thinking'.[51] The three categories are not mutually exclusive, and a single conversation can include features of all three kinds of talk. But they provide us with a useful model for thinking about the kinds of talk we want to see less of, and what we would like to see more of.

As the name would suggest, **disputational talk** is characterised by disagreement. Here, we see lots of interactions of the 'Yes it is'/'No it's not' variety. The atmosphere is competitive rather than collaborative, and participants are more concerned with point-scoring than they are in engaging critically with one another's ideas or getting to the truth of the matter.

We often see disputational talk in public life as well as in schools, in things like Prime Ministers Questions and combative political interviews. For example, Person A might say: 'We have an unprecedented recruitment and retention crisis in nursing. This is a stain on this government. When are you going to resign?' To this, Person B might reply: 'I don't know what figures the right honourable member is referring to. We have put record investment into the recruitment of nursing. Numbers now are at an all-time high!' As an observer, you think, helplessly: 'This is ridiculous! How many nurses are there? Has the number gone up or down?' But you never find out, because in disputational talk, there is rarely any critical engagement through evidence or reasoning, or any attempt to reach a shared understanding. Disputational talk might make for entertaining (if maddening) political theatre, but it is extremely unhelpful from an educational standpoint.

At its most basic level, **cumulative talk** is what happens when people just wait for their interlocutor to stop talking so they can say their thing. A typical example in school would be a PSHE lesson on road safety. All the children's hands go up because they all want to share a story about how their best mate's next-door neighbour's cat nearly got run over by a milk float. In more sophisticated forms of cumulative talk, people may listen intently to one another and they may even build on one another's ideas – but again, there's a lack of critical engagement. As a basis for pooling ideas and creative ideation, cumulative talk can be useful, but it's not helpful in every situation. Very few people change their mind as a result of cumulative talk.

When the SLANT researchers were coding the data, they found that most interactions were either disputational or cumulative, and it was all a bit depressing, because it didn't seem that children were able to talk together in educationally productive ways. But then they started to see glimpses of more productive interactions, and this developed into a third category – **exploratory talk**. By coincidence, similar research was taking place in the US around the same time, and they called it accountable talk, but it's basically the same thing.[52] This is not a comprehensive list, but exploratory talk is characterised by the following features:

- Everyone is encouraged to contribute.
- Everyone listens actively.
- People ask questions.
- People share relevant information.
- Ideas and opinions are treated with respect.
- There is an atmosphere of trust.
- There is a sense of shared purpose.
- Contributions build on what has gone before.
- People give reasons for their thinking.
- Ideas may be challenged.
- The group seeks agreement for joint decisions.[53]

In exploratory talk, the thinking, reasoning and critical engagement is tangible. The group interacts as a well-oiled unit, engaging in collaborative group discussion that is greater than the sum of its parts – like a 'hive mind'. Clearly, it is exploratory talk that is of most interest to teachers wishing to help their students learn to think together in more productive ways. The question is, how do we get children to engage in exploratory talk more? And the answer is: talk rules. Embedding the use of talk rules is one of the most simple, powerful and transformative things you can do as a teacher.

What does it look like in practice?

The first thing to understand is that we are all guided by rules all the time – they're just usually invisible, implicit, and unspoken. These are the habitual rules of thumb that govern the way we behave in different contexts. Often, these are cultural norms that can vary from one country to another. In the UK, this includes things like not jumping the queue in the supermarket, trying to catch the waiter's eye in a restaurant rather than clicking your fingers, and understanding that if there's only one passenger on the bus, it's not OK to go and sit next to them.

Such rules may go unspoken, but you will soon see how seriously people take them if you transgress them. In school, an example might be that at the start of a lesson the children sit down at desks while the teacher remains standing. This rule makes practical sense – the teacher can see all their students and vice versa. If a student remained standing, or if the teacher sat on the floor facing the wall, it would be weird and people would say something.

Sometimes, however, there are implicit rules in play that are unhelpful. For example, in group discussions, children are often guided by the following unspoken rules:

- If you have a good idea, keep it to yourself.
- Don't disagree with your friends – back them up, come what may.
- Let the most confident person dominate the discussion.
- It's unwise to challenge the most popular group member.
- Don't speak if you aren't 100% sure about what you want to say.

Such implicit rules of thumb can lead to groupthink, the widespread phenomenon whereby people make bad decisions because of dysfunctional group dynamics.[54] In schools, it is the final entry in the list above – enshrined in the adage 'it's better to remain silent and be thought a fool than to speak and remove all doubt' – that is the most common and the most insidious. If we can't create a classroom culture where all young people feel safe to articulate their emerging thoughts and views without fear of ridicule, then it's going to be a lot harder for them to develop those thoughts and views and therefore to learn and grow as people.[55]

So the first thing to do is to talk with your pupils about how invisible rules govern our behaviour in all kinds of settings. Help them understand that people follow unspoken rules like these all the time, often without even realising it. Talk through the consequences of pupils following unhelpful rules such as those listed above in class discussions – and then set about creating a better set of explicit talk rules. There are some excellent resources to help you do this on the University of Cambridge *Thinking Together* website.[56] You can also use a variation of the 'hat method', which we will describe later in this chapter in the section on inclusive practice. In secondary schools, you can establish a set of talk rules easily within the space of a single lesson; with younger children, it can take a bit longer. The *Thinking Together* website contains some excellent resources for teachers, including three lessons that you can run through to establish talk rules with younger children.

It is important that the class goes through the process of co-creating a set of talk rules rather than having them imposed by the teacher. The teacher can contribute to the process, but should not control it completely. Co-construction means that the pupils are invested in the process and feel a sense of ownership over the content. It's a good idea to aim for around five to seven talk rules, and to phrase them positively (dos, rather than don'ts). A typical set of 'child friendly' talk rules usually looks something like the following:

1. We will share what we know with each other.
2. We will ask everyone to say what they think.
3. Everyone will listen carefully to others and consider what we hear.
4. We will give reasons for what we say.
5. We will pay attention and try to think of good ideas.
6. We will decide what to do only when everyone has said all they want.
7. We will try to agree about what we think.[57]

Talk rules like these are useful for guiding group discussions, but they don't cover all aspects of group work. For group work, you might also want to include things like 'Everyone should contribute equally to the group goal', or 'Everyone should have a job that they are happy with'. Once agreed, the talk rules should be displayed on the wall in such a way that they can be seen from every seat in the room.

Before any talk or group task, remind your pupils of the talk rules. If it's a while since you last revisited them, you may wish to ask a different pupil to read each one aloud and to check that the students understand what each one looks like in practice. If time allows, it's also a good idea to ask pupils to use the talk rules to set themselves a target for the lesson: 'I will make sure everyone gets the chance to speak', 'I will give reasons for my thinking', or 'I will try to speak less today, to give others a chance to speak'. It's also a good idea to refer back to the guidelines after a talk task, or at the end of a lesson: 'How easy did we find it to work toward agreement today?', 'Was everybody able to contribute to the discussion?', 'What can we do to make sure group work is even better in the future?' – and so on.

The message from the research literature is simple. If you want your students to work productively in groups, you have to teach them how to do so. No teacher would say, 'Today, Year 7, we're doing literacy – now off you go!' They would model some aspect of literacy, explain it, break it down, give the students opportunities to practice, provide them with feedback and so on. And so it is with group work. When you use talk rules, it transforms the quality of group work overnight. And it does much more than that. Changing the way children speak, listen and interact in groups changes their understanding of themselves and of one another. It helps them learn to get along with one another better, and it can also help them learn knowledge and skills more effectively. It is to this question of 'learning to get along with one another' that we now turn our attention.

COLLABORATION AND COMPLEXITY

Rationale

It is standard practice in many schools to have a seating plan in every classroom, designed by the teacher. Because many children are prone to 'talk off-task' when they sit with their friends, teachers often arrange their seating plans so that this doesn't happen. In co-educational schools, boy–girl–boy–girl seating plans are often used for this reason.

When children are in a seating plan, if you ask them to discuss something with the person next to them, there are many reasons why that conversation might not go well. They might never have spoken to one another before, and feel awkward, nervous or anxious for that reason. One pupil might have bullied or made fun of the other at some point in the past, and the residue of a grudge hangs over their table like a silent cloud. One of them might be deemed more 'popular' than the other, and that popularity differential might be too steep to allow an extended conversation about their learning. One might secretly admire the other... and so on.

To enable high-quality spoken communication to blossom and flourish in every conceivable direction, we need to find ways to help our students overcome such interpersonal barriers that are often invisible to us as teachers.

What does it look like in practice?

One of the aims of the *Learning Skills* curriculum is to make sure that by the end of the year every student is able to have a high-quality conversation – steeped in the features of exploratory talk – with anyone, in any group size. This is the end point. It's not where you begin. Instead, you begin by telling the children the first sentence of this paragraph, and then repeating this message regularly throughout the year. It's really important to make sure that they hear this message as often as possible.

At first, to avoid the awkwardness of seating plan-based discussions, we allowed the students to sit with a talk partner of their choosing. We then spent the whole of the first half-term getting them to practise using talk rules, until they reached the point where they were able to use some or all of the features of exploratory talk within a lesson. In these talk lessons, we often used a book called *Thinking through Philosophy* by Paul Cleghorn, which includes many fantastic open-ended discussion tasks.[58] During these lessons, the teacher would circulate, and wherever we saw exploratory talk taking place, we would stop and ask the students to model what they were doing to the rest of the class. In this way, we provided individuals with positive reinforcement and gradually steered the whole class toward more productive ways of speaking and listening together.

The following half-term, we repeated this process with three students in each group – again of the children's choosing. A group size of three is a lot more complex than a pair, because you have three times as many lines of communication (A–B, B–C and A–C rather than just A–B). So already, the sparks begin to fly. Again, we would spend the whole half-term getting them to a point where they could engage in discussions – in groups of three – that featured many or all of the characteristics of exploratory talk.

Next, we moved to a group size of four. Again, this increases the complexity considerably, with six relationships now (A–B, A–C, A–D, B–C, B–D, C–D). And again, we worked the cycle until all students were able to communicate effectively in groups of four.

In the second half of the year, we repeated this cycle again – but this time, the teacher chose the groupings. Over time, we gradually worked up to the most challenging groupings, but we didn't avoid any particular combinations of pupils. The aim was to make it so that any pupil would be able to engage in an exploratory conversation in any pair or group they found themselves in. To recap:

- Half-term 1 – pairs, students choose
- Half-term 2 – threes, students choose
- Half-term 3 – fours, students choose
- Half-term 4 – pairs, teacher chooses
- Half-term 5 – threes, teacher chooses
- Half-term 6 – fours, teacher chooses

Running alongside these oracy lessons, we also had weekly philosophical inquiry sessions where students were expected to embody the features of exploratory talk in whole-class discussions.

Combined with the use of talk rules, this method proved highly effective as a way to systematically nudge our pupils out of their comfort zones, learning to collaborate effectively in increasingly complex groups as they moved through the year. As we will see in *Chapter 6: The evidence for Learning Skills*, the students really valued the way in which *Learning Skills* required them to mix with one another in this way, and we agree. We can't recommend it highly enough.

STRUCTURED DEBATES

Rationale

We mentioned in *Chapter 3* that Eton College recently spent an eye-watering £18 million on building a new debating chamber, Jafar Hall.[59] It looks a bit like the House of Commons, with rows of benches facing one another.

Eton now counts no fewer than 20 British prime ministers among its alumni.

At Harrow School, there is something called a 'super-curriculum', which 'includes (but is not limited to) wide and habitual reading, extended project work, debate, public speaking, research, competitions, lectures, study trips...'[60] Recently, a group of Harrovians travelled to India to debate 'the best speakers from Calcutta at the Indian Cultural Commission's auditorium in front of a large audience that included media.'[61]

Harrow has produced seven prime ministers.

At Westminster School, there are a range of societies 'run by the pupils themselves [which]… involve a mixture of external speakers and internal pupil-led discussions and presentations'. As the school's website explains:

> The nature of Westminster's approach to learning means that a debate-style challenging of ideas and development of arguments is common to most of the societies; however, there are also several specific debating societies, teams and programmes. As well as internal opportunities such as House Debating, Westminster pupils can get involved in external inter-school competitions both nationally and internationally.[62]

Westminster has produced six prime ministers. You get the idea.

Clearly, there is more to gaining access to the corridors of power than having a way with words. The fact that each of the schools mentioned above is incredibly expensive to attend (the annual fees are considerably higher than the average national salary) – and that they are exclusive to the male of the species – cannot be overlooked. Other factors play a role, as can be seen in the following account of a year 9 'balloon debate', published on the Eton College website, in which students imagine that they are in a sinking hot-air balloon and must decide which Old Etonians are worth saving and which should be considered ballast:

> The Debating Society's final meeting of a successful half packed out the Marten Library, with a predominantly F Block [year 9] audience, to decide who has been the best Old Etonian of all time. The debaters were all F Blockers who had been recruited by a Debating Society committee member who helped to prepare their argument. The candidates ranged from George Orwell to Hugh Laurie and included the less well known Captain Julian Gribble, whose heroic actions in the First World War were an interesting cameo to such well known figures as Keynes. The quality of debating from all the F Block involved was exceptional and surprised the audience in their humour and particularly their ability to think on their feet. Such mature performances from young debaters made the evening's balloon debate an excellent competition. The round where they criticised each other's characters was a highlight, Boris Johnson's representative putting in a fittingly humorous and offensive performance. The final left Boris and Hugh Laurie in the balloon (the audience having dismissed Keynes, Orwell, Wellington and Gribble as credible candidates for the greatest OE of all time) and Hugh

Laurie eventually prevailed. The evening showed the strength of Eton's young debaters who certainly entertained the audience, who will have felt it was another evening well spent with the rejuvenated Debating Society.[63]

Here we can see how, as well as taking debating seriously, the tradition of belonging to a school that has produced so many people of influence helps inculcate a sense among students that they too can one day be similarly influential, should they so choose. Nevertheless, it is surely no coincidence that so many prime ministers (as well as famous politicians, economists, authors, actors, etc.) have been the alumni of a small group of schools that take public speaking and, in particular, debating, extremely seriously.[64]

Here's how seriously they take it. In a form of debate commonly practised in schools like these, the team arguing in favour of the motion is referred to as the 'Government', while the team arguing against is referred to as the 'Opposition'. Moreover, the individuals opening the debate are referred to as the Prime Minister and Deputy Prime Minister, and those opposing are referred to as the Leader and Deputy Leader of the Opposition.

Just take a moment to let this sink in. At schools such as Eton, Harrow and Westminster, students regularly get to play a game of 'Government versus Opposition'. They are literally rehearsing for when they get to run the country. This is a good thing: we should rehearse such things. But if we really want to draw on all the available talent to fill these vital roles – and a brief survey of the current crop of the world's politicians suggests that this might not be an entirely bad idea – surely we should be playing this game in every school on the planet. What kind of a world would we have if such knowledge, skills and opportunities were truly democratised rather than being limited to the (mainly male) children of the super rich? It's an interesting question to reflect on. It would be even more interesting if, as a teaching profession, we decided to find out for real.

What does it look like in practice?

At Sea View, one of the projects was to have a structured debate each week. Having not attended elite private schools ourselves, the *Learning Skills* team was not experienced in the art of running formal debates, and so we had to learn with the students as we went along. Since we left Sea View, we have become aware of the English Speaking Union (ESU), a wonderful organisation with lots of excellent programmes and resources for promoting debate in primary and secondary schools.[65] Had we known about the ESU ten years ago, we would probably have done things differently. But, for what it's worth, here's how we ran debate lessons at Sea View:

1. The students would propose a range of motions for debate (e.g. we should ban violent video games; footballers are paid too much money; the internet is a force for good). We would discuss each in turn, considering how well suited it was to extended debate (e.g. Do we know enough about this topic? Are there several strong arguments on either side?), and then we would vote to choose one.

2. All students would then spend two lessons researching arguments for and against the motion, making detailed notes and flash cards. We would discuss the importance of understanding both sides of the debate and the power of the counterargument as a method for undercutting your opponent's position before they have even spoken ('Our opponents will argue that zoos are cruel. However, zoos have saved over a thousand endangered species from going extinct and many species have been returned to the wild. Zoos are the opposite of cruel!').

3. Five students would then be allocated to the speaking positions (one chair, two arguing for the motion, two against). These allocations were drawn from a hat to ensure that all students had a speaking role at least once during the half-term (5 students a week × 6 weeks = 30 speaking roles across the half-term). The class would then be split in half – half arguing for the motion, half against – and the two teams would prepare their case, ranking the various arguments in order of how persuasive they felt they were and deciding who would say what in the opening statements. During this lesson, the chair would work across both groups to ensure that they understood what each side was planning to say.

4. The debate lesson itself would take the following format:

   a) Audience votes on the motion (for/against)
   b) Opening statement by Prime Minister
   c) Opening statement by Leader of the Opposition
   d) Opening statement by Deputy Prime Minister
   e) Opening statement by Deputy Leader of the Opposition
   f) Chaired discussion, where the for and against teams respond to the opening statements and question one another
   g) Questions/comments from the floor
   h) Summing up/closing comment from either side
   i) Audience votes on the motion (for/against)

j) Audience provides verbal feedback on what each person had done well

k) Audience provides written feedback on what went well/even better if (on slips that they fill in during the debate – so that each of the five speaking members receives four or five slips with written feedback on how they had performed).

As you can see, this is a time-consuming process – it would take a whole week of lessons to prepare for and then carry out one debate. Even though we spent a whole half-term on it, most students only got the chance to play a speaking role once within that period. It is important that you spend the time building up the students' knowledge of the topic to be discussed, and it isn't easy to see how the time could be cut down considerably. This alone is an excellent reason why we need to significantly scale up the number of debates that happen in state schools, so that every student regularly gets the opportunity to sharpen their debating skills. Ideally, this should be done in lessons rather than simply running an after-school debating club for a small number of interested students. Once the technicalities and skills of debate have been mastered through the taught *Learning Skills* course, the practice of debates can be imported into subject learning across the curriculum much more easily.

PRESENTATIONAL TALK

Rationale

Depending on which survey you read, somewhere between 25% and 75% of people say they have a fear of public speaking.[66, 67] This fear runs deep. As we mentioned in *Chapter 3: Learning to Learn on trial*, surveys have repeatedly found that many people rank their fear of public speaking higher than their fear of death.[68, 69] As Jerry Seinfeld observed, this leads to the alarming conclusion that if they were at a funeral, many people would rather be in the coffin than deliver the eulogy!

Like many aspects of human psychology, the fear of public speaking is a spectrum condition. At the extreme end is 'glossophobia', a recognised social anxiety disorder. Thankfully, glossophobia is relatively rare. However, it is clear that many people experience at least some degree of anxiety and/or nervousness around public speaking, and endeavour to avoid it at all costs. As the oracy expert Alan Howe put it recently:

Even if we don't suffer from the phobia, many of us are familiar with the feeling of heightened anxiety associated with speaking in front of an audience, especially when the stakes are high, for example: when talking about a topic for the first time; to a large, unknown audience; or to an audience of known peers. We may worry about being judged (both on what we say but also because of how we sound). The knowledge that everyone is watching, waiting on your next words, can be debilitating. Or simple lack of experience may make the demands of the context seem overwhelming.[70]

Much of this is perfectly rational. When you address a group of people, you're in the spotlight and naturally you want it to go well. But no matter how well you have rehearsed what you want to say, when you aren't used to that kind of exposure, your body can betray you with wildly unhelpful responses; your hands shake; your mouth goes unbelievably dry; your mind goes blank under the pressure.

We can both recall that feeling of abject terror at the prospect of public speaking that we felt as students and even as early career teachers. Nowadays, we both regularly address large rooms of people – a prospect that would have filled us with terror only a few years ago – often without so much as a second thought. We are far from unique in this regard. It has long been known that the most powerful way to overcome a fear is to expose yourself to the thing that terrifies you – so-called exposure therapy.[71] There is abundant evidence that the best way to help people overcome their fear of public speaking is to get them doing public speaking.[72, 73, 74] Indeed, the sense of anxiety often declines significantly once you get up there, a phenomenon known as 'within-session habituation'.[75] In this case, the words 'Just do it, you'll be fine' are actually true!

This does not mean that we should throw students in at the deep end. We don't want to completely overwhelm them and reinforce their fears. We need to allow the gradient to be as shallow or as steep as each student needs it to be in order to push them to the edge of their comfort zone. The journey to success is fast for some students; for others, it can require many steps – modelling, explaining, deconstructing, coaching, mentoring and allowing students to practise in non-threatening ways (e.g. to just two or three people, or just to the teacher, or only saying a few words at first, or using cue cards). The main thing is to continue to gradually increase the difficulty level for each student – speaking to more people, or different groups, for increasing lengths of time, without cue cards and so on – until they can present confidently, from memory, using a range of rhetorical language devices.

Sometimes, people object to this idea, saying things like, 'If a student doesn't want to do public speaking, it's cruel to force them to do it.' But do we allow them to opt out of other things they find challenging or unpleasant – some aspect of maths, say? Of course not – and nor should we make excuses for their fear of public speaking. We should acknowledge it, show them we understand it, and then calmly but persistently support them in getting to the point where they can experience success.

In a small number of cases, a student might have a recognised social anxiety condition where we may wish to make an exception. But such instances are extremely rare. By the time they leave school, the vast majority of young people should be able to comfortably address a class, if not a hall full of adults, without notes. The boost such an experience can give to a young person's confidence and self-esteem is quite remarkable; we have seen it happen many times. We now run a one-day 'Language of Power' workshop for students (and for teachers), and you can almost see some of the students walking an inch taller by the end of the day. Realising that they *can* be the person at the front of the room changes their perception of who they are and of what they can achieve in the future.

It is perfectly possible to go through life without ever addressing a large group of people. However, this should be based on choice rather than on an inability to cope should the situation arise. It is important, therefore, that we teach young people these skills.

What does it look like in practice?

At Sea View, there was an expectation that at the end of each project, all students would present an aspect of their work to their teacher and their peers in a 'teachable moment'. As we described above, some students required a gentler gradient – at first, we would allow them to present just to a small group, or to the teacher in a one-to-one session. Whenever we did this, audience members would fill out an A5 feedback sheet, using the time-honoured 'What Went Well/Even Better If' format. At first, we were a bit nervous that student feedback might be dangerously blunt, but we found that our students were often highly adept at softening the edges of their critical feedback. No doubt it helped to know that they too would take their turn in the spotlight!

Within a half-term, we found that even the most nervous students were keen to give it a go, having seen their friends do it and seeing the buzz that surrounds public speaking. They wanted a piece of it for themselves – even if they were terrified. We allowed students to dictate the level of challenge they would attempt to meet – speaking with no notes was the highest level of challenge.

Since we left Sea View, we have become better acquainted with the ancient art of rhetoric – thanks in part to an excellent TEDx talk by the speechwriter Simon Lancaster, referred to earlier in this chapter, which outlines several tricks of the trade.[76] If we had our time again, this is an aspect of the *Learning Skills* course that we would pay more attention to – we'll explain how at the end of this chapter. We would also provide the 'Language of Power' training for all teaching staff, so that whenever teachers ask children to present their findings to the class, we would be able to use consistent language and expectations for how to achieve success in public speaking.

PHILOSOPHY FOR CHILDREN (P4C)

Rationale

The origins of Philosophy for Children (P4C) can be traced to the global period of student unrest in 1968, when Matthew Lipman, a philosophy professor at Columbia University, became concerned by the lack of critical thinking and reasoning evident among his students and colleagues:

> There was so much rigidity among both students and the university administration, so little communication, so little recourse to reason. I was beginning to have serious doubts about the value of teaching philosophy. It didn't seem to have any impact on what people did. I began to think that the problem I was seeing in the university couldn't be solved there, that thinking was something that had to be taught much earlier, so that by the time a student graduated from high school, skilful, independent thinking would have become a habit.[77]

Lipman began to make enquiries as to how thinking skills might be better developed through the school system.

> But I didn't want to teach children logic in the way we taught (or pretended to teach) college students logic... Someone suggested to me that I somehow present logic in the form of a children's story. The possibility intrigued me: a story... of the

discovery by a group of children of how their own thought processes work, and how more effective thought processes could be distinguished from less effective ones.[78]

The following year, Lipman wrote a children's book, *Harry Stottlemeier's Discovery* (Aristotle... geddit?), and began using it as a stimulus for extended philosophical discussions among fifth grade (year 6) students, which took place twice a week for nine weeks. The impact of this intervention was evaluated in a controlled study involving pre- and post-intervention measures of logic and logical reasoning ability. According to Lipman, the intervention led to an 'increase of 27 months in mental age of the pilot study group at the end of the 9-week program. I could hardly believe we'd made such an impact on the kids in the study.'[79]

Encouraged by these early experiences, Lipman wrote a range of books and teacher manuals to cater for students ranging from age 6 to 16. In 1974 he established the Institute for the Advancement of Philosophy for Children (IAPC) at Montclair University, New Jersey, which is still going strong. Since then, the use of P4C has grown significantly, and the approach is now practised in more than 60 countries worldwide.

Over the last 50 years, the impact of P4C has been studied extensively, and there is a wealth of evidence that the approach is associated with significant gains across a range of academic, cognitive and affective (attitudinal/emotional) domains. Several early studies found that children taking part in twice weekly P4C sessions significantly outperformed students in control groups in measures of formal and informal reasoning.[80, 81, 82] Intriguingly, another early study found that students receiving P4C performed significantly better than control students in maths and reading comprehension.[83] This was a surprising finding, because P4C sessions do not involve maths or reading, suggesting that the thinking and reasoning skills developed through P4C were able to transfer to other areas of the curriculum – an early example of 'far transfer', as we discussed earlier.

This finding that P4C develops transferable knowledge and skills has been repeated on several occasions since. For example, a systematic review of controlled studies spanning 30 years found that P4C led to significant gains in logical reasoning, reading, maths, self-esteem and turn-taking.[84] More recent studies of P4C have found evidence of lasting cognitive gains, improved maths and reading comprehension, improved interactive behaviour and enhanced self-esteem.[85, 86, 87, 88] There is also evidence that P4C benefits teachers as well as students, leading to greater use of open-ended questioning and encouraging teachers to critically engage with their practice.[89, 90] This certainly chimes with our own experience as teachers who have run hundreds of P4C inquiries over the years.

So if it's evidence of impact you're after, P4C has it in spades. But by far the strongest rationale for P4C comes from seeing it in action. It's absolutely gripping. Happily, there are now dozens of videos online of P4C in action, with even very young children engaging in thought-provoking extended discussions. Just type 'P4C' into YouTube – you'll soon see what we mean.[91]

What does it look like in practice?

> The aim of P4C is for children to become 'more thoughtful, more reflective, more considerate and more reasonable individuals'. Most of these skills and the dispositions to use them are learned best through language, by creating a 'community of enquiry', where children engage in dialogue as a co-operative venture.

> Robert Fisher (1990)[92]

Running a philosophical enquiry lesson is very different from teaching subject knowledge, and it can take a bit of practice to get good at it. The first thing to do is to get trained in the approach. In the UK, the main training provider is the Society for Advancing Philosophical Enquiry and Reflection in Education (SAPERE, Latin for 'to be wise'), and there are equivalent bodies in several countries. In the UK, it takes two days to do the Level 1 course, which is all you need to get started. You can also host a training event at your school, which is a good idea if you want to get a few people trained at once. We don't recommend trying to run a P4C session until you have been properly trained in the approach. However, we will briefly outline what a P4C lesson typically looks like.

Nowadays, people tend not to use the original Lipman texts. Instead, most P4C sessions begin with some kind of a stimulus – a short piece of writing, a poem, a photograph, a news article, an object, or a piece of music perhaps. Following this, the children generate questions for discussion, which they then vote on. Before you can do this, however, you need to do some work with your pupils on what kinds of questions lend themselves to philosophical discussion. To do this, many practitioners of P4C refer to the 'question quadrant' (see Figure 5.1, below).[93]

Figure 5.1. The question quadrant

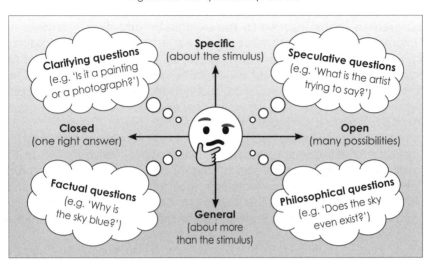

Let's say the stimulus for discussion is a hyper-realistic painting of the sky. If you're not familiar, look up hyper-realistic paintings online – they're amazing! There are many questions that could arise from a stimulus such as this. Often, children tend initially to ask closed questions that seek to clarify understanding about the stimulus: for example, 'Is it a painting or a photo?' or 'Who is the artist?' These are perfectly reasonable questions to ask, but they don't lend themselves to extended philosophical discussion.

Alternatively, they might ask more open, speculative questions – questions that they might use their imagination to answer. For example, 'What feeling is the artist trying to convey?' or 'Why would you want to paint something that looks like a photograph?' As a basis for discussion, these are better than closed questions, but they are still focused on the stimulus. In P4C lessons, what we really want is for pupils to look beyond the stimulus to explore the 'big ideas' that lurk behind it. Nature, beauty, perception, consciousness, the idea of something being fake, deceptive or artificial, the nature of reality – all that good stuff.

Sometimes, children ask questions that sound big and profound at face value: for example, 'Why is the sky blue?' This is an improvement in the sense that it goes beyond the stimulus to enquire about the broader concepts of 'sky' and 'colour'. However, it is a closed question in that you can look up the answer in a book or online. Scientists can answer this question, but it soon becomes quite technical, and again, it doesn't really lend itself to extended discussion.[94]

In a P4C lesson, what we really want is for pupils to ask questions that sit in the lower right quadrant in Figure 5.1 – open-ended questions that are about general ideas, inspired by the stimulus but not directly related to it. For example, they might ask, 'Does the sky even exist?' or, 'Is a photograph more real than a photorealistic painting?' or, 'Can something that is fake be as beautiful as something that is real?' These are questions that lend themselves to extended discussion, partly because the answers depend on what we mean when we use words like 'exist' and 'real' and 'beautiful'.

Once your pupils have learned how to ask the kinds of questions that lend themselves to extended, philosophical discussion – and it doesn't take long to teach them – you're good to go. There is no single way to run a philosophical enquiry lesson. However, most practitioners of P4C get the class to sit in a circle (this is actually kind of important, as we will discuss later in this chapter) and follow a variation on the following 10-step procedure:

1. Some kind of settling activity – e.g. a guided visualisation to calm the pupils down – or you might play a short game if they need waking up a bit.
2. Present the stimulus – give some quiet time for reflection and discuss it – make sure everyone understands what it is and what it's not.
3. Identify the big ideas that sit behind the stimulus.
4. Generate philosophical questions inspired by the stimulus.
5. Share the questions and make sure everyone understands what they mean.
6. Vote on the question most people want to discuss. This can take a bit of time, e.g. you might want to group some questions together on the way to choosing one.
7. First words – whoever wrote the question explains why they chose it. It's a good idea to go around the circle to ask everyone for their initial thoughts – they can pass if they wish.
8. Build and challenge – through skilful questioning, the teacher/facilitator can encourage pupils to deepen the collective understanding (e.g. 'Can you provide an example?' or, 'Why do you think that?') and also to challenge ideas (e.g. 'Can anyone think of an instance where that might not be true?' or, 'Are there any hidden assumptions here that we haven't considered?').
9. Construct an answer – see if you can get to a point where the group agrees on the wording of an answer.
10. Final words – give everyone an opportunity to make a final comment, either about the question or about the inquiry itself. Again, they can pass if they so choose.[95]

The list above makes it look simple, and in some ways it is. But there is more to P4C than meets the eye. Running a philosophical enquiry is very different from teaching a lesson, and to get good at it requires considerable planning, discussion and reflection, repeated over time. As Fisher (1990) pointed out:

> *Productive discussion does not of course just happen. There are practical problems to face. Children often find it difficult to take turns in a debate. It is not always easy to persuade them to follow a line of argument through, or once they have developed their own idea to listen to the ideas of others. The success of a discussion depends on the teacher's skill in facilitating dialogue.*[96]

It is also worth emphasising that apart from the choice of stimulus, which is normally made by the teacher or another member of the group in advance, decisions about how the enquiry proceeds are consensual: 'without that presumption, there is no "Community of Enquiry"'.[97] For this reason, the teacher/facilitator should strive to be the neutral chair of discussion. However, this question of neutrality can give rise to some misunderstanding. The teacher is not expected to relinquish the need to manage behaviour, nor to provide some degree of quality control over the discussion. Instead, you are required, 'albeit in a subtle manner, relentlessly to feed rationality into the discussion'.[98]

It's also useful if the teacher knows a thing or two about critical thinking. P4C works best once the children have become adept at identifying assumptions, building arguments and counterarguments, and recognising logical fallacies. At Sea View, the teaching of critical thinking was the central aim of the year 9 taught course, and the P4C enquiries really moved up a gear at this point. If we had our time again, we would have introduced the teaching of critical thinking much earlier. We will return to the thorny matter of teaching children how to think critically – and whether this is even possible – later in this chapter.[99]

METACOGNITION

Rationale

We looked at the research literature relating to metacognition and self-regulation in detail in *Chapter 2: A brief history of Learning to Learn*, so there's no need to revisit it here. Instead, in this section we will provide a further rationale for weaving a bit of the old metacognition into your lessons by considering the powerful role it plays in helping children become more confident, curious, independent learners.

The phrase 'inextricably linked' is overused, but it describes the relationship between metacognition, self-regulation and oracy admirably. They really are very intertwined indeed, and while we can write nice separate headings in a book, in practice it's incredibly difficult to tease them apart. Which is just as well, because why would you want to? It's the very way in which these ideas and practices interact with and feed into one another that gives them such power.

For example, one of the many brilliant things about exploratory talk is that it is inherently metacognitive. When you use talk rules to increase the amount of exploratory talk that happens in your classroom, your pupils become increasingly mindful not only of what they think, but also of their reasons for thinking what they think, the quality of that reasoning and how their views relate to the views of others. They also become increasingly mindful of the need to articulate their thoughts so that they are accurately expressed and easily understood.

So talk rules – at face value, a simple set of agreed principles to govern how we talk together – are really a powerful engine that drives your students' ability to engage in their learning on a metacognitive as well as on a cognitive level. In turn, this metacognitive 'noticing' increases your students' ability to regulate their behaviour – setting goals to help them get better at engaging in group discussions, thinking through what they want to say before they say it, thinking about how what they say links to their chosen goals and so on.

Metacognition and self-regulation are also powerfully developed through P4C – so much so that we found it difficult to decide which heading P4C should fall under. Is it mainly about developing your students' speaking and listening skills, or is it about increasing their awareness of thinking and reasoning? It's both! Helping your pupils learn to look beyond everyday objects to contemplate the big ideas that lurk behind them; teaching them how to ask brilliant philosophical questions and discuss them at length; insisting that they give reasons for their thinking and that they demand it of others until they do so automatically – all of these elements of P4C, and many more besides, require that pupils look beyond the 'what' and engage powerfully with the 'how' of learning.

Likewise, metacognition and self-regulation are powerfully developed through debating and public speaking and by increasing the complexity of group interactions. In each case, students firstly monitor and then take increasing control over their thinking and learning behaviours. For the most part, this can be done using quite traditional teaching methods:

1. The teacher models, explains, deconstructs.
2. Students get opportunities for deliberate practice.
3. Students receive rich, formative feedback.
4. Students are given the time to reflect on how things are going, to set goals and to plan next steps.

If you just want your students to learn stuff, you can achieve that quite effectively simply by repeating the first three stages. But if you also want them to *get better at learning stuff* – if you want to achieve the dream of helping them become confident, independent learners, less characterised by the kinds of helpless utterances we saw in the Introduction – it's the fourth stage that is the most important, because it is only through reflection that we can make sense of the past and make plans for the future. In the first three stages, we teach students X, give them the chance to practise X and tell them how close they are getting to achieving or mastering X. The fourth stage, however, is qualitatively different, because it engages the autonomy of the student. This is the stage where the journey to independent learning begins, ends and begins again.

In *Chapter 2: A brief history of Learning to Learn*, we defined metacognition as the process of 'monitoring and controlling your thought processes'. As Flavell (1979) suggested, these thought processes might include what we know about:

- Ourselves (Am I any good at this? What do I think about this?)
- Other people (Who do I know who is good at this? Who might be able to help?)
- The task before us (What do I need to do? What do I have that can help me? What don't I have?)
- Strategies (Is there only one way of doing this? What alternative methods might I use?)

In each case, we are faced with choices – what questions to ask of ourselves and others, what strategies are available to us, and so on – and each of these choices carries consequences. In childhood, before we have learned to be metacognitive, these choices are not visible. Children are given a task and they can either do it or they can't. The aim of teaching metacognition, then, is to help children see the choices that are open to them at any given point in time, to think through the likely consequences of those choices, and to get better at asking the kinds of questions – of themselves and others – that will propel them toward success.

Within reason, there is nothing we cannot do without an understanding of how we can use questions and self-talk to drive our progress. For example, when faced with a complex task, a child might think, *Oh no, I don't know how to do this. I'm so useless,* and sit there not even asking for help – the very definition of helplessness. Or, they might employ a bad strategy like, *I know, I'll surreptitiously glance at what my neighbour is writing, and then I'll copy that.* Alternatively, a student with a repertoire of metacognitive knowledge might question and/or self-talk their way out of trouble:

Task level

- Do I understand the task/problem properly?
- Have I faced a problem like this before? What did I do then?
- How long do I have to do this task?
- What do I have that can help me with this task? What do I not have? What do I need?

Person level

- Others
  - Who is good at doing problems like this?
  - What do they usually do?
  - I've noticed that effective learners make little lists of what needs to be done, and then tick things off as they go.

- Self
  - How do I feel about this task? Am I confident or uncertain?
  - Am I usually good at solving problems like these?
  - Do I need to ask for help at this point, or can I go this alone?
  - Maybe I can do this by myself. I'll give it a go – I can always ask for help if I get stuck.

Strategy level

- I seem to remember something about breaking the problem down into small, manageable steps. Maybe I can try that.
- Then I'll decide which order to do each of the steps in.
- Then I'll make a list of what needs to be done, and tick it off as I go. That way, I'll know for sure if I've done everything that needs to be done.

And so on. Once the nature of a task is clear, there are decisions to be made in terms of how to progress, and those decisions become apparent through such metacognitive questioning and self-talk. If it's a written task – and in schools, it usually is – students often just start writing in the hope that the answer will come to them as they go. This is why we often find quite weird sentences in children's exercise books, because they write themselves into a corner with no exit strategy in place. Alternatively, a student trained in the art of metacognition might think, *I'll start by making a skeleton plan for what I want to say, and in what order*, or, *I'll make a list of the key vocab I need to use.*

In short, metacognition requires a proactive, conscious engagement with the *processes* of learning and the micro-decisions we make (or don't make) along the way. Teaching children how to do this begins when you ask them to start noticing, monitoring and describing their thought processes. The more aware of their thought processes children become, the more they come to realise that they have options at every step along the way. They come to learn through experience that the next time they are faced with a similar problem or task, if they ask different questions and make different choices, different consequences will follow: better consequences, like more efficient learning, or a deeper understanding, or better grades.

This is all well and good, you might think, *but I can't see inside my students' heads, and they aren't very good at describing what's going on inside their heads either.* This is often true – at first, at least. If you ask a student how they learned something, they will often reply, 'I dunno, I just did', or maybe, 'I read it and then I just knew it.' This is why metacognition is so closely related to oracy. To develop metacognition in our students, we must firstly teach them how to articulate their thoughts so that they can reliably relay what they're thinking, what they know and what they're struggling with, whether they feel confident to build on their learning by themselves or whether they need additional support. Preferably, all of this should take place before they are tested at the end of the term, because by then it's too late.

This is why time for metacognitive reflection needs to be built into the curriculum. In recent years, many schools have introduced DIRT (Directed Improvement and Reflection Time). This is a welcome development. However, in practice DIRT often means giving students a few minutes at the start of a lesson to compose a short written response to some written feedback in their exercise book, or possibly to correct some marked-up mistakes. This might be a valuable thing to do, but it falls short of the deep reflective practice that develops metacognition and enables children to become confident, effective learners.

How often do we hear from students that they spent hours reading the revision guide in order to revise for a test that they resoundingly flunked?

There are some students with savant-like qualities who can flick through the revision guide the night before a test and smash it. But such students are in a very small minority. For most, reading the revision guide isn't going to be of much help if what they actually need is to develop their ability to retrieve relevant chunks of information and express it accurately and concisely, using subject-specific vocabulary. When students have a clear idea of the goal they are aiming for, and when they become familiar with the look and feel of different strategies and activities that will help them achieve that goal, then they can begin to weigh up the relative efficacy of those different strategies, figure out what works for them and plan and act accordingly.

In the wild, these processes and strategies are implicit, which means that they are invisible. Through regular metacognitive reflection, we draw them out into the light and make them visible, tangible – and therefore learnable. When you do this, the mystery of why some students are good at learning while others struggle becomes clear. Sometimes, students do something so impressive – they learn a complex concept or skill so quickly and apparently effortlessly, that it looks almost like magic. But successful students don't use magic, and they don't have wildly different brains or special powers. As with magic, if you look behind the curtain, there is always a humdrum method at work.

Usually, effective students simply know a few methods that work for them, and they use them diligently. They use strategies for memorising like making lists, mnemonics or silly little songs; they make flash cards with images and colours to make them easier to visualise and remember; they quiz themselves regularly in order to make sure their knowledge is where they can find it; they talk through their thinking with other people to make sure it's in the right order and makes sense; they have systems for keeping track of what they know for sure, what they need to work on and what they need help with; and they seek out that help rather than waiting for the universe to hand it to them on a silver platter.

In short, effective learners are deliberate and methodical and that's what makes them successful at learning stuff and performing well in tests. They know what works for them in a range of situations, and they know what to do when they don't know what to do because they have tried-and-tested strategies that they know they can rely on. Based upon past experience, they can recognise the characteristics of tasks they are likely to find easy and those they may struggle with. When children learn to take responsibility for their own learning, to dissect their learning behaviours and to examine them with curiosity rather than judgement, they can then make plans for how to address any shortfalls and to build on their strengths.

This is what it means to be a confident, effective, independent learner. It doesn't mean that you learn by yourself all the time, or that you don't need teachers or peers to learn alongside. It just means that you have a bunch of tools at your disposal that mean you can learn what you want, when you want, rather than when the education system decides the time is right. When we help students see these invisible processes of learning – when they learn to name them and describe them and recognise what it feels like when they're happening – we are giving them a gift that will last a lifetime. And the good news is, it's really quite straightforward. All you need is a bit of time and know-how.

What does it look like in practice?

To a significant extent, metacognitive reflection is something that needs to be driven by the teacher's questioning. There are loads of examples online of questions you can ask to promote metacognition in the classroom, so we aren't going to dwell on that here.[100] Instead, in this section we will outline four explicit methods we used to develop metacognition through the *Learning Skills* curriculum:

- Learning journals
- Meditation/guided visualisations
- Shared language of learning
- Thinking and reasoning skills

As above, for each we will outline a rationale and then consider what it looks like in practice.

LEARNING JOURNALS

Rationale

In the first year of the *Learning Skills* curriculum at Sea View, students had scrapbooks in which to record evidence of their use of their learning, both in and out of school. Students were expected to write down which skills they had used, where, with whom and so on. This was useful as a way to begin thinking about transfer, but it wasn't tight enough. In the second year, the journals evolved to become more focused on subject learning as we became increasingly mindful of the need to proactively promote the transfer of knowledge and skills out of the *Learning Skills* classroom and into subject learning across the curriculum. So, the short version of the rationale is that learning journals are a method for promoting transfer, although they do much more than that.

There isn't a wealth of research evidence relating to the use of learning journals in schools – there are no randomised controlled trials (RCTs) or systematic reviews that we are aware of. However, there is emerging evidence that the use of learning journals among high school students is associated with improved learning outcomes, elaboration and transfer gains[101] as well as improved comprehension, interest and critical reflection.[102] Furthermore, Glogger et al. (2012) reported that:

> Learning strategies assessed by learning journals [predict] learning outcomes. The more sophisticated cognitive learning strategies were especially good predictors of successful learning outcomes: The more elaborative and organizational strategies students used during writing and the higher the quality of these strategies, the better their learning outcomes were.[103]

Thus, there is evidence that learning journals are beneficial for improving students' learning – and when learning journals are specifically used to aid metacognition, it is particularly beneficial. Elsewhere, there is emerging evidence that learning journals aid metacognition, boost creativity and help reduce anxiety.[104, 105, 106]

More widely, there is compelling evidence that getting people to write about things they find difficult is a good idea. The practice of 'expressive writing', a technique pioneered by the psychologist James W. Pennebaker, has been studied extensively and has been associated with an incredible array of benefits, including reduced stress, improved blood pressure, immune function, wound healing, sleep, depression and pain.[107] Pennebaker's work has also given rise to other writing-based interventions such as self-authoring, a systematic approach to goal-setting that has been found to improve student retention and attainment in undergraduates.[108]

To be clear, expressive writing is a therapeutic approach whereby the participant writes about trauma for 15 minutes each day, while in self-authoring, the participant is 'encouraged to consider the nature and desired quality of their future experience on a number of important life dimensions – family, intimate relationships, activity outside of work, career, education and so on'.[109] This is not how learning journals were used within the *Learning Skills* programme, although as we will see in *Chapter 6: The evidence for Learning Skills*, students often wrote quite openly about difficulties they were facing in their lives. Nevertheless, it is interesting to note the many positive outcomes associated with scrawling some ink across a page. Writing about yourself runs deep.

What does it look like in practice?

Once a fortnight, all students in year 7 had one lesson dedicated to metacognitive reflection. These lessons began with a short meditation or guided visualisation exercise to establish a calm atmosphere in which students could reflect on their learning; we'll discuss this in the next section. Following this, there would be a period of silent writing in their learning journals, which students were allowed to decorate and personalise. The aim here was to encourage the students to develop a positive relationship with their learning journal and to view it differently from their other exercise books.

First, students would respond to comments and questions made by the teacher in their journals, written in response to their previous entry. Next, they would respond to a set of generic questions that remained more or less constant throughout the year:

- Thinking back over the last 2 weeks:
  - What has gone well? (And why?)
  - What have you found challenging? (And why?)
  - Is there anything you currently feel 'stuck' with? (What and why?)
  - What strategies have you tried?
  - What other strategies might you try?

Finally, students would respond to a series of prompt questions relating to transfer. The focus of these transfer questions would vary from one lesson to the next to enable the focus to respond to whatever was happening that week and to ensure that each subject took a turn in the spotlight at least once. For example, in the excerpts we will look at in *Chapter 6: The evidence for Learning Skills*, students were asked to write about their experience of the '7-day challenge', an exercise we ran for anti-bullying week, whereby students attempted to get through seven days without saying anything negative about, or to, any other person. More typically, prompt questions were designed to engage students in metacognitive reflection around a particular subject, such as:

- How well do you feel you learn in *Learning Skills* lessons?
- What kinds of things do you learn in *Learning Skills* lessons?

- What do you actually *do* in order to learn in *Learning Skills* lessons?
- Is this the same or different from how you learn in other lessons?
- How is it the same/different?

Or:

- How well do you feel you learn in French?
- What obstacles stand in the way of you learning more effectively in French?
- What strategies have you tried?
- What might be worth trying in future?
- How might *Learning Skills* lessons help you learn more effectively in French?
- Who do you know that learns well in French?
- What things do they do that enable them to learn effectively in French? How might you find out?

The lesson would end with a discussion of emerging issues and next steps, to enable the students to 'compare notes', as it were. This would take place firstly in pairs and then as a whole-class discussion.

After each session, learning journals were marked using a dialogic approach, where the teacher would respond to what the student had written, usually with questions designed to seek clarification or to stimulate further thinking. Essentially, this meant that each student took part in an ongoing written dialogue with their *Learning Skills* teacher as they progressed through the year. We took the decision not to mark the learning journals for spelling and grammar, because we felt this would detract from the purpose of the exercise.

Marking learning journals in this way enabled the *Learning Skills* teachers to develop deep insights into the minds and lives of our students. It provided us with a regular opportunity to identify any obstacles or challenges they were facing and to help them identify strategies for developing or expanding their range of learning strategies and behaviours. It also enabled a bond of trust to develop – more so with some students than others – but many felt they could share their feelings and frustrations honestly in their learning journals without them being judged or shared publicly.[110] We now work with other schools to help develop *Learning Skills* curricula, and we find that learning journals are often one of the first things schools are keen to put in place as a low-cost, high-impact initiative.

MEDITATION/GUIDED VISUALISATIONS

Rationale

People have practised meditation for thousands of years. The earliest documented evidence is Indian wall art dating from around 5000 to 3500 BCE, depicting people sitting in meditative postures with half-closed eyes.[111] Ever since – from ancient history through the so-called dark ages to the present day – meditation never really seems to have fallen from favour. Clearly, there's something to it.

Meditation has predominantly been practised by followers of Buddhism and Hinduism and mystical off-shoots of mainstream religions like Sufism and Kabbalah. However, throughout the last 100 years or so, the realisation that meditation might be associated with physical and mental health benefits has led to its increased use within Western public health and education systems. In the last 20 years in particular, there has been an exponential growth in column inches on the topic in both the scientific literature and the mainstream news media.[112]

Meditation in the health literature

Meditation and mindfulness practices have been researched more in healthcare than in education.[113] In the medical and health literature, there is evidence that meditation can provide benefits across a wide range of outcomes, including improved blood pressure and reduced cardiovascular disease,[114] improved pain relief,[115] reduced negative symptoms of schizophrenia,[116] reduced insomnia,[117] improved cognition among the over 60s,[118] improved outcomes for adults with Attention Deficit/Hyperactivity Disorder (ADHD),[119] and reduced anxiety, depression and stress among students.[120]

Clinical benefits for children have also been reported in the medical literature. For example, a 2009 RCT investigated the impact of mindfulness-based cognitive therapy for children (MBCT-C) on attention, anxiety and behaviour among 9- to 13-year-olds.[121] This study found that MBCT-C led to a reduction in attention problems compared with children in the control group, and that these improvements were maintained at three months following the mindfulness intervention. In addition, there were significant reductions in anxiety symptoms and behavioural problems among children who exhibited high levels of anxiety at pre-test. This study concluded that

MBCT-C 'is a promising intervention for attention and behaviour problems, and may reduce childhood anxiety symptoms'.[122]

Brain imaging studies point towards a potential causal mechanism as to how meditation leads to such a wide variety of health benefits. A 2005 study conducted at Harvard Medical School found that meditating regularly physically alters the structure of the brain, increasing cortical thickness, suggesting that regular meditation may slow the neural degeneration associated with age.[123] Furthermore, a follow-up study in 2011 found that an eight-week meditation-based stress reduction programme led to increases in grey matter density 'in brain regions involved in learning and memory processes, emotion regulation, self-referential processing and perspective taking'.[124]

Meditation in the education literature

Because of findings such as these, various forms of meditation and mindfulness practices are now increasingly practised in schools. The rationale for this has partly been an attempt to help alleviate mental health issues such as stress and anxiety, but also to help improve behaviour and even to boost academic attainment. In some schools, meditation is used as an alternative to detentions.[125] In the following section, we will summarise some of the key research findings from recent meta-analyses, systematic reviews and RCTs relating to the use of meditation in education.

A 2014 systematic review looked at the impact of school-based meditation programmes on well-being, social competence and academic achievement, combining 15 studies of around 1800 students from around the world.[126] This study found that 'school-based meditation is beneficial in the majority of cases and 61% of the results were significant'.[127] In most studies, there was only a small impact on student outcomes, although '33% of the effect sizes were medium or strong'.[128] The authors drew two conclusions from this review: that meditation increases cognitive functioning and that it improves emotional regulation. They also suggest that the impact of meditation can be increased 'by increasing programme duration, by encouraging twice daily (or more) meditation and by having the teacher deliver the programme'.[129]

A 2013 RCT looked at the impact of a two-week mindfulness training course on attention and cognitive performance.[130] This study found that mindfulness training 'improved both... reading-comprehension scores and working memory capacity, while simultaneously reducing the occurrence of distracting thoughts during completion of the [reading comprehension task] and the measure of working memory.' The authors concluded that 'cultivating mindfulness is an effective and efficient technique for improving cognitive function, with wide-reaching consequences'.[131]

A 2015 systematic review examined the impact of mindfulness meditation (MM) on reducing stress and improving health outcomes among adolescents.[132] The authors found evidence of wide-ranging benefits both in school and outside of school, and concluded that:

> MM appears to have positive effects on adolescent psychological health including reduced depression, anxiety and stress, increased overall well-being, self and emotion regulation, positive affect, and resilience. Academic related outcomes include increased attention, cognitive, and academic performance. Results also point to feasibility, acceptability, and efficacy throughout a broad range of adolescent groups including males and females, learning disabled, those with ADHD and other psychological disorders, along with those in diverse cultural settings.[133]

We don't want to overstate the evidence base for the use of mindfulness and meditation in schools. The studies tend to be quite small, and there are limitations to the methods that can be used to study the effects of meditation.[134, 135]

However, anyone who practises meditation regularly would likely tell you that absence of evidence does not equate to evidence of absence. And there is sufficient evidence in the research literature to justify introducing mindfulness and meditation practices into schools more widely – if only to introduce all young people to a practice that elicits a wide range of physical and mental health benefits for relatively little time investment, which may be of lasting benefit throughout their lives. For any teachers or school leaders thinking of introducing mindfulness or meditation practices into their school, based on our experience and on the research literature, we would advise the following:

- Have a good reason as to why you're doing it.
- Start small and see how it goes.
- Only do it if the teacher feels comfortable doing so, and only if they have experienced the positive consequences of meditation/guided visualisation themselves.

What does it look like in practice?

At Sea View, the 'good reason' was that we wanted to have one lesson a fortnight dedicated to metacognitive reflection, in which the main activity was for students to write in their learning journals and then to share their thoughts in a whole-class discussion. Such reflective lessons are very different from other lessons, which are typically pacy affairs driven by the need to 'cover content'. We therefore wanted to do something at the start of the learning journal lesson to enable our students to regulate their nervous systems and to adjust to a slower, more reflective mode of being.

We introduced meditation in the second year of the programme. To begin with, we used guided visualisations rather than meditations. There are loads of brilliant guided visualisation scripts on the internet if you have a look around. Some are general relaxation scripts – go to your happy place, float on a cloud, that sort of thing. But there are also scripts for different situations – to help you concentrate better, or to alleviate anxiety around exams, or for dealing with friendship issues.

When using guided visualisations, through trial and error, we found that it's far better to have the teacher read a guided visualisation script rather than using a recording of someone else's voice. However, if and when you decide to practise meditation – the mindfulness of breathing, say – it's a good idea to use a recording unless the teacher is very comfortable and confident at leading meditation sessions. It's not really something you can 'wing'. Again, there are many free recordings available online, through apps or podcasts.

In terms of logistics, we would put a 'please do not disturb' sign on the door and make the room as dark and as comfortable as we could. At first, we asked all children to sit upright in their chairs with their feet planted firmly on the ground and their hands on their knees. However, we soon found that many of them found this difficult, and so before long we agreed to let the children sit however they wanted. Some would sit upright with a straight back, others sat normally, others still might choose to rest their head on the table. Some preferred to sit under the table or even lie on the floor. Some closed their eyes; others preferred to keep them open. Some would even sit on the desk with their legs crossed, fingers pinched together in the classic meditation pose. We allowed them to do whatever made them feel most comfortable.

At first, some of the students found these sessions awkward or even challenging, and there was some nervous giggling and sideways glances. But they soon settled down, and before long they came to really value these sessions. We mainly did it with year 7, but we also used it occasionally with years 8 and 9. A typical guided visualisation or meditation session would last between five and ten minutes. After each session, when they opened their eyes and 'returned to the room', we would do a think/pair/share whole-class discussion. How did they find it today? What did they notice? What did they find difficult? What did they find surprising? What could they see? And so on. They were always keen to share their experiences with one another, and no two experiences were ever completely alike – which is interesting in itself.

We did not systematically evaluate the impact of this aspect of the *Learning Skills* programme, other than that some students mentioned it in the interviews. For example, when asked at the end of year 9, 'What do you most remember about *Learning Skills* lessons?', one student, Louise, replied:

> *The bonding with friends. Making new friends because of the seating plans... The anorexia project because it was awesome and I'm still doing it now. I liked learning about something that was close to my heart. I also remember the meditating and how it let me focus more.*

This use of the word 'let' is interesting. Louise did not say that meditation *helped* her focus more, but that it *let* her – as though the ability to focus was not something she had to learn, but that meditating enabled her to discover this ability within herself.

We do not make any grand claims for the use of meditation within the *Learning Skills* programme. Essentially, we used guided visualisations and mindfulness meditation as a kind of buffer – a short decompression exercise that allowed students to calm down, slow their thinking and become more internally reflective. Schools are intensely stimulating places, and many of those stimuli are not conducive to reflection – busy corridors, strip lighting, the constant hubbub of background noise. These sessions simply allowed them to chill their boots for a few minutes and focus their attention on their own internal thoughts and feelings rather than constantly reacting to the busy world 'out there'.

Despite our initial reservations, students and teachers at Sea View soon found that these short meditation sessions became a part of the *Learning Skills* lesson cycle that we really looked forward to. A deliberate space to unwind and just *be*. As teachers, we often feel the imperative to 'look busy' at all times. It isn't an easy thing to hold a space while nothing tangible is taking place. It takes a certain amount of self-regulation on the part of the teacher not to cave in when there is pressure to just 'get on with it'. But in our experience, it is really worth the small time investment. As anyone who meditates regularly will attest, knowing that there is a peaceful space within you – and that you can go there for free, whenever you need to – is a precious thing indeed.

SHARED LANGUAGE OF LEARNING

Rationale

Have you ever shadowed a student for a day? If you have, you'll know that it can be a pretty intense experience. Primary or secondary, it doesn't matter which, although secondary is even more bewildering because you move around so much and the physical environments are so varied, as well as the subject matter. From our own experience of doing this, the main thing we remember is that it's really *tiring* being told what to do all day. Line up, enter in silence, get your planner out, answer your name, listen carefully, talk to your partner, write this, do that, stand behind your chair, leave when your table is called, single file, no pushing. And that's just tutor time!

At 9 a.m., you're out on the school field learning to throw a javelin. At 10 a.m., you're writing a letter to your Spanish penfriend to tell them about life in the UK. By 11 a.m., you're doing a science experiment on how to test for sugar and protein in food samples. After lunch, you're learning to play a piano piece in the mathematical style of Johann Sebastian Bach. Then a bell rings and suddenly you're analysing a grizzly poem by Carol Ann Duffy. The next day brings another whirlwind of similar activities – and the next, and the next, and the next.

At face value, there doesn't seem to be much in common between javelin throwing, writing Spanish, squirting things into test tubes, playing the piano and analysing poetry. Each lesson looks and sounds very different from the last, and each teacher and each subject discipline has different ways of using language to describe what the pupils are supposed to be doing.

If you look beneath the surface, however, there are many commonalities between learning in different subjects. The typical learning cycle in any subject will include many similar processes – the teacher explains and models, the students practise and discuss what they're doing and, at some point, they will receive feedback and try to respond to it. If all teachers made explicit that this is what they're doing – following the same set of principles and using the same vocabulary to describe the learning cycle

– students would find it far easier to make connections between how they learn in PE and how they learn in Spanish, science, music and English.

So, one argument for developing a shared language of learning is simply to provide students with a more joined-up diet of learning. When a school has a shared language to describe the processes of learning – using memory techniques like mnemonics, rehearsal or retrieval practice, drawing diagrams, making links between ideas, using metaphors, asking good questions, embracing failure, engaging in exploratory talk – it helps the students understand that these learning strategies and skills apply equally well across most or all of their subjects.

But the rationale for a shared language of learning goes beyond the need for teachers to use similar terminology when discussing 'today's learning objectives'. It's about weaving the common threads of metacognition, self-regulation and oracy throughout the curriculum. It's about providing students with the language and the regular opportunities for dialogue they need in order to monitor and control their thoughts, feelings and behaviours across a range of contexts, and to become more confident, articulate, self-regulated learners.

Imagine you're a science teacher and you're teaching a unit on electricity. At some point in the planning process, you will probably identify a list of key words that the students need to know by the end of the unit: current, voltage, resistance and so on. Helping them understand these concepts might involve a range of activities – drawing diagrams, doing experiments and reading books. But when it comes to checking their understanding, they really just need to be able to use the key words in a sentence: 'Current is the electricity in the wire' – needs more work. 'Current is a flow of charge in a circuit' – that's more like it. If they can acquire the key vocabulary and use it appropriately, then we can assume that they have learned what we wanted them to learn. In a sense, much academic learning can be viewed primarily as a process of language acquisition.

Similarly, if our aim is to help our students get better at learning stuff, we need to provide them with the vocabulary they need in order to describe the processes of learning and to describe themselves as learners. As we have discussed, Learning to Learn is, to a significant degree, a process of making the implicit, invisible, tacit processes of learning explicit, visible, tangible – and, therefore, learnable. To do this, we need to help students acquire a shared lexicon for describing their inner and outer worlds as accurately and as reliably as possible. For this reason, a shared language of learning should be seen as something that is shared not only across subjects, but shared between students and their teachers and among the students themselves.

What does it look like in practice?

In the paragraph above, we used the phrase 'provide them with the vocabulary they need', and this was very much our thinking when we started out. Over a period of three years, we learned the hard way that actually you can't really 'provide it'. Rather, a shared language of learning is something that has to be co-constructed. We'll come to that shortly.

In 2010, the government had recently published a language of learning known as the Personal Learning and Thinking Skills (PLTS). The PLTS framework comprised six 'generic skills' – teamwork, creative thinking, independent learning and so on – and each of these were divided into six descriptors. Being more experienced in these matters, Kate suggested that we should come up with our own framework rather than taking the PLTS framework off the shelf. However, the *Learning Skills* team was a little bit freaked out by the blank sheet of paper we had been given – to design a Learning to Learn curriculum from scratch – and so we grabbed hold of the PLTS framework as something we could use as a language of learning and as a basis for assessing pupil progress.

We should have heeded Kate's advice. We soon found that the PLTS framework was ill-suited to either of these purposes. For one thing, it was too bulky – by Christmas, many of our students were unable to recall the 6 broad categories, never mind the 36 descriptors that underpinned them. Part of the reason for this is that the PLTS framework is quite managerial in tone: 'the language of the committee and the bureaucrat', as Martin Robinson (2013) put it.[136]

So at the end of the first year, we sat down to create a new language of learning, inspired by the 'Habits of Mind' framework developed by Art Costa and colleagues in the US.[137] We really liked our Habits of Mind model. We thought it was elegant – it was much simpler than the PLTS, being based around the three areas of thinking, being and doing. So, with no real consultation either with students or staff, we duly launched it as a whole-school language of learning. You can probably see where this is going.

During the second year of the *Learning Skills* programme, we invited a couple of students from a local university to help us research how well the transfer out of *Learning Skills* and into other lessons was going. As the Head of *Learning Skills*, Kate had the impression that whenever she popped into lessons or did a 'learning walk', she was being treated to a special performance. We wanted to know what was really happening for students. Where was it working already, and where was there more work to be done?

The student researchers did an amazing job, and handed us an excruciating 100-page report detailing all the ways in which the Habits of Mind framework wasn't working. The main problem was that students and teachers alike seemed only vaguely aware of its existence. We had run a twilight session where each department had to write a policy detailing how they were going to incorporate the Habits of Mind into their lessons, marking and feedback policies, thinking that if it was policy it would have a greater chance of being done. But in practice, the Sea View Habits of Mind was just a poster stuck to the wall in each classroom that was roundly ignored by students and teachers alike.

Upon reflection, we realised that we were imposing *our* ideas on our pupils and colleagues in an attempt to model the values, habits and behaviours we felt were most important. We hadn't involved either our colleagues or our students in the design of the Habits of Mind. It may have been a language of learning, but it certainly wasn't shared.

By this time, we'd got the hang of designing an inclusive curriculum with our students rather than for them – co-constructing class charters and talk rules and success criteria for the projects. But we were still trying to dictate the language they were supposed to use to describe themselves as learners. Old habits die hard, it seems. We realised that if we were going to develop a shared language of learning that would truly be useful, we were going to have to involve students and teachers in the process. In this way, we hoped, there would be a greater sense of ownership and therefore more chance that it would become a living, breathing thing. Third time lucky and all that.

At the time, the school had just become an academy, and our academy sponsor had a number of 'attributes' they were keen on embedding across all their schools: risk-taking, problem-solving, determination and so on. We realised that if these broad attributes were going to be useful, we had to drill down to identify the specific processes, practices and behaviours that drive learning forward. To say, 'We need to use teamwork in this lesson' is so vague as to be meaningless. Teamwork is a complex thing comprising many individual processes working (hopefully) in harmony. If, instead, we say things in lessons like, 'Today, we need to make sure we listen to one another really carefully', or, 'We need to discuss in groups using talk rules', we can set really clear expectations for how we want our students to work together in teams.

We set up working parties with students and teachers and began by asking questions like, 'What does good teamwork look like?' and, 'What might risk-taking look like in a lesson?'[138] Through this process, we identified a number of specific learning processes and behaviours that drive learning forward, many of which were common across different subject disciplines. We also wanted to come up with a way of representing the language of learning visually. We showed the students an image from a book by Claxton et al. (2011) where a brain is divided into sections, and they wanted to make a version for our school.[139] The result of this process can be seen in Figure 5.2. In this scheme, the large words are the overarching 'attributes' and the smaller words are how we translated those broad attributes into specific actions or learning behaviours in lessons.

Figure 5.2. The Learning Brain: A shared language of learning

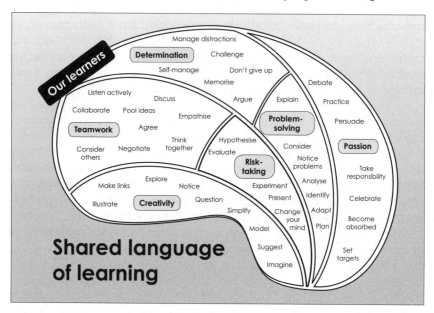

Now, images like this have a tendency to rub people up the wrong way, and we understand why. It looks a bit like a modern-day variation on phrenology, the 18th century pseudoscience where it was thought that you could predict a person's personality by measuring tiny bumps on their skull. So just to be clear: we aren't holding this up as a scientifically accurate model of how the mind works. This is just the visual that we came up with, in collaboration with our students, at the third time of trying.

Following Claxton et al. (2011), we referred to the words in small font as 'learning muscles'. Again, we are aware that this phrase rubs some people up the wrong way. However, this language of 'learning muscles' really resonated with our pupils. In particular, it helped them understand that you can get better at any of this stuff with practice. You can get better at asking good questions, at debating, at memorising stuff. It was an effective way of embedding Carol Dweck's notion of a 'growth mindset' without ever having to utter the words 'growth mindset'.

Using Claxton's metaphor of school as a learning gymnasium also helped our students understand that learning stuff can sometimes feel unpleasant – and that this is a good thing. In a gym, you have to get hot and sweaty in order to get fit. Sitting motionless on a rowing machine watching MTV is not a recipe for rock-hard abs. Similarly, when you're learning new stuff, you often have to go through a period of feeling confused and frustrated before the penny drops. But that sense of confusion and frustration should really be embraced as a sign that you are on the right track and that a breakthrough is imminent if you can just stick with it a little longer.

These reservations aside, there were two significant advantages to the 'Learning Brain' model compared with the PLTS and Habits of Mind frameworks. First, we co-constructed it with our students rather than implementing it in a top-down way. It made sense to them, and they felt a sense of ownership over it that had previously been missing. And second, lesson observations and learning walks suggested that the Learning Brain was referred to by students and teachers in lessons across the school in a way that the PLTS and Habits of Mind frameworks had not been (e.g. starting a lesson by saying, 'Here's what we're learning today. Which learning muscles might we need to use...?', and then referring back at the end of the lesson: 'How well were we able to practise/set meaningful targets/explain our thinking today...?'). It still wasn't referred to by every teacher in every lesson – but it was a step in the right direction.

We know that there is a strong causal link between spoken language and brain development.[140] It's really hard to be metacognitive if you don't have the words to describe what's going on in your head. It's really hard to self-regulate if you can't name what you are feeling. It's really hard to express yourself without the words you need to describe your ideas. The more students talk about learning using words that make sense to them, the more confident they become in describing themselves as learners across a range of contexts, and the more likely they are to view themselves as effective learners.

If we did it again, we would likely produce something quite different from the Learning Brain. However, we do think that co-constructing a shared language of learning is an important part of the equation. At Sea View, it really helped establish Learning Skills as a whole-school approach to teaching and learning rather than it just being a lesson taught for a few hours a week in Key Stage 3. Spoken language is the invisible thread that ties it together as a whole-school approach to teaching and learning, and the primary medium through which transfer happens. It takes time to develop, and you need to set aside the time to go through a process of coming up with something that makes sense to the students. The Learning Brain model is not perfect, but it's the least bad version we came up with after three years of trying. And we do not recommend that other schools should use this model – in fact, we strongly recommend that you don't. We would encourage you to come up with your own version, and not use anybody else's. But most of all, involve your students and colleagues in the process. That's the most important thing of all.

THINKING AND REASONING SKILLS

Rationale

As we mentioned in the *Introduction*, when the first *Learning Skills* cohort reached the end of year 7, the timetabled lessons expanded into year 8, for three lessons a week; the following year, it expanded again into year 9, for five lessons a fortnight. The year 8 programme was primarily a 'personal effectiveness' course concerned with helping the students get better at organising their time and resources. We'll explore this in more detail in the next section on self-regulated learning. With the year 9 programme, we wanted to do something different.

People often say that children should be taught critical thinking skills in school – that we teach them *what* to think but we don't teach them *how* to think. In recent years, the teaching of critical thinking skills has become a hot potato in the education debate. Everybody agrees that children should learn to think critically – but as we saw in *Chapter 3: Learning to Learn on trial*, there is fierce disagreement on how best to get there.

On one side of the debate, you have people who suggest that critical thinking is entirely dependent on what you know. Therefore, the argument goes, schools should focus on teaching knowledge: the critical thinking will take care of itself. On the other side of the debate, it has been suggested that critical thinking skills are purely generic. The aforementioned PLTS framework was based on the idea that it is possible to teach generic skills that can be applied across a range of contexts, for example. This view has been roundly criticised in recent years. As Daniel Willingham wrote in 2007: 'Can critical thinking actually be taught? Decades of cognitive research point to a disappointing answer: not really',[141] although it is worth noting that Willingham later changed his mind on this.[142]

We take the middle ground in this debate. It is beyond doubt that domain-specific knowledge is foundational in being able to think critically within a given subject discipline. Clearly, you can't think deeply or critically about something you know nothing of. However, as we argued in *Chapter 3: Learning to Learn on trial*, it is also clear to us – and to the majority of psychologists and cognitive scientists who study these things – that there are also a number of generic, transferable elements of critical thinking. These include things like being able to construct a coherent argument, recognising that arguments can be structured in different ways, being able to identify questionable assumptions, being able to identify logical fallacies like straw man arguments and *ad hominem* attacks, and problem-solving strategies such as looking for patterns, anomalies and analogous examples of similar problems.

It's also a good idea to know about the wide range of human cognitive biases – the many and varied ways in which we delude and deceive ourselves on a daily basis. Perhaps the mother of all cognitive biases is confirmation bias, whereby people pay attention to evidence that reinforces their existing worldview, while dismissing or explaining away evidence to the contrary.[143] As Willingham has pointed out elsewhere: while knowledge may be necessary for critical thinking, it is by no means sufficient. Instead, 'we must ensure that students acquire background knowledge *in parallel with* practicing critical thinking skills'.[144]

In short: in order to be able to think critically about something, you need to be knowledgeable within that domain. But you also need to know a thing or two about critical thinking itself – and, preferably, you should have had plenty of opportunity to practise it and become skilled at it. This was the rationale for the year 9 component of the *Learning Skills* curriculum: to teach the students about critical thinking itself and to provide them with opportunities to use this knowledge in discussions and debates and through extended writing.

What does it look like in practice?

Critical thinking courses are often taught at independent schools, either within the curriculum or as part of the extracurricular provision.[145] However, they are less common within the state sector, and good-quality resources for teaching critical thinking and reasoning are pretty thin on the ground. Within the *Learning Skills* team, we didn't have any experience or expertise at teaching critical thinking courses, and so we looked at what was available on the market.

As luck would have it, in 2011, OCR (Oxford, Cambridge and RSA – an exam board) launched a fantastic Level 2 (GCSE-equivalent) course called *Thinking and Reasoning Skills* (TARS), which has sadly since been discontinued. The TARS course comprised ten skills that provide such a useful introduction to critical thinking and reasoning skills it's worth briefly setting out the course content here:[146]

1. Understanding arguments
   - Arguments vs rants vs lists of information vs explanations
   - Recognising and identifying the parts of simple arguments (reasons, intermediate conclusions and conclusions)
   - Using visual argument maps

2. Evaluating arguments
   - Recognising some common logical fallacies (*ad hominem*, straw man, *tu quoque*, slippery slope, false dilemmas)
   - Recognising loaded language and irrelevant appeals in an argument
   - Judging the strength or weakness of an argument in terms of degree of fit between reasons and conclusion

3. Presenting and developing arguments
   - Presenting simple arguments in support of a precise conclusion
   - Recognising, identifying and developing counterarguments
   - Responding to counterarguments

4. Evaluating the credibility of sources
   - Examining individual witnesses, documents, images, using the credibility criteria of vested interest, bias, reputation, relevant expertise, and ability to see
   - Recognising and identifying a range of factors (political, religious, cultural, regional, economic) that can influence the presentation, selection and interpretation of evidence

5. Evaluating evidence
   - Recognising and identifying common weaknesses in polls: sample size, unrepresentative samples; bias in the framing of questions
   - Recognising and identifying the distinction between fact and opinion
   - Recognising and identifying strengths or weaknesses in evidence in terms of relevance (the degree of fit between the evidence and the claim it supports) and selection
   - Seeking and creating alternative explanations for evidence in order to question its significance

6. Seeking and evaluating explanations
   - Generating alternative explanations
   - Recognising and identifying the distinction between necessary and sufficient conditions in an explanation
   - Recognising and identifying that one thing can follow another in time without being caused by it
   - Recognising and identifying that correlations are open to many different explanations

7. Decision-making and ethical reasoning
   - Identifying different options
   - Identifying relevant criteria for deciding between options
   - Applying criteria to reach a decision in the light of relevant evidence
   - Clarifying the meaning of everyday ethical concepts such as fairness, equality, freedom and happiness

8. Conceptual thinking and clarifying the meaning of concepts
   - Using Venn diagrams to explore similarities and dissimilarities
   - Using mind mapping to explore connections between ideas
   - Identifying common properties in a range of examples
   - Generating examples and counterexamples to clarify the meaning of concepts
   - Recognising and identifying the distinction between necessary and sufficient conditions
   - Recognising, identifying and evaluating analogies

9. Information processing and problem-solving
   - Scanning and skimming sources for relevant information
   - Identifying relevant data
   - Recognising and identifying patterns
   - Using simple matrices to organise data in order to solve a problem
   - Drawing conclusions from data

10. Creative thinking
    - Generating questions – who, when, where, why, what – in response to stimulus
    - Generating ideas and hypotheses for the purposes of explaining, interpreting or organising evidence
    - Generalising and extrapolating from data
    - Exploring and evaluating possible consequences through suppositional and counterfactual thinking.

These ten skills were taught through an engaging curriculum that centred around the following themes, which were great because our students found the topics inherently interesting:

Personal and social issues:

- Teenage violence and antisocial behaviour
- Crime and punishment
- Drugs and alcohol abuse
- Sex and gender (e.g. male underachievement; teenage pregnancies)

Bioethical issues:

- Genetic engineering
- Euthanasia
- Rationing and allocation of medical resources
- Animal welfare and animal experiments

Political issues of freedom and justice:

- Freedom of expression and tolerance
- Civil disobedience and the law

Global issues of poverty, conflict and environment:

- Global warming and the environment
- Third World poverty (e.g. fair trade; consumerism)
- International conflicts and their resolution

Science issues:

- Human origins: evolution and design
- Life after death: reincarnation, near death experiences and the soul
- UFOs, alien visits and alien abductions
- Astrology, alternative therapies and alleged supernatural phenomena

Mysteries and conspiracies:

- Conspiracy theories
- Murder mysteries
- Historical mysteries

Although TARS was a taught course with a set curriculum that we worked our way through, teaching children about critical thinking and reasoning skills involves a significant metacognitive component because it requires them to monitor and control their own thinking and reasoning skills and to become increasingly aware of the extent to which their thinking (and that of others) is based on solid foundations.

We aren't aware of any other taught courses in critical thinking and reasoning skills that are as comprehensive or as engaging as the Level 2 TARS course was. If you know of any, please drop us a line at rethinking-ed.org/contact. We certainly wish that we had been taught this stuff at school. And OCR, if you're reading this: *#BringBackTARS!*

SELF-REGULATED LEARNING[147]

The 'learning' aim of any set of lessons is to get students to learn the skills of teaching themselves the content and understanding – that is, to self-regulate their learning.

John Hattie (2012)[148]

In *Chapter 2: A brief history of Learning to Learn*, we outlined a model for understanding the difference between metacognition, self-regulation and self-regulated learning. To recap:

Figure 5.3. Metacognition, self-regulation and self-regulated learning

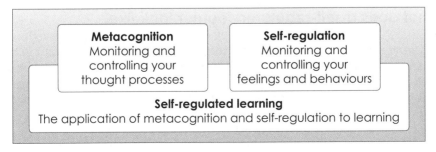

When we started the *Learning Skills* curriculum, we talked a lot about self-regulated learning – helping our students learn to take more ownership over their learning through things like goal-setting, weekly reviews and setting their own homework. However, we underplayed the importance of self-regulation – monitoring and controlling your feelings and behaviours – as a precursor to, and as an important part of, self-regulated learning.

At the end of this chapter, we will outline a number of things we would do differently if we had our time again and focusing more explicitly on self-regulation is at the front of the queue. In this section, we will focus on how the *Learning Skills* curriculum set out to help our students learn to take more ownership, and therefore more control, over their learning.

As we have argued, schools are really good at teaching stuff to children, and less good at helping them learn stuff by and for themselves. This is because the agenda for learning is usually decided by the teacher, by the curriculum and by pre-determined deadlines. This makes for an efficient use of time, but has the unfortunate side effect that the children can become very dependent on their teachers, resulting in the examples of helpless classroom talk we saw in the Introduction. As Boekaerts (2002) memorably put it:

> *Remarkably, in traditional classrooms there is not much room for self-regulated learning. Students are cognitively, emotionally, and socially dependent on their teachers who formulate the learning goals, determine which type of interaction is allowed, and generally coerce them to adjust to the learning environment they have created.*[149]

Coerce is a strong word, but you can see her point. We believe the obvious conclusion to draw from this is that teachers need to find ways to step back from time to time – judiciously, of course – to provide young people with the opportunity to find out for themselves what they can and cannot do without being told what to do, and how, and by when all the time.

What does a self-regulated learner look like?

Before we explain how we did this through the *Learning Skills* curriculum, let's remind ourselves what we're trying to achieve here. Schunk and Ertmer (2000) suggest that self-regulated learning refers to 'self-generated **thoughts**, **feelings** and **actions** that are planned and systematically adapted as needed to affect one's learning and motivation.'[150] This can involve some or all of the following:

- Setting goals for learning
- Attending to and concentrating on instruction
- Using effective strategies to organise, code and rehearse information to be remembered
- Establishing a productive work environment
- Using resources effectively
- Monitoring performance
- Managing time effectively
- Seeking assistance when needed
- Holding positive beliefs about one's capabilities, the value of learning, the factors influencing learning and the anticipated outcomes of actions
- Experiencing pride and satisfaction with one's efforts.[151]

Nobody would argue that we don't want all people – young or old – to be able to do all of these things as a matter of course. The question, as ever, is: How do we get there? What can we do in schools to help all young people become effective, self-regulated learners? Here is our answer to that question, and it comes in four parts: inclusive practice, project-based learning, curated autonomy and personal effectiveness. As above, we will provide a rationale for each of these, followed by what it looks like in practice.

INCLUSIVE PRACTICE

Rationale

The *Learning Skills* programme started in 2010, following a decade of inclusive education initiatives such as *Every Child Matters*,[152] the *Social and Emotional Aspects of Learning*[153] and policies seeking to increase 'social inclusion... to close the gap between the achievements of different groups of young people so that they can fulfil their potential and contribute purposefully to society'.[154]

The debate about whether, when, why and how schools should include or exclude some students rages on to this day, with issues such as fixed-term exclusions, off-rolling and isolation booths rarely out of the headlines. We do not wish to rehearse the arguments on either side of this debate here, other than to say that the *Learning Skills* programme is very much situated within the tradition of inclusive practice.

Learning Skills isn't an 'intervention' for a targeted group of students; this is something entire cohorts go through together. We want this to be the rising tide that lifts all boats. Our aim is to help every student find their 'on switch', find their feet, and find something that they can succeed at and feel proud about. More than anything, we want every student to find their voice and to learn to express their thoughts and feelings with confidence as they enter the often-challenging terrain of the teen and tween years. We knew that in order to achieve this, we had to focus on how the students interacted with one another.

We were influenced by the work of Professor Robin Banerjee at the University of Sussex, and the importance of identifying those students who isolate themselves, those who struggle to connect, and those who seem to deliberately reject others.[155] Kate had worked with Robin at her previous school to help her map peer relationships among her students, to see how she could best support children with autistic spectrum conditions who were being integrated into the mainstream for the first time. So we set out to build a curriculum that would provide the space and time for relationships between our students to form and flourish.

What does it look like in practice?

The first thing to say is that Learning Skills is a mixed attainment approach. But creating the classes is just the beginning. In schools, children quickly settle into groups, cliques and ghettos. Like attracts like and there's safety in numbers. If you want to teach them to take risks and do new things, you need to gently but persistently nudge them out of the safety of their friendship groups and be explicit about why you're doing it. So within those mixed prior attainment classes, we mixed up the groupings regularly, as we outlined above in the section on 'collaboration and complexity'.

Ultimately, our aim was to get every student to the point where they could learn independently, teach one another and work harmoniously with anyone. This is easier said than done; to be a truly effective independent learner requires a complex combination of knowledge, skills, habits and dispositions. Some of our students had many of these pieces in place right from the get-go, but many had much further to travel. Some could barely copy down the date correctly from one lesson to the next. Some had less impulse control than a puppy. Some felt that they were so far behind that they isolated themselves from their peers or obfuscated at every available opportunity.

Some students had been through four years of primary school in the same class and didn't even know each other's names. Others had fallen out in previous years and bore deep-rooted, seemingly intractable grudges. Some had a history of either bullying or having been bullied, and were afraid of being made to work with their old adversaries. Many had challenging home lives; and some had a toxic cocktail of most or all of the above.

None of this stuff is visible to the untrained eye, and yet all of it can impact on how physically and emotionally safe a student feels in a classroom. If a student doesn't feel safe – if they don't feel they have friends that will 'have their back' when they need it, for example – their fear and sense of isolation can become overwhelming. In these circumstances, they are understandably reluctant to add to their woes by stepping out of their comfort zone and taking a risk in front of their peers.

Earlier in this chapter, we discussed the importance of trust between the *Learning Skills* team and school leadership. In order to get to a point where students can take risks and be courageous in their learning, there needs to be trust among the students as well. When students don't know one another, the outliers are acutely at risk. So we had to find ways for the students to get to know one another and to build a network of trust between them.

Circle time lessons

One way in which we built a sense of trust and mutual appreciation within each class was through circle time lessons. We did this a lot at the start of the year, and then once a week for the rest of the year in philosophical inquiry sessions. In case you aren't familiar, a circle time lesson is simply when you push all the tables to the sides of the room and sit in a big circle with empty space in between. There are many ways in which circle time lessons can be used, and some excellent books have been written on the topic.[156]

Circle time solves one of the perennial problems of being a classroom teacher: the whole-class discussion. Say the class are all sitting in rows facing the front – or if they're sitting in groups for that matter. You ask the class a question. A student in the front row responds. Because they're quite near to you, they often speak at a volume that can't be heard at the back of the room. Even if you ask them to repeat what they said more loudly or repeat it for the benefit of others, the other students can't see their body language or facial expressions, which are really important aids to understanding. Also, they tend only to address the teacher, and rarely one another. Normal classroom layouts – whether in rows or groups – are just not conducive to having a sustained conversation between 30 people.

In a circle time lesson, these logistical issues disappear. They all speak at a volume that everyone can hear. Everyone can see everyone else's face and body language. They build on one another's ideas more freely rather than just responding to the teacher. But the big advantage of circle time is that it enables a dialogic approach to teaching and learning that is very difficult to achieve when the children are sitting behind desks. It enables the students to really listen to one another, which means that whenever anyone speaks there are 30 minds focusing on what they're saying and how they're saying it, thinking about the reasons that person gave to support their ideas and whether they agree or disagree, relating the contribution to what has gone before – and so on. Circle time amplifies the educational potential of every utterance. It makes talk count.

It's a good idea to use some kind of visual cue to make clear whose turn it is to speak – a bean bag, say. We tended to use thumbs: you sit with one thumb up if you have something to say, resting your hand on your knee (not waving it around!). If you want to respond to what someone has just said rather than making a new point, you hold your upright thumb in your other hand (like the children's game one-potato, two-potato). This helps the conversation flow more easily. With training, you can run the lesson so that whenever a child has finished what they want to say, they scan the circle and select the next person to speak. In this way, the students can engage in long periods of discussion with little need for the teacher to intervene.

When such a discussion is in full flow, it is a wonderful thing to behold. All students have regular opportunities to contribute – you might use a 'round', for example, where you work around the circle asking for contributions – students can 'pass' if they prefer to just listen to others. Or you might ask them to discuss things in pairs before sharing their thoughts with the wider group. After a few weeks, when a hitherto silent student tentatively sticks their thumb out and contributes to a whole-class discussion, we would often get one of those shivers down your spine that remind you why you became a teacher.

Creating a class charter

Another powerful way to create an atmosphere of safety and trust is to involve all pupils in a process of deciding how the class will operate. To do this, you need to create two sets of ground rules – a 'class charter' that governs behaviour and routines, and a set of 'talk rules' that govern how the students speak and listen to one another.[157] We explored talk rules earlier in this chapter; here, we'll briefly discuss one way of creating a class charter (or a set of talk rules): the hat method.

1. Give each student a sheet of scrap paper and ask them to tear it in half. On one half, they write down one or two examples of things that help them learn in lessons. Then they fold them up and place them in a hat that gets passed around. It's important that you tell the students in advance that this will happen, because they need to know that their responses will be anonymous. For example, a student might not want to put their hand up and say openly, 'I don't like it when people touch my things/nudge my arm when I'm writing/talk over me', because it might be perceived as a sign of weakness. The hat method means they can say what they really think without fear of repercussion.

2. Read them out. It's best if the teacher does this, because you might find that some wag has taken advantage of the anonymity to write something silly, so you can vet the responses. Ask a student who can type quickly to collate them into a list on the board.

3. Repeat this process for 'things that can make it difficult to learn in lessons'. Again, pass the hat around and collate the suggestions into a list on the board. The two lists should sit side by side so that they can be seen together.

4. Get the students into pairs and ask them to write a set of ground rules to make sure that all the good things happen and none of the bad. There are three criteria:

   - Try to use positive language (dos rather than don'ts).
   - Try not to use the word 'and' (i.e. each rule has to be about one thing only).
   - Combine rules together to reduce the list down into the fewest rules possible.

5. Collate these into a new list, ignoring any duplicates. It's best to do this overnight, as it can take a while to do it in a lesson. Next lesson, review the list and again whittle it down to the smallest number of ground rules that the whole class agrees would ensure that all the good things happen and none of the bad. It's a good idea to aim for around five to seven rules; too many and it all becomes unwieldy.

6. Once you have agreed your list, create a wall display so that the class charter can be seen from every seat. You might also ask every student

to sign their name to it as a visual reminder that these are rules that everyone has agreed to together.

The class charter should be a living, dynamic document – throughout the year we would regularly revisit the charter at the start or end of a lesson, amending the rules if the class felt anything should be added, edited or removed. Here's an example of a set of ground rules one of our classes came up with:

1. If there is a problem, we will try to solve it ourselves before asking the teacher for help.
2. What is said in the room stays in the room, unless there is good reason.
3. It's OK to take risks and to make mistakes.
4. Laugh *with* people, but not *at* people.
5. Be respectful when other people are talking.
6. Respect people's property and leave the classroom as you found it.

Note that these ground rules are not designed to replace school rules about uniform, consequence ladders and handing in your homework. Instead, a class charter sets a positive mould for how each group agrees to operate throughout the year. This is part of a wider strategy to include the pupils in decision-making as often as possible – to break them out of the mindset that education is something that is 'done to them'.

At Sea View, students and teachers made decisions together until it became normalised. We also set ourselves challenges and played ice-breaker games that we all participated in. Recently, some teachers on social media have expressed concern that students would play games when we should be busy filling them up with cultural capital. We think these teachers are not only missing out on the fun; they are missing the point entirely. Games can be a cause of laughter, but we should not be distracted by the frivolity. As a method for building relationships, confidence and trust within a group – and for including those isolated, hard-to-reach students in non-threatening ways – the playing of games is deadly serious.[158]

In *Learning Skills*, we purposefully and deliberately built our classes into cohesive, inclusive units one step at a time. It wasn't always a smooth path. Young people often have a lot happening outside of school that can impact on their ability to cope with the daily requests made upon them by others. However, when an atmosphere is established that expects students not only to sometimes stumble, but also gives them the space they need to figure how best to pick themselves up and repair any damage caused after they have, that too becomes normalised. It's not an all or nothing approach. Inclusion requires flexibility, understanding and compassion. It's not a question of every pupil staying in the room come hell or high water in the name of inclusion. The school rules still apply, as well as the class charter. Inclusion means that every student knows and trusts that there is always a way that they can stay in the room and learn alongside everyone else, even when they are really struggling. Some days, that may mean being fully immersed in their learning and taking the lead; on other days, it may mean working in parallel with others or watching from the wings. But there is always a way for them to participate.

To help our pupils learn to take responsibility for the choices they make, we deliberately provided them with opportunities for failure without consequence – a kind of amnesty for all the things they wanted to try but hadn't been allowed to do before:

'What will happen if I don't write anything?'
'What will happen if I don't do my homework?'
'What will happen if I learn about whatever topic I choose?'

Pupils needed to be able to answer questions like these for themselves. The answers would be different for different pupils, but they all needed to trust that this was not a place where such things would be met with warnings or consequences imposed from above. If a pupil didn't do the homework they had set for themselves, then they wouldn't make as much progress with their project as they otherwise would have made. They would own both the choice and the consequence, and it would be reflected in their work. What mattered was that they all knew that there were rules of engagement they were expected to try their best to adhere to, even if they couldn't always manage it. Before long, pupils learned to trust that the *Learning Skills* classroom was a fair and safe place to be, because everyone was trying their best, and when mistakes were made, they were expected to repair any damage caused and learn from them as best they could.

Through working in this way, students and teachers came to know one another really well – far more so than is possible within the context of subject learning. In fact, the students knew one another's strengths far better than we did. By the end of the first year, they were able to build teams according to what they wanted to achieve. They all got a chance to achieve something that elicited a little victory dance – and they all had their inner mettle tested along the way.

There were moments of disappointment and experiences that didn't hit the mark and left them feeling vaguely unsatisfied – but they went through these experiences together. They built the trust and the support networks they needed in order to be able to stop worrying about friendships and status and all the interpersonal micro-politics of the classroom, and to focus on their learning.

The aggressive and passive-aggressive comments and behaviours that so often come with the territory of being a teenager – from light-hearted 'banter' through to name-calling and sustained campaigns of bullying and intimidation – undermine learning and cause children to live in fear. In response, some children make themselves more brash, 'giving as good as they get'; others make themselves smaller or more verbose or become paralysed with overthinking.

Such fear responses tend not to manifest as outright terror. Sometimes, the fear is almost imperceptible; you can detect its presence through the behaviours that you see and don't see. Schools can be fractious places, and every teenager faces challenges within their peer group from time to time. But when children learn how to navigate this arena without fear of failure – when they learn how to respond in healthy ways when they feel afraid or challenged or threatened in some way – they feel safer, relationships become stronger, and learning can flourish.

PROJECT-BASED LEARNING

Rationale

In *Chapter 2: A Brief History of Learning to Learn*, we discussed the idea that in order to allow children to develop the skills of self-regulated learning, at some point teachers need to take a step back and hand over the responsibility for deciding what to learn, and how, and in what order, over to the children. At Sea View, the *Learning Skills* team took the view that the best way to do this would be through project-based learning. This felt like a no-brainer: it seemed obvious that we would have to set them tasks with sufficient breadth, time and challenge for them to find out what they were capable of doing by themselves.

This association between self-regulated learning and project-based learning makes logical and intuitive sense, and it is also a link that has been made many times in the research literature over the years.[159, 160] However, project-based learning is a broad church – it means different things to different people – and, as might be expected, research looking at the impact of project-based learning on academic outcomes reveals a mixed picture.

For example, a recent RCT looked at the effect of project-based learning on literacy among year 7 students.[161] This study, which had 12 secondary schools in the treatment group and 12 in the control group, found that project-based learning had 'no clear impact on either literacy... or student engagement with school and learning'.[162] It also found that 'project-based learning may have had a negative impact on the literacy attainment of pupils entitled to free school meals'.[163] However, this study begs the question: *why should* project-based learning help children develop their literacy skills? Some things lend themselves more to explicit instruction, and the teaching of literacy surely falls into this category. If reading and writing is the goal, put the project-based learning down and teach students how to read and write!

When the curriculum aims are better suited to self-regulated learning, there is evidence that project-based learning can be effective at improving outcomes – including in academic subject learning. For example, a 2018 meta-analysis of 48 studies of project-based learning in science reported a large effect size of 1.063, and concluded that project-based learning was significantly more effective at improving outcomes in science than were traditional methods – especially in secondary schools.[164]

Elsewhere, research has found that problem-based learning – closely related to project-based learning – is associated with improved long-term retention of content knowledge, problem-solving and attitudes to learning.[165, 166]

There is also evidence to suggest that teaching the skills of self-regulated learning explicitly – such as through modelling, project-based learning, granting children greater autonomy and collaborative learning – can have a positive impact on student learning. For example, a review by Duckworth et al. (2009) reported that 'there is a positive overall relationship between self-regulation and academic achievement. Children and young people with more adaptive personal skills and learning resources are more likely to succeed academically'.[167] They also report that 'individual elements of self-regulation – e.g. attitudes toward learning, attention and persistence – are also related to academic achievement'.[168]

Despite such positive research findings, it is widely acknowledged that project-based learning can be difficult to implement effectively within the context of a busy school curriculum.[169] This was reflected in a recent review of the literature, which described the association between project-based learning and improved academic outcomes as 'promising but not proven'.[170] Helpfully, the authors make a number of recommendations for how to make project-based learning effective. These include having design principles that:

a) are measurable and observable, so that the impact of project-based learning as a method of achieving your goals can be evaluated
b) pay close attention to the content you want the students to learn, and use authentic assessment methods
c) are informed by practice and/or designed with practitioners, so that the teacher feels a sense of ownership over the process
d) are adapted to fit the local context – planning project-based learning with explicit curriculum goals in mind.[171]

This final point is of paramount importance. As we mentioned above, project-based learning is not suited to all tasks. If your aim is to teach the children how to conjugate the verb 'to be' in French, or about how electromagnetic induction works in science, explicit instruction is likely to be far more effective. If, however, your aim is for the children to learn how to regulate their own learning, then project-based learning is definitely the way to go, because it allows the teacher to step back and the children to find out what they can and cannot do under their own steam. It also allows you to set challenging targets that the children think are beyond their ability – things that may take several weeks to complete. When you pitch this right, so that all pupils achieve things they thought were beyond them just a few short weeks ago, project-based learning can be incredibly powerful.

What does it look like in practice?

In the years 7 and 8 taught course, all students carried out six projects a year – one per half-term. The key features of the projects we ran in years 7 and 8 are summarised in Table 5.4.

Table 5.4. The years 7 and 8 projects, in the 3rd year of the programme

Year	Half-term	Project title	Individual or group?	Central themes	Outcome
7	1	Who am I?	I	Identity/ organisation	Project artefacts & presentation
	2	Christmas Market	G	Collaboration/ interpersonal	Christmas Market stall
	3	Independent research	I	Study skills/ public speaking	Oral presentation (individual)
	4	Debating	I & G	Debating/ public speaking	A series of class debates
	5	Group research	G	Study skills/ interpersonal	Oral presentation (group)
	6	Teaching others	G	Collaboration/ organisation	Lessons taught to year 6 at open day

8	1	Sex and relationships	I & G	Collaboration/ research	Educational resource & presentation
	2	Universal Declaration of Human Rights	I & G	Citizenship/ communication	Children's book & presentation
	3	Drugs education	G	Students as researchers	Research report & presentation
	4	Allotment	G	Community/ collaboration	Allotment bed & presentation
	5	Campaigning	I & G	Community organising	Campaign artefacts, letters & presentation
	6	£2 challenge	I	Enterprise/ organisation	Accounts/payment for trip

As can be seen in the right-hand column, each project had a tangible outcome, so that the students were clear what they were working towards. Each project also required the students to present to their classmates (either to the whole class or to a small group) at the end of each half-term. Some of the projects worked better than others; some we would recommend; others we probably wouldn't do again or we'd do them differently. Here's a brief summary of what each project involved.

Who am I?

To help your new teachers and classmates learn all about you, answer this question in as many ways as possible (see Figure 5.4 for the project brief, below)

Christmas Market

Working in a group of 3 or 4, create a stall for the year 5 Christmas Market. The stall should be hand-made and should include an engaging activity that teaches year 5s about an aspect of the Learning Skills curriculum.

Independent research

Carry out a piece of independent research on a topic of your choosing. Choose how to present your findings and share them with the class at the end of term.

Debating

Take part in a series of structured debates, taking an active speaking role as well as contributing to the performance of your team.

Group research

Carry out a piece of research on a topic of your choosing. This worked far better than the independent research project, because a) we limited the topics to 'academic subjects you might learn at University but not at school', and b) each group had to negotiate, compromise and agree on a topic. These constraints led to some really creative decisions, as we saw in the vignette about 'Year 7 projects that sound like PhDs' at the end of *Chapter 4: The story of Learning Skills*.

Teaching others

For their end-of-year project, students wrote a series of short lesson to teach year 6 students about some aspect of the *Learning Skills* curriculum. They practised them on one another, gave, received and acted on feedback, and then taught them to year 6 students as part of the open day.

In year 8, projects were based around aspects of the PSHE curriculum:

Sex and relationships

Students had to work in groups to research and then produce a range of age-appropriate resources and activities to teach year 7 students about some aspect of sex and relationships education. Most groups chose to produce a series of leaflets on topics ranging from puberty and relationships to contraception and the development of the embryo *in utero*. They were also required to provide information on where children can go for free, confidential advice, including maps, directions and opening times. These were checked for accuracy and the best examples were shared with year 7s.

Human Rights

Working in groups, students had to produce a children's story book with the aim of teaching younger children about the Universal Declaration of Human Rights.

Drugs education

In this 'students as researchers' project, pupils worked individually to carry out an original piece of research (involving data collection and analysis) to find out about people's knowledge, attitudes and opinions about legal and illegal drugs, as well as researching the effects different drugs have on the body. They then produced a written report summarising their findings, addressing misconceptions and providing advice about where people can go to get help if they have any concerns about drugs or alcohol.

Allotment

Groups of four pupils were each allocated a plant bed in the school allotment. They had to dig it up, create a border using scaffolding boards, research the lifecycles of various plants and vegetables, buy seeds within a budget on a class trip to the local garden centre, plant the seeds, and attend to the growth and health of their plants. Some groups chose instead to work together to build a greenhouse out of plastic bottles.[172]

Campaigning

This was probably the least successful of all the projects we ran. The students had to choose something to campaign for, and then write letters, put up posters, arrange meetings and so on in order to raise awareness and achieve their goal. Examples included lobbying the local council to install a zebra crossing outside the school; lobbying the headteacher to abolish school uniform (we told them it was probably a non-starter, but they wanted to persevere anyway); and campaigning to have pro-anorexia websites banned within the academy chain.

The problem with a six-week campaign project is that campaigns usually exist for as long as it takes to achieve success. This usually takes a lot longer than six weeks, and many students expressed dissatisfaction at the end of this term that their work had been in vain. This led to some interesting conversations as we 'owned' the failure of this project and resolved to do better next time. In the case of the pro-anorexia websites, one student persevered with her campaign into year 9 with remarkable tenacity, and ultimately achieved her goal in getting a number of sites blocked within the school.

£2 challenge

For this enterprise project, we gave each student £2 and read them the Parable of the Talents, the Bible story where a father gives some money to each of his three sons, with varying degrees of success. Working individually, each student had to use the money to raise enough to pay for a school trip to a location of their choosing. Naturally enough, the students chose a local theme park. Some bought and sold drinks and snacks to sell (though they weren't allowed to sell sugary snacks within school). Some bought a bucket and sponge and washed cars. One girl made a small fortune buying bottled water in increasing quantities and selling it in her mother's cafe. All students had to keep accounts and be able to show receipts for any transactions they had made along the way. The students also organised the entire trip, including choosing the venue, booking the tickets, researching and booking the transport, writing letters to parents and carers – even completing the risk assessment!

At the start of each half-term, students were presented with a project brief no longer than one side of A4. An example of the project brief for 'Who am I' can be seen in Figure 5.4. Because this was the first project they did, we provided quite a lot of guidance in this case. Throughout the year, we gradually provided less detail up front, to allow the students to decide how to interpret the project brief for themselves.

Figure 5.4. The 'Who am I' project brief

Now that you've settled in, your new teachers and classmates want to know all about you! To help us get to know you, we would like you to spend this half-term completing a project to tell us all about you. At the end, you will present your project to your classmates. Here are a few suggestions. You don't have to do all of these – and feel free to make up some of your own!

- **Pet profile:** Do you have any pets? Have you ever had a pet? Tell us about them! If you interviewed your pet, what would they say?!

- **My ideal day:** How would you spend your ideal day, if money was no object?

- **My friends:** Why not write a profile of some of your friends – likes, dislikes, memories…

- **The year of my birth:** What happened during your birth year/month? (hint: search the internet!) You might wish to include local, national, and international news. What song was number one on the day you were born? What sort of technology was being invented?

- **My Geography:** Where were you born? Where do you live? Can you draw a map or find one to label? What is the area like? Which places have you visited on holiday? What are the similarities and differences? How could you show this?

- **My portrait:** How have peoples' faces been recorded through history? Can you find an interesting way to record your own appearance? Think of different media (paint, pastel, collage, digital media)

- **My story so far:** Make a timeline with memories of your life so far. What major (or minor) events have made you who you are today? Would it make a good film script? How could you show this? Which parts would you include and which would you leave out?

- **My family:** Introduce and describe your family. You might wish to create a family tree – there are some genealogy websites that can help you with this (although you often have to pay – check with an adult), or you can ask family members.

- **My body:** How does your body work? Think about your brain, muscles, skeleton, digestive system, memory, senses etc.

- **My career in sport:** How would a sports commentator or biographer describe your progress and achievements in sport? What have been your best moments?

- **An interview with____:** Interview someone important in your life – your best friend, a family member, a neighbour etc... record it, write it up and share it!

- **My future:** Describe what you think you will be like in the future. Choose different ages to describe (e.g. 16, 18, 21, 30, 50, 70, 100...). Could you draw a labelled picture?

- **My passions and talents:** What else could you add that will really allow people to understand what makes you, you?

- **My ideal school:** If you could design your own school, what would it be like & why? You might wish to draw a map, or an ideal day (it must be educational: no theme park rides!)

- **My hopes and dreams:** What do you want to achieve in your life? How would you change the world, if you could? What do you wish people would do differently?

- **Who am I really? Try listing all the different ways in which you can define yourself:** e.g. human, mammal, citizen, child, colony of cells, pile of atoms, musician, sister...

- **A letter to myself in 5 years:** Write a letter to your 16-year-old self. Keep it safe until you reach Year 11!

Following this, each student used the project brief to create a set of success criteria to determine what success would look like for them, on four levels: Distinction, Merit, Pass and Fail (the students preferred this to Gold/Silver/

Bronze, or using standard grades). In essence, the students were creating a kind of mark scheme that they would later be assessed against. Some students struggled with this at first, but we were often pleasantly surprised at how good students were at setting themselves 'Goldilocks' targets that were neither too challenging nor too easy. Table 5.5 details the success criteria one student chose for her 'Who am I?' project.

Table 5.5. Student-derived success criteria for the 'Who am I?' project

Fail	• If I don't hit the criteria for 'pass'
Pass	• My ideal day • Photos – family, pets, friends • Year of my birth • Family tree • Folder is neat and colourful
Merit	All of the above, and: • My future • My geography • Hopes and dreams • Check spellings
Distinction	All of the above, and: • Who am I really? • Letter to myself in 5 years • Interview my nan • Set myself homework every week – and remember to do it!

Each student then set short-, medium- and long-term goals for how they would organise their time throughout the half-term. This included deciding how they would spend their time in lessons each week, as well as setting themselves homework tasks for each week of the project. At the start of each week, there was a short 'weekly review' session to allow students to monitor their progress against their goals and to refine their planning for the week ahead.

At the end of each half-term, each project was peer-, self- and teacher-assessed, and an overall grade was agreed upon. Interestingly, we often found that the students would award their own work a lower grade than the teacher and their peers thought it deserved.

Stepping back: a vignette

By way of a final word on project-based learning, here's a brief story about what 'stepping back' feels like in the classroom. In the early individual projects in year 7 – the 'Who am I' project and the independent research project in particular – it soon became clear that some of the students found it incredibly difficult to work under their own steam. Many students relished the freedom to work on their own and were quite adept at organising their time and resources and just generally getting on with stuff. But some of them just kind of did the deer-in-the-headlights thing. They hadn't ever been asked to do anything this big before, and nor had they ever been handed control over their own learning. They just didn't know what to do with all this freedom, and they were paralysed by it.

As teachers, we found it really difficult not to swoop in and tell these students what to do. We wanted to support them, but we also wanted them to navigate their own way out of the situation they found themselves in. If we were teaching our subject specialisms, we would absolutely swoop in and intervene, because time is in short supply and there's a lot to get through. But teaching Learning Skills is not like teaching a specialist subject, and so we had to figure out how to support our students in different ways.

For example, one student – let's call him Alex – had chosen to do an independent research project about how televisions work. He had printed out some rather technical notes from the internet, and he also planned to take an old-fashioned (cathode ray tube) TV apart and figure out what all the various parts did. We assumed that he was some kind of electronics whizz, and that this was already a passion of his, but this turned out not to be the case – he was just curious, and saw this as an opportunity to find out. He just didn't really know how to find things out for himself – yet.

At first, Alex did a good job of looking busy. He would surround himself with printouts from the internet, making notes in an exercise book. It really looked like he was getting on with it. But when the teacher caught up with him, it was clear that he was just copying out chunks of text without really understanding what he was reading. He hadn't skim-read the notes before printing them out, and he didn't seem to have any idea of how to prioritise different parts of the task. His short-, medium- and long-term goals were very vague and didn't really provide him with a clear plan for what needed doing, in what order. He had chosen a huge topic and he felt overwhelmed. It was clear that he lacked the organisational skills to make any headway with his ambitious project.

So Alex's teacher sat down with him and asked him how it was going. At first, he responded that he was doing fine, but after a little gentle questioning, he admitted that he was struggling, and that he didn't really know what he was supposed to be doing. Lots of other students around him were getting on with their projects, and so his teacher suggested that he spend some time watching what the others were doing and then report back on what he had noticed. After five minutes or so, he came back and said, 'Well, Amy's written a list of all the things she needs to do, and then she ticks things off as she goes.'

Remarkably, Alex had never heard of a 'to-do list' before. After a short conversation, he decided that he would try writing one, listing what he could do in that week's lessons and in what order. Soon, however, he changed his mind. Instead, he would make a list of all the different parts of a TV and find out what each part does, and, if possible, find a photo or a diagram of each. Then, when he took apart an actual TV, he would know what he was looking for. He went back to the computer and, instead of searching for 'how does a TV work', he searched for labelled diagrams of TVs. Then he started looking up what each of the words meant and made notes on each. His project was under way.

This small piece of classroom practice did not transform Alex into a proactive, self-regulated learner overnight. But the story illustrates how project-based learning, combined with the teacher stepping back rather than swooping in, enables students to begin to identify strategies – in this case, making lists – and then to adapt those strategies to serve the goal they are trying to achieve. These small steps then become 'teachable moments' – at the end of a lesson, we would highlight and celebrate such moments with the class. In this way, the students would learn how to do things vicariously as well as through their own individual endeavour.

If Alex's teacher had come into the lesson and said, 'Right, class. Today we are going to learn about the importance of to-do lists', he would likely have glazed over within minutes. Project-based learning enables you to immerse your students in the situation where they need to identify, trial and adapt strategies in order to meet some goal or objective that they themselves have committed to. This is why project-based learning is so helpful as a method for helping young people become self-regulated learners – it allows you to throw them in at the deep end, commit to taking on something much more ambitious than they would normally commit to, and then provide them with the minimal amount of guidance they need in order to learn how to 'flounder intelligently'.

CURATED AUTONOMY

Rationale

One of the problems Learning to Learn has faced in the past is that the goal – to teach children how to get better at learning stuff – has been confused with the method for achieving that goal. Specifically, some people have assumed – understandably, but wrongly – that the way to create independent learners is to give the students complete independence – i.e. to let them learn what they want, how they want – at the novice stage. In our experience, novices learn the skills and habits of independent learning most effectively using the traditional methods of teaching and learning – observing and questioning (in the case of Alex, above), modelling, explaining, practising, receiving and responding to feedback, and so on.

That said, it goes without saying that if you're trying to help people become more effective, independent learners, at some point you have to give them at least some degree of freedom over what and how they learn. That's literally what independent learning means. If your aim is for your students to independently learn precisely what you want them to learn, you're kind of missing the point. For this reason, several researchers and practitioners of Learning to Learn have singled out the concept of autonomy as being of particular importance.[173]

The word autonomy derives from the ancient Greek *autos*, meaning 'self', and *nomos*, meaning 'rule', so it basically means being your own boss. Autonomy has been the focus of much research from the world of work in recent years, where several studies have found that autonomy in the workplace is linked to higher intrinsic motivation, improved performance, increased job satisfaction, enhanced health and wellbeing, and decreased absenteeism and turnover,[174] which is rather a ringing endorsement! It is therefore easy to see why the concept of autonomy should be of interest to practitioners of Learning to Learn. As we pointed out in *Chapter 2: A brief history of Learning to Learn*, to develop metacognition and self-regulation is to promote independent learning; by definition, self-regulation cannot be imposed from above.

Following a wide-ranging review of practices that focus on learning as opposed to performance, Chris Watkins (2001) concluded that 'promoting learners as active and collaborative constructors of meaning with autonomy and self-direction can enhance performance'.[175] Watkins cites research from a range of fields – education, sport, business – to suggest that the more people are supported to be autonomous in their behaviours, the better they perform.[176] However, this is not a binary choice between total control and total freedom: the *amount of choice* people are given is important. For example, Kirschner & van Merriënboer (2013) suggest that 'providing some autonomy – but not too much – appears to us to be broadly consistent with the motivation research'.[177]

To understand what 'some autonomy – but not too much' might look like within the context of a top-down organisation like a school, it is important to understand that people differ in the extent to which they seek to be autonomous or controlled by others. Deci and Ryan (1985) suggest that there are three orientations that people can have with regard to how they regulate their behaviour: *control, impersonal* and *autonomous*.[178]

In the **control** orientation, people regulate their behaviour through externally or internally imposed controlling events, such as rewards and deadlines. For example, a student might do their homework so as to avoid getting a detention rather than because they feel intrinsically motivated to do so.

People with an **impersonal** orientation tend to believe that things are beyond their control, and therefore feel unable to regulate their behaviour to achieve desired outcomes. For example, a student might wish they had more friends, but they don't feel that this is something they can do anything about.

In contrast, **autonomy-oriented** individuals tend to regard their environment as a resource with which they can achieve their goals. For example, a student might want to join a band, but they don't know anyone else who plays an instrument. So they stick a sign on the student noticeboard saying, 'Fancy a jam? Come to the music room after school on Wednesdays.' In short: if you are autonomy-oriented, you believe that you are able to effect change in the world and so you are more likely to be the kind of person who *makes things happen*.

It is clear, therefore, that it's probably a good idea to help children become more autonomy-oriented – in some situations, at least. It seemed to us that the way to do this is to grant our students some autonomy – not too much, not too little – and to allow them to experience what successful autonomous learning feels like. We thought that if we could achieve this, they might get a taste for it and become more autonomy-oriented in the future. In the following section, we will consider how autonomy plays out in the *Learning Skills* curriculum on two levels: first, for us as teachers, and then for the students, via a co-regulated phase we refer to as *curated autonomy*.

What does it look like in practice, for teachers?

As we have discussed, from the outset of this project, the *Learning Skills* team was given an unprecedented degree of autonomy: five lessons a week, with the whole of year 7, to do with as we saw fit. None of us had ever worked in this way before, having the freedom to choose what to teach, and when, and how. As we will see in the teacher interviews in *Chapter 6: The evidence for Learning Skills*, we found having such a high degree of autonomy incredibly energising and motivating. We began by asking ourselves questions, such as:

- What do the students most need to know, or to be able to do?
- What's relevant?
- What's important?
- What do we know a lot about?
- What do we really care about?
- What do we feel excited about teaching?
- What do our students really care about?
- Will this take our students on a meaningful journey?
- Will they be inspired to continue learning by themselves?

Of these, the last three were the most important. We wanted to teach in such a way that our students would feel the same degree of energy and enthusiasm that we felt as teachers. We realised that in order to do this we would need to pass some of the autonomy on to our students. As a result, we built a curriculum with a lot of space in it. We filled the curriculum with structures: philosophical inquiry lessons, project-based learning, weekly reviews, metacognitive reflection lessons and oracy lessons. But within each of those structures, there were significant opportunities for students to determine the direction of travel.

What does it look like in practice, for students?

At Sea View, students were able to exercise autonomy in a range of ways, including:

- Choosing the topics for several of their projects in year 7
- Choosing the topics for discussion in philosophical inquiry and oracy lessons
- Choosing how to set about working on a project, and deciding the order in which things needed to be done
- Choosing who they worked with and where in the room to sit (at least in some lessons)

- Choosing how to share their learning to the rest of the class
- Setting their own homework
- Co-constructing class charters, talk rules and success criteria for projects
- The regular use of peer- and self-assessment.

That said, in keeping with the advice of Kirschner & van Merriënboer (2013), none of these freedoms was granted without careful consideration, and, in some cases, without strings attached. In particular, we were guided by the principle of *curated autonomy*. To illustrate this idea, we will briefly outline the way in which the students chose topics for their research projects.

Giving 11-year-olds complete freedom over what they learn and how is not always a good idea. For one, the fear over making a 'good choice' can render some pupils incapable of making any choice and actually getting started. For another, you may find yourself sitting through a lot of PowerPoint presentations about pop singers, footballers and fast cars. A balance between the 'what' and the 'how' is required if you want the children to learn project-management skills while also accruing a bit of the old cultural capital.

Clearly, there are degrees of freedom that already exist within the education system. In primary schools, for example, teachers often give pupils the choice between mild, medium and spicy maths problems. They're all learning about triangles, but they're doing it at different levels. This is a narrow example of what we would call curated autonomy. The novice children can choose what to do, within reasonable parameters that have been established by adult experts.

We strongly believe that there is great value to be gained from significantly widening the degree of autonomy at times – in particular, running independent research projects that run for a half-term. Once children are able to read and write to a decent level – equipped with a few pointers in sourcing reliable material from libraries and the internet – they have everything they need to learn powerful knowledge for themselves. However, it's important to set parameters around the autonomy they have.

The individual group projects had begun with a visit to the library; however, libraries contain books about many things, not all of them steeped in cultural capital. For subsequent research projects, the *Learning Skills* teachers visited the library beforehand to map out which areas of the library we wanted the children to explore, and which shelves were off limits. First, we narrowed it down to non-fiction, and then we identified particular shelves that we wanted them to draw from. Our broad aim was for students to study topics that you can study at college or university, but not at school - at least, not in any great depth at school.

This included biographies, reference books and textbooks on topics such as archaeology, architecture, astronomy, calligraphy, forensic science, health and medicine, human geography, journalism, photography, politics and so on.

Students brought their books back to the classroom, and while they explored them and started planning their projects, each student had a brief conversation with the teacher to make sure that their chosen topic would be suitable for a six-week project – primarily, to check whether there were sufficient, age-appropriate resources available for them to access and easily digest. As we described in *Chapter 4: The story of Learning Skills*, the students then went through a process of negotiation and compromise within their groups, to agree on a topic they could all get behind.

Similarly, when we ran speaking and listening projects, in which students took part in debates and delivered speeches on topics of their choosing, their choices were often derived from a list of suitable topics such as:

- School sports should not be gender-based.
- Pupils should be able to leave school at 14.
- Teachers should be paid more the better their exam results.
- Attending school should be optional.
- Science, maths and English are more important than art, music and drama.
- Everyone should be vegan.
- Too much money makes you unhappy.
- Footballers' wages should be capped.
- The internet is a force for good.
- The internet is a force for evil.
- Social media encourages bullying.
- Organ donation should be compulsory, with the legal right to opt out.

Some students wanted to do something that wasn't on the list. For example, one boy wanted to do a presentation on why recycling is pointless – something he didn't believe himself, but he wanted to challenge himself to argue against what he believed. Naturally, we granted his wish. But providing a curated list sets the tone for the kinds of topics that make for educationally worthwhile projects and presentations.

The aim of project-based learning is that the students will learn how to do things like set goals, identify strategies to help them meet those goals, access and evaluate the quality of different sources of information, organise their time, monitor their progress toward those goals, teach one another what they have learned and so on. Learning how to do all of this is no mean feat, and so in order to ensure your students are intrinsically motivated to learn, it's a good idea to let them choose something they find interesting. If they learn something about the history of feminism in China and South America along the way, so much the better; but in *Learning Skills* lessons, subject knowledge is the vehicle, not the destination.

ORGANISATIONAL SKILLS

Rationale

By the time the first cohort reached the end of year 7, there was emerging evidence that the *Learning Skills* curriculum was having a positive impact on the students. For the most part, this evidence was observational and anecdotal rather than reflected in the progress data: these students carried themselves differently, they were more switched on in lessons, and people were starting to notice. It was therefore agreed that timetabled lessons would extend into year 8, for three lessons a week. As part of the compromise, we would have to teach the PSHE curriculum through the *Learning Skills* programme.

In year 7, it was clear that the project-based learning had been effective in helping students learn to regulate their learning. However, the year 7 projects were not very tightly structured, since there was no requirement for the students to present their work in any particular way. As subject teachers, we were acutely aware that students often lack organisational skills. Where GCSE courses required students to keep a folder or a ring binder, these would often be stuffed full of sheets in the wrong order, with work frequently going missing. In the year 8 course, therefore, we decided to tighten up our practice around project-based learning to ensure that all students learned a range of vital organisational skills – including, but not limited to, organising a ring binder – before they progressed into their GCSE years.

To do this, we turned to the Award Scheme Development and Accreditation Network (ASDAN) Award of Personal Effectiveness (AoPE) course, a short version of the Certificate of Personal Effectiveness (CoPE). The ASDAN personal effectiveness courses have been a source of controversy in recent years, with some commentators holding them up as examples of the 'Mickey Mouse' vocational courses that proliferated under the 1997–2010 New Labour government.[179] In 2012, the Liberal Democrat/ Conservative coalition government announced that vocational and skills-based qualifications such as CoPE would not be included in school league tables from 2014, on the grounds that they have 'no equivalency' to traditional qualifications such as GCSEs, AS and A levels.[180]

However, there is evidence that these so-called 'Mickey Mouse' courses are more valuable than some politicians and newspaper headlines would have you believe. For example, a study of over half a million students carried out by researchers at the University of the West of England found that completing the ASDAN CoPE course was significantly associated with improved attainment in traditional subjects such as maths and English.[181] In particular, this study found that students who completed the Level 2 CoPE course had a 10% increased likelihood of achieving GCSE English at A* to C, and a 5% increased likelihood of achieving 5A*CEM compared with students in comparable schools not offering CoPE.

In particular, CoPE was found to benefit pupils with low Key Stage 3 attainment, those with special educational needs and disabilities, those from black and minority ethnic communities, and those eligible for free school meals. It is important to recognise that this study establishes correlation rather than causation. For example, it is possible that more able students also happened to sit the CoPE course. However, this does seem unlikely, since CoPE has traditionally been taken by lower achieving students. It therefore seems that regardless of the tough-sounding rhetoric about 'Mickey Mouse' courses, teaching students personal effectiveness and organisational skills may help them achieve higher grades in the more traditional, academic subjects that some politicians deem more worthwhile.

What does it look like in practice?

For budgetary reasons, we were not able to enter students to be accredited for the AoPE qualification. Instead, we used the AoPE specification as a guide, but did our own assessments and certification. To gain the AoPE qualification, students are required to produce a physical portfolio of evidence to show that they have met the success criteria relating to some or all of the following skills areas:

- Teamworking
- Planning and reviewing learning
- Dealing with problems in daily life
- Planning and carrying out research
- Group discussion
- Preparing for and giving a presentation
- Developing self

We mapped these against the six areas of the PSHE curriculum we planned to cover in year 8 (e.g. 'Teamworking' was Sex and Relationships Education, 'Planning and carryout out research' was Drugs Education and so on). Each project involved some teacher input – sharing high quality information and resources around sex and relationships education and drugs education, for example – before handing control of the project to the students. As well as fulfilling the project brief, students had to provide evidence that they had met a range of assessment criteria for each project. For example, the AoPE Level 2 assessment criteria for 'Teamworking' can be seen in Table 5.6.[182]

Table 5.6. Teamworking: assessment criteria

Learning outcomes *The learner will:*	Assessment criteria *The learner can:*
Plan how to work effectively with others	• Describe what makes groups or teams effective
	• Identify what the team needs to achieve together
	• Share relevant information to clarify what needs to be done, and individual responsibilities
	• Confirm the arrangements for working as a team
Work co-operatively towards achieving identified objectives	• Organise and carry out tasks to meet own responsibilities: a) safely b) using appropriate methods
	• Describe how individual behaviour can have a positive or a negative effect on a team achieving its objectives
	• Check progress, seeking advice from an appropriate person when required
	• Describe how he/she supports cooperative ways of working
Recognise own contribution to teamwork and agree ways to improve work with others	• Identify own role in helping to achieve things together
	• Share relevant information on what went well and less well when working with others
	• Explain how improved interpersonal skills could contribute to the effectiveness of group/teamwork in the future

These criteria could be met through a combination of written and verbal evidence. There were advantages and disadvantages to this approach. Having such a rigorous assessment framework required our students to develop their ability to manage their time and resources more effectively, including how to organise a ring binder!

Many of our students found organising a ring binder incredibly difficult, especially at first. It often felt like a thankless task to sit with them and help them organise their folder, only to look on in despair as they returned to a state of complete disorder – sometimes within a matter of minutes! In addition, the requirement to record written or verbal evidence for all the success criteria was burdensome for both students and teachers. There was too much emphasis on assessment and evidence, and not enough on the PSHE and learning skills. Upon reflection, we realised that perhaps we had set the bar too high: ASDAN recommends that their AoPE and CoPE courses are taken by students aged 14 or older. When it comes to organisational skills, there is a big difference between a 12-year-old and a 14-year-old!

We learned our lesson. The following year, instead of following the AoPE qualification, we created our own slimmed-down version of a personal effectiveness course. We still required the students to evidence their work in folders, but we returned to the form of assessment we used in year 7 (Distinction, Merit, Pass, Fail), with grades determined through a combination of peer-, self-and teacher-assessment. And although we still used the AoPE criteria, we would discuss them and use them formatively rather than as a summative checklist. This was vastly preferable, and we would advise other schools to beat their own path in this regard – especially at Key Stage 3.

As the *Learning Skills* curriculum expanded throughout the school, a number of our 6th form students went on to achieve the more challenging Level 3 CoPE and AoPE qualifications. We highly recommend these qualifications, as they encourage students to venture out of their comfort zones, to work collaboratively to solve problems, and to engage with their local communities in productive and creative ways.

OTHER GOOD IDEAS

A university professor once told us that the first question she asks in a PhD viva is: 'What would you do differently if you had your time again?' If the candidate can't answer this question convincingly, she fails them. She makes a good point: if you don't have any regrets, you're not paying attention. Having spent the last 15 years designing, teaching and now disseminating the *Learning Skills* approach, we have learned an incredible amount about ourselves, our students and about learning itself. But perhaps more than anything, we have learned how not to do things!

In this chapter, we have outlined in detail the components of the complex *Learning Skills* intervention as it existed after three years of research and development. We have also described how *Learning Skills* evolved from a year 7 transition initiative into a joined-up, whole-school approach to teaching and learning. However, there are a number of things that we didn't do in the Sea View pilot study that we now think would be worthy of consideration to anyone planning on implementing a *Learning Skills* curriculum.

In schools, time is the most precious resource of all, and it would not be advisable to implement a *Learning Skills* curriculum that incorporates everything we have covered in this chapter. That said, we will conclude this chapter by outlining a few more ideas that we think are worth thinking about should you find yourself in the priveleged position of implementing a *Learning Skills* curriculum of your own. The first of these, and the one we give the most space to because it's such an important topic, is self-regulation: monitoring and controlling our feelings and behaviours.

SELF-REGULATION

There comes a point where we need to stop just pulling people out of the river. We need to go upstream and find out why they're falling in.

Desmond Tutu

Rationale

To begin this section, here's another reminder of the model that reflects our current understanding of the difference between metacognition, self-regulation and self-regulated learning.

Figure 5.5. Metacognition, self-regulation and self-regulated learning

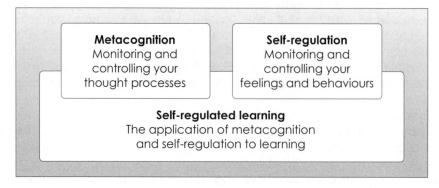

238

As we mentioned earlier, when we began the Sea View pilot study ten years ago, we didn't think about self-regulation in this way. This is not to say we didn't recognise the importance of emotional self-regulation. We understood that teaching children how to learn involves emotions as well as thoughts and behaviours, and much of the work we did reflected this understanding. For example, within the *Learning Skills* teaching team, we talked a lot about things like 'behaviour for learning', 'building trust' and 'creating positive relationships'. We understood the importance of getting to know our students through the learning journals. We set identity-based projects such as 'Who am I?' and interpersonal challenges such as the 7-day challenge. And we mixed up student groupings as much as possible so that students developed emotional resilience by stepping out of the apparent comfort of their friendship groups.

However, we didn't have the knowledge, understanding or vocabulary we now have about how the nervous system mediates our feelings and behaviours and how we can take control of our nervous system – and therefore our emotions and behaviours – as we will outline below. As a consequence, we didn't make self-regulation – monitoring and controlling our feelings and behaviours – explicit in our conversations with our pupils. Instead, when we talked about self-regulation, we talked about things like goal-setting, identifying strategies, reviewing progress and so on – what we now understand to be self-regulated learning.

We have since come to understand that if you really want your students to get better at learning stuff – and if you really want to get to the bottom of the endemic fear of failure that afflicts so many young people – it is important to be explicit about helping them learn to monitor and control their feelings and behaviours, just as it is important to help them monitor and control their calendars, to-do lists and ring binders. All too often, the emotional dimension of learning is overlooked in an education system that prioritises knowledge of subjects over knowledge of self. We aren't saying that schools *should* prioritise knowledge of self over knowledge of subjects. It's not an either/or thing. The question is: Have we got the balance right?

What does it look like in the classroom?

To help children learn to regulate their emotions and behaviours, we need to teach them a) how the nervous system functions to keep us safe; b) how our nervous systems can sometimes work against us; and c) how we can learn to monitor and control our nervous systems in order to regulate our feelings (and therefore our behaviours) on a deep level. To do this, we need to teach them about a few key concepts. Depending on the age of your students, you may wish to adapt the following information to suit their needs. Here we will give you the full-fat version as we currently understand it, although our ideas in this area are evolving all the time. In particular, we will look at seven key ideas:

- The zone
- Feelings come first
- We can learn to control our feelings - and therefore our behaviours
- The human brain vs the chimp brain
- The autonomic nervous system
- Fear of failure: an evolutionary hangover
- Manual overrides: mind, body, breath

Let's consider each in turn.

'The zone'

A useful way to start talking to children about self-regulation is to consider 'the zone'. It's not always clear what people mean when they speak of 'the zone', but everybody seems to accept a) that it exists, and b) that it's where you want to be. For example, if a student has an unusually successful lesson, their teacher might say, 'Wow, you are really in the zone today!' Conversely, if a student has experienced 'friendship issues' at lunchtime, or if there are challenging circumstances in their home life, for example, it might be extremely difficult for them to engage in their learning. They might try to focus, but find that they keep 'zoning out'.

At this point, three questions arise:

1. How can we make it so that students spend more time 'in the zone'?
2. How can students return to the zone if they have parted ways with it?
3. Are students' feelings and behaviours best regulated externally (e.g. through rewards and sanctions), or is it possible to teach them how to navigate their own way around 'the zone'?

Feelings come first

To answer these questions, it is important to distinguish between feelings (the internal self) and behaviours (the external self). Ultimately, self-regulation is about behaviour – making informed rather than impulsive choices about how we interact with the external environment. To make such informed choices, we need to understand that there is a wide range of behaviours from which we can choose – and that we don't always have to be the slave to our feelings. In the same way that not all of life's disappointments can be fixed with a stiff gin and tonic, not all difficulties in school require students to remove themselves from the situation by any means possible, whether that's by pretending to need the loo, going to sharpen their pencil six times a lesson, or swearing at the teacher to get themselves removed. To get to the point where we can take control of our behaviours, we need to understand that our behaviours are often driven by our feelings, whether we realise it or not. These can be physical feelings (I am hungry, I have butterflies in my stomach, I am too hot) or emotional feelings (I feel upset, I feel confused, I feel frustrated). In short: feelings come first.

The ability to regulate your feelings – both physical and emotional – is critical to becoming a more confident, effective, independent learner, because what you feel (or don't feel) significantly influences your ability to learn stuff. Our thoughts are not separate from our feelings. The two are integrated, and each has the power to affect the other. When we are angry or afraid, an overwhelmed or hyper-aroused nervous system restricts the blood supply to certain parts of the brain, reducing the choices available to us. This is what happens when people 'lose it' or 'see red'.

Conversely, a brain that senses threat (whether real or imagined) will set your heart racing, make your breathing shallower and get your muscles primed for action. Such biological responses are hard-wired, having evolved over millennia to keep us safe from harm. But we don't have to remain their slave. Understanding how the nervous system works helps us learn to recognise the early signs of such hard-wired responses, to develop strategies to remain in the zone for longer, and to return to the zone when we are feeling overwhelmed.

We can learn to control our feelings and therefore our behaviours

Schools are always going to need rules, and the teacher is always going to be the adult in the room. But it is possible to build a classroom culture where students work toward mutually agreed goals, individually and collectively, without the need for a teacher to monitor and control their behaviour externally by continually administering rewards and consequences. We know this because we have worked in such classrooms, and now we help others build them too. A self-regulated classroom does not undermine the authority of the teacher; it reduces the need for it.

We can't give you a wand that will magically transform your students into self-regulated learners. But we can give you some tips on how to teach them in such a way that they learn to do it for themselves. Just as we can control our physical feelings (I am too hot → take your blazer off, open a window, drink some water), so we can control our emotional feelings (I fear failure → talk it through, take a measured risk, reframe failure as feedback).

When we teach students how to monitor and control their feelings – and when we give them opportunities to practise the techniques we will outline below – they develop the ability to regulate the internal workings of their minds, guts and nervous systems, to regulate how they respond to the external environment, and to get from where they are to where they want to be without ever losing the feeling of being in control.

The reason there isn't a magic wand is that, as the name would suggest, self-regulation is something that you can only do for yourself. As with many aspects of Learning to Learn, developing self-regulation involves making the implicit processes of learning explicit, and then providing students with regular, low-stakes opportunities to develop, practise and rehearse a range of strategies that work for them. Too often, we 'administer' self-regulation to young people in schools, instead of finding ways for them to develop these skills for themselves. This can easily backfire. For example, if you tell a young person in full-blown fight-or-flight mode to 'take a deep breath' or 'count to ten', you may very well find that your well-meaning intervention makes things worse. Similarly, telling a flustered child that they should 'have a growth mindset' is more likely to make them inwardly flinch than to quietly resolve to take heed of your wise words.

Depending on how an individual is wired, they may need to devise their own solutions to their own unique experiences. You can't force someone to self-regulate by telling them what to do when they are overwhelmed. First, we may have to co-regulate – modelling and practicing strategies with them – before withdrawing that support over time. Before we outline some practical strategies for how co-regulation and self-regulation can be achieved, we need to step inside the body to look at what is going on when a student has become so overwhelmed that they have parted company with 'the zone'. In particular, we'll look at two related ideas that are really helpful to understand: the human brain vs the chimp brain, and the autonomic nervous system.

The 'human brain' and the 'chimp brain'

In his 2012 book *The Chimp Paradox*, the psychiatrist Dr Steve Peters proposed a powerful model for explaining how our brains work – and why they often do things we don't want them to do.[183] Peters suggests that we can view the brain as comprising two distinct entities, each capable of independent thought and action: the human and the chimp. The 'human brain' is a conscious, thoughtful, analytical entity that is concerned with things like facts, narratives and logical thinking. This is the bit that you often think of as 'you'. When the human brain is online, you have the sense that you are in control.

The 'chimp brain', on the other hand, is very much not under your command. The chimp trades in emotions and instinct; at any given moment, the chimp can hijack the steering wheel and act on your behalf, without your permission. This can happen in any number of ways. Imagine you have to give a presentation as part of a job interview. You spend hours preparing it, and practise it to within an inch of its life. That night, you go to bed early – but you can't sleep. Your mind starts racing, thinking of all the ways in which your presentation could go wrong. You try some strategies to calm you down – a body scan or a breathing exercise, perhaps. Eventually, it works and you grab a few precious hours of sleep. The next morning, you have a strong coffee and get ready for the interview. It seems to be going well – but as you start your presentation, your tongue suddenly becomes unbelievably dry. You pause to take a sip of water. As you do so, you feel yourself blushing. When you restart your presentation, you find that your polished words are somehow beyond your grasp. You miss out a whole section, and to make up the time, on the spur of the moment you find yourself telling a loosely related story that wasn't part of the plan at all…

No wonder so many people have a fear of public speaking! In this example, for reasons real or imagined (in this case, firstly imagined and then all-too-real), the chimp brain feels threatened by the impending presentation and starts pulling all kinds of levers that cause all manner of trouble. No sleep… dry mouth… sudden tangents… thanks a bunch, brain!

Other classic chimp behaviours include finding yourself halfway through a packet of biscuits that you intended to leave unopened… impulsive online purchases that you can't really afford… and, perhaps the uber-example, road rage. The chimp brain is the reason supermarkets put chocolate by the checkout: your human brain can steer you clear of the chocolate aisle, but when temptation is within arm's reach, your chimp brain can hijack such lofty ambitions in a heartbeat. In short, things don't tend to pan out terribly well when chimps are at the helm – and, if left untrained, chimps can take that helm whenever and wherever they choose.

To return to the classroom, imagine a student is being distracted from their work by something – their neighbour is tapping their pen, or talking off-task, or trying to get their attention while the teacher is talking. They could react in a rational, proactive way – using a non-verbal signal to tell the student to stop, or alerting the teacher to the annoyance by asking to move seats, perhaps. Instead, they decide to ignore the distraction. It works for a while, but suddenly they snap. They turn and swear at the person causing the annoyance, and suddenly find themselves in trouble with the teacher. They find themselves getting told off for something that wasn't really their fault, and understandably feel hard done by. 'But *they* were talking...this is SO UNFAIR' is a catchphrase that will perhaps be familiar to every teacher who ever existed. How quickly chimps can send things spiralling out of control!

To understand the 'human vs chimp' dichotomy on a deeper level, we will now look at what's going on inside the body when we are struggling to remain 'in the zone'.

The autonomic nervous system

Without wishing to get too technical – and to simultaneously risk offending any neuroscience purists reading this – the 'human brain' is primarily situated in the prefrontal cortex, the area of the brain that sits behind the forehead. This is the region of the brain that allows us to think and reason, concentrate, set goals, form strategies, make links, and learn stuff. It is also where we can learn to control our impulses, feelings and behaviours. Some people are better at doing this than others, but we can all get better at it; as with most things, improvement comes with practice.

The prefrontal cortex is the part of the brain that evolved the most recently. There are, however, other parts of the brain that are much older, evolutionarily speaking, which have been keeping our ancestors safe for millions of years – long before we started doing clever things like speaking and writing and going to school. These older parts of the brain are home to the autonomic nervous system.

The autonomic (think automatic) nervous system regulates things within our bodies like heart rate, digestion, breathing, and so on. It works a bit like an autonomous car, with an accelerator and a brake pedal that are activated in response to external stimuli. The accelerator is known as the sympathetic nervous system (SNS) and the brake pedal is known as the parasympathetic nervous system (PNS).

The SNS is activated in response to stress or physical exertion: our pupils dilate, we take faster, shallower breaths, our heart rate increases and the blood moves away from our gut and out to the muscles, ready for action. When gently activated, this is sometimes referred to as being in 'run and fun' mode. This is the children doing their thing in the playground at lunchtime. When strongly activated, however, the SNS can trigger a 'fight and flight' response. When you're about to be eaten or attacked by something with sharp teeth and claws, you either need to hurt it or exit the scene, pronto – and it may even be wise to do both.

The PNS does all the opposite stuff to the SNS, and is activated when we're chilling out: our pupils contract, we take slower, deeper breaths, our heart rate slows, and the blood flow returns from the muscles to the gut to aid digestion. When gently activated, this is sometimes referred to as being in 'rest and digest' mode. This is the children back in the classroom, ready to learn, having burned off a few calories in the playground. However, the PNS can also be strongly activated in response to stress, triggering a kind of shutdown that is sometimes referred to as 'freeze/faint', 'rabbit in the headlights' or 'playing dead'.

Central to all of this is the amygdala, a kind of sensor in the brain that continually scans the environment for threats to safety. If it senses a threat, the amygdala can 'hijack' your mind and override whatever you're doing – there is danger, and to remain safe you either need to fight, run or freeze. When you walk into a room that you thought was empty, suddenly see someone and jump out of your skin – that's your amygdala trying to keep you safe, albeit with hilarious consequences.

By way of analogy, it is useful to think of your brain as being a bit like a computer. If your laptop has 18 browser tabs and eight applications open, two movies downloading, email notifications pinging, and perhaps background music on, it is likely that it will slow down and perhaps even crash. Similarly, a pupil might have many 'browser tabs' open at any one time. These might be things such as friendship issues, forgotten PE kits, arguing parents, a younger sibling that they care for, a looming maths test, feeling hungry – and so on. All of this can place an incredible load on the autonomic nervous system, which wants to minimise stress and keep them safe. If a child becomes overwhelmed and the SNS/chimp response is activated, they might shout, swear or punch a nearby wall. If the PNS response is activated, they might become incredibly quiet and withdrawn.

To return to the idea of 'the zone', we can visualise the autonomic nervous system as a kind of sine wave, with 'run and fun' and 'rest and digest' within the normal parameters of a healthy, functioning nervous system, and 'fight and flight' and 'freeze and faint' at either extreme (see Figure

5.6). When you're in the zone – whether in 'run and fun' or 'rest and digest' mode – you can access the 'human brain' and think, reason and learn effectively. However, when your nervous system becomes overwhelmed or dysregulated – whether through fight/flight or freeze/faint – your human brain gets hijacked by your chimp, amygdala, call it what you will, and you find that you are no longer 'in the zone'.

Figure 5.6. 'The zone'

Fight & flight

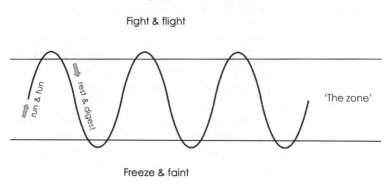

'The zone'

Freeze & faint

A well-regulated nervous system is able to effectively go up and down with the ebb and flow of a day's events and all communications channels remain open. When the prefrontal cortex is online and firing on all cylinders, we can look people in the eye, we have access to the full range of our vocabulary, and we can speak, move and gesture freely because we feel safe in our surroundings. A well-regulated nervous system is able to take a human being from a thrilling roller-coaster ride into a deep meditation without ever losing control of their mental faculties.

A dysregulated nervous system is not able to do these things. It gets overwhelmed easily and pulls primitive levers to take evasive action. It can find direct eye contact threatening and it can make us tongue-tied and feeling physically self-conscious. When our nervous systems are overwhelmed, every new person and request on our time or attention can feel like a potential threat. In the parlance of our times, a person in this state may find that they are easily 'triggered'. When this happens, the chimp brain leaps into the driving seat and we see the kinds of impulsive, out-of-control behaviours we described above.

To recap: the chimp brain is a hard-wired, defensive reflex mechanism that can override our mental and physical faculties in order to keep us safe. When there's a threat to your safety, there's no need to involve the human brain in decision-making. Humans dither. Chimps act fast. This is really helpful if your house is on fire, or if there's a lion in the vicinity. Not so long ago, that split-second dither might have been the difference between being lion lunch and surviving long enough to pass on your genes.

In evolutionary terms, humans have only been at the top of the food chain for the blink of an eye. Unhelpfully, our nervous systems haven't had an upgrade since being eaten by a lion was the biggest threat to our existence, and so our autonomic nervous systems are constantly bypassing our human brain and activating our defence mechanisms if any threat is sensed. There doesn't need to be an actual threat, just a sense of one, for these mechanisms to be triggered.

Fear of failure: an evolutionary hangover

What does all this have to do with teaching children how to get better at learning stuff and helping them overcome a fear of failure? Well, in schools we often see children exhibiting 'fight/flight' and 'freeze/faint' type behaviours – especially among younger children, although these responses can persist into adulthood. Often, these extreme responses can be triggered by what may seem to be perfectly innocuous stimuli – try this maths problem, read something to the class, go and fetch the felt tips from the other side of the room. A teacher's instruction that might seem harmless and even fun to one child might very well strike fear into the heart of another. When children melt down over seemingly inconsequential things, it can seem irrational and extreme, and that's because it is. But when a child's amygdala has sensed a threat – whether that threat is real, imagined or overblown – the subjective, emotional response is all too real.

When you ask a student to look you in the eye and they don't, that might be wilfully defiant behaviour. However, it might also be the case that their ability to engage in prosocial behaviour – located in their prefrontal cortex – is not currently available to them. If they are in 'freeze/faint' mode, they may want to make themselves look as small and non-threatening as possible. Their shoulders hunch, their head dips down, and they look at the floor until the threat has passed. Looking an adult in the eye is the last thing they want to do.

Looking an adult in the eye isn't a smart move when you're in 'fight/flight' mode, either. You might give away your intention. The teacher doesn't pose a real threat (one would hope!), but the child's autonomic nervous system is pretty convinced that they represent one. Chimps don't deal in reason. Afterwards, when they can finally talk about what happened, if they tell you that they don't know why they swore/kicked the chair over/ walked out, they may not be being deliberately obtuse. It's unlikely that they will have run through a series of options and chosen their course of action with their human brain: 'Hmmm, shall I swear, kick the chair or slam the door...? Decisions, decisions... I know, why not all three!' Instead, it will probably feel to them like it 'just happened'. Losing control in this way can feel very frightening.

To be clear, we are not condoning or excusing fight/flight behaviours in the classroom or indeed in the wider society. However, helping children understand why our bodies have evolved with these defence mechanisms – and how they can kick in at unhelpful times – can help them shift their thinking from the passenger seat to the driving seat. They learn to monitor and control their feelings and to take ownership and responsibility for their actions. They begin to recognise their early warning signs and to learn how to put their chimp back in its box before it can grab hold of the steering wheel.

For one person, an early warning sign might be using stronger language than usual. For others, it's feeling twitchy or irritable. For others still, it might be that they aren't able to find the words they want to use, or that they can't pay attention to what people are saying. Unless children learn to monitor and respond to these early signs, many of these subtle cues go unnoticed, and it isn't until a rage erupts or they find themselves having a heated argument they don't really care about or crumple into a heap of tears on the floor that they realise their nervous systems have become overwhelmed. The journey to that point has probably been significant; they just didn't notice the signs early enough to change course.

Fear of failure is perhaps the ultimate example of a chimp behaviour that we see in the classroom. From when they are very young, children are often told things like, 'We learn from our mistakes', 'FAIL stands for First Attempt In Learning', or, 'If at first you don't succeed, try, try and try again'. Despite this, as we have seen, many young people silently carry around with them a paralysing fear of failure. They will tear a page out of their exercise book and write it out again rather than have a single word crossed out. They will sit before a blank sheet of paper for half a lesson – not out of laziness, but because as soon as they commit pen to paper, they run the risk of making a mistake. When revising, many children either just read the revision guide or copy out pages of notes rather than putting it in their own words or trying to summarise the key points, because the version in the revision guide is the 'perfect version' – at least in their eyes – and in translation or summation lies the risk of introducing an error or an omission.

When a child is in the grip of fear of failure, they may not realise it on a conscious level, but on an unconscious level, they have detected a perceived risk – 'I might get it wrong and people will laugh', for example – and this can trigger a range of behaviours designed to avoid that possibility at all costs. This is not a fight-or-flight, hungry lion, life-in-danger situation. It's more like, 'There is a low-level risk that I might get this wrong. People might laugh. Take evasive action'.

Say the teacher asks a question, and a student is confident that they know the answer. They go to raise their hand, but at the last minute their heart skips a beat and so they keep their hand down. The student's 'human brain' understands that this is not a life-or-death situation – after all, they are confident that they know the answer, and even if they do make a mistake, nothing really bad is going to happen. And there are upsides either way: if they get it right, they confirm to their teacher and to themselves that they are on the right track, and perhaps grow a little in confidence; and if they get it wrong, they receive valuable feedback that will help them understand the world better in future. But chimps do not deal in logic. Instead, the 'chimp brain' catastrophises the situation such that no matter how low-level the threat, it will avoid detection at all costs. And so the student chooses not to raise their hand – even when they *know* they know the answer. They play it safe.

In most cases, fear of failure does not trigger the kind of extreme responses we described above. The child does not enter a catatonic state, and nor do they tend to flee the classroom, slamming the door off its hinges. Instead, we see dysfunctional microbehaviours. They sit with their pen hovering over the page, looking like they're working when really they're afraid of having a go at something they aren't sure about in case they make a mistake. They procrastinate, they glance at what their neighbour is doing, they change the subject. They spend half the lesson colouring in the title of a poster they're making – and start all over again if they 'go over the line'. We often tell children they should take risks, but taking risks literally means risking failure – and many children will engage in all sorts of tricks, habits and routines to prevent this from happening.

Some of this stuff can be regulated by the teacher. For example, by setting clear expectations in combination with tight classroom management, you can make sure your students don't spend half a lesson colouring in bubble writing. But that's external regulation, which solves the problem in the short term and deepens it in the long term. The question is: what can teachers do to help children learn to regulate *their own* feelings and behaviours so that they are more willing to take risks and spend more time in the zone – and so that they know how to return to the zone when they become emotionally (and therefore behaviourally) dysregulated?

Manual overrides: mind, body, breath

The good news is that teaching children how to monitor and control their feelings and behaviours is actually quite straightforward. As with many aspects of Learning to Learn, we can teach self-regulation using the traditional teaching cycle: explain, model, practise, feedback, repeat. There are three key elements.

1. Teach them a child-friendly version of the above. Talk about chimps, humans, lions, internet browsers, fear of failure – whatever it takes to help them understand how the human nervous system can override our minds and that we can take back control if we know how.
2. Carve out some time for self-regulation each week: time to teach your pupils a range of strategies; time for them to try them out; time to write, think, reflect, discuss, receive and respond to feedback. We recommend a weekly 'check in' of around 10 to 15 minutes.
3. As adults, we need to walk the talk. If we aren't modelling self-regulation – if we aren't explicitly demonstrating what it looks like on a daily basis – then the children are going to struggle with it far more than if they have a model of good practice to emulate.

When teachers are 'in the zone', we can work countless minor miracles every day. A pause, a look, a quiet word of appreciation – all of these microbehaviours keep things ticking along, de-escalating potential flare-ups and averting problems before they even arise. Among experienced teachers, much of this becomes automated. We do it without thinking. When our pre-frontal cortex is fully online, we can achieve a state of 'flow' where we can access all of our prosocial tricks, habits, strategies and tools without breaking a sweat. But teaching can be a tough gig, and nobody is superhuman. Sometimes we get overwhelmed too – and students know this better than anyone.

Consider the following scenario: two pupils enter a lesson late, laughing. An overwhelmed teacher might snap, 'How dare you come in late, disturbing the start of my lesson? The exam's in two weeks and we haven't even covered all the material yet! Go out and walk in again, in silence this time!' Suddenly, 28 pupils who were thinking about their starter task are now focused on a psychodrama that these two latecomers and the teacher have co-created – and the teacher has modelled to the children that snapping is something that adults do. The students also probably feel slightly more anxious about the upcoming exam. We have certainly both been this teacher – too many times.

On another day, when the teacher is 'in the zone', they might instead respond by saying, 'Wow, you're in a good mood today. Settle down quickly please – I'll speak to you later about why you were late.' This sends a very different message – that as an adult, you are positive, upbeat, not rattled by disruptions, that even latecomers are welcomed to your lesson – but also that you are no pushover, and that you will pick them up on their lateness at a time of your choosing. It reassures the students that you are in control and that they can feel safe, relax and focus on their learning. We aren't saying that all teachers should be 'in the zone' for 100% of the time. But if you ever find yourself snapping at a pupil – or even just wanting to – you should probably recognise that as an early warning sign that your own nervous system is getting a bit jittery and that it would be a good idea to hit the reset button fairly soon.

All of us – adults and children alike – need to learn how to recognise the signs that can alert us to the fact that we may be heading down an unhelpful path. Fortunately, this is quite easy to do, because our mental and emotional state is often reflected in our bodies, although precisely how this happens varies from one person to another. Stress might manifest as a furrowed brow; a clenched jaw; hunched shoulders; a tight chest; shallow breathing; acid reflux; fidgety fingers; jittery legs; tapping feet. In contrast, a relaxed, confident state of mind might manifest as a spring in your step; smiling a lot; singing; making jokes or using playful language; moving lightly on your feet; even dancing.

Our bodies not only provide us with a set of clues and cues as to our emotional state; they also provide us with a set of levers for controlling our thoughts and feelings. Mind–body duality is a two-way street. When we learn to observe and notice our telltale tics and early warning signs, this provides us with a clue as to what action to take.

There are three broad categories of moves we can make to reset our nervous systems: the mind, the body and the breath. People usually have a preference for one over the others. It's likely that you already have strategies that you use to keep yourself 'in the zone': things like walking the long way round to the staff room so as to stretch your legs at breaktime; going to the gym or a yoga class after work; or walking away from a confrontation when you feel your blood rising. The wider your repertoire of such strategies, the easier you will find it to stay 'in the zone' when life becomes challenging – as life tends to do from time to time.

The mind, the body and the breath are inextricably linked. Your breathing affects how you think and feel; your thoughts affect how you breathe and feel; and your feelings affect how you breathe and think. The key is finding ways to monitor and control all three so that they work to your advantage. There is no 'right answer' and no universal formula for success – each of us finds some techniques more powerful than others. The more you find what works for you, the better you get at self-regulating and co-regulating with others. In this way, you can model and explain aspects of self-regulation to your students so that they too can learn how to monitor and control their internal and external worlds.

In our workshops, we teach people a range of techniques for how to regulate their feelings and behaviours through the mind, body and breath. There isn't space to explore this in detail here, but here are a few 'quick fixes' that we and others have found useful. In each case, it is useful to think about self-regulation in three stages: tune in → monitor over time → take action.

Breath:

First, bring your attention to the breath. How are you breathing currently? Don't change your breathing yet – just observe what it is doing over time, or at different times in the day. Is it fast or slow? Deep or shallow? Loud or silent? Is it different in the morning from the afternoon? How about before, during and after meals? If you notice that your breathing has become shallow or fast, you can fix this easily by exhaling for longer than you inhale: in for 4, out for 6. This is how we breathe when we are at rest, and when we're about to fall asleep. We don't tend to fall asleep when we feel unsafe, so longer exhalations are a safety cue.

There is an excellent short video online of Dr Andrew Weil demonstrating a variation on this exercise (the 4–8–7 technique, where you inhale through your nose for 4, hold for 8 and exhale through your mouth for 7).[184] It can send you straight off to sleep with a little practice. Alternatively, if you need waking up, you might wish to reverse the order of longer/shorter timings; a few 7–8–4 breaths, for example, can be the equivalent of nature's Red Bull.[185]

Body:

Start by checking in. How do you feel physically? How do you feel emotionally? Where does stress or tension manifest in your body? Is it in the neck? Back? Stomach? Shoulders? Jaw? If you do this regularly, you will start to notice patterns. What does your body tend to do? What does your body want to do? How does it feel at different times of the day, week or term? How does this relate to movement or to how you sit when you're at a desk?

Noticing how your body feels over time will help inform the kinds of activities you can do when you need to refresh or reboot your nervous system. Introducing simple movements can help to shift your thoughts, feelings and energy. You might choose to focus a stretch or a repetitive motion on the area of your body where stress manifests. Experiment with a few simple, physical routines that give you a sense of physical wellbeing – rolling your neck or wrist, stretching the backs of your legs, twisting your spine, pushing your feet into the floor, balancing on one leg, taking a short walk – whatever works for you.

Mind:

Again, begin by noticing your current state of mind. Are your thoughts racing, are you perfectly alert, or are you staring into space and finding it difficult to concentrate? Are you mulling over past events or worrying about the future? Try to 'sit behind' your thoughts – observe them as they come and go. How do your thought patterns change at different times in the day?

If we notice that our internal dialogue is becoming more negative than normal – thinking *I can't do this anymore*, playing out conflict scenarios, or thinking of all the ways in which we have made a fool of ourselves recently – there are many simple techniques we can use to divert our train of thought onto a more healthy, helpful track. For example, we can 'flip the script' by reframing our negative thoughts with some positive self-talk (*I am useless at X* → *I am really good at A, B, C…*). We can write down our catastrophic predictions about the future – a powerful technique for helping us realise how unlikely it is that the worst case scenario will actually come to pass. And we can detach from our unhelpful thoughts and observe them as they go sailing off into the distance.

These 'quick fixes' exemplify three powerful manual override levers with which we can regulate our feelings, and therefore our behaviours: the mind, the body and the breath. The common thread is that in each of these examples, we are bringing ourselves into the moment. This is really helpful, because whatever might be on your mind – past events you are mulling over or concerns about the future – it is very unlikely that you are actually in any real and present danger. This has the effect of sending a message to your autonomic nervous system: whatever else might be going on, you are currently safe from threat. Your chimp gets back in his or her box and you can return to the zone where learning, thinking and prosocial behaviour can flourish.

In sum

Learning is not something that occurs in a disembodied state. In fact, our ability to learn stuff is powerfully determined by our sense of physical and emotional wellbeing. And learning itself can be an incredibly emotive process – from the frustration, despair and anger that we can feel when we find something difficult to the elation, satisfaction and exhilaration of reaching a goal we have worked our socks off to achieve.

Therefore, if we really want children to maximise their ability to learn stuff, we have to pay attention to the self-regulation of feelings and behaviours. We need to teach children how their nervous system works, how it can sometimes work against them, and how they can use the manual override levers of the mind, the body and the breath to get themselves back on track when they notice the early warning signs that they might be feeling overwhelmed or under threat. We also need to regularly provide students with the time and support they need to monitor, explore and discuss their feelings and behaviours – and to practise using those manual override levers – to enable them to build up a repertoire of tried and tested strategies that they can draw upon when the chips are down.

We understand that for many teachers, teaching self-regulation is beyond their comfort zone. We also appreciate that there is a big difference between primary and secondary school teachers with regard to self-regulation, because a secondary school teacher will typically see a pupil for two or three hours a week, compared with 25 hours for a primary school teacher.

If you're a secondary school teacher and you just want to teach your subject, that's great – we need teachers who are passionate about their subjects! However, we also need teachers who are passionate about teaching children how to regulate their feelings and behaviours, how to speak and listen effectively, how to organise their time and resources, and so on. This is another strong argument for having timetabled *Learning Skills* lessons in secondary schools, taught by teachers who understand and believe in the importance and the efficacy of this stuff.

In the remainder of this chapter, we will outline a few more ideas for things we might have considered including in the *Learning Skills* curriculum at Sea View, had we known ten years ago what we know now. We will keep these fairly brief.

META-MEMORY AND META-LEARNING

Since the *Learning Skills* curriculum started in 2010, there has been a groundswell of interest in cognitive science in education. A recent review of selected reading published by the Chartered College of Teaching provides an excellent summary of the field, with dozens of articles, blogs and podcasts exploring things like retrieval practice, cognitive load theory and Rosenshine's principles of instruction.[186] As well as the modest explosion in the literature on cognitive science – much of which has been written by serving or former teachers – several grassroots organisations have also emerged in this area, providing research summaries and practical resources for teachers.[187, 188, 189]

Rather like Learning to Learn in the 1950s, the current wave of interest in cognitive science – and, in particular, memory – is predominantly aimed at teachers, as a lens through which to view curriculum planning, pedagogy and assessment. However, there is good reason to believe that teaching pupils about memory – developing their so-called meta-memory – is a good idea also, and a *Learning Skills* taught course would be ideally suited to this purpose.[190]

Meta-memory is defined by Dunlosky and Bjork (2008) as 'people's knowledge of, monitoring of, and control of their own learning and memory processes'.[191] It is a sub-set of metacognition – and like metacognition, the word was coined by our old friend John Flavell, in response to the genius question, 'What is memory development the development of?'[192] Flavell responded:

> *It seems in large part to be the development of intelligent structuring and storage of input, of intelligent search and retrieval operations, and of intelligent monitoring and knowledge of these storage and retrieval operations – a kind of 'meta-memory', perhaps.*[193]

Perhaps unsurprisingly, there is evidence that teaching children how their memory works helps them remember stuff better. For example, a 2009 review of the literature found abundant evidence of a correlation between memory and meta-memory, and concluded that 'with help, children can improve their metamemory skills and, thus, become better learners.'[194]

So teaching children about how memory works seems to be a no-brainer. As Kirschner, Sweller and Clark (2006) suggested: 'if nothing has changed in long-term memory, nothing has been learned'.[195] However, we would go further than teaching children about meta-memory. It may be true that learning requires a change in long-term memory, but there is more to learning than memorising stuff. A *lot* more. Recently, James compiled a glossary of 225 learning terms.[196] The list is not comprehensive – far from it – but the range of concepts and ideas in the glossary, from 'Accidental Learning' to 'the Zone of Proximal Development', powerfully illustrates just how complex and multifaceted learning is.[197] This glossary – or an edited version of it – would be an excellent stimulus for a student research project into how learning happens – including, but not limited to, how memory works.

Thus, the effort to develop children's meta-memory should be couched within what Chris Watkins refers to as meta-learning. Drawing the distinction between metacognition and meta-learning, Watkins (2001) describes metacognition as 'awareness of thinking processes, and executive control of such processes', while 'meta-learning (making sense of one's experience of learning)… covers a much wider range of issues than metacognition, including goals, feelings, social relations and context of learning'.[198] A student-led, six-week research project on meta-learning – including, but not limited to, meta-memory – would be a wonderful thing to include in any future iteration of the *Learning Skills* curriculum.

TOUCH-TYPING

Why are all children not taught to touch-type at school? It's a mystery. Not only does touch-typing save a tonne of time, but there is also evidence that it has knock-on benefits, including improved quality of writing,[199, 200] performance on standardised tests[201] and improved spelling and narrative writing skills.[202] Being able to touch-type also significantly reduces the cognitive load on a student as they write: they're more likely to be able to reach for that searching metaphor if they aren't simultaneously searching for the 'R' key.

The problem with learning to touch-type is that it's repetitive and therefore a bit boring, and children tend not to do boring, repetitive things under their own steam. This is why touch-typing should be taught in schools. If there's one things schools are good at, it's getting children to learn and do things that they wouldn't otherwise learn and do. There are some excellent websites that can help you learn to touch-type. *Typing Club* seems to be a particularly good one – there are lots of slick videos and interactive exercises, you can set up a profile to track your progress, and it's free, although there's also a paid version that allows schools to track their students' progress.[203]

van Weerdenburg et al. (2019) suggest that you can teach children to touch-type in around 15 to 20 lessons, and that it's best done when they're aged around 10 to 12.[204] It is also necessary for them to practise for around 20 minutes each day during this period. This is a fairly significant time investment – but, when we consider the evidence that teaching children to touch-type leads to the improved outcomes listed above, it is likely that over the course of a school (and indeed work) career, this investment would repay itself many times over. In total, children take part in over 10,000 lessons over the course of a school career. Surely we can spare 15 to 20 lessons to teach them a skill that will set them up for life?

DIGITAL LITERACY

We are currently living through a period of unprecedented transformation in the way we consume news media - and information more widely. In this post-truth age of deep fakes, fake news and 'alternative facts', it is incredibly important that all people – young and old – learn how to navigate the daily deluge of emotive adverts, biased reporting and downright propaganda, how to locate reliable sources of information, and how to tell when they are being lied to or manipulated.

Recent research carried out by Sam Wineburg and colleagues at Stanford University focused on helping students learn how to do just this.[205, 206] The researchers found that young people are often too trusting of what they read on the internet – assuming that the first hit on a search engine is the most reliable source, for example, when in fact search results can vary significantly depending on where you are, your online behaviour profile and your internet search history.

The research team developed a curriculum of strategies for helping students learn how to identify more reliable sources of information. These include 'reading laterally' (judging the credibility of a website from other sources); showing 'click restraint' (scanning a range of search results before choosing one); and referring to the 'talk' page on Wikipedia, which often includes informative discussions of controversial or contested topics. When these strategies are taught to students, the researchers found that they 'arrive at more warranted conclusions in a fraction of the time'.[207]

Writing about Wineburg's research, Daniel Willingham commented:

I've been very skeptical of 21st century skills... My skepticism grew out what I perceived as a neglect of domain knowledge among the proponents of 21st century skills and (to a lesser extent) a sense that the truly new part of '21st century' is a relatively small part of what students need to learn: most of students' time should be devoted to math, science, reading, civics, history, etc., much the way it looked in the 20th century. Sam Wineburg's recent research shows that I was wrong... I think my assessment of 21st century skills as a small part of what students need to know was inaccurate, because evaluating sources on the internet is such a substantial part of student work today.[208]

As Willingham points out here, given how big a role the internet plays in a young person's education and the formation of their worldview, teaching students strategies for fact-checking and evaluating online sources is an example of a generic skill that a) can reliably be taught, and b) is likely to contribute significantly to a young person's educational attainment over the course of their school career.

These are promising findings. However, there is more to digital literacy than reading laterally, click restraint and checking the Wikipedia 'talk page'. Finland leads the world in terms of fighting the good fight against fake news, and their success has been attributed to the explicit teaching of critical thinking as a pre-International Baccalaureate course.[209] So studying digital literacy as part of a wider taught course in critical thinking seems to be a sensible idea, as well as ensuring that both are embedded, at least to some extent, across the curriculum. As ever, strategies also need to be in place to ensure that these skills transfer from one context to another.

SELF-AUTHORING

Although we focused on a different subject each week in the learning journal sessions, our pupils sometimes complained that it was a bit repetitive, writing about similar things from one session to the next. This was kind of the point – we really wanted to hammer it home in order for the transfer to happen – but it's possible that we over-egged the pudding in this regard, and that we could have embraced a wider variety of writing exercises in these sessions.

Since the Sea View pilot study ended, we have learned of other kinds of autobiographical writing that appear to have an incredibly profound impact across a wide range of outcomes. In particular, an approach known as 'self-authoring' looks like it might be worth exploring. Self-authoring is a variation on the idea of expressive writing – an approach developed by the social psychologist James W. Pennebaker that we discussed earlier in the chapter – and comprises three broad activities: past authoring, present authoring and future authoring.

In past authoring, you divide up your life to date into different sections and write about the defining events of each period. Past authoring might be difficult to do with children, partly because their lives have been short so far, but also because past authoring can prompt people to revisit challenging, painful or traumatic experiences. We would advise extreme caution before embarking on past authoring with children, and recommend limiting their focus to their school life, for example. However, present and future authoring look like they might be simpler to implement.

Present authoring is essentially a kind of SWOT analysis (strengths, weaknesses, opportunities, threats), where you write about what you see as your faults and virtues. In the faults section, you take a long, hard look at yourself – warts and all – and take responsibility for any areas where you feel you currently fall short. You then identify strategies for improving on your shortcomings. In the virtues section, you write about your strengths, and consider how you might build on these to help yourself and others in the future.

In the future authoring exercise, you divide up your life into different areas – friends, finances, career, etc. – and envisage what it would be like a) if your life went unbelievably well, and b) if your life went unbelievably badly. In this way, you build up a richly detailed picture of where you'd like to end up, and of what to steer clear of along the way.

Self-authoring has been studied fairly extensively, albeit mainly with undergraduates, and it has been found to lead to improved academic attainment and reduced drop-out rates.[210, 211, 212] We think it could be really valuable to adapt this approach to a school setting, as an exercise for students to work on as they begin their secondary education. It would also be interesting to revisit the exercise later on – say in years 9 and 11, before they choose their options for GCSE and A level – to enable students to explore whether and how their values, beliefs and ambitions change over time.

METACOGNITION A–Z

In 2019, a fantastic little volume was published called *Thinking Moves A to Z: Metacognition made simple*.[213] It's a brilliant resource that we wish had been around ten years ago as a tool for helping ensure that metacognition is a) understood in practical terms, and b) embedded across the curriculum.

The book outlines 26 'thinking moves' – one for each letter of the alphabet. Whenever we hear of things like this, we're usually pretty sceptical. The universe does not organise itself into alphabets or acronyms, and all too often, such things are an attempt to shoe-horn ideas into a memorable format for little gain. But *Thinking Moves A to Z* might just be the exception that proves the rule.

What's great about this approach is that it focuses on a number of practical 'moves' to help children learn to navigate the world of thoughts, ideas and beliefs. We can't do justice to the book here, but here's the alphabet, with an example of a coaching question you might ask to stimulate metacognitive processing among your pupils:

A   AHEAD *What do you think will happen?*
B   BACK *What were the last two ideas?*
C   CONNECT *How do those connect?*
D   DIVIDE *How is that different?*
E   EXPLAIN *How do you mean?*
F   FORMULATE *What ideas have people got?*
G   GROUP *How would you sort these into groups?*
H   HEADLINE *How would you say that in one sentence?*
I   INFER *If that's true, what else is true?*
J   JUSTIFY *Can you say why?*
K   KEYWORD *Which five words are most important here?*
L   LISTEN/LOOK *What do you notice?*
M   MAINTAIN *Who is a 'yes'?*
N   NEGATE *Who is a 'no'?*
O   ORDER *What's the best way to organise this?*
P   PICTURE *What do you see when you picture this?*
Q   QUESTION *What's the juiciest question here?*
R   RESPOND *What do you say to that?*
S   SIZE *What sort of number are we talking?*
T   TEST *How could you tell if that's true?*
U   USE *How can you use it?*
V   VARY *How else could we think?*
W   WEIGH UP *Which choice has more back-up?*
X   EXEMPLIFY *Can you give me an example?*
Y   YIELD *Can you disagree with yourself?*
Z   ZOOM *What's the big/little picture?*

There is more to the approach than this list of questions – the book includes many activities and examples of subject-specific applications, and we heartily recommend that all teachers get their hands on a copy. It would also be a good idea to have a poster in every classroom with these questions on, to help students and teachers nudge their thinking into the metacognitive dimension.

THE ORACY SKILLS FRAMEWORK/ ORACY BENCHMARKS

This is another example of something that didn't exist ten years ago, but we really wish it had. As we discussed earlier in this chapter, in recent years, oracy has not been given the recognition it deserves in the majority of schools. There are many reasons for this, but perhaps one reason is that people often refer to oracy simply as 'speaking and listening', without really appreciating that 'speaking and listening' are extremely broad categories comprising many discrete skills and abilities.

In 2014, researchers from the University of Cambridge, working with Voice 21, developed the *Oracy Skills Framework* (see Table 5.7).

Table 5.7. The Oracy Skills Framework

Physical	Voice	• Pace of speaking • Tonal variation • Clarity of pronunciation • Voice projection
	Body language	• Gesture & posture • Facial expression & eye contact
Linguistic	Vocabulary	• Appropriate vocabulary choice
	Language	• Register • Grammar
	Rhetorical techniques	• e.g. metaphor, humour, irony, mimicry
Cognitive	Content	• Choice of content to convey meaning & intention • Building on the views of others
	Structure	• Structure and organisation of talk
	Clarifying & summarising	• Seeking information and clarification through questioning • Summarising
	Self-regulation	• Maintaining focus on task • Time management
	Reasoning	• Giving reasons to support views • Critically examining ideas and views expressed
Social & emotional	Working with others	• Guiding or managing interactions • Turn-taking
	Listening & responding	• Listening actively & responding appropriately
	Confidence in speaking	• Self-assurance • Liveliness & flair
	Audience awareness	• Taking account of level of understanding of the audience

The *Oracy Skills Framework* identifies four dimensions along which we can think about the development of speaking and listening – physical, linguistic, cognitive and social/emotional – and each of these can be further broken down into smaller skills. There is a version of the *Oracy Skills Framework* on the Oracy Cambridge website, including a glossary to explain what each of these terms means.[214]

The publication of the *Oracy Skills Framework* marked a significant leap forward in providing schools with practical guidance about the range of ways in which they can develop speaking and listening, alongside written reading and writing. The *Oracy Skills Framework* was evaluated by the Education Endowment Foundation in 2015,[215] who concluded that it 'provides a useful tool for schools wishing to review and develop their approach to oracy [and] can be used diagnostically and to track students' progress in developing oracy skills'.[216] We agree.

More recently, Voice 21 published *The Oracy Benchmarks*, a really helpful document that sets out in detail how classroom teachers and school leaders can give spoken language the status it deserves.[217] The teacher-level and school-level benchmarks are summarised in Table 5.8.

Table 5.8. The Oracy Benchmarks

Teacher benchmarks	School benchmarks
1. Sets high expectations for oracy	1. Has an ambitious vision for oracy
2. Values every voice	2. Builds a culture of oracy
3. Teaches oracy explicitly	3. Has a sustained & wide-ranging curriculum for oracy
4. Harnesses oracy to elevate learning	4. Recognises oracy as central to learning
5. Appraises progress in oracy	5. Is accountable for the impact of oracy

The *Oracy Benchmarks* provide schools with simple, effective guidance – exemplified with case studies from real schools – on how to take the development of speaking and listening skills seriously. Regardless of whether or not you're implementing a *Learning Skills* curriculum, we recommend that all teachers and school leaders read, digest and act upon the *Oracy Benchmarks* forthwith.

THE LANGUAGE OF POWER

Speaking of oracy, one thing we didn't focus on enough in the Sea View study was public speaking. The main reason for this is that we weren't particularly good at it ourselves back then, having never received any training in it or had much experience of doing it ourselves. We expected our pupils to present to the class regularly, and we tried to support them as best we could. But at that time, we were only able to give fairly basic advice – practise beforehand, make eye contact with your audience, use stories – that sort of thing.

Since then, our thinking and our practice has developed a lot – both as teachers of public speaking, and as public speakers ourselves. For example, we now run a one-day Language of Power workshop for students and teachers, inspired largely by the work of the speechwriter and author Simon Lancaster referred to earlier in this chapter. In his TEDx talk *Speak Like a Leader*, Simon identifies six rhetorical devices, language features, tricks of the trade – call them what you will – that have been used to great effect by history's movers and shakers for hundreds of years.[218] In fact, there are really seven, because the tricolon – the rule of three – is here, there and everywhere! To give you a flavour (metaphor! – these, too, are everywhere), here's a brief description of each, with examples:

- **Asyndeton**. Technically, asyndeton is a style of speech or writing where conjunctions (e.g. and, yet, but) are omitted. This produces short, breathless sentences that are faster than normal speech, creating a sense of pace, excitement and determination. This technique is often combined with the rule of three. A famous example is '*Veni, vidi, vici*' (I came, I saw, I conquered – Julius Caesar).
- **Anaphora**. This is where the first part of a sentence or clause is repeated at the beginning of two or more successive sentences. This creates a sense that the speaker is fixated on their topic – that they have thought about it for a long time and that they have a lot to say on the matter. Some of the most powerful speeches and passages of writing from history have featured anaphora. Perhaps the most famous is Winston Churchill's infamous battle cry:

    > We shall not flag or fail. We shall go on to the end. We shall fight in France, we shall fight on the seas and oceans, we shall fight with growing confidence and growing strength in the air, we shall defend our island, whatever the cost may be, we shall fight on the beaches, we shall fight on the landing grounds, we shall fight in the fields and in the streets, we shall fight in the hills. We shall never surrender. [219]

We shall, we shall, we shall.

- **Antithesis**. This is when two seemingly contrasting ideas are placed alongside one another in a single statement. When you do this, it provides the illusion of balance, because it creates the impression that you've weighed up both sides of the argument. Examples include 'Ask not what your country can do for you – ask what you can do for your country' (John F. Kennedy), or 'Tough on crime, tough on the causes of crime' (Tony Blair).
- **Metaphor**. Metaphors often get confused with similes, which is when you say 'x is like y'. A metaphor is when you say 'x *is* y', and this is why metaphors are so powerful – they enable the speaker to transform reality. Metaphors are everywhere – on average, we use one every sixteen words. In fact, it is quite difficult to write about metaphors without resorting to using metaphors. Metaphors are an incredibly powerful tool (metaphor!) for manipulating people into doing, believing or accepting things that they would ordinarily be opposed to. In his brilliant 2018 book *You Are Not Human: How Words Kill*, Simon Lancaster provides a fascinating insight into how metaphors have been used to shape and distort the world – and, in particular, to dehumanise particular groups of people, with horrifying consequences.[220] This book should be required reading for children and adults alike, and many excerpts could be used in a *Learning Skills* curriculum as a stimulus for philosophical inquiry, debate or even an extended research project.
- **Hyperbole**. Exaggeration used for emphasis or humour. Hyperbole is often used to liven up a narrative, or to make a story more interesting or compelling. An example would be the song by The Proclaimers: 'I would walk 500 miles', or the phrase 'I'm so hungry I could eat a horse'. Politicians have really embraced the power of hyperbole in recent years; even though everyone knows they're lying, as long as it's an entertaining or a novel lie, people seem not to mind. Which is worrying. Noam Chomsky recently wrote, 'I am always put off by people who are called good speakers, by those who can rouse an audience. That's just what you do not want. If you have the capacity to do it, you should suppress it'.[221] He makes a good point. This is another powerful argument for why we should teach this stuff in schools - not so as to teach young people to exaggerate and manipulate their way through life, but to help them detect when others are using these powerful language devices for nefarious ends.
- **Rhyme**. Incredibly, research shows that people are more likely to believe something is true if it rhymes. This is known as the 'rhyme as reason' effect. It's to do with the 'processing fluency' of language – how easy language is to swallow. Long words and sentences are hard to digest, whereas short rhyming phrases just slip straight in. For example, many people believe the phrase 'i before e except after c' is true. Which it is, in 44 cases. However, there are over 900 words

in which it is not true. Advertisers are wise to the power of rhyme – 'A [*popular chocolate bar*] a day helps you work, rest and play', or describing toilet tissue as 'soft, strong and very long' (note how advertisers also often make use of the tricolon). Another example is the phrase repeatedly used by OJ Simpson's lawyer, Johnie Cochran – 'If the glove don't fit, you must acquit!' – which many believe was a powerful factor in Simpson's surprise acquittal.

- **Tricolon**. The all-pervading rule of three. As Simon Lancaster says, when you say things in threes, 'it makes you sound more credible, convincing and compelling!'[222]

There are many more rhetorical devices than these, but these are a good start, because you can use them, in the order they appear above (with the exception of the tricolon, which is often used in combination with the others), to write a short speech on almost any topic. Since we got the rhetoric bug, we've really gone down the rabbit hole (to mix metaphors!). You start noticing these language features everywhere, and how they are used to pull the wool over people's eyes (metaphor!).

Learning about rhetoric makes you a more confident, compelling speaker. But the main reason we should teach children about rhetoric is that it helps you learn how to read the world. A powerful exercise is to get your pupils to write two speeches using these rhetorical devices – one in favour of something (e.g. animal testing, the death penalty, euthanasia) and then another against that same thing. Once children realise how easy it is to use language to present a credible, persuasive case both for and against a given issue, they develop a healthy scepticism toward people in public life who use such language features to great effect. And in the 'post-truth' age – that can't be a bad thing.

THE VESPA MODEL

Some students can do pretty well at GCSE just by turning up to lessons and paying attention. Some can even achieve top grades across the board without too much effort. This is not the case at A level, however, where in order to achieve top grades, students really need to hit the ground running with lots of independent study. If they aren't used to working in this way, many students hit the 'year 12 wall'. This can be pretty brutal. If a student isn't set up for independent learning – if they don't already have systems in place, a proactive attitude to learning and a range of tried and tested independent learning strategies – they can soon find themselves slipping behind, and their whole time at 6th form college can turn into a massive uphill struggle. We also know that the transition from GCSE to A level is particularly challenging for children from disadvantaged backgrounds and those from non-selective state schools, making it far harder for them to go on and succeed in higher education.[223]

In 2016, Steve Oakes and Martin Griffin published a brilliant book called *The A Level Mindset*.[224] Drawing on their combined 40 years of experience as teachers, their own research into the habits of effective students and the wider research literature, Oakes and Griffin came to the conclusion that non-cognitive factors (defined as 'attitudes, behaviours and strategies that are thought to underpin success in school and at work, such as motivation, perseverance, and self-control'[225]) are more important determinants of academic success than a student's prior attainment. They then developed a framework of five key non-cognitive factors that students need to have in place if they are to succeed at A level – Vision, Effort, Systems, Practice and Attitude – which they refer to as the VESPA model.

The A Level Mindset includes diagnostic tools to identify the areas where students are lacking – in our experience, it's often vision, systems and practice – and there are lots of activities to help you get to the point where students are cooking on gas in all five domains. More recently, Oakes and Griffin have published several other books, including *The GCSE Mindset*, student workbooks for GCSE and A level, and a more general book for 'anyone learning anything'.[226]

There is clearly a huge amount of overlap between the VESPA model and the *Learning Skills* approach, and we are keen to strengthen these links in the years to come. We think all students should have worked through the GCSE mindset book by the end of year 9 and the A level mindset by the end of year 11. But really, you need to start this work much earlier, which is why we suggest *Learning Skills* lessons should run from years 7 to 9. We also think the VESPA model might lend itself to forming a framework for a whole-school shared language of learning, although you would need to drill down into each of the five strands to look at the individual learning behaviours that underpin each, as we did with the 'Learning Brain' model.

AN OVERLY COMPLEX INTERVENTION?

And so concludes our grand tour of the components of the complex *Learning Skills* intervention: past, present and future. We are aware that there is a lot in this chapter, and as we have mentioned, we don't think people should implement everything we have covered here. But we hope the chapter has been useful in giving readers a sense of what *Learning Skills* looks like in practice.

Before we look at the evidence for *Learning Skills* from the 8-year Sea View study, we would like to return to a question raised in the cross-examination at the end of *Chapter 3: Learning to Learn on trial*, when the prosecution asked: is *Learning Skills* too complicated to be implemented at a system level? We don't think so, but at the end of such a long chapter, we can understand why some people might have this concern.

There are two key points to make here. First, to reiterate: we do not present the ideas and practices in this chapter as a comprehensive recipe for success. If you take the contents of this chapter and implement them in a top-down way, you've got the wrong end of the stick. The ideas presented in this chapter are examples of the kinds of things teachers and school leaders might wish to consider in creating *their own* complex intervention – whatever combination of ideas and practices they think makes the most sense within their context. But you do not have to implement all of these ideas at once for it to work. That's not how *Learning Skills* was implemented at Sea View, and nor should it be anywhere else.

The second point is that, although *Learning Skills* is a complex, whole-school intervention, the whole-school element is fairly light-touch: the *Learning Skills* teachers, and ultimately the students themselves, do most of the heavy lifting. As a starting point, a typical secondary school might simply have two expectations for teachers across the curriculum: 1) to refer regularly to the 'how', as well as the 'what' of learning, in ways that make sense to the teacher and their subject context; and 2) use 'talk rules' to structure class discussions. Just doing these two things will get you a really long way toward providing your students with a more joined-up diet of learning.

Other schools may wish to take this further. For example, you may wish to create a shared, whole-school language of learning for structuring those 'how of learning' discussions. Alternatively, you may wish to have aspects of metacognition and self-regulated learning woven into classwork and homework – finding ways to enable students to plan, monitor and evaluate their learning, for example. It's really a matter of finding what works in your context, deciding where the balance should sit between focusing on the 'what' and the 'how' of learning, and working in a 'tight but loose' way so that all colleagues are able to exercise a degree of autonomy in how they choose to interpret and make sense of this joined-up approach to teaching and learning. We will return to the question of 'tight but loose' implementation in *Chapter 8: An implementation (and evaluation) checklist*.

CHAPTER 6

THE EVIDENCE FOR *LEARNING SKILLS*

'I thought about everything that I have learned and how I can use that in other lessons. And it kind of sticks with you, and then it becomes a part of you and your routine.'

Olivia, year 8, Sea View

In *Chapter 5: Components of a complex intervention*, we outlined the main features of the *Learning Skills* curriculum as it existed after three years of trying out a range of ideas and tweaking, discarding or doubling down on them as we went along. However, it is important to understand that we assembled our complex intervention slowly over that three-year period. We started out with a blank sheet of paper, and we recommend others do the same.

At the outset, we had a team of five teachers who had applied to be on the team, and we had five lessons a week, with the whole of year 7, to do with as we wished. We realised at the outset that this was an unprecedented opportunity to do something bold and different, and we were keen to capture what we were doing by carrying out the most rigorous impact evaluation we could muster.

At the time, James had just completed a research-based MA in person-centred education, and he was keen to find out how deep the teacher-research rabbit hole goes.[1] Evaluating the *Learning Skills* curriculum as the focus of a PhD seemed like the logical next step. Our initial plan was to follow the first *Learning Skills* cohort from year 7 through to GCSE, i.e. over a five-year period, evaluating the impact of the programme using a range of cognitive and non-cognitive measures. In the event, we used the pre-*Learning Skills* cohort as a control group, and we also followed the second and third *Learning Skills* cohorts through to GCSE. In total, therefore, the

Sea View pilot study incorporated data collected over an eight-year period – from 2009 to 2017. It has taken rather a long time to write this book, as you can see!

FIVE RESEARCH QUESTIONS

As we discussed in *Chapter 3: Learning to Learn on trial*, there is more to an education than exam results. That said, we felt it was important that the primary outcome measure in the Sea View study would be the extent to which the *Learning Skills* curriculum impacted on subject learning across the school, using existing indicators (i.e. teacher assessments and exam results). We did this by comparing the academic attainment of *Learning Skills* cohort 1 with the pre-*Learning Skills* control cohort in year 9 (the end of Key Stage 3) and year 11 (the end of Key Stage 4). As we will see in the baseline analysis, the two cohorts had similar prior attainment at entry to the school, which was fortunate because it made for a fair comparison. This brings us to the first of the five research questions that drove the Sea View study:

RQ1: What is the relationship between *Learning Skills* provision and student attainment in subject learning across the curriculum?

At the end of the first year, the *Learning Skills* team was successful in campaigning for timetabled lessons to extend into year 8, for three lessons a week. Naturally, this created an increased teaching load within the *Learning Skills* department. However, as Robert Burns famously observed, the best-laid schemes of mice and men often go awry. For financial reasons, in 2011 there were a number of redundancies at Sea View, and two members of the original *Learning Skills* team had to go back into their departments to fill gaps. The remaining *Learning Skills* lessons were allocated to non-specialist teachers with spare time on their timetable – the aforementioned 'sceptical conscripts',[2] a point we will return to later.

This was further compounded by an unforeseen timetabling issue. The year 7 *Learning Skills* timetable was 'backed' against English, in which pupils were set by ability. This meant that for the second *Learning Skills* cohort, rather than being in mixed ability groups – a key design feature of the approach – the classes were ability groups based on the students' prior attainment in English. This combination of factors presented a serious challenge to the quality of *Learning Skills* provision in its second year.

In the third year of the programme, the *Learning Skills* taught course expanded again into year 9, this time for five lessons a fortnight. By this time, year 7 classes were once again mixed ability, and all lessons were taught by specialist teachers. This unintended 'blip' in the quality of *Learning Skills* provision in its second year enabled us to pursue a second line of inquiry, by retrospectively testing the hypothesis that *Learning Skills* leads to gains in subject learning across the curriculum:

RQ2: To what extent does the quality of *Learning Skills* provision in year 7 predict student attainment at GCSE?

Nationally – and internationally – there is a stubbornly persistent pattern of educational underachievement among children born into social or economic disadvantage. By age 16, according to a 2019 report by the Education Policy Institute (EPI), disadvantaged pupils are 18.1 months behind their peers.[3] Following the introduction of the Pupil Premium (PP) in 2011 – a measure brought in by the UK's coalition government in an attempt to boost the attainment of children from disadvantaged backgrounds by channelling additional funding toward them – some modest progress was made in closing the attainment gap. Between 2011 and 2018, the gap between disadvantaged pupils and their peers at GCSE narrowed by 1.6 months, from 19.7 to 18.1 months.

However, even this modest trend is beginning to falter. In 2018, the disadvantage gap at GCSE widened for the first time in eight years – more so for persistently disadvantaged pupils. This prompted the authors of the EPI report to caution that 'there is a real risk that we could be at a turning point and that we could soon enter a period where the gap starts to widen'.[4] Based on current trends, it would take 560 years to close the gap,[5] which of course means it's never going to happen unless we can come up with a radical new approach to improving outcomes among disadvantaged children that can be reliably replicated on a national or international scale.

Closing the attainment gap was a central concern for the *Learning Skills* team at Sea View, where the proportion of pupils eligible for Free School Meals (FSM) was described by Ofsted as 'well above average'. In the Sea View study, disadvantage was defined in terms of whether a pupil was eligible for the PP. Pupils are eligible for the PP if they have been in receipt of FSM at any time in the previous six years, if they are looked after or have left care through adoption or other routes, or if they have been identified as being the children of servicemen and women in the school census at any point in the previous five years.

PP eligibility is a conservative measure of disadvantage, since many eligible families do not apply for FSM for fear of being stigmatised as poor.[6] However, it is a measure that is widely used within the research literature, and its use as a proxy for disadvantage in the Sea View study is in keeping with the wider tradition of research and practice concerned with reducing the extent to which a child's educational outcomes can be predicted by their post code. All of which brings us to our third research question:

RQ3: What was the relationship between *Learning Skills* provision and the attainment of students from disadvantaged backgrounds?

These three research questions sought to quantitatively determine whether there was any correlation between *Learning Skills* provision and student outcomes in terms of subject learning as they progressed through to GCSE. However, as (almost) everybody knows, correlation does not mean causation. It doesn't rule it out – but it doesn't rule it in, either. For this reason, we were keen to explore the 'space between' the *Learning Skills* curriculum and the students' exam results. What did students say, think and feel about the *Learning Skills* curriculum? What did teachers say, think and feel?

An important lesson from the past is that Learning to Learn initiatives have an Achilles heel – transfer – or, more specifically, the lack of it. This is because the development of knowledge and skills is, to a significant degree, context dependent. It's all very well teaching children how to manage their own projects and work productively in groups in a Learning to Learn classroom, but when they go into other lessons, they tend to revert to type. Old habits die hard. This doesn't mean that transfer is a lost cause – the entire project of education would be questionable if nothing transferred beyond the school gates. It just means that the process of transfer has to be carefully managed, at both ends of the process: transfer *out* of the *Learning Skills* classroom and transfer *in* to subjects across the curriculum.

If we were going to succeed, we had to find ways to transfer the knowledge, skills, habits and dispositions developed through the taught course out into subject areas across the school. And from a research perspective, we needed to capture the extent to which any gains in subject learning (or lack thereof) might reasonably be attributed to the *Learning Skills* taught course. Here we arrive at our fourth research question:

RQ4: To what extent did the knowledge, skills, habits and attitudes, developed through the *Learning Skills* curriculum, transfer into other subject areas?

As well as aiming to help our pupils get better at learning stuff, part of the rationale for the *Learning Skills* programme was to help students learn to regulate their feelings and their behaviours. Partly, this is because enhancing self-regulation helps improve academic learning, and partly it's because non-cognitive outcomes are valuable educational aims in themselves. In particular, we wanted to find out about the social and emotional aspects of the programme, and to explore the impact of *Learning Skills* on things like the pupils' attitudes to learning, their organisational and interpersonal skills, and their beliefs about themselves as people and as learners. For this reason, we set out to answer a fifth and final research question:

RQ5: What was the non-cognitive impact of the *Learning Skills* programme?

These five research questions, and the quantitative and qualitative methods through which they were investigated, are summarised in Table 6.1.

Table 6.1. Five research questions, and the methods used to investigate them

Research question	Quantitative methods	Qualitative methods
What was the relationship between *Learning Skills* provision and student attainment in subject learning across the curriculum?	• Baseline SATs, CATs • Student attainment across the curriculum (control vs treatment at three and five years)	• Student interviews • Teacher interviews • Learning journals
To what extent does the quality of *Learning Skills* provision in year 7 predict student attainment at GCSE?	• Baseline SATs, CATs • Student attainment at GCSE (control vs treatment cohorts 1–3)	• Teacher interviews
What was the relationship between *Learning Skills* provision and the attainment of students from disadvantaged backgrounds?	• Baseline SATs, CATs • Student attainment subgroup analysis	• Teacher interviews

Research question	Quantitative methods	Qualitative methods
To what extent did the knowledge, skills, habits and attitudes, developed through the *Learning Skills* curriculum, transfer into other subject areas?	• Language of learning evaluation (in year 2) • Student attainment across the curriculum (control vs treatment at three and five years)	• Student interviews • Learning journals
What was the non-cognitive impact of the *Learning Skills* curriculum?	• Attitude to learning • Psychometric questionnaires	• Student interviews • Teacher interviews • Learning Journals

In the remainder of this chapter, we will present the findings from five of the data strands – student attainment across the curriculum at three and five years, attitude to learning scores, learning journals, student interviews and teacher interviews. We will present these in two broad sections: the stats (quantitative stuff) and the stories (qualitative stuff). In *Chapter 7: The case for Learning Skills*, we will consider these findings in light of the five research questions outlined above, and consider potential explanations for how the *Learning Skills* programme may have significantly boosted the students' attainment in their subject learning across the curriculum.[7]

THE STATS
STUDENT ATTAINMENT ACROSS THE CURRICULUM

Student attainment across all curriculum subjects was analysed at two time points: an interim analysis at the end of year 9 (three-year outcomes), and a final analysis of GCSE results at the end of year 11 (five-year outcomes). The primary outcome measure of the study was to compare the attainment of *Learning Skills* cohort 1 with that of students in the control (pre-*Learning Skills*) cohort. To examine longer-term trends, the attainment at GCSE of students in *Learning Skills* cohorts 2 and 3 was also included in the study.

As well as comparing the overall attainment of each cohort, we evaluated the impact of the *Learning Skills* programme on the 'disadvantage gap' by comparing the relative attainment of PP and non-PP students within and across the treatment and control cohorts.

Baseline measures

When you're comparing the academic progress of two cohorts over a number of years, it's important to make sure that, as far as possible, you're comparing like with like. To do this, we compared the prior attainment of the control and treatment cohorts at entry to the school in three ways:

1. Cognitive Attainment Test (CAT) scores (tests of verbal, non-verbal and quantitative reasoning completed at the start of year 7)
2. Key Stage 2 Standard Attainment Test (SAT) scores (tests of English, maths and science completed at the end of year 6, prior to transition)
3. Key Stage 2 SATs – the PP gap in the treatment vs control cohorts.

In each of these measures, the prior attainment of the control and treatment cohorts was very similar at entry to the school. In fact, the average CAT score was slightly higher in the control cohort (97.4 control vs 96.5 treatment), although the average Key Stage 2 SAT scores were very similar (4.04 control vs 4.03 treatment). There was, however, a disparity in terms of the PP gap at entry to the school. In the control cohort, PP students slightly outperformed non-PP students in their Key Stage 2 SATs. This bucks the national trend, where students from disadvantaged backgrounds typically achieve lower grades than their peers at Key Stage 2. In contrast, in the *Learning Skills* treatment cohort, there was a gap between PP and non-PP students at entry to the school, in line with national trends. As a consequence, in the subsequent comparisons of the PP gap at three and five years, the *Learning Skills* treatment cohort would be at a relative disadvantage, since they started from a position of greater disparity.[8]

Statistical analyses

If you look at any population – blades of grass in a field or cars in a car park – you will usually find that there are many differences between the individuals that make up the population: colour, size, age and so on. In addition, populations tend to change over time. So, when you compare two cohorts of students and one of them performs better than the other, it is possible that the difference was caused by natural variation – chance, in other words – rather than being driven by some particular known or unknown factor.

To determine the extent to which any differences in the academic attainment of the treatment and control cohorts might reasonably be attributed to the *Learning Skills* curriculum rather than just being due to chance, we carried out statistical significance testing. That's why you'll see asterisks (*) on some of the graphs in this chapter: * means we can be 95% sure the difference was not due to chance, ** means we can be 99% sure, and *** means we can be 99.9% sure.[9]

Interim (three-year) analysis

Because students no longer take external examinations at the end of year 9 (Key Stage 3 SATs were abolished shortly before this study began), the year 9 analysis was based on teacher assessments. Naturally, the nature of these assessments varied from one department to the next, and even from one teacher to another. From a research perspective, this is problematic, because teacher assessments are generally considered to be more unreliable and more subjective than standardised instruments such as GCSE exam results.

Indeed, it is difficult to even test the reliability of teacher assessments in some subjects, because they can be based on activities such as dance, drama, musical ability, sporting ability or public speaking, none of which generate a paper trail that can easily be cross-checked or moderated.[10] However, steps are taken within schools to ensure that teacher assessments are as robust as possible. At Sea View, the teacher-assessed grade in each subject was based on summative termly assessments – either test scores, or assessments using levelled criteria that were shared with students beforehand. In addition, the levelling process was subject to moderation (quality assurance) as per standard departmental practice.

To compare the progress of students in the treatment and control cohorts, we looked at the proportion of students either hitting or exceeding their target grade at the end of year 9 (age 14, after three years of *Learning Skills*). To allow for the fact that any single point of assessment might not give an accurate representation of each student's ability level in a subject – a student may be absent on the day of the assessment, for example, or they might have had an 'off day' for some reason – for each subject, the teacher assessment grades from each 'data harvest' throughout year 9 (autumn, spring and summer) were combined and an average grade was calculated.

In this study, the treatment and control cohorts had similar prior attainment at entry to the school; they had the same teachers, the same behaviour policy, the same uniform, the same curriculum, the same kinds of assessments, and so on. During the study period, there were no known changes to policy or practice at the school that would be likely to have affected one cohort and not the other. By far the most significant known difference between the two cohorts is that the treatment cohort took part in over 400 lessons of *Learning Skills* over a three-year period. In contrast, therefore, compared with the *Learning Skills* cohort, the control cohort had over 400 more lessons of subject-based learning throughout Key Stage 3. So, if anything, you would think that in any subsequent measures of subject learning, the control cohort would have had a fairly significant advantage.

It is therefore quite remarkable that by the end of year 9, there was a significant increase in the proportion of students either hitting or exceeding their target grade in the *Learning Skills* cohort compared with the control cohort. As we can see in Figure 6.1, these improvements were more pronounced among disadvantaged students (those eligible for the PP), although the gains among non-PP students were statistically significant also, compared with their counterparts in the control cohort.

Figure 6.1. Student attainment at the end of year 9 (all subjects combined)

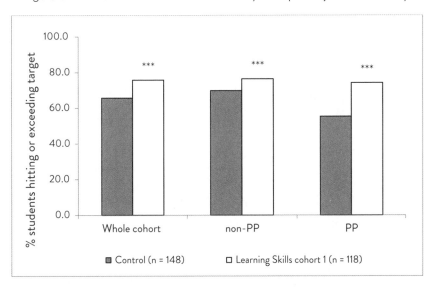

*** *Statistically significant differences vs control group, P ≤ 0.001*

To explore this narrowing of the PP gap in more detail, we analysed what happened in each subject. Figure 6.2 breaks down the PP gap by subject. As can be seen in the five white bars with negative values, in five of the subjects (English, maths, science, art and geography), after three years of *Learning Skills* the PP gap had reversed, with PP students outperforming non-PP students.

Such a balanced picture, with PP students outperforming their peers in some subjects and not in others, is what you would expect to see if disadvantage were not a predictor of educational attainment. However, most striking here are the two bars on the right-hand side of Figure 6.2. When we combine the students' attainment data for all subjects at the end of year 9, we can see that the overall attainment gap between PP and non-PP students was 25% in the control cohort. In the treatment cohort, following three years of *Learning Skills*, the PP gap was just 2%.

Figure 6.2. Pupil Premium gaps at the end of year 9: treatment vs control cohort

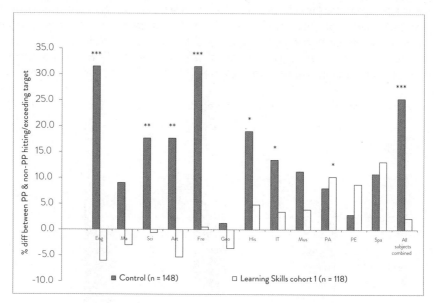

* Statistically significant difference vs control, P ≤ 0.05; ** P ≤ 0.01; *** P ≤ 0.001

In three of the subjects (performing arts (PA), physical education (PE) and Spanish), the PP gap was larger in the *Learning Skills* cohort at the end of year 9 compared with the control group. However, the findings relating to these three subjects can be explained by other factors. In the case of Spanish (and also French, where the PP gap was 31.6% in the control cohort and 0.5% in the *Learning Skills* cohort), the numbers of students taking the subject at the end of year 9 was much lower than the other subjects (around 40 students for each language), and the proportion of students eligible for the PP was much lower than for the other subjects.

Consequently, the findings for both French and Spanish are far less robust than for the other subjects. In the case of PA and PE, it is important to bear in mind that the students' target grades in these subjects (as with all subjects) are based on their attainment in the English, maths and science SAT exams taken at the end of primary school. For many years, teachers have complained that SATs results are a particularly poor predictor of a student's future attainment in more practical subjects such as PA, PE and music. We were therefore not overly concerned about the fact that the idiosyncratic findings for these subjects were not in keeping with the general pattern of results, although we would of course prefer if there were no gap at all.

To recap: the interim analysis at the end of year 9 suggests that there was a positive correlation between *Learning Skills* and academic attainment in subject learning across the curriculum, with accelerated gains among students from disadvantaged backgrounds. Indeed, following three years of *Learning Skills*, the PP gap had all but disappeared in the treatment cohort. It is also worth noting that the gap closed from the bottom up rather than from the top down; there is more than one way to close a gap, and some ways are better than others!

These findings were encouraging, and suggest that by year 9 *Learning Skills* might be helping the students learn more effectively in their subjects across the curriculum. However, this interim analysis was based on teacher assessments rather than on external exams. The possibility therefore remains that these findings could be explained by anomalies in the way individual teachers assessed their students, rather than being driven by the *Learning Skills* programme. To resolve this question, we would have to wait two more years for the *Learning Skills* cohort to take their GCSEs. Fortunately, you only need to wait until the next paragraph. Maybe you should go and make a cup of tea or something to build up the anticipation a bit!

Final (five-year) GCSE analysis

When this study was carried out, school achievement was usually measured by looking at the proportion of students achieving 5 A*–C grades at GCSE, including English and maths (5A*CEM). Figure 6.3 shows the proportion of students achieving 5A*CEM in the treatment and control cohorts. As can be seen here, the results followed a very similar pattern to the interim results at the end of year 9, with statistically significant gains in subject learning among the *Learning Skills* cohort as a whole and among students from disadvantaged backgrounds (i.e. those eligible for the PP).

Figure 6.3. Student attainment at GCSE: treatment vs control cohort

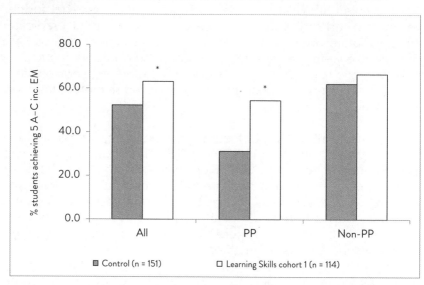

Statistically significant differences vs control group, P ≤ 0.05

To break this down: in 2014, 52.3% of students in the control cohort achieved 5A*CEM at GCSE. At the time, these were the best results in the school's history. When *Learning Skills* cohort 1 sat their GCSEs a year later, 63.2% of students achieved 5A*CEM – a raw improvement of 10.9%. As with the three-year interim analysis, non-PP students in the *Learning Skills* cohort performed better than their counterparts in the control cohort, although the difference was not statistically significant (66.7% attaining 5A*CEM in the treatment cohort vs 62.1% control). However, once again, the gains were most pronounced among students from disadvantaged backgrounds (54.6% of PP students attaining 5A*CEM in the *Learning Skills* cohort vs 31.3% in the control cohort – a statistically significant increase of 23.3%). Once again, the disadvantage gap closed from the bottom up. It hadn't closed completely, but it was heading in the right direction.

As with the interim analysis, we also looked at the PP gap in each subject at GCSE. These five-year outcomes provide us with a more robust measure than the interim analysis, because they are based on GCSE scores rather than teacher assessments. Figure 6.4 shows the gap between PP and non-PP students achieving a C grade or higher at GCSE in each subject. The bars on the left correspond with the data in Figure 6.3, showing the gap between PP and non-PP students in each cohort at the end of year 11.

Once again, the most striking result can be seen in the two bars on the right-hand side of Figure 6.4, which compares the average PP gap in the proportion of students in each cohort achieving a C grade or higher, for all subjects combined. In the pre-*Learning Skills* control cohort, the PP gap was 25.7%. In the *Learning Skills* treatment cohort, the PP gap was 8.5% – a 66.9% decrease in the gap between disadvantaged students and their peers. Because these data relate to the proportion of students achieving a C grade or higher at GCSE, they are not directly comparable with the interim three-year analysis (where the PP gap was 25.3% in the control cohort and 2% in the treatment cohort). However, it is clear that once again we saw the PP gap decrease dramatically at GCSE – by more than two-thirds – from one cohort to the next.

Figure 6.4. Pupil Premium gaps at the end of year 11: treatment vs control cohort

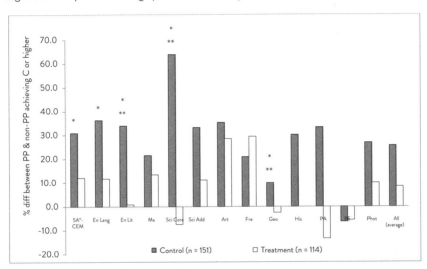

* P < 0.05; PP students achieving C or above, treatment vs control

** P < 0.05; PP students grade distribution, treatment vs control

Pupil Premium analysis: local and national contexts

Sea View is located within a former local authority that included nine secondary schools. To contextualise this closing of the PP gap within the local cluster of schools, Figure 6.5 shows how the PP gap changed from 2014 to 2015 for each school. Since it was not possible to access attainment data for non-PP students from all schools, these data do not represent the gap between PP and non-PP students; rather, it shows how the gap changed, from 2014 to 2015, between the proportion of PP students achieving a C grade in both English and maths and the whole-school population. Because the whole-school population includes PP students, this is a conservative estimate of the PP gap as a whole. As can be seen here, Sea View achieved the largest reduction in PP gap in the local cluster of nine schools, in a year when the PP gap increased across the cluster (and indeed the country) as a whole.

Figure 6.5. Change in Pupil Premium gap across the local cluster, 2014–15 (5A*CEM)

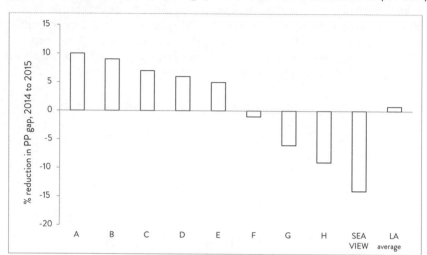

The year 7 'blip' analysis

As stated above, in the second year of the *Learning Skills* programme, there were a number of unforeseen changes in the department, such that classes were no longer mixed ability, and half the classes in year 7 were taught by non-specialist 'sceptical conscripts'. This unforeseen disruption to the quality of provision in the second year of the programme – this 'blip', if you will – allowed us to test the hypothesis that *Learning Skills* leads to measurable improvements in subject learning across the curriculum, by asking: To what extent does the quality of *Learning Skills* provision in year 7 predict GCSE results five years later?

The GCSE results of the pre-*Learning Skills* control cohort and *Learning Skills* cohorts 1, 2 and 3 are summarised in Table 6.2. The way in which GCSEs are measured changed between 2016 and 2017, with the introduction of a numerical grading system for English and maths (other subjects followed suit in 2018). Here, 'Basics EM' refers to the proportion of students who achieved an A*–C grade (2014 to 2016), or a 9–4 grade (2017) in both English and maths.

Table 6.2. Comparing year 11 GCSE results: control vs treatment cohorts 1, 2 and 3

GCSE year	Cohort	5A*CEM	Basics EM
2014	Pre-*Learning Skills* cohort (control)	52.3%	54.2%
2015	*Learning Skills* cohort 1	63.2%	68%
2016	*Learning Skills* cohort 2 (the cohort for whom *Learning Skills* provision was compromised in year 7)	53.1%	61%
2017	*Learning Skills* cohort 3	-	70% (FFT5)

As can be seen here, in both the 5A*CEM and the Basics EM metrics, there was a spike in student attainment for *Learning Skills* cohort 1, followed by a dip in cohort 2. This dip only lasted for one year; in 2017, 70% of students in *Learning Skills* cohort 3 achieved a grade 9–4 in both English and maths, placing them in the top 5% of similar schools nationally.

Given that these are five-year outcomes, it is of course likely that these results were influenced by factors other than the *Learning Skills* curriculum. However, it is worth noting that this analysis of attainment at GCSE aligns with the central hypothesis being tested in this study – that *Learning Skills* helps students learn more effectively, in ways that are detectable using existing indicators.

When the quality of *Learning Skills* provision was compromised in its second year as a result of staffing changes and timetabling issues, there was a corresponding dip in results five years later. It may seem to be a bold claim that the quality of *Learning Skills* provision in year 7 could have such a direct impact on GCSE attainment five years later, but there are many studies detailing such long-term effects in the research literature. To share just one recent example, a longitudinal study of around 45,000 students carried out at Durham University found that the quality of teaching in reception (age 4–5 years) was 'significantly related to later attainment at age 16'.[11]

In sum

To recap: the primary outcome analysis found that students in the treatment group (who took part in more than four hundred *Learning Skills* lessons throughout years 7, 8 and 9) went on to achieve significantly higher grades in subject learning across the curriculum compared with students in the control cohort (who had more than four hundred additional lessons of subject-based learning). This pattern was evident in both the interim (three-year) and final (five-year GCSE) analyses.

It is striking that the patterns of attainment were very similar in the interim and final analyses, both in terms of overall attainment and in terms of the PP gap. While non-PP students in the treatment cohort performed better than non-PP students in the control cohort in both the interim and final analyses, the gains in subject learning were particularly pronounced among students from disadvantaged backgrounds.

Given these findings, it is interesting to recall the baseline analysis, which revealed that there was a difference at entry to the school in terms of the PP gap between the treatment and control cohorts. When the control cohort entered the school, the PP gap was not yet apparent; indeed, PP students in the control cohort performed slightly better than non-PP students in their Key Stage 2 SATs. We can therefore see that the PP gap in the control cohort clearly opened up significantly as the students progressed through Key Stage 3, in line with national trends. Conversely, in *Learning Skills* cohort 1, a PP gap was apparent at entry to the school. When one considers the subsequent closing of the PP gap in the *Learning Skills* cohort, it should therefore be recognised that the accelerated progress of PP students was even more pronounced than is apparent in the graphs above, since that cohort started from a position of greater disparity between disadvantaged students and their peers.

The primary aim of this study was to determine the extent to which the *Learning Skills* curriculum impacted on academic learning across the curriculum. However, even if academic attainment were to increase among the *Learning Skills* cohorts relative to the control cohort, that would not necessarily mean that the improvements had been *caused* by the *Learning Skills* curriculum.

To examine this question of causation, a number of measures were used to explore the 'space between' the input variable (the *Learning Skills* curriculum) and the output variable (student attainment across the curriculum). This question of causation was explored by capturing the views of students and teachers relating to the impact of *Learning Skills* on subject learning across the curriculum. We did this by analysing four sources of data: attitude to learning scores, learning journals, student interviews and teacher interviews. We will now consider each in turn.

ATTITUDE TO LEARNING SCORES

As well as looking at academic attainment at three and five years, naturally we also sought to evaluate the Learning Skills curriculum in real time as the programme progressed. This was particularly important as the first Learning Skills cohort reached the end of year 7 and the leadership team considered whether we should extend timetabled lessons into year 8. It was still too soon to tell whether Learning Skills had significantly impacted student attainment across the curriculum, and so we had to look to other measures to determine the ways in which Learning Skills was playing out across the school.

As is the case in many schools, when entering termly assessment data, teachers at Sea View were required to enter an attitude to learning (ATL) score for each student on a 6-point scale (see Table 6.3). So one way in which we evaluated the impact of the Learning Skills programme in year 7 was by comparing the students' ATL scores with previous cohorts.

Table 6.3. *Criteria for determining a student's attitude to learning score at Sea View*

Attitude to Learning	Grade	Likely Outcomes	Expectation
Excellent and sustained attitude to learning, aware of targets and striving to meet or exceed them. Always working to the best of their ability, eager to learn and help others learn.	6	Will achieve academic potential.	Meeting or exceeding target grade.
Positive attitude to learning, aware of targets and striving to meet or exceed them. Usually working to the best of their ability, motivated and engaged in their learning.	5	Is likely to achieve academic potential with encouragement and determination.	Working towards or meeting target grade.
Usually a positive but inconsistent attitude to learning. Aware of their targets and the attitude required to achieve them. Completes work set and engages most of the time but showing signs of potential under-achievement.	4	Needs encouragement to maintain good standards. A little extra effort will quickly move student back into the 'Green' area.	Unlikely at the moment to achieve target grade.
Reluctant to work and few signs of wishing to achieve target grades. Their attitude to learning affects their own and other students' progress at times. Needs occasional encouragement in order to be involved in the lesson.	3	In danger of underachieving and not consistently demonstrating an appropriate attitude to learning.	Unlikely to achieve target grade.

Attitude to Learning	Grade	Likely Outcomes	Expectation
Poor attitude to learning which frequently affects their own and other students' progress. Needs regular encouragement in order to take part and get the grades they can.	2	Underachieving and subject to regular sanctions. Can expect to be monitored by teachers and student services. May receive exclusions.	Well below target.
Very poor attitude to learning with serious disruption to their own learning and that of others. Frequent sanctions and very little desire to achieve the grades they are capable of.	1	Is likely to face lengthy exclusions. In danger of permanent exclusion or managed transfer to another school.	Well below target.

Year 7 ATL scores for the treatment and control cohorts are shown in Figure 6.6. As can be seen here, the ATL scores were higher in the *Learning Skills* control cohort in English, maths and science and other subjects combined. In maths, the difference was small (81.8% of students being awarded a grade 5 or 6 in the control cohort vs 82.5% treatment). However, the differences in other subjects were much greater (English 75.6% control vs 86.2% treatment; science 61.9% control vs 92.0% treatment; other subjects combined 84.8% control vs 92.0% treatment).[12]

Figure 6.6. Year 7 ATL scores: treatment vs control

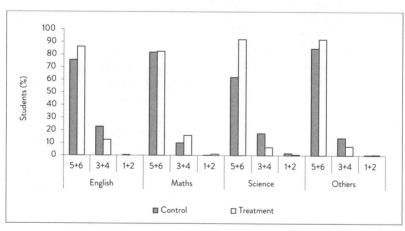

When we combined the data for all subjects together, the proportion of students achieving an ATL grade 5 or 6 in the control cohort was 76% compared with 88.2% in the treatment group – a 12.2% improvement from one cohort to the next. As can be seen in Figure 6.7, this pattern continued into year 8 (71.4% control vs 78.8% treatment). Interestingly, by year 9 there was virtually no difference between the two cohorts (70.4% control vs

70.7% treatment), and so it seems that the attitude to learning 'bump' may only have lasted for two years. However, this may have been enough to set the *Learning Skills* students on a different trajectory.

Figure 6.7. ATL scores throughout Key Stage 3: treatment vs control

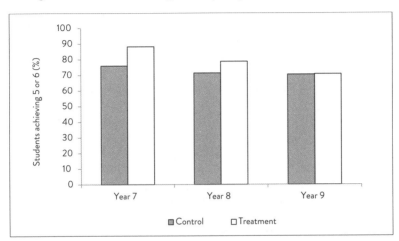

As we mentioned in *Chapter 4: The story of Learning Skills* and in the 'blip analysis' above, in the second year that *Learning Skills* ran there were significant issues relating to staffing and timetabling, such that the quality of provision was compromised. It is interesting to note, therefore, that when comparing the year 7 ATL scores of *Learning Skills* cohorts 1, 2 and 3, there was a clear dip in *Learning Skills* cohort 2 (Figure 6.8).

Figure 6.8. Year 7 ATL scores: Learning Skills cohorts 1, 2 and 3

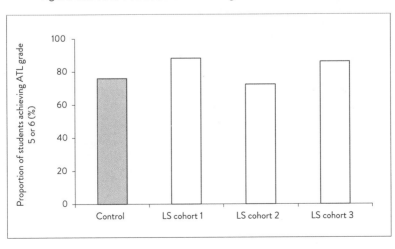

Here, the proportion of students achieving an ATL grade 5 or 6 in fact dipped below the level seen in the control cohort (76.0% control vs 72.4% *Learning Skills* cohort 2). The following year, the *Learning Skills* team returned to being taught by dedicated teachers in mixed ability groups, and the proportion of students achieving grades 5 or 6 for ATL across all subjects rose again (86.1% for *Learning Skills* cohort 3). Again, we must remain cautious not to conflate correlation with causation. However, it is interesting to note this correlation between the quality of *Learning Skills* provision and ATL scores and the way in which this aligns with the 'blip' analysis outlined above. This provides us with a potential mechanism of action: if *Learning Skills* helped improve the pupils' attitudes to learning, this could explain why they went on to achieve higher grades in subject learning across the curriculum.

THE STORIES
LEARNING JOURNALS

Once a fortnight in year 7, all students in *Learning Skills* cohorts 2 and 3 wrote entries in a learning journal, as described in *Chapter 5: Components of a complex intervention*. To analyse this data source, a random sample of 30 students' learning journals from cohort 3 was collected. Five pages of each journal were sampled, covering the same date range.

A date range was chosen that included a representative spread of journal entries, where pupils wrote about their views on *Learning Skills* and other subjects, as well as social and emotional issues arising from the 7-day challenge (pupils had to go 7 days without saying anything negative about another person). These were analysed using a method known as 'thematic analysis', whereby each phrase or sentence is allocated a code, and then the codes are grouped into themes.[13] This method allows the researcher to construct a 'bottom-up' account of the data set rather than analysing the extent to which the data support preconceived categories or questions. A summary of the codes and themes to emerge from the learning journals can be seen in Table 6.4.

THEMATIC ANALYSIS
A 'bottom-up' approach to analysing textual data. The text is broken up into chunks, which are then coded and organised into emergent themes.

Table 6.4. Learning journals: codes and themes

Theme	Theme tally	Code	Code tally
Interpersonal relations	50	7-day challenge – difficult	27
		7-day challenge – success	18
		7-day challenge – strategies	5
Other subjects	46	Other subjects – favourites	19
		Other subjects – least favourites	27
Learning Skills positives	26	*Learning Skills* – confidence/helps	15
		Learning Skills – favourite lesson/enjoy	11
Transfer	24	Transfer	16
		No transfer	3
		Transfer maybe	5
General school	22	General – challenge	7
		General – strategies	7
		General – proud	8

The aim of this strand of the study was to provide an insight into whether the students felt *Learning Skills* lessons helped them learn more effectively in other subjects. However, it was expected that other codes and themes would emerge from the data, since students were asked to write about a range of topics beyond the issue of transfer. In particular, the date range covered a period of time in which the students attempted to complete the '7-day challenge' for anti-bullying week. As a consequence, many of the students' comments that week related to interpersonal relationships – in particular, their struggle to not speak ill of their siblings!

Following this, the largest theme was 'other subjects'. This is because students were responding to prompt questions that often focused on how they were getting on in different subjects. In the entries sampled, students were asked to respond to the following prompt questions, which were about *Learning Skills* lessons and 'other subjects' in general:

- On a scale of 1 to 10, how much have you enjoyed *Learning Skills* lessons so far this year?
- Why did you give it this number?
- Do you feel that *Learning Skills* lessons help you learn better in other subjects?
- If so, how? If not, why not?

Four of the five themes to emerge from the students' learning journal entries are considered in turn below, with illustrative excerpts from the students' journals.[14] The fifth theme (favourite and least favourite subjects) is not relevant to this evaluation of *Learning Skills*, and so is not included here.

Interpersonal relations

The most frequent pattern to emerge within this theme was the surprising finding that almost all the students found it incredibly difficult to not say a bad word, either about or to their friends and family members, as required by the '7-day challenge' – even for a single day. As can be seen in the following excerpts, very few students made it through the entire week, and even then, only with great difficulty:

'Unfortunately, I only lasted until the Friday of the first week. It all began when I asked my baby cousin to hurry up, then my auntie started having a go at me so I turned around and started giving her a piece of her own medicine and then she stopped having a go at me.'

'Thursday – I done really well again but my sister knows about [the 7-day challenge] now, so I think it might get harder. Friday I broke it because my sister was winding me up, so I called her names. Saturday my mum and my sister was really annoying, so I was annoying back and being horrible so I broke it.'

'Tuesday – told my brother to go away. Wednesday gave up. Stopped. Not doing it. Thursday gave up. Stopped doing it. Don't think I am strong. I lasted three days. I will be kind to my brother when he is mean. I've learnt I am really angry with myself.'

[Teacher comment: What do you mean by this?]

'I get mad about things people do to me and try and change things I've done. I find it difficult to do it because I get really angry when my brother winds me up. I ask a question and my family don't get it. I am fed up. I have tried my hardest. I can't do this anymore.'

As can be seen here, students often wrote quite openly and honestly in their learning journals about difficulties they faced at home as well as in school. In some cases, as in the final excerpt above, the learning journals enabled teachers to identify potential safeguarding issues. Over time, with teachers commenting each week and students responding, learning journals enabled teachers of *Learning Skills* to build a deep understanding of their students and the challenges they faced.

While many students found the '7-day challenge' difficult, a number of students reported notable successes, as can be seen in the following excerpts:

'On the Wednesday when we started, I did really well, I did not say anything or do anything negative. I was so happy with myself because I just ignored rude people and walked away. The next day when I was asleep, one of my brothers was banging on my door and I said "Go away" and forgot the challenge because I was not really awake.'

'Today was really tricky. My brother was really annoying. I had to go upstairs to my room because he was really making me mad. I went upstairs so I wouldn't say anything back.'

'Today has been quite good. I haven't done anything or said anything so I think today has gone alright. I confused my brother by being really nice to him. Asking if he would want anything before he said anything annoying.'

As the week wore on, some of the students began to identify strategies they could use to avoid or de-escalate conflict, as can be seen in the following excerpts:

'I usually go to my room and punch my pillow and stay in there until I calm down.'

'I am pretty sure that I didn't crack. "I love pizza," I said to myself when I got annoyed.'

'I was nice to the person that annoyed me. The reason I was nice to them is because I really thought it would help them to stop being nasty to me and it sort of worked. The person was a bit confused at first but then they just walked away from me.'

Learning Skills positives

Many of the students were extremely positive about *Learning Skills* lessons in their learning journals. It could be argued that this data set is biased, since the students knew that their *Learning Skills* teacher would read their responses. However, as we will see below, our students did not hold back from criticising *Learning Skills* where they felt it was necessary. The main code to emerge within this theme was that the students felt the course had enabled them to become more confident, or that it helped them in some other way, as can be seen in the following excerpts:

> *'I learn best in Learning Skills. I would give it 10/10 because I get along with the teacher and learn a lot. The thing I have enjoyed doing most in* Learning Skills *is the projects, because they have helped me get closer with my brother.'*

> *'Awesome teacher and I learn about what happens in life. It helps me understand the world's problems.'*

> *'The thing I am most proud of this year is the "Who am I" project because I learnt how to stand up in front of a big group of people confidently.'*

The way in which *Learning Skills* (referred to at the time as 'Learning to Learn') helped students is also apparent in the excerpt in Figure 6.9. This theme of students finding their voice, standing up for themselves and communicating more effectively recurred in many of the students' learning journal entries throughout the year.

Figure 6.9. Learning journal, excerpt 1

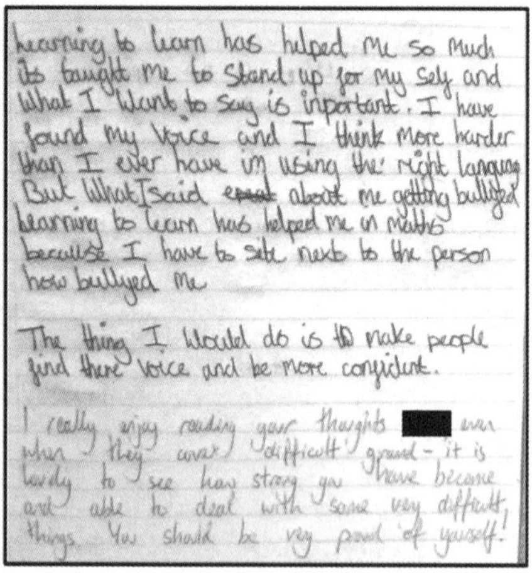

learning to learn has helped me so much its taught me to stand up for my sely and what I want to say is inportant. I have found my voice and I think more harder than I ever have im using the right languag But what I said ~~speak~~ about me getting bullyed learning to learn has helped me in maths because I have to site next to the person how bullyed me

The thing I would do is to make people find there voice and be more confident.

I really enjoy reading your thoughts [redacted] even when they cover difficult ground – it is lovely to see how strong you have become and able to deal with some very difficult things. You should be very proud of yourself!

The penultimate sentence in Figure 6.9 is worth drawing out. Here, the student writes about how *Learning Skills* had helped her in maths because she was able to sit with someone who had previously bullied her. Elsewhere in the learning journal, she wrote about how she had helped that person with their work, and how it had changed their relationship. This excerpt provides an insight into one way in which *Learning Skills* lessons positively impacted on students' learning in other subjects – by helping students learn to navigate the often difficult terrain of interpersonal relations within their peer group.

Transfer

In learning journal lessons, students were often asked to reflect on whether they felt that *Learning Skills* lessons helped them learn more effectively in their other lessons – and if so, how. The theme of transfer therefore emerged strongly within the learning journal data. In most cases, students did feel that *Learning Skills* helped them learn better in their other subjects, and they were able to provide examples of how this happened:

> 'Learning Skills *has helped me learn better in subjects because I've got a lot more confident. If I have* Learning Skills *before a lesson, I'm more calm (most of the time).'*

> 'Learning Skills *has helped me learn better in my other subjects because it has helped me communicate with the other people in my classes and helped me to be more confident when I'm talking in a large group of people.'*

> 'Learning Skills *has helped me to have a good memory, and now I have the courage to speak in all of my classes.'*

As can be seen here, the reasons the students gave frequently referred to a sense of greater confidence leading to improved spoken communication in other lessons. Indeed, the majority of the 16 instances of positive transfer in the learning journal sample referred either to confidence or to a newfound ability to speak up in other lessons. Some students were able to elaborate further on the theme of transfer, as can be seen in Figures 6.10 and 6.11.

Figure 6.10. Learning journal, excerpt 2 *Figure 6.11. Learning journal, excerpt 3*

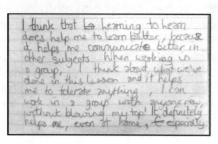

In Figures 6.10 and 6.11, we can see evidence of how knowledge and skills that were developed through the *Learning Skills* taught course transferred not only to other subjects but also to life beyond the school gates, helping students learn to 'ace a job interview' or 'handle life crises', and explaining how *Learning Skills* helps students regulate their emotions 'even at home'.

It should be noted, however, that not all students were convinced that *Learning Skills* lessons helped them learn more effectively in other lessons, as can be seen in the following excerpts:

> *'I haven't really thought about it. Maybe it helps in some ways.'*

> *'Sometimes. Sometimes they're not linked.'*

> *'Not really. Because we don't do a lot of class talking in other lessons.'*

Furthermore, a small number of pupils (3 of the 30 sampled) were quite adamant that *Learning Skills* did not help them learn more effectively in their other subjects, as can be seen in the following excerpts:

> *'It doesn't really help with anything.'*

> *'I think* Learning Skills *is fun but it hasn't helped in other lessons.'*

> *'It doesn't help me. I think it is a waste of time.'*

As the saying goes, you can't win 'em all! The *Learning Skills* teachers were keen to follow up on such comments with the students, to try to unpick what they felt the barriers were for them in terms of finding *Learning Skills* lessons valuable. Some students definitely needed more persuading than others, as might be expected for an intervention involving every student in a year group. However, as can be seen in Figure 6.12, even where students did not feel *Learning Skills* helped them in other subjects, they were able to identify, when asked, ways in which it may have done – in this case, helping the student with their listening skills and confidence in making themselves heard.

Figure 6.12. Learning journal, excerpt 4

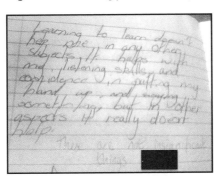

General school

The final theme to emerge from the learning journals was a group of comments relating to school life in general. As can be seen in the following excerpts, some of these comments related to interpersonal issues similar to those seen in the entries relating to the 7-day challenge:

> 'One thing I have found challenging this year is sitting with Student X and near Student Y.'

> 'Something I have found challenging this year is getting pushed away from my friends because I don't think anyone likes me anymore.'

> 'The thing I am most proud of from my first year at Sea View is confidence because I'm a lot smarter [and] I can speak up more.'

A number of students wrote about the challenges they faced in terms of the amount and difficulty of work expected of them in year 7, as can be seen in the following excerpts:

'Something I found challenging this year is some assessments that I have to do, because some of the questions are really hard.'

'I have found maths quite challenging this year because we are learning new stuff that we have never done.'

'Something I have found challenging this year is homework because there is lots of stuff to do and I have so much homework that I can barely fit any time in to do fun stuff.'

More promisingly, several students in the learning journal sample wrote about strategies they had identified to help them overcome such challenges:

'I used to get in trouble for not having pens. Now I have a pencil case that has four pens. I help my friends as well with giving them pens to borrow.'

'One strategy I have developed for overcoming difficulties [if I'm] getting stuck in classes [is] I now ask teachers. This helps me because I can get on with my work and know what I'm doing.'

'One strategy I have developed for overcoming difficulties is trying to be nice to [people] when they are being mean to you.'

'The thing I have learnt is being nice to people that are annoying so I sit next to someone and I'm really nice and it annoys them.'

'One strategy I have developed for overcoming difficulties is I just walk away from my brother and sister when they are annoying me. This helps me because they know it is annoying me so they leave me alone.'

Through this thematic analysis of the students' learning journal entries, we can see that by providing students with regular opportunities to reflect on challenges they were facing, and by helping them identify strategies to overcome them, *Learning Skills* lessons had a positive impact on student wellbeing and learning across the school in a number of clearly identifiable ways.

STUDENT INTERVIEWS

Rationale

As with the learning journals, the main reason for conducting student interviews was to explore what was happening in the 'space between' the input and output variables (i.e. the *Learning Skills* programme and student attainment across the curriculum). In particular, the aim of the student interviews was to find out:

a) what our students thought about the *Learning Skills* taught course
b) what they thought about their other subjects
c) whether they felt the *Learning Skills* taught course helped them learn more effectively in other subjects, and
d) if so, how.

Methods of data collection and analysis

In total, interviews were carried out with 31 students from *Learning Skills* cohorts 1, 2 and 3. Students were sampled at random so as to represent a range of demographic groups (i.e. students eligible for the PP, students who speak English as an additional language, students with identified Special Educational Needs and Disabilities (SEND), students with high prior attainment, and label-free students). To encourage discussion and interaction, interviews were conducted in groups of three or more students.

In each interview, students were asked about their favourite and least favourite subjects, about *Learning Skills* lessons, about school in general and about life in general. The rationale for this approach was to frame the students' views about *Learning Skills* within a broader context.

All student interviews were transcribed and subjected to a line-by-line thematic analysis, as used with the learning journals. The codes and themes to emerge from the student interview data are summarised in Table 6.5.

Table 6.5. Student interviews: codes and themes

Theme	Theme tally	Code	Code tally
Learning Skills positives	31	Learning Skills fun/enjoy	21
		Learning Skills helped/useful	5
		Learning Skills learn best in	5
		Intelligence/higher attainment	3
Learning Skills negatives	14	Criticism of Learning Skills lessons	14
Transfer	19	Transfer	16
		No transfer/not sure	3

Learning Skills positives

The most common theme to emerge from the student interviews was that students had many positive things to say about the taught Learning Skills course. Within this theme, the most common code related to students describing the lessons as enjoyable or fun. Reasons given for the students' enjoyment of Learning Skills lessons included:

- a sense of community involvement
- the fact that the projects had real-world outcomes
- learning to get along with others
- taking part in philosophical inquiries and debates
- the fact that they were allowed to choose which topics to research and discuss
- the meditation sessions
- writing in the learning journals
- the fact that students felt they could relax / the sense that there was less pressure to 'perform' or worry about their grades.

As can be seen in the following excerpts, students often spoke at length about their enjoyment of Learning Skills lessons, and were able to provide a range of reasons for their enjoyment:

'I like working in groups because you can bounce your ideas off the other people in the groups and... I feel like I'm less pressured to work hard, because they're able to do some of the work instead of me doing all of it. And I like the fact that in Learning Skills, you didn't really need to focus on what level we got – because I'm in top sets I feel a lot of pressure to get top

grades, and... it's like I feel pressured to get a good level, and even though I do get good levels, I still feel like... I'd feel more comfortable if I didn't feel so pressured.'

'I found it really fun and I like that... you pushed us to work with other people that I've never worked with, so I can see what it's like working with someone that I'd never usually work with. It makes you make more friends and you learn that you might not always work with the people that you want to work with, but you have to get to like them or at least be civil if you want to get along. Because otherwise you won't be able to do what you need to do... I also loved the journal thing – I liked reflecting on my feelings and how I found the work in class so that you could read it and see what I needed improving on.'

'The bonding with friends. Making new friends because of the seating plans... The anorexia project because it was awesome and I'm still doing it now. I liked learning about something that was close to my heart. I also remember the meditating and how it let me focus more. I remember the building of the house and the hairdryer that blew it down, because I had a lot of fun... It was kind of competitive with the people around me... Also, I remember the learning journals and you would feed back saying, "Oh I like what you've done here and well done for the wording.' And you did really good feedback because you didn't grade it in the same way as other subjects... you just gave us lots of detailed comments.'

'I loved the debating because we were set a side to be on, and we had to think of a way to agree with something that we disagreed with. I liked it because I felt challenged to think about what it actually was about and why I disagreed with it, and I wondered what it would be like coming from the other side. Knowing that I had to think about it from both sides, and that I had to agree with a point even if I really disagreed with it.'

Two other codes emerged within the theme of 'Learning Skills positives': students saying that they felt Learning Skills was the subject they learned best in, and the idea that Learning Skills lessons helped the students, or that they found them useful in some specific way. In the following excerpts, students describe how they learned 'life skills' in Learning Skills lessons, while one student (in the third excerpt) commented on the responsibility that came with some of the challenges they were set:

'I believe that it's taught us life skills, like working independently but also in a team, and being able to organise your time well.

Like the Christmas fair, because I could see there was a lot of stuff to get done, and there was a deadline, and you had to make sure everything got done at the right time.'

'I thought it was useful because it taught me how to work well in a team and it taught me how to solve problems.'

'The tasks that we did, like the £2 challenge and... the Christmas market... it was really good to have something to work towards. Like the Thorpe Park trip. And it helped us develop life skills. But it was quite a lot of weight on our shoulders, like we were only young...'

In one of the interviews, the interim (three-year) findings of the study were shared with the students. We did not consider it appropriate to discuss the closing of the disadvantage gap with students. However, students were asked for their thoughts as to why students in *Learning Skills* cohort 1 might have achieved higher grades in their subject learning across the curriculum compared with the previous cohort:

'I think it's because when you're in Learning Skills, *you learn how to do other things that you can use in other lessons. And you learn how to be more confident and what you learn sticks with you, and teaches you to act the same in other lessons.'*

'Because... because you always made us say because. Like if there's a question and you think you know the answer, but then you go, OK, so maybe it's not that, maybe it's this. And you can say, "Well why is it that?" And then you go, "Ooh, so actually it's this!" And then you go, "I'm smarticles!"'

'Well, you sort of... it seems like they're able to take things from that lesson and then put it in all of their other lessons. With me, I wasn't really able to do that, but most people seem able to take it with them and use it in other situations. And even with me, it was a more relaxed environment in Learning Skills *than in other lessons, it was just a different sort of environment. It was more calm and relaxed, and it makes you able to concentrate a bit more because it's more quiet and I don't know, it's just easier to concentrate... we're able to feel more confident with what we're doing because there aren't any consequences if you don't do it, like we didn't really get levelled – it was really just, "Well done, you've done this" and it didn't focus on what you haven't done. It's easier to learn how to do something when you're being told what you can do, and not what you can't do.'*

Learning Skills negatives

Students were also asked about aspects of the *Learning Skills* course that they found challenging. Primarily, these took the form of criticisms of *Learning Skills* lessons related either to the amount of paperwork involved in the year 8 'personal effectiveness' course or to the aforementioned staffing problems in the second year of the programme, as can be seen in the following excerpts:

> '*It got a little bit repetitious, we were doing the same folder work, paperwork, it just got a bit boring in a way. I feel like the teachers could have done a bit more to help us. We had to fill out quite a bit about how we were progressing, and I felt the teachers could have taken more time and effort to help us. I think we maybe made it more stressful than it was.*'

> '*We didn't do anything, it was just boring. We had Teacher X and Teacher Y. We did the research projects but that's all we did. We never really got told what to do.*'

Transfer

Students were also asked whether they felt *Learning Skills* lessons helped them learn more effectively in other lessons, and if so, to provide examples. A number of students felt that this was the case, and they were able to provide a range of reasons, as can be seen in the following excerpts:

> '*It helped answering skills. Questioning skills. Like if someone tells you something, like in science, I'll ask, "Why does it do this? Why does it do that?"*'

> '*The skill things, critical thinking and problem-solving and stuff, we'd go over those in Learning Skills and it would... I don't know, it just strengthened our ability to use those in class because we'd practised using them so much in Learning Skills and it just became stuck in our heads, like it just became the way of learning. Like now, when I'm in a lesson I still do think about those... skills, and if I'm using them like working in a team, and working on my own, and making sure I don't give up, like I'm resilient and stuff, and I always make sure I try as hard as I can to achieve my goal.*'

> '*I think it did because it developed my ability to manage a folder, because we pretty much have folders in every single*

lesson. So I'm a lot more organised and aware of my time in those situations. And like it helped me with marking and stuff, like we did a lot of "what went well/even better if", peer assessment and stuff, and we do that a lot in lessons now.'

'Because you learn other lessons in Learning Skills without the pressure. Because in other lessons, say in English, they give you pressure – like, "You have to do this, and you have to achieve this" and you're like... summarised in a group of people. Like, "Some of you can do this and most of you can do this". And you didn't have that in Learning Skills, because you're like, "Ah, the pressure is lifted off." And... if you'd just been in Learning Skills and then went into English, you would do much better because you've just been in Learning Skills where you had no pressure.'

Here again, we find students talking about the how lack of pressure to perform in *Learning Skills* lessons helped them learn more effectively in other lessons. This was a finding that we did not anticipate or expect, but which came through strongly in the student interviews - we are keen to explore this phenomenon further in our future research.

Finally, there was also some evidence in the student interview data of students transferring knowledge, skills, habits and attitudes not just to other lessons, but to their lives more widely, as can be seen in the following excerpts:

'It's not just my lessons that it helps me in, it's also helped me in my assemblies to speak up more, it's helped me so I can debate more in class. If I have a debate topic, and if someone's in class and they've said something, then I can say, "Wait a minute!" and I can say my points, and then I can say, "I don't disagree with you, I disagree with your point", like I can do the structured thing like where if you say, "OK I see it from your perspective but I am still outraged. I get that you think that, but it's all wrong to me, I have a different perspective of it." And I could take him down more easily! I took him down that day.'

'I was really disappointed when I found out that we aren't going to have Learning Skills this year. But then I thought back to last year, and I thought about everything that I have learned and how I can use that in other lessons. And it kind of sticks with you and then it becomes a part of you and your routine.'

TEACHER INTERVIEWS

Alongside the learning journals and student interviews, teacher interviews were conducted as an additional method for exploring the 'space between' the *Learning Skills* programme and student learning across the curriculum.

In total, seven teachers were interviewed. One of these was the head teacher whose idea it was to implement the *Learning Skills* programme in the first place, and five were teachers of *Learning Skills*, each of whom also taught at least one other subject. All non-*Learning Skills* teachers at the school were also invited for interview; however, only one volunteered to take part in the study (the head of PE). The teacher interviews were conducted individually, transcribed in full and subjected to thematic analysis. The codes and themes to emerge from the teacher interviews are summarised in Table 6.6.

Table 6.6. Teacher interviews: themes and codes

Theme	Theme tally	Code	Code tally
Origins of *Learning Skills*	107	Origin of *Learning Skills* at Sea View	56
		First heard of/thoughts on Learning to Learn	22
		Rationale for *Learning Skills*	17
		Early meetings of the *Learning Skills* team	12
The *Learning Skills* taught course	83	Lessons – content, processes, projects	26
		Early *Learning Skills* lessons	18
		Assessment	15
		Language of learning	14
		Mixing up the groups	10
Evaluating *Learning Skills*	139	Impact on subject teaching/learning	25
		Closing the disadvantage gap	23
		Even better if...	20
		Independence/metacognition	14
		Dedicated teaching team	12
		Observing change in *Learning Skills* students	11
		Fear of failure	7
		Public speaking/confidence	6
		What went well?	6
		Previous cohorts spoon-fed	4
		Taught vs embedded vs both	4

In the remainder of this chapter, we will briefly explore each of the three broad themes to emerge from the teacher interviews.

Origins of *Learning Skills*

Prior to initiating the *Learning Skills* curriculum at Sea View, the head teacher, Stuart, had worked with Kate at a previous school, City High, where they had implemented three different versions of year 7 Learning to Learn curricula over several years. These iterations were discussed by Kate in *Chapter 4: The story of Learning Skills*. Explaining how his thinking developed during this period, Stuart explained:

> 'It started when I was at City High... we were trying to develop the skills young people need to be effective learners... just by following the National Curriculum, those skills weren't naturally developed because the way the National Curriculum is set up, it tends to be content driven, and actually the processes of learning are something that... there are skills there that need to be taught discretely, I always felt. And... you need to actually make sure that you build them into the curriculum in a very identifiable way... So I decided that we would give some discrete time in the timetable, to actually ensure that through sort of project-based, cross-curricular learning students actually identified those skills. So the first thing is identifying what the skills are, and the second thing is creating the time and then creating the curriculum to make sure they're actually developed.'

As we discussed in *Chapter 4*, the *Learning Skills* teachers at Sea View were not massively familiar with the research literature on Learning to Learn when they applied to become a part of the team. However, the interview with Stuart revealed that the initial vision for Learning to Learn was informed by research evidence – in particular, by the work of Chris Watkins, who had written a number of compelling review articles[15, 16] on the wisdom of moving away from a performance orientation and toward a learning orientation:

> 'You know, I don't think it matters which skills or attributes you identify... it's the fact that you're focusing on learning as opposed to performance. And there's so much evidence, you know, Chris Watkins' stuff up at the Institute [of Education], it shows that schools that focus on learning get better outcomes than schools that focus on performance.'

One of the main lessons Stuart had learned from the City High experience was the need for Learning to Learn to be taught by a team of dedicated teachers, as we can see in the following excerpt:

'At Sea View, the five hours or whatever that we give to Learning Skills is lost by other subjects, and that is a real pressure. Obviously, with the demand to keep the standards in English and maths going up... you know, it would be very easy to take time off Learning Skills and give it back to English and maths. So that's a real pressure. And I think the second pressure is, there's always a danger with a subject like Learning Skills, that it becomes the last thing that goes on the timetable, and it becomes a bit of a back filler for people who've got spare time on their timetable.

'Where it was successful at City High, and where it was successful when we set it up at Sea View, is that we had a dedicated team who wanted to make it work and who were prepared to give the time to plan and work together, way above what you would expect people to do. The fact that they would meet in the evenings over a bottle of wine to think about it and go, "Let's get this right." And I think unless you've got that dedicated team it won't work. I think you have to almost hand-pick your teachers, because it does require very highly skilled teachers to make it work. If it's just seen as an add-on to your timetable, people won't give it the commitment that it needs.'

The importance of volunteering and applying to be a part of the team can be seen in the following excerpts (the third of which is from the interview with Kate), in which several of the *Learning Skills* teachers spoke about the excitement of the early meetings:

'We met in my classroom, and it was nice because... I remember it was just bouncing ideas around, and anything went – you know, there were very few restrictions about what we could and couldn't do. Everything was on the table, and there was a real feeling that we could make a difference, you know? And we had a budget, so we had a bit of money to play with, and we had the will from the senior team, especially Stuart, who was throwing his weight behind it. There was a real feeling of being let off the lead, being able to take the best of the ideas from [other approaches] and get rid of what didn't work, and being able to put our stamp on it. That was exciting.'

'I wanted to be part of something bold and interesting... I remember feeling very excited about it.'

'I can remember [the early meetings] being very productive, enthusiastic, it was quite exciting. There were quite a lot of raised eyebrows I remember, at the beginning. And, you know... you guys didn't know me, I had come in from somewhere else and I was encouraging behaviours that were outside of the norm... I was encouraging you... and asking everybody's opinion and input. So I remember them being really creative meetings. Lots of ideas generated, lots of conversation. I remember there being, you know, they felt like a buzz, it felt like we were going to be doing something really interesting, And that you were on board. I never for a minute felt like I was dragging anybody with me. I felt like we were definitely all keen to do this kind of work.'

The *Learning Skills* taught course

In contrast to the excitement of the early meetings, the teachers' recollections of early *Learning Skills* lessons were somewhat mixed. Largely, this stemmed from the fact that a key feature of the *Learning Skills* approach was to set the students off on six-week projects and then to take a step back to allow them to find out what they could and couldn't do for themselves. This was a marked shift away from our experience of subject teaching, where the teacher drives the learning agenda and often intervenes as soon as a pupil shows signs of difficulty. An account of this early struggle can be seen in the following excerpt, also from the interview with Kate:

'When you hand over the responsibility for learning to 11-year-olds, who have never had that given to them before, sometimes... they are just there with the responsibility but they don't know what to do with it. And that can take quite a long time. And so the nervousness that someone would look through the door and see some children really actively engaged and purposeful, and others just staring out the window because they're not quite sure what to do... it takes quite a lot as a teacher to tolerate that feeling, especially at that time... there were learning walks and mock Ofsteds and we were in 'special measures' and everybody was looking at us all of the time.

'So I remember it being something that I was conscious of, of staying with it and trusting in the process. Because to the outside, it could have looked too risky. What if they don't come through? What if they don't pick up their responsibility and learn how to run with it? What if they don't thrive as a result of this experiment?

So I remember living with that, that kind of being on my mental dashboard a lot. Because I was asking other people to do the same thing. But fortunately, that didn't last very long because by Christmas... by the second half-term, there was a visible difference, even in the students who had really struggled, who had been like rabbits in the headlights for the whole of the first half-term.

'There was kickback from some students who had been very good at being good at school, at primary school, and so they knew how to perform for their teachers, they knew how to write beautiful essays and underline the title and behave and line up... And then they were being told that those things were not valued above other things, and that they had to learn to get along with other students and they had to learn to plan and they had to... think for themselves. And that felt quite frightening for some students. They didn't enjoy that. They didn't know how to be good at that. They didn't know what to do for their teacher. So there was a real... that first half-term was quite hairy, until it settled.'

The notion that *Learning Skills* lessons enabled teachers to spend more time getting to know their students and to build relationships with them was highlighted by several of the teachers interviewed, as can be seen in the following excerpts:

'It was all about relationship building... It was about gaining their trust, and making them feel comfortable within the classroom, making them feel comfortable and confident about their learning. So the classes were always really positive, and we knew that... we knew how to identify students who weren't confident or comfortable, or who had those particular issues. And we knew how to approach them, and we had the time to understand them individually as learners, and to help them with those particular learning needs. Which was exactly what Learning Skills really was great at.'

'After three years... I felt that they trusted me more, I felt that they were more proud of the school, because they had been doing things and they had been listened to. So the response and the openness learned was very different... also the fact that because I had them for a few lessons, you can build up those relationships and get to know them underneath a bit better.'

When asked to share examples of *Learning Skills* lessons that they had found to be particularly useful or effective, a number of teachers singled out the Philosophy for Children (P4C) lessons. Interestingly, several of these comments referred to these sessions being as useful for the teachers as for the students, as can be seen in the following excerpt:

> *'I saw the value in it very quickly, for noticing how long some students need in order to work out what they think. And how we almost never allow them that time and space in a normal lesson. So I learnt a lot from P4C as a teacher. I learnt how to wait and how to notice, how to listen and participate rather than be a leader. So I found it quite a powerful tool for me, for my personal development as a teacher. As with all things, some students liked it more than others, but they got a lot from it because it created a safe space where they could say what they wanted and it was fine. It was just talking, shooting the breeze, asking the big questions, muddling through things together, understanding that not everything has a right or wrong answer. That's a big thing for young people to learn.'*

As we saw in the student interviews, a number of students suggested that they benefited from *Learning Skills* precisely because it wasn't assessed or levelled in the way other subjects are, and that there was less pressure to perform. This can also be seen in the following excerpt, from the perspective of a *Learning Skills* teacher, in response to the question: 'Why do you think the Pupil Premium gap closed?'

> *'Because sometimes, when the kids are not performing well, it's because they think they are no good at anything. And* Learning Skills *gives them the opportunity to feel that they are good at something. And they actually feel that people care... I think the important thing is that they don't feel like they are being assessed in a particular way. So they just go for it because they're not so afraid of failing. Because they aren't being assessed in a way that can be seen in black and white. Does that make sense? I think it builds their confidence and... they think, I might not be good at this, but I am good at that, and I'm actually part of this team and together we're doing something, and so it will be all right. And it actually makes them feel that they are part of the school, that they are doing things for the school and it helps them to like the school better. And it makes their attitude in the classroom more relaxed... I think that's the big thing.'*

Evaluating *Learning Skills*

The third and final theme to emerge from the teacher interviews related to comments that were essentially evaluative in nature. In particular, a number of the teachers remarked that they had noticed changes in the students as a consequence of the *Learning Skills* programme. This is particularly apparent in the extended excerpt from the interview with Caroline, the head of PE, which appeared at the end of *Chapter 4: The story of Learning Skills*.

As the only teacher who replied to the request for interviews from teachers across the school, it's important to recognise that Caroline's views may not have been representative of all teachers across the school. However, this notion of a transformation within the student body as a result of the *Learning Skills* programme was mentioned by other teachers as well as visitors to the school, as can be seen in the following excerpt from the interview with Stuart McLaughlin, the head teacher:

> '*I think it operates on different levels... certainly, teachers have noticed that children that have been through* Learning Skills *are better equipped to deal with the approaches that we have adopted now at Sea View towards learning, like group work and more independent learning. They seem to have the skills built in because they've been working on them. So that's on one level. I think it also affects the students, their attitude to learning... they're more positive about learning and why learning is important. And I think that comes through... certainly in the last Ofsted inspection when they spoke to the students... because the lead inspector was not convinced by the whole idea of Learning to Learn. I think she was prejudiced against the whole programme. And... it came through very clearly when she spoke to the students that they really valued it, and that they could identify what the qualities of a good learner were. Because we'd identified what they were... They're starting to develop a vocabulary of learning, and I think that's going to have a profound impact in the long term.*'

The interviews with the *Learning Skills* teachers took place after the interim analysis had been carried out, when the first *Learning Skills* cohort reached the end of year 9. As we saw above, that interim analysis revealed that in the *Learning Skills* cohort, the PP gap for all subjects combined was just 2% compared with 25% in the control cohort. When they were asked 'Why do you think the Pupil Premium gap closed?', teachers proposed a number of potential causal mechanisms, as can be seen in the following excerpts:

> '*I think it boils down to time. These students had the time to develop themselves in ways outside of just academics. So if they are PP students or SEND students or any other cohort of disadvantaged students, then they have a range of issues that*

they are bringing into the classroom, and of course that has an impact on their learning. So the students need time to be able to learn to control all of these issues within their lives and feel good about themselves, because they can then start to develop their own learning...

'I think Learning Skills gives them the time that they need to gain a sense of confidence, reassurance, trust. These are all the issues that are affecting their personal lives, and these are the issues that are affecting their learning. With Learning Skills, there's time for them to build positive relationships with their teachers or even their peers. Otherwise they're just going into a classroom, a subject where they don't have that time and they are expected to achieve what other students are achieving, and it's really difficult for them. So I think time is definitely one of the most important factors for these students. For them to just have the time to process, and have the time to develop their self-esteem is really important.

'And... I think Learning Skills itself is just a really positive curriculum... because it's easy to see that the student is right at the heart of the curriculum... there's no denying that. I think all of the projects and objectives of Learning Skills are there to promote the person, the individual. Not just the learner but the person. So I think Learning Skills supports these students more than any other [subject]... Because they come into school with a whole range of issues and I think they need that support, they need that time. And they need somebody to be able to introduce them to their own learning process so they can also take control.

'I think control might be an important aspect as well. Where they might not have control in other areas of their lives, they can perhaps come into the classroom and some of the projects are 100%, or at least 95% controlled by them. And the sense of ownership might give them a particular emotional release or some sort of response that might make them feel a bit more positive over their lives, that they have some sort of control over something.

'I think these students, once they get over that hurdle of processing their personal issues, whatever issue it is that they are battling... once they get over that, if they ever do, then they are absolutely amazing and they can achieve anything they want to achieve... they are ambitious, they do want to learn, they do want to be really positive and supportive and they love their *peers... you know, friendship is the most important thing and they would do anything for their peers... these are some really great individuals. So I think* Learning Skills *did some amazing things for a lot of students from disadvantaged groups.'*

IN SUM

The evidence we have reviewed in this chapter falls under two broad categories. Firstly, the evidence from the quantitative analyses of student attainment and ATL scores (the stats) established that there was a positive correlation between *Learning Skills* and subject learning across the curriculum.

Secondly, through the evidence from the learning journals, the student interviews and the teacher interviews (the stories), we have considered the extent to which we might reasonably attribute some degree of causation to this relationship – to make the bold claim that the *Learning Skills* curriculum, at least in part, contributed to these improvements in subject learning.

In the next chapter, we will consider this evidence in light of the five research questions we set out at the start of this chapter, before looking beyond the evidence to consider the following, crucial question: if it is true that *Learning Skills* helps students get better at learning in ways that can be detected using existing indicators... how exactly might it work?

CHAPTER 7

THE CASE FOR *LEARNING SKILLS*

---

*'Children have the right to surprise us.
Children have the right to enable us
to believe that they can do amazing
things. Too often, our education system
unintentionally stops that happening...'*

Dame Alison Peacock (2016)[1]

In his 2013 book *The Art of Thinking Clearly*, Rolf Dobelli outlines 99 ways in which we humans unwittingly fool ourselves.[2] Perhaps the biggest beast in this compendium of cognitive errors, biases and fallacies – described by Dobelli as 'the mother of all misconceptions' – is *confirmation bias*, which he defines as 'the tendency to interpret new information so that it becomes compatible with our existing theories, beliefs and convictions'.[3]

In the context of the Sea View study, it is important to recognise that both the authors of this book chose to join the *Learning Skills* team, all the way back in 2010. This was not foisted upon us. The very fact that we volunteered to be on the team means that we both believed – as we still do – that it is possible to teach children how to get better at learning stuff.

For the last ten years or so, we have been immersed in this work on a more or less daily basis. Obviously, we believed in what we were doing and wanted it to succeed, or else we wouldn't have spent a significant chunk of our lives trying to make it happen. James self-funded a PhD to evaluate the impact of the programme over eight years, and now we're writing a book in which we're effectively staking our professional reputations on the fact that we might actually be on to something here.

Thus, as well as being mindful not to succumb to confirmation bias, we also risk falling prey to the *sunk cost fallacy*. As Dobelli explains:

> The sunk cost fallacy is most dangerous when we have invested a lot of time, money, energy or love in something. This investment becomes a reason to carry on, even if we are dealing with a lost cause. The more we invest, the greater the sunk costs are, and the greater the urge to continue becomes.[4]

With all of this in mind, we will attempt in this chapter to set out a balanced case for the *Learning Skills* curriculum, recognising the limitations of the Sea View study while also putting forward the positive argument that all schools should consider implementing a *Learning Skills* curriculum. As Professor Adrian Simpson recently remarked,[5] in seeking to make the case that an educational initiative is worth implementing, research and evidence will only get you so far. You also need to make the *narrative case* – explaining why you think it works, or at least why it might be better than the prevailing model.

Before we do this, we will briefly recap the key findings from the Sea View study in light of the five research questions we outlined in *Chapter 6*.

SUMMARY OF FINDINGS

RQ1: What was the relationship between *Learning Skills* provision and student attainment in subject learning across the curriculum?

Key finding: Students in the Learning Skills cohorts achieved statistically significant gains in subject learning across the curriculum, compared with the control cohort..

The strongest evidence to suggest a link between *Learning Skills* and subject learning comes from the comparison of student attainment in the treatment and control cohorts at three and five years. This analysis reveals a consistent pattern of accelerated subject learning in the treatment cohort, compared with the control cohort. When you consider that the control cohort had more than four hundred additional lessons of subject-based learning throughout Key Stage 3, this finding of significantly improved attainment across the curriculum is all the more remarkable.

As we have discussed, it is important to recognise that correlation may not equate to causation. However, the hypothesis that the *Learning Skills* programme was at least partly responsible for the subsequent gains in academic attainment is supported by the findings from the learning journals, student interviews and teacher interviews. Although a small number of students questioned the value of *Learning Skills*, the learning journal and student interview analyses reveal that the majority of students thought that *Learning Skills* had impacted positively on their subject learning in other subjects, with many of them able to articulate how this had happened, either for themselves or for others.

Although a number of mechanisms of transfer were identified, the most commonly cited were increased self-confidence and enhanced communication skills, meaning that students were able to assert themselves and participate more fully in other lessons. All of the teachers interviewed reported that they had observed more proactive learning behaviours among *Learning Skills* cohorts, compared with previous cohorts. Teachers were also able to articulate a range of ways in which *Learning Skills* helped students learn more effectively in other subjects, and why the programme may have been particularly beneficial for students from disadvantaged backgrounds.

RQ2: To what extent does the quality of *Learning Skills* provision in year 7 predict student attainment at GCSE?

Key finding: The 'blip analysis' suggests that the quality of Learning Skills provision in year 7 correlates with student attainment at GCSE.

As a result of unforeseen changes to staffing and timetabling in the second year of the programme, it was possible to test the central hypothesis further. If the quality of *Learning Skills* provision in year 7 is a predictor of academic attainment at GCSE, then we would expect to see a spike for cohort 1, a dip for cohort 2 and then a spike again for cohort 3. This is precisely the pattern of results that was observed. When *Learning Skills* was taught by specialist teachers in mixed ability groups, the results significantly improved; when the quality of *Learning Skills* provision was compromised by staffing and timetabling issues in the second year, the results dipped; and when mixed ability grouping and a dedicated teaching team were restored for cohort 3, the results improved again.

RQ3: What was the relationship between *Learning Skills* provision and the attainment of students eligible for the Pupil Premium?

Key finding: Learning Skills was associated with accelerated gains among students from disadvantaged backgrounds, with a closing of the disadvantage gap at GCSE by over 65% from one cohort to the next.

The baseline analysis revealed that in the *Learning Skills* treatment cohort, there was a statistically significant Pupil Premium (PP) gap at entry to the school. This is in line with national trends, whereby students from economically disadvantaged backgrounds typically achieve lower grades than their peers. In the control cohort, however, the gap was reversed at entry to the school, with students eligible for the PP marginally outperforming their peers.

Over the next three years, this pattern reversed. By the end of year 9, the PP gap in the control cohort was 25% (all subjects combined); in the *Learning Skills* cohort, it was just 2%. If we take into account the difference between the two cohorts at entry to the school, the improved attainment of disadvantaged students in the *Learning Skills* cohort is even greater than it appears, since they started from a position of greater disparity than was evident in the control cohort. This pattern of accelerated attainment among PP students in *Learning Skills* cohort 1 was also seen in the year 11 GCSE analysis, where the PP gap was reduced by 66.9% from one cohort to the next.

Secondary data analyses revealed a number of reasons why the *Learning Skills* programme may have been particularly beneficial for disadvantaged pupils. For example, by valuing a range of skills, such as leadership, organisational skills and speaking and listening skills, students found themselves on a more level playing field than in traditional subject disciplines, where there is often an almost exclusive emphasis on written literacy. A wider range of students were able to achieve success in this environment, because there were more ways for them *to* succeed.

Related to this, the fact that *Learning Skills* was not assessed in the same way as other subjects enabled students to shift their focus from a performance orientation to a learning orientation. The fact that *Learning Skills* is a mixed ability approach – combined with the fact that we continually mixed up the groupings – was also likely instrumental in closing the gap, because the students were able to learn a lot from one another.

But perhaps the biggest factor in closing the disadvantage gap is that the *Learning Skills* curriculum provides all students with the time, the opportunities and the support they need to find their voice, to find their feet, and to develop the confidence and the vision for a positive future that underpins so much academic success. It stands to reason that students who had previously struggled to compete on a narrower playing field that focused mainly on written literacy – and who therefore lacked the confidence that comes with achievement and success – would stand to gain the most from such an intervention.

As well as closing the disadvantage gap, it is important to recognise that in the *Learning Skills* cohorts, non-disadvantaged students also performed significantly better than their counterparts in the control cohort. Therefore, in contrast with interventions that target only disadvantaged students, the *Learning Skills* programme appears to have closed the gap in an equitable manner, with all students gaining from the programme, and accelerated gains among students from disadvantaged backgrounds.

RQ4: To what extent did the knowledge, skills, habits and attitudes, developed through the *Learning Skills* curriculum, transfer into other subject areas?

Key finding: Evidence from progress data, teacher interviews, student interviews and learning journals suggests that students were able to transfer their learning from Learning Skills into other subject areas in a range of ways.

The success of a taught Learning to Learn initiative rests on the extent to which the knowledge, skills, habits and attitudes developed through the taught course are able to transfer into other subject areas. Transfer does not always happen automatically, and some have suggested that this is a fatal flaw in the idea of a taught Learning to Learn curriculum. In this view, Learning to Learn is seen as something that should be embedded throughout all subject areas rather than being taught through a separate course. In contrast, the *Learning Skills* approach is premised on the idea that transfer is possible – it just needs to be carefully and explicitly managed at both ends of the process (transfer *out* of *Learning Skills* lessons and transfer *in* to subject learning across the curriculum).

The fact that academic attainment across the curriculum was significantly higher among the *Learning Skills* cohorts than in the control cohort suggests that some degree of meaningful transfer was able to happen in this instance. In the student interview and learning journal analyses, the majority of students felt that what they learned in *Learning Skills* lessons *did* transfer to other subjects, and they were able to articulate a range of ways in which this happened. Similarly, the teacher interviews revealed a number of mechanisms by which *Learning Skills* may have led to improved subject learning across the curriculum.

RQ5: What was the non-cognitive impact of the *Learning Skills* programme?

Key finding: There is evidence that Learning Skills led to improvements in attitudes to learning, curiosity and exploration, personal growth, interpersonal skills and public speaking.

As well as evaluating the impact of *Learning Skills* on the students' academic attainment, this study included data collection and analysis relating to a number of affective domains. This includes the students' attitude to learning scores and the use of psychometric questionnaires, administered at the start and end of year 7. To save space, we haven't included the psychometric questionnaire data in this book.[6] To summarise, however, they revealed statistically significant gains in two domains from the start to the end of year 7 – (1) curiosity and exploration and (2) personal growth.

Methodologically however, the use of questionnaires in this study was problematic. In particular, there was no control group in this strand of the study. It is therefore not known whether the improved scores were related to the *Learning Skills* course; it is quite possible that the students' scores would increase on some measures if tested a year apart regardless of any intervention effect. The questionnaire findings should therefore be treated with a good degree of caution.

More convincing evidence relating to the students' non-cognitive development came from the qualitative data analyses. In the learning journals, many students wrote about how *Learning Skills* had helped them learn how to get along with others, at school and in their home lives. In the interviews, teachers spoke about how the *Learning Skills* course helped students overcome their fear of failure and to achieve things that they did not previously think they were capable of. These included quite rare occurrences, such as overcoming a fear of public speaking, as well as everyday experiences, such as being able to sit with a former bully in maths or learning strategies that enabled them to get along with their siblings better.

CAUSALITY AND GENERALISABILITY

Taken together, the findings summarised above suggest that the *Learning Skills* programme at Sea View achieved a considerable degree of success in meeting its aims – to help students get better at learning in ways that are detectable using existing indicators of learning. However, it is important to recognise the limitations of this small study and to remain open to alternative interpretations of these findings.

One of the advantages of mixed methods research is that it helps overcome the limitations of any single method. However, increasing the number of methods also increases the number of ways in which the methods of data collection and analysis need to be qualified and carefully considered. A comprehensive account of the limitations relating to each strand of the Sea View study can be found in James's PhD.[7] In this section, we will focus on two issues – (1) the question of causality (how confident can we be that the improved results were caused by the *Learning Skills* programme and not some other factor or factors?) and (2) the generalisability of findings.

THE QUESTION OF CAUSALITY

In this study, *Learning Skills* cohort 1 achieved significantly higher grades than the control cohort in both the interim (year 9) and final (GCSE) analyses. However, the grade a student achieves in a GCSE exam is primarily a product of the hard work, knowledge and skills of that student and their teacher (and, in some cases, a private tutor). To suggest that the improved GCSE results may have been caused, at least in part, by the *Learning Skills* curriculum, is therefore a bold claim, and it is not one that we make lightly. To test the strength of this claim, we must consider alternative interpretations of the data.

There are three main considerations here. First is the fact that the study period began at a time when the school's exam results had been in a period of decline. In 2009, just 26% of students achieved 5A*CEM, around half the national average; in 2010 – the year the *Learning Skills* programme began – this figure increased to 36%. It could therefore be argued that the school's results were already on an upward trajectory, and that the improved attainment in *Learning Skills* cohort 1, five years later, was simply an extension of this.

Second, the improved attainment could be an example of 'regression to the mean', a statistical phenomenon whereby it is likely that an outlier (an unusually high or low data point), when measured again after a period of time, will have moved closer to the mid-point (the average). Put simply: when you're at the top, the only way is down, and when you're at the bottom, the only way is up. Therefore, any improvements in the school's GCSE results may simply have been a consequence of the elastic way in which numbers work, whereby outliers have a tendency to move toward the average over time.

Third, Sea View was in 'special measures' during the first two years of the study period. Since the *Learning Skills* programme was not the only change to take place at the school during this period, it could be argued that the improved attainment may have been driven by other factors – an increased emphasis on marking books, for example – rather than the *Learning Skills* programme.

At face value, each of these alternative interpretations appears plausible. The question is, are they more or less plausible than the idea that the improvements were driven, at least in part, by the *Learning Skills* curriculum?

To determine whether the improved results were the result of an upward trajectory, regression to the mean, or some other factor, the most important question to ask is: Why did the results improve far more for the *Learning Skills* cohort than for the control cohort? This leads us to a second question: What are the main known differences between these two cohorts of students?

Having worked at Sea View throughout the study period, we are aware of no major changes to policy or practice that would have affected one cohort significantly more than the next – with one exception. By far the biggest known difference is that students in the *Learning Skills* cohorts took part in over four hundred *Learning Skills* lessons throughout years 7, 8 and 9 – a research-informed complex intervention designed to help students in those particular cohorts become more effective, self-regulated learners in ways that transfer to other subject areas – while the control cohort had the equivalent number of lessons of subject-based learning.

Here, we must return to the question of 'correlation vs causation'. The best way to explore the question of causality is to triangulate the findings from a range of data sources. If, for example, the results went up but students and teachers consistently said that *Learning Skills* did not help them learn in other subjects, then it would be sensible to conclude that the improvements were more likely due to some other factor.

However, in the Sea View study there was a high degree of alignment between the different strands of data collection and analysis. When the control cohort reached year 11, they got the best results the school had ever achieved (52.3% 5A*CEM). Clearly, it is true that the school was on an upward trajectory. However, one year later, *Learning Skills* cohort 1 achieved 63.2% 5A*CEM, a raw improvement of 10.9% and a relative improvement of 21% – a far greater rate of improvement than had been seen in previous years. Data from the attitude to learning scores, the students' learning journals, student interviews and teacher interviews point to a range of ways in which the *Learning Skills* curriculum helped pupils achieve higher grades in their subject learning across the curriculum. But perhaps the most compelling evidence of all is the way in which the disadvantage gap closed.

In the three-year interim analysis, the PP gap for all subjects combined was 25% in the control cohort and just 2% in the treatment cohort. In the five-year GCSE analysis, again we saw the PP gap close by 66.9% from one cohort to the next. None of the three alternative interpretations outlined above explains why the PP gap closed so significantly from one cohort to the next. By far the biggest known difference is that the treatment cohort had more than four hundred *Learning Skills* lessons throughout Key Stage 3 – lessons that were designed to help them become more effective, proactive, self-regulated learners. It is therefore not unreasonable to conclude that the gains in academic attainment were driven, at least in part, by the *Learning Skills* curriculum.

That said, this was a relatively small pilot study, carried out in a single school. The only way to determine whether the *Learning Skills* approach reliably leads to improved academic attainment, especially for young people from disadvantaged backgrounds, would be to scale up the approach and subject it to a rigorous, large-scale evaluation. This is what we intend to do in the coming years – indeed, the approach is already spreading to other schools around the world.

GENERALISABILITY OF FINDINGS

To summarise our central claim: the combination of findings from multiple strands of data collection and analysis suggest that the *Learning Skills* curriculum contributed to the students' significantly improved attainment in subject learning across the curriculum, with accelerated learning among students from disadvantaged backgrounds. Given the moral imperative to do whatever can be done to 'level up' the disadvantage gap – to minimise and ideally to eradicate the extent to which the education system perpetuates disadvantage and inequality – these findings are encouraging, and provide a strong basis for considering whether and how *Learning Skills* might be scaled up for use in other settings.

At the start of the study period, the attainment of students in both the treatment and control cohorts was some way below the national average. The question of whether these findings can be replicated in schools with different demographic profiles – or even in other schools with similar profiles – remains to be seen. As mentioned in the *Introduction*, this intervention was implemented by a dedicated group of teachers who had been involved in the design of the *Learning Skills* programme. In a very real sense, the teaching team 'owned' the intervention, and we built it from the ground up. There is no reason to believe that such enthusiasm, autonomy and agency cannot be replicated in other settings – we will return to this question in the next chapter. However, it would be unrealistic to expect these findings to be replicated in other schools through the top-down implementation of the ideas in this book, and we strongly advise schools not to pursue this course of action.

Should *Learning Skills* be implemented in enough schools to warrant a larger-scale evaluation, based on this study (and learning lessons from previous large-scale evaluations of Learning to Learn initiatives) it would make sense to apply strict criteria for inclusion in the study. The implementation checklist we present in *Chapter 8* would form a good basis for deciding which schools to include in such a study. Should enough schools meet these criteria, it would be possible to carry out a large-scale evaluation of the approach, either using previous cohorts as a control group as in the Sea View study, or potentially through a large-scale Randomised Controlled Trial. However, we have a number of reservations about the use of RCTs in education, as we will discuss in the next chapter.

THE NARRATIVE CASE FOR *LEARNING SKILLS*

The Sea View study advances the Learning to Learn field in two key ways – in terms of outcomes and in terms of theory. First, the *Learning Skills* curriculum shows promise in achieving what previous Learning to Learn initiatives have failed to achieve: to bring about demonstrable improvements in learning outcomes across the curriculum, with accelerated gains among young people from disadvantaged backgrounds. This alone provides a strong basis for further developing and refining this approach, to determine whether these findings can be replicated in other settings as part of a strategy for school and system improvement.

However, as well as being able to point to evidence, it is also important that we are able to explain how *Learning Skills* helps children get better at learning stuff. Second, then, we must provide an explanation of how the *Learning Skills* curriculum might drive improved attainment across the curriculum. We've seen the evidence of improved outcomes – but how does it work on a theoretical level? There are six key features to consider:

1. The *Learning Skills* curriculum reconceptualises Learning to Learn as a **complex intervention** – a whole-school approach to teaching and learning that combines the use of many active ingredients. The *marginal gains* to accrue from each of these active ingredients stack up and interact, producing a larger effect size overall.

2. The *Learning Skills* curriculum places an explicit focus on **metacognition** – helping students monitor and control their thought processes. Through such practices as reflective writing, a shared language of learning and transfer plenaries, students were regularly provided with the space, the time and the linguistic tools to discuss and think deeply about how they learn in different contexts – what they find easy, what they find difficult, and how they might overcome any particular challenges they currently face. Through such practices, *Learning Skills* takes the implicit, tacit, invisible processes of learning and makes them explicit, tangible, visible – and, therefore, learnable.

3. The *Learning Skills* curriculum provides regular opportunities for students to develop the skills of **self-regulation** – learning to monitor and control their feelings and behaviours. Through the approach described in *Chapter 5: Components of a complex intervention* under the heading 'collaboration and complexity', *Learning Skills* lessons regularly required students to venture from the safety of their friendship groups and learn how to engage in educationally productive 'exploratory talk' with anyone, in any group size. In addition, through activities such as meditation and guided visualisations, the '7-day challenge' and reflective writing, students had the time and space in which to learn how to monitor and control their feelings and behaviours – both in school and in their lives beyond the school gates.

4. The *Learning Skills* curriculum recognises that the teaching of **oracy** is not only a powerful driver of learning (learning *through* talk) – it is

an important educational end in itself (learning *to* talk). Teaching children how to speak and listen effectively in a range of contexts – from small talk and group discussions, through formal debates to delivering a knockout speech – helps them find their voice, literally and metaphorically. The importance of this cannot be overstated. The *Learning Skills* curriculum recognises that there is more to education than exam results – that education should really be seen as a process of human self-actualisation, helping every young person develop the knowledge, the skills and the confidence they need to meet the world on their own terms.

5. Through this combination of three powerful ideas – metacognition, self-regulation and oracy – students were able to become more confident, articulate, **self-regulated learners**. Through half-termly projects and weekly reviews, students had the space and time to discover their strengths and weaknesses and to take increasing ownership over their learning – setting goals, identifying strategies to meet those goals, and evaluating their progress along the way. By judiciously stepping back to allow them to learn how to 'flounder intelligently', teachers of *Learning Skills* instill in their students arguably the most important lesson of them all: that ultimately, they alone are responsible for the choices they make, and for the consequences that follow.

6. The *Learning Skills* approach includes a number of explicit strategies to ensure that the knowledge, skills, habits and dispositions developed through the taught course are able to meaningfully **transfer** out of the *Learning Skills* classroom and into subject areas throughout the school, driving improved attainment across the curriculum.

Taken together, these six key features provide a compelling narrative as to how the *Learning Skills* curriculum helps students become more confident, articulate, effective learners, enabling them to learn more effectively and threfore to achieve higher grades in subject learning across the curriculum. This is what the *Learning Skills* team set out to achieve ten years ago, and the evidence outlined above suggests that we have made some purposeful strides toward meeting our goals. We are also quite convinced that if we did it again, knowing what we know now, the outcomes would have been even better.

Since the Sea View study ended, we have built on our early experiences and adapted the *Learning Skills* approach to a range of contexts – from early years to universities, from schools in disadvantaged areas to elite international colleges, from workplaces to refugee camps. As James argued in a recent blog, metacognition, self-regulated learning and oracy also form the basis of what makes for effective professional development for teachers – reflecting on our practice, taking ownership over our own professional development, and doing so in collaboration with others.[8] We have not yet undertaken robust evaluations of *Learning Skills* in these new contexts. However, the early feedback we have received in each of these settings has been extremely encouraging, and we look forward to developing our work in each of these areas in the years to come.

In the next chapter, we will turn to the thorny issue of implementation. For now, we will conclude this chapter by listing a few reasons why we think it's a good idea to implement a *Learning Skills* curriculum:

- It significantly improves academic attainment across the curriculum.
- It closes the disadvantage gap from the bottom up.
- It makes teaching more enjoyable:
  - In *Learning Skills* lessons, there is less teaching from the front of the room and more time for one-to-one conversations with individuals and groups of students. As a result, you get to know your students like never before.
  - It reduces the frequency of helpless questions asked by students, such as those we saw in the *Introduction*.
- Although it's a complex intervention, it isn't complicated to implement from a whole-school perspective. The *Learning Skills* team and the students themselves do most of the heavy lifting.
- As well as helping students pass exams, it prepares them for a life of learning beyond the school gates by helping them become more confident, independent learners.
- It enables students from state schools to leave school as confident and articulate as those from expensive independent schools.
- It doesn't cost anything to implement – and everything you need to get started is in this book.

When you see the case for *Learning Skills* summarised like this... it's kind of a no-brainer, don't you think?

CHAPTER 8

AN IMPLEMENTATION (AND EVALUATION) CHECKLIST

'Implementation Science is remarkable on two counts. Few scientists and fewer practitioners have heard of it, and most scientists and most practitioners require it immediately!'

Dr Barbara Kelly (2014)[1]

Given the possibility that the widespread implementation of the *Learning Skills* curriculum might significantly enhance the educational and life outcomes of current and future generations of children – especially those from disadvantaged backgrounds, who seem to gain disproportionately from the approach – we believe that there is a strong moral imperative to continue developing and evaluating the approach in new settings in the years to come. On really optimistic days, we can envisage a time in the not-too-distant future when there is a version of a *Learning Skills* curriculum in every school on the planet.

We use this phrase 'a version of' advisedly. We are not suggesting that the particular approach we implemented at Sea View is the best or the only way to do it. There are so many variables in play that to make such a claim would be foolish. We don't know whether five lessons a week is the optimal amount of time to allocate to a year 7 taught course. No doubt some people would say this is too much; others may think it is not enough. The truth is, it's too early to say. We do know that it didn't do any harm at Sea View – quite the opposite, in fact.

Equally, we don't know whether the particular combination of classroom practices we outlined in *Chapter 5: Components of a complex intervention* is the best way to teach children how to get better at learning stuff. As we outlined at the end of that chapter, there are a number of things we would do differently if we had our time again. That said, we do believe that *Learning Skills* marks a significant advance toward fulfilling the vision John Flavell had all those years ago – that a concern for metacognition may one day be translated into approaches to teaching and learning that help young people make 'wise and thoughtful life decisions', as well as helping them learn more effectively in formal educational settings.[2]

Flavell's dream is closer to being realised than ever before. But if *Learning Skills* is going to become a permanent fixture in the way we educate future generations, we need to collect evidence of impact in many more schools. We are as excited by this prospect as we are daunted: excited, because of the potential these practices hold for helping every young person on the planet find their feet, find their voice, and become confident, switched-on, articulate, self-regulated, self-actualising human beings; and daunted, because we know that scaling up educational innovations so that the efficacy is maintained at scale... well, let's just say it's no picnic.

We discussed the difficulty of scaling up good ideas in *Chapter 3: Learning to Learn on trial*, when we looked at the example of Assessment for Learning (AfL) – an approach that started out life as a simple enough idea (assessment that is used to adapt teaching to meet student needs), but which underwent a series of 'lethal mutations' to become a multi-headed, Hydra-like beast that roamed the nation's classrooms waving WALT and WILF signs (*We Are Learning To... / What I'm Looking For...*), juggling traffic-light cups and lollipop sticks and insisting that every child knows what alphanumeric level they're on in every subject.

But as well as serving as a warning of what can go wrong, AfL also provides us with important insights into how to implement good ideas at scale. As we discussed in *Chapter 3*, there is a tension when you scale up an educational initiative. You want it to remain close to the original idea – what researchers refer to as 'fidelity' – without being so rigid that you don't take account (or advantage) of local contextual factors. But at the same time, you don't want things to become so flexible that fidelity is compromised by a series of lethal mutations.

In an attempt to strike a balance between the simultaneous need for fidelity and flexibility, Thompson and Wiliam (2008) propose a 'tight but loose' approach to implementation:

The Tight but Loose formulation combines an obsessive adherence to the central design principles (the 'tight' part) with accommodations to the needs, resources, constraints, and particularities that occur in any school or district (the 'loose' part), but only where these do not conflict with the theory of action of the intervention.[3]

In recent years, thanks in part to some excellent books on productivity, people have really come to appreciate the power of checklists.[4], [5] With this in mind, in the remainder of this chapter we will outline a checklist of 'central design principles' for *Learning Skills* – elements that we think are non-negotiable if you want to replicate or improve upon the outcomes of the Sea View study.

There are six central design principles in our checklist: 1) vertical slice implementation team; 2) timetabled lessons; 3) embedded practices; 4) strategies for transfer; 5) ongoing monitoring and evaluation; and 6) visible leadership. To maximise the chances of successful implementation, each of these elements needs to be in place. However, it should be up to each school to determine how to adapt these design principles to suit the local context.

When it comes to effective implementation, 'tight but loose' is a good rule of thumb, but it will only get you so far. In recent years, a new field of study has emerged – implementation science – that we believe holds great promise as a framework for school improvement.[6] There isn't space here to do justice to implementation science; this will be the focus of James's next book. However, items 1, 5 and 6 in the checklist are features of effective implementation generally that we think are necessary to ensure that this thing really flies.

Whether you work in early years, primary, secondary or beyond – and whether you are in the state, independent or alternative sector – there are loads of ways you can get started in putting the ideas in this book into practice. However, we are especially interested in exploring whether the findings from the Sea View study can be replicated or improved upon in secondary schools, and so the checklist is written with secondary schools in mind.

THE CHECKLIST

1. VERTICAL SLICE IMPLEMENTATION TEAM

If you're planning to roll out a whole-school initiative, the most important thing is to secure buy-in from people throughout the school. A really powerful way to do this is to assemble a 'vertical slice' implementation team.[7] It's a simple enough idea: you put together a team comprising representative stakeholders from throughout the organisation. In the case of *Learning Skills*, the vertical slice team might include the assistant head with responsibility for teaching and learning, a middle leader, an early career teacher, an experienced classroom teacher, *Learning Skills* teachers, a teaching assistant and the Special Educational Needs and Disabilities Coordinator. Depending on the size of the school, around eight to ten people is a good number to aim for. If you're doing something around behaviour management, you might include pastoral staff, the data manager, lunchtime supervisors or representatives from the student body – whoever is directly affected by whatever is being implemented.

The aim of the vertical slice team is to write and execute a detailed implementation plan covering three to five years (the timeframe will depend on the complexity of the innovation), looking at the process of implementation from multiple perspectives. The work of this team will be front-loaded – the writing of a comprehensive implementation plan is the most important thing – but members of the team should also be responsible for executing aspects of the plan over time. We recommend that the implementation team is hand-picked – people you know are ready for a challenge, and who are confident enough in their own practice to be able to take on the additional responsibility of helping implement a whole-school initiative.

The implementation team should operate as a glass box, as opposed to a black box. Communication is key. At regular intervals, the team should communicate with the wider staff body what they're doing, why and how. It should be made clear that everyone in the organisation is represented on the team, and that if anyone has any questions or concerns, they can speak with a member of the team.

Early on in the process, it's a good idea to carry out a data collection exercise whereby the team captures the views of their colleagues on whatever the initiative is. The teaching assistant collects data from other teaching assistants, the middle leaders collect data from other middle leaders (or possibly from their departments, or both) – and so on. Good questions to ask include:

- What do you think about the idea of [helping our students get better at regulating their own learning]?
- What are our current areas of strength in this area?
- Here are some ideas we have been discussing...
  - What do you think?
  - What might be improved upon?
  - What concerns do you have?
  - What ideas do you have?
  - What further questions do you have?

This initial phase of data collection and consultation should involve interviews/focus groups – never underestimate the importance of face-to-face communication – but it may also involve a short online survey, which can be useful as a way of collecting people's views anonymously. This data collection exercise can be incredibly powerful as a way of finding out what people throughout the organisation really think, and to make sure that you have robust discussions at the outset where people feel free to air their honest thoughts and feelings without fear of repercussion.

The implementation team then works collaboratively over the course of a year, working through some of the ideas in the remainder of this chapter, to create a detailed implementation plan that addresses the following questions:

- What problem are you trying to solve? (And how does this problem play out at the level of the student, teacher, parent?)
- What's the innovation you are seeking to implement to solve this problem? (And what are the 'active ingredients' of this innovation?)
- What's your plan for implementation? Who will do what, by when? Who will check it's been done? Who is ultimately responsible? (Ideally, the responsibility should be carried collectively by the implementation team)
- What obstacles or barriers do we anticipate we might encounter along the way? What plans can we make now to help us address problems when – not if – they arise?
- What short, medium and long-term changes do we want to see in terms of teacher outcomes and pupil outcomes?
- How will we monitor and evaluate the impact of the innovation over time? (See below)
- What resources do we need (e.g. staff training, coaching, mentoring, triads, ICT infrastructure etc) to ensure a high quality of provision is achieved and maintained?

On the implementation team, it is important that everyone is treated as being equally important. This means everyone on the team is equally responsible for contributing to the writing and execution of the implementation plan, as well as for voicing any concerns as they arise. This approach helps prevent groupthink from happening (the phenomenon whereby people make bad decisions because of dysfunctional group dynamics, which we discussed briefly in *Chapter 5: Components of a complex intervention*), and makes it far more likely that the initiative will be followed through by the "hive mind", regardless of any changes to key personnel that will inevitably happen over a three-to-five year implementation period.

2. TIMETABLED LESSONS

There should be timetabled lessons for all students in each *Learning Skills* cohort, in mixed ability groups. You may wish to start small and build up. However, we recommend that you allocate at least three lessons a week – ideally four or five – and, if possible, these should be timetabled either on the same day or on two consecutive days. If you're in a secondary school, this should start in year 7; as students progress through the school, you might also consider extending timetabled lessons into years 8 and 9.

Timetabled lessons should always be taught by a dedicated team of teachers, appointed through a competitive selection process. If possible, these teachers should also be year 7 tutors. If you aren't able to assemble a team of teachers who are well suited to the task of designing and teaching a *Learning Skills* curriculum and who are motivated to do so, now is probably not the time to pursue this particular avenue of school improvement.

The content of the timetabled lessons should be determined by the dedicated teaching team. However, here are five tried-and-tested ideas that you may wish to consider:

1. Project-based learning (half-termly)
2. Weekly philosophical enquiry lessons
3. Oracy lessons (group discussions, structured debates, presentational talk)
4. Learning journals
5. Weekly reviews (monitoring progress, identifying strategies for success, setting goals and reminders for the coming week).

3. EMBEDDED PRACTICES

Alongside the timetabled lessons, as far as possible, the self-regulated learning agenda should also be reflected in teaching and learning practices throughout the school. This may include some or all of the following:

- Focusing on the 'how of learning' as well as the 'what of learning', ideally using a shared language of learning. A balance needs to be struck here, and where this balance lies will differ from one school/department/teacher to the next. Some may wish to discuss the 'how of learning' in every lesson; others may prefer to use weekly or half-termly reviews.
- Talk rules displayed in every classroom and used routinely to guide class discussions.
- Departmental policies for developing self-regulated learning.
- Promoting the self-regulated learning agenda consistently through things like assemblies, tutor time, homework, feedback and report-writing.

4. STRATEGIES FOR TRANSFER

As mentioned above, it is a good idea to appoint a 'vertical slice team' to write and execute a three-to-five year implementation plan. In the case of *Learning Skills*, one of the central aims of such an implementaiton plan is to ensure that the knowledge, skills, habits and dispositions developed through the taught *Learning Skills* course are able to meaningfully transfer into subject learning throughout the curriculum. The implementation plan should therefore include strategies for transfer, such as:

- Transfer *out* of *Learning Skills* lessons:
  - Learning journals
  - Transfer plenaries
- Transfer *in* to subject learning across the curriculum:
  - A shared whole-school language of learning, developed by students and teachers working together
  - A shared understanding as to the meanings of key words, e.g.:
    - metacognition – monitoring and controlling thought processes
    - self-regulation – monitoring and controlling feelings (physical and emotional) and behaviours
    - self-regulated learning – the application of metacognition and self-regulation to learning

○ A joined-up approach to whole-school CPD (e.g. instruction, coaching, peer observations, action research or lesson study focusing on different aspects of self-regulated learning).

5. ONGOING MONITORING AND EVALUATION

Ultimately, the proof in the pudding is not whether you can demonstrate progress within *Learning Skills* lessons themselves – this is a losing game, as we explained in *Chapter 4: The story of Learning Skills* – but whether there is an impact on academic attainment in subject learning across the curriculum.

As well as using existing indicators of progress (e.g. teacher assessments and exam results), it is important to have a multi-layered approach to monitoring and evaluation, incorporating a range of quantitative and qualitative measures (e.g. student progress data, psychometric questionnaires, student interviews, student work, teacher interviews, small group observations).

Monitoring and evaluation should be overseen and co-ordinated by key members of the vertical slice implementation team. Each strand of data collection and analysis should be viewed as a lens that brings into focus a different part of the whole. Data collection should be non-judgmental, and used formatively to inform future decision-making and resourcing (e.g. CPD, peer observations, coaching/mentoring as required), as well as summatively (i.e. to determine the impact of *Learning Skills* on academic learning across the curriculum).

6. VISIBLE LEADERSHIP

It is not necessary, or indeed desirable, for senior leaders to have day-to-day involvement in the running of the *Learning Skills* curriculum. However, it is important that school leaders are regularly seen to actively support *Learning Skills* as a joined-up, whole-school approach to teaching and learning. This can be achieved through the writing and execution of a communications plan that incorporates the following elements, implemented over several years:

• A range of voices (e.g. senior leaders, middle leaders, teacher leaders, support staff, governors, parents, students)

- A range of channels (e.g. staff briefings, the CPD programme, newsletters, assemblies, lessons)
- A range of audiences (e.g. students, parents, governors, support staff, teachers)
- A range of frequencies (e.g. some messages are worth emphasising daily, others weekly, termly or annually).

With the exception of timetabled lessons, the content of which should be determined by the *Learning Skills* teaching team, many of the design principles listed above can be overseen by the vertical slice implementation team. However, care should be taken to ensure that the self-regulated learning agenda is not seen to have been 'outsourced' by the school's senior leadership team. School leaders need to play their role in 'creating the weather' by visibly, audibly and consistently reinforcing the collective goal – to support all students in becoming more confident, proactive, self-regulated learners.

FUTURE EVALUATIONS OF *LEARNING SKILLS*

As we saw in *Chapter 2: A brief history of Learning to Learn*, previous large-scale evaluations of Learning to Learn initiatives have generally reported a net finding of 'no clear impact, either positive or negative, on academic attainment'. However, within the evaluation reports, an intriguing pattern emerged: where whole-school implementation was achieved, there were signs of improved academic attainment.

However, not all of the schools sampled in these evaluations met this important criterion. It is therefore likely that previous large-scale evaluations of Learning to Learn initiatives threw the net too wide – there was too much variance within the sample. In such large-scale evaluations, the signal gets lost in the noise and the baby gets thrown out with the bathwater. And as we argued in *Chapter 3: Learning to Learn on trial*, the field has moved on significantly since the last large-scale evaluations were carried out.

Following the publication of Guy Claxton's book *Building Learning Power* in 2002, 'thousands of schools and classrooms around the planet... experimented with BLP'.[8] Should this book lead to a similar widespread implementation of *Learning Skills* curricula, then in the coming years it should be possible to carry out large-scale evaluations of the approach.

The checklist above is therefore designed to serve two purposes. First and foremost, it is intended as a practical guide to help schools replicate or improve upon the outcomes of the Sea View study. However, we also hope that it may eventually serve as a set of selection criteria for deciding which schools to include in future evaluations of the approach. To be clear: schools should only be included where *Learning Skills* has been implemented in accordance with the six central design principles outlined in the checklist, and where no 'lethal mutations' have been introduced.

If and when we get to that point, we need to consider what kinds of research methods would best be suited to evaluating a complex intervention of this nature. In recent years, there has been a rapid increase in the number of medical-style RCTs in education. The UK's Education Endowment Foundation, formed in 2011, recently published the findings of its 100th RCT. The idea of an RCT is simple enough: you get, say, a hundred schools to sign up to your study, randomly allocate 50 schools to the treatment condition and 50 schools to the control condition (who just do 'business as usual'), and then compare the attainment of the treatment and control groups after a period of time. In medicine, RCTs are considered the 'gold standard' in terms of evidence, and it's easy to see why – it really is a very powerful and elegant research design.

However, there are a number of problems with the use of RCTs in education that are rarely discussed. Here, we will briefly outline three concerns.

First, in medicine, RCTs are almost always placebo-controlled, which means that patients in the control group receive a dummy pill that is known to have no clinical effect. In education, to have a placebo-controlled study, you would have to have those 50 schools in the control group spend an equivalent amount of time (in the case of *Learning Skills*, several lessons a week) doing things that we know will have zero educational benefit – which would be a tough one to get past the ethics board! In education, therefore, we lose one of the most significant benefits of medical RCTs: the ability to rule out the placebo effect (i.e. the teachers believing they are doing something effective, and that conviction giving rise to 'false positives' in the data).

Second, those 50 schools in the control group won't all be doing the same thing; in fact, 'business as usual' will vary enormously across a sample of 50 schools. The control group isn't a single, neat, univariate thing that you're comparing your treatment effect with – it's a massive, messy, multivariate thing. So to compare 'treatment schools' with 'control schools' – as though 'control schools' represent a single point of comparison – is deeply problematic.

To make matters worse, having a control condition in an educational study can create perverse incentives. Schools generally apply to join a trial because they're interested in the thing being evaluated – but then half the schools get told they're in the control group. And what's the point of a control group in an RCT? The point of a control group is to be a bit rubbish compared with whatever's going on in the treatment group. This has been known to prompt some control schools to respond by saying, 'Right, we'll show them – let's really double down on our year 7 English and maths teaching this year' – which just muddies the control data even more.

Finally, in medicine, RCTs are typically double-blinded. This means that not only do the patients not know whether they are getting the drug or a placebo (a single-blind) – the clinicians don't know either (they are just given bottles with coded labels). In education, to double-blind an RCT, you would literally have to have teachers who did not know what they were doing!

Taken together, these reservations seriously undermine the confidence we can have in any results to arise from an education RCT. For this reason, and many more besides, we think that in the short term at least, a naturalistic approach to evaluating *Learning Skills* is the most appropriate approach to pursue, whereby researchers seek to provide a bottom-up account of the impact of *Learning Skills* in multiple, real-world situations.

Such an approach to evaluation would likely resemble the kind of mixed methods evaluation used in the Sea View study. In addition to the criteria outlined in the checklist above, future evaluations of *Learning Skills* should ideally include schools that have previous cohorts with similar prior attainment that can serve as a historical control group. If you are in such a school and you would like to a) implement and b) evaluate the impact of *Learning Skills* over several years, please drop us a line via rethinking-ed. org/contact – we would love to hear from you.

CONCLUSION

ANTIDOTES TO FEAR

'Fear has a large shadow,
but he himself is quite small.'

Ruth Gendler (1988)[1]

'Some failure in life is inevitable. It is
impossible to live without failing at
something, unless you live so cautiously
that you might as well not have lived
at all – in which case, you fail by default.'

JK Rowling (2008)[2]

'Everything you've ever wanted
is on the other side of fear.'

George Addair (n.d.)[3]

To wrap things up, we would like to return to the discussion we started in the *Introduction* – in particular, the question of what education is for. One answer to this question is that education is a process of learning subject knowledge and trying to pass exams. Helping young people gain qualifications is a good thing to do, and we should definitely continue to do it.

However, this is a narrow conception of what education is for. We can also think of the purpose of education more broadly as a process of personal growth, or self-actualisation – helping young people find their feet, find their voice and become the best version of themselves that they can possibly be. That might involve passing exams, but it might also involve learning to speak and listen effectively, developing project management skills, and learning to take control of their own learning – becoming a proactive, as well as a reactive, learner. The *Learning Skills* curriculum addresses both these aims – broad and narrow – and that's why we're hopeful that the approach will go from strength to strength in the years to come. We'll return to this discussion at the end of this chapter. First, here's a quick recap.

THE STORY SO FAR...

We started the book by mapping out the history of Learning to Learn, the field of theory and practice within which the *Learning Skills* curriculum is situated. In *Part I*, we discovered that Learning to Learn is not new – people have been thinking and writing about this stuff for centuries – but that the field really took off with the coining of the word 'metacognition' in the 1970s.

In *Chapter 1: High impact for low cost, or snake oil for hipsters?*, we discovered that the field is rooted in apparently contradictory research findings. On the one hand, educational researchers tell us that 'metacognition and self-regulation' – the two most central concepts in Learning to Learn – provide 'high impact for very low cost, based on extensive evidence'.[4] However, we also discovered that Learning to Learn involves group work, which has a bad rep in some circles. Elsewhere, we find educational researchers confidently asserting that you can't teach 'generic skills' like speaking and listening, and that schools should focus instead on teaching knowledge. In short, we learned that Learning to Learn is educational Marmite: it's either the best thing since sliced bread or it's the road to ruin. All of which begs the question: Which is it?

In *Chapter 2: A brief history of Learning to Learn*, we attempted to unpack these puzzling findings by digging into the research literature. We explored the difference between being learning-oriented and performance-oriented (a learning orientation improves performance more effectively, counter-intuitively). We also reflected on the wisdom of 'marginal gains', the theory that provides a rationale for using complex interventions in education – interventions with more than one moving part. We grasped the nettle of definitions in an attempt to bring clarity to the meaning of three key concepts – metacognition, self-regulation and self-regulated learning – while also considering what these ideas look like in the classroom. And we examined the evidence for and against Learning to Learn, both within the UK and internationally.

Here we found an abundance of evidence in support of educational initiatives oriented around the development of metacognition, self-regulation and oracy. However, much of this evidence comes from meta-analyses of small studies. When people have tried to scale these ideas up into whole-school approaches to teaching and learning – and there have been several large-scale attempts to do so – the benefits seem to fall away. We concluded this chapter by setting out our belief that it is possible to advance the field further, and to learn from earlier attempts to scale up the promising research on metacognition and self-regulation into whole-school approaches to teaching and learning.

It is fair to say that not everybody has yet been persuaded of the value of Learning to Learn. Partly, this is because of the conflicting research evidence outlined above, but it is also because some people don't think it's possible to teach children how to get better at learning stuff – that any attempt to do so is rooted in an ignorance of 'human cognitive architecture', and that schools should focus on teaching knowledge instead.

There are some fascinating insights to be gleaned from this debate, and so in *Chapter 3* we put Learning to Learn on trial. Here, we looked beyond the research evidence to examine a number of arguments for and against teaching children how as well as what to learn. The prosecution drew on three lines of argument: knowledge is foundational; children are novices; and generic skills can't be taught/don't transfer.

Having rebutted these arguments, we offered three counter-arguments: the field has developed since it was last evaluated; scaling up is hard to do, but implementation science is a thing now; and the death of Learning to Learn has been greatly exaggerated. In sum, we concluded that the reason large-scale evaluations of whole-school Learning to Learn initiatives have had mixed results to date may not simply be a failure of the idea that it is possible to teach children how to get better at learning stuff.

Instead, we argued that the 'mixed results' of large-scale evaluations of Learning to Learn are likely to arise from a combination of patchy implementation, being a product of their time, and overly inclusive evaluation methods (throwing the net too wide rather than only evaluating schools where whole-school implementation had been achieved). Finally, we identified several promising lines of enquiry that remain unexplored – lines that we drew together into a complex, whole-school intervention when we began our journey into Learning to Learn 15 years ago.

In *Part II*, we turned our attention to the *Learning Skills* curriculum, a whole-school approach to Learning to Learn that we developed, taught and evaluated over eight years at Sea View, a secondary comprehensive school in a disadvantaged area in the south of England. Often, educational researchers describe things in quite scientific language – interventions, data analysis, input and output variables and so on. But in our experience, when you're a teacher you don't feel much like a scientist. Teaching feels more like a vocation – something that involves your whole identity as a human being; something it isn't always easy to switch off when you go home. So, in *Chapter 4*, we relayed the story of *Learning Skills* as we experienced it as teachers – warts and all.

One important way in which the *Learning Skills* curriculum moves the field forward is that it reconceptualises Learning to Learn as a complex intervention – an initiative with several moving parts. In *Chapters 4* and *5*, we explained why we think teachers and educational researchers should embrace the idea of complex interventions, and how this thinking shaped the design of the *Learning Skills* curriculum.

Following this, we explored the components of the *Learning Skills* curriculum in detail. These fall under four broad categories: structural elements, oracy, metacognition and self-regulated learning. For each component, we provided a rationale for its inclusion in the curriculum and considered what it looks like in the classroom. We concluded *Chapter 5: Components of a complex intervention* with a number of ideas that were either absent or underdeveloped in the *Learning Skills* curriculum at Sea View, but which we think may be worth considering in future iterations of the approach.

In *Chapter 6: The evidence for Learning Skills*, we set out the key findings of the evaluation we carried out over the course of eight years at Sea View, as we followed four cohorts of students from year 7 through to year 11 – one control cohort and three *Learning Skills* cohorts. Here we found that *Learning Skills* was associated with significant gains in academic attainment across the curriculum, with accelerated gains made by students from disadvantaged backgrounds.

We also examined several additional strands of data collection and analysis, with a view to exploring the 'space between' the input variable – the *Learning Skills* curriculum – and the output variable – academic learning across the curriculum. Here, we found a significant degree of alignment between the various strands of the study. Evidence from a range of sources (student progress data, attitude to learning data, the students' learning journals, student and teacher interviews) suggested that *Learning Skills* was successful in helping students get better at learning stuff in ways that could be detected using existing indicators of learning (i.e. teacher assessments and GCSE grades). Secondary data analyses also revealed a number of ways in which the knowledge, skills, habits and dispositions developed through the *Learning Skills* curriculum transferred into other subject areas, enabling students to achieve higher grades in subject learning across the curriculum – as well as to their lives beyond the school gates.

In *Chapter 7: The case for Learning Skills*, we pulled all of this evidence together in relation to the five research questions that underpinned the Sea View pilot study. We also considered the questions of causality and generalisability of findings, before setting out a narrative account of how we think *Learning Skills* contributed to the significant gains we saw in academic attainment across the curriculum.

In particular, we identified six key features of the *Learning Skills* curriculum that combined together to produce the improved student outcomes: the fact that it was a complex intervention, combining the use of several research-informed practices (1); the fact that it focused explicitly on developing metacognition, self-regulation and oracy (2, 3 & 4); the fact that together these three concepts combine to help students become effective, self-regulated learners (5); and the fact that we put in place a number of strategies to ensure that the knowledge, skills, habits and dispositions developed through the *Learning Skills* taught course were able to transfer to subject learning across the curriculum (6). And in *Chapter 8*, we provided a six-point checklist that we hope will serve two purposes: to help teachers and school leaders implement the *Learning Skills* approach effectively in new and diverse settings, and to serve as a set of selection criteria for deciding which schools to include in any future evaluations of the approach.

THE LITANY AGAINST FEAR

As we have been writing this book, many people have asked us: why on earth have you chosen to call a book about education *Fear is the Mind Killer*? The short answer is that it came from one of the teacher interviews James did for his PhD – at least that interview provided the thread that we tugged at, shortly before we realised that this phrase comes close to encapsulating everything we've been doing for the last 15 years. The relevant excerpt comes from an interview with our friend and maverick science teacher Paul Meredith, in response to the question: 'Do you think teaching *Learning Skills* has had any impact on the way you teach science, and if so, how?'

Massively. Massively... so many things. Even the language of how I teach. I don't think a day goes by where I don't refer, whether it's to the whole class or to a student individually, to how fear of failure is paralysis for the brain. How just being afraid of getting things wrong will stop you learning faster than anything. How true confidence comes not from getting things right, but from being prepared to be wrong. I use that language pretty much every day, in pretty much every lesson, to reinforce that it's only from making mistakes that we learn.

And by using this language myself, I'm constantly promoting metacognition in my students. And when I see it in them, when I see that fear in them, I can remind them that they are afraid, and I can point out, "Look what the fear has done to you, it's made you sit in front of a blank bit of graph paper for 20 minutes. The person next to you has had a go, and people who have a go and get it wrong and have a go and get it wrong and have a go – they will get it right eventually. If you sit in front of a blank sheet of paper, you will never get it right." It's all about referring to that fear of failure, and getting them to think about what that will do to their learning. It's just become second nature to me. Because it's true. It's like in Dune, isn't it? Fear is the mind killer.

In case you aren't familiar, *Dune* is a brilliant book by the science fiction author Frank Herbert, later made into a film by David Lynch.[5] In *Dune*, there's a religious order called the *Bene Gesserit*, a powerful and ancient sisterhood whose members spend years training their minds and bodies to obtain superhuman abilities. The *Bene Gesserit* have a mantra known as *The litany against fear*, which they use to help focus their minds in times of peril. We included it at the start of the book, but it's such an incredible piece of writing that we will repeat it here:

The litany against fear

I must not fear.
Fear is the mind killer.
Fear is the little-death that brings total obliteration.
I will face my fear.
I will permit it to pass over me and through me.
And when it has gone past, I will turn the inner eye to see its path.
Where the fear has gone, there will be nothing.
Only I will remain.

When we started writing this book, we asked ourselves: What is the 'big idea' that encapsulates the *Learning Skills* approach? As you are by now (hopefully!) aware, the *Learning Skills* curriculum is a complex intervention, comprising multiple moving parts. It was therefore not immediately obvious whether there is a single 'big idea' that underpins *Learning Skills* – the whole point is that it comprises many component parts, and that the 'marginal gains' to emerge from each component stack up and interact, producing a larger effect size overall.

But as we wrote, this phrase 'Fear is the mind killer' returned to us again and again. As we have mentioned throughout the book, there is an endemic fear of failure among young people, and it typically serves to stop them from doing things. It can stop them from raising their hand in class; it can lead them to avoid public speaking at all costs; and it can prevent them from doing anything to deviate from a narrow range of behaviours deemed acceptable among their peer group. Of course, this is not unique to children: fear can affect adults in quite similar ways. Fear can stop us from speaking up in a meeting, or asking a question of a speaker; it can prompt us to take evasive action rather than have a conversation with someone we recognise in the street; or it might prevent us from applying for a job that would take us away from what we know. Fear can manifest in many different ways, but its effect is usually the same: it keeps people in their lane, and stops them from trying new things.

But fear is weird. Powerful though it undoubtedly is, it is also surprisingly fragile. When people confront their fears, they often find that they simply vanish without a trace. For example, if you are able to overcome that gut-wrenching feeling that stops you from public speaking – a feeling that both of us can recall only too well – you may soon find that public speaking is actually kind of fun and really not worth losing sleep over. Likewise with the fear of putting your hand up to ask a question of a speaker, or the fear of starting a conversation with someone you want to talk to: when we take the plunge, we often find that the water isn't so icy after all. Time and time again, experience tells us: fear's bark is a lot worse than its bite.

Psychotherapists have known about this for years.[6, 7] In exposure therapy, also known as immersion therapy, patients who are exposed to the source of their anxiety/phobia/trauma often find that the fear disappears in a puff of smoke, like a vampire exposed to direct sunlight. This is because fear is often simply a conditioned response to particular environmental stimuli. If you change the environment – for example, making it safe for people to confront their fears by having high expectations enforced with kindness, clear guidance and unconditional support – the fear soon dissipates. In psychotherapy circles, this process is referred to as 'fear extinction'.[8] It needs to be done carefully – you can make things worse if you don't know what you're doing, and you can't force people to face their fears against their will – but exposing people to their fears is well established as a therapeutic approach.

In writing this book, we have come to understand that if there is a 'big idea' that underpins the *Learning Skills* curriculum, it is this: *Learning Skills* is a systematic attempt to eradicate the fear of failure that permeates so many of our classrooms, silently undermining everything we are trying to do as teachers. By gently but firmly (and repeatedly) pushing our students out of their comfort zones, we helped them identify, confront and overcome their fears, one by one.

By requiring them to take part in a range of class discussions – from paired and group work to whole-class philosophical discussions to structured debates to presenting to the class and even to speaking in assemblies and taking part in school plays – we helped our students overcome their fear of public speaking. By setting them long-term projects and then stepping back judiciously, we helped them overcome the paralysing fear that many students experience when they aren't told what to do, and how, and by when. Through the approach to mixing up pupil grouping that we described in *Chapter 5: Components of a complex intervention* under the heading *Collaboration and complexity*, we systematically nudged our pupils out of the comfort of their friendship groups to help them overcome their fear of speaking with students from different backgrounds and friendship groups. And by working with our students to set ambitious goals that many of them felt were beyond their reach at the start of the course, we helped them overcome their fear of failure, because all of · them experienced varying degrees of failure and frustration many times as they progressed through the course.

Through such practices, our students learned how to feel comfortable with feeling uncomfortable. In so doing, they learned through experience to view failure for what it is – feedback in a Halloween mask. It may appear scary or unpleasant at first, but you soon realise that it isn't worthy of your goosebumps. When students confront their fears in this way, not only do their fears evaporate and become 'extinct', but other things appear in their place – knowledge of self, personal growth, confidence, organisational skills, communication skills, good memories – just as the 'litany against fear' describes: *Where the fear has gone, there will be nothing. Only I will remain.*

ANTIDOTES TO FEAR

It may be a cliché, but teaching is a wonderful job. It really is a privilege to be able to play such a formative role in young people's lives. And it can be a lot of fun: spending so much time around young people doesn't half keep you on your toes. Regrettably, however, there is also no shortage of fear swirling around within the teaching profession itself. An online search of 'teachers fear' yields an incredible 200 million results, with no shortage of hair-raising headlines. Here are just a few from the last couple of years:

FEAR IS THE DOMINANT EMOTION FOR TEACHERS NOW

TOO MANY TEACHERS FEAR SPEAKING OUT

THERE'S A FEAR IN SCHOOLS THESE DAYS – MY UNION WORK HAS GONE FROM 3 CASES A YEAR TO 300

TEACHERS REPORT 'FEAR-MONGERING' TACTICS USED TO OFF-ROLL STUDENTS

OLDER TEACHERS BULLIED TO BREAKING POINT

TEACHERS IN FEAR OF KIDS AGED JUST 4

No doubt there is an element of newspapers writing sensational clickbait headlines here. But make no mistake: the fear within the teaching profession is no media confection. Fear of making a mistake in front of the class; fear of having a bad lesson observation; fear of not making pay progression; fear of not getting good enough grades, and worse, being publicly named and shamed for it; fear of being put on 'capability measures' or even summarily dismissed; fear of being 'found out'; fear of burnout; fear of what might happen if you speak out about questionable practices like onerous written marking policies or unethical practices such as off-rolling; the fearful spike of adrenaline that floods your body whenever you hear the door handle go during an Ofsted inspection.

We do not mean to suggest that all teachers live in fear of these things all the time – far from it. But as experienced teachers ourselves, we know these fears all too well, and we know many gifted teachers who are now ex-teachers as a consequence. It is little wonder that the profession has such a significant recruitment and retention problem.[9]

The fear within the teaching profession in the UK is as real as the fear of failure felt by so many children. Indeed, the two are closely linked, since both are ultimately caused by the prevailing culture of high-stakes testing and high-stakes accountability. It is important to understand that this high-stakes culture comes from a good place – we all want young people to get the best start in life that they possibly can. But as the saying goes, the road to hell is paved with good intentions. In recent years, these good intentions have often taken the form of a series of policy initiatives, such as school performance league tables, performance management and performance-related pay – policies that play an instrumental role in creating and maintaining the culture of fear described above. Note the repeated use of the word performance in these policy initiatives. It would be fair to say that UK education policy is in the grip of a performance orientation, a phenomenon that has been described as a culture of 'performativity'. As Professor Stephen Ball suggests, this policy environment creates schools in which:

> ... day-to-day practice is flooded with a baffling array of figures, indicators, comparisons and forms of competition. Within all this, the contentments of stability are increasingly elusive, purposes are made contradictory, motivations become blurred and self-worth is uncertain. We are unsure what aspects of work are valued and how to prioritise efforts. We become uncertain about the reasons for actions. Are we doing this because it is important, because we believe in it, because it is worthwhile? Or is it being done ultimately because it will be measured or compared? It will make us look good!

> Do we know we are good at what we do, even if performance indicators tell a different story? Do we value who we are able to be, [or who] we are becoming in the labyrinth of performativity?... These things become matters of self-doubt and personal anxiety rather than public debate... The policy technologies of market, management and performativity leave no space for an autonomous or collective ethical self. These technologies have potentially profound consequences for the nature of teaching and learning and for the inner life of the teacher.[10]

Thankfully, even within the current policy environment, there are many things teachers and school leaders can do to replace this culture of fear with a culture of self-regulated learning – for students and teachers alike – and the fulfilling of human potential. In the following section, we will outline six 'antidotes to fear' – safety, confidence, knowledge, experience, closing the gap and courageous leadership – and explain how these can be enacted through implementing a Learning Skills curriculum.

SAFETY

Fear is a primitive response to anything that might threaten our safety – physical or emotional, real or imagined. As teachers, we are limited in our ability to influence the things beyond the school gates that can threaten a child's sense of safety. However, we do have the power and the responsibility to ensure that when they are in school, we are able to provide children with a space where their physical, psychological and emotional safety is paramount. There are many aspects to safeguarding children. As well as making sure that the school site is physically safe and secure, we also need to pay attention to helping students develop a sense of safety within themselves. When children feel safe internally as well as externally, they are in an optimal state for learning effectively.

The *Learning Skills* curriculum enables children to feel internally safe in a number of ways. Through a focus on self-regulation, we teach children how to monitor and control their feelings and behaviours. For example, in the '7-day challenge', we saw several examples of how students learned to recognise the signs that they were coming into conflict with family members or peers, and to take action to process their feelings and prevent the conflict from coming to a head.

Through having randomly allocated classes – and by systematically and repeatedly mixing the children together within those classes – *Learning Skills* enables and encourages all students to venture out from the apparent safety of their friendship groups and form more diverse friendship groups, broader support networks, and stronger relationships among a wide group of their peers than is usually the case. This is invaluable in the tumultuous period of early adolescence, when close friendships can all too easily turn to rejection and recrimination.

Through practices such as creating class charters, talk rules and co-constructed success criteria, *Learning Skills* allows students to exercise more autonomy and ownership over the rules that govern their lives. If they don't like a talk rule or a success criterion, they learn that they can raise it, discuss it and change it, should they so choose.

And through the regular use of philosophical inquiry and circle time lessons, students listen intently to one another and get to know how others think about a wide range of issues. They also model to one another how to interact, and they learn to find their own voice. When you get to the point where all students feel safe to air their views without worrying about what others might think or say, that's when you know you've cracked it.

CONFIDENCE

Confidence is a powerful antidote to fear. When children feel confident in themselves, they worry less about making mistakes. When you have plenty of memories of positive experiences and successes 'in the bank', you can afford to take a risk and make the odd mistake – even in public – without it impacting too greatly on your sense of self-worth.

Through a relentless focus on developing students' speaking and listening skills, the *Learning Skills* curriculum helps all students develop confidence in a range of contexts – from paired and small group work to taking part in whole-class debates and delivering speeches from memory. When we have strong oracy skills, we can put our feelings and thoughts into words and make ourselves understood – even to express thoughts and feelings that we don't fully understand yet. Being able to express your confusion creates opportunities for new understandings to emerge.

Understanding that all human beings err, that all of us have gaping holes in our knowledge base and that we are capable of changing our minds is an incredibly powerful weapon for combatting fear of failure. When children come to view themselves as works-in-progress, they learn to embrace failure as feedback and use it to propel them further along a journey of personal development, growth and learning, rather than a stick with which to beat themselves up.

In *Learning Skills* lessons, students learn to find their voice – literally and metaphorically – and the boost this gives to their sense of self-confidence is palpable. This newfound self-belief spills over into their relationships with friends and family members. It changes their perception of themselves and helps them think more expansively about the kinds of things they might go on to achieve in their lives. They become more willing to take risks and more able to take setbacks in their stride when they comes along – as they inevitably do from time to time.

EXPERIENCE

People often ask: 'How can we teach children to be more resilient?' To which the answer is: you can't. Resilience is not something that can be taught; it is something that is grown through experience. In schools, there are often some children who almost never fail, and others who almost never achieve recognition for their work. This situation doesn't help either child develop resilience.

To grow resilience, children need to step outside of their comfort zone, take a few calculated risks, fail a few times, dust themselves off and work persistently toward achieving an agreed level of meaningful success or progress. This will look different for different children, and that's why we need to build flexibility into the *Learning Skills* curriculum – to allow each child to set targets and success criteria that are in the Goldilocks zone for them (not too hard, not too easy, but just right).

It is also important to understand that resilience is not a generic trait. A child may be incredibly resilient in some situations and incredibly brittle in others. Many children care for family members, or play a sport that they aren't very good at yet, or work a part-time job come rain or shine. If they appear frozen before a maths challenge, panic when they see a microphone, or dissolve into tears before a blank piece of paper, this does not mean that they aren't resilient. It just means they haven't built up a resistance to overcoming that particular challenge yet. If we can raise children in an environment that provides them with diverse experiences and involves an ongoing dialogue about overcoming such challenges, then we can help them move beyond making decisions based on fear of failure (consciously or unconsciously) and begin to identify, confront and overcome their fears.

Through the ongoing use of project-based learning, with students setting their own goals and monitoring and evaluating their own progress toward challenging targets, the *Learning Skills* curriculum provides all students with repeated, low-stakes opportunities to face their fears, flex their emerging relationship-building and problem-solving muscles, bite off more than they can easily chew and not only survive the ordeal if it goes horribly wrong, but learn from it and bounce back stronger.

Through the experience of facing and overcoming adversity, children are able to develop the art of self-regulation – monitoring and controlling their feelings (physical and emotional) and behaviours. They learn to feel the fear, take a breath, decide how best to respond and then override it if they choose to. This ability to control their internal environment is something that they must practise until they know it in their bodies. Through experience, they learn to trust that even though they may be feeling utterly terrified at this particular moment, they will soon overcome that feeling and emerge on the other side stronger, braver and with new knowledge and skills to help them manage the next challenge.

KNOWLEDGE

Knowledge is the antidote to fear... Knowledge is the encourager, knowledge that takes fear out of the heart, knowledge and use, which is knowledge in practice. They can conquer who believe they can.

Ralph Waldo Emerson (1870)[11]

Linked to confidence and experience is the notion, expressed so lucidly by Emerson, that knowledge can be a powerful antidote to fear. As we saw in *Chapter 3*, knowledge is foundational. It is the stuff that understanding, skills and so-called 'higher order' processes such as creativity and critical thinking are made of. It therefore stands to reason that the more knowledge and understanding a child has stored in their long-term memory, the more resources they have to draw on at a moment's notice when faced with a new or daunting situation – without having to look anything up on their smartphone.

Being knowledgeable by itself doesn't insulate you against fear, although it certainly doesn't hurt. But the process of becoming knowledgeable also teaches you that you are someone who is able to learn effectively. Knowing that you are able to learn your way out of a tight corner can be hugely powerful in diminishing the fear of not knowing what to do in any given moment. As we have seen, there is abundant evidence that developing children's knowledge and skills around metacognition, self-regulation and oracy leads to significant, demonstrable and sustained gains in subject learning – especially among children from disadvantaged backgrounds. In this way, too, *Learning Skills* helps children reduce the power that fear can hold over them.

But there is more to knowledge than knowledge of school subjects. Through an explicit focus on metacognition (monitoring and controlling thought processes) and self-regulation (monitoring and controlling feelings and behaviours), the *Learning Skills* curriculum helps children develop knowledge of self.

This is developed through things like the *Who am I?* project, and through allowing children to set short-, medium- and long-term goals and then track their progress (or lack of it) toward those goals over time. When children have a clear idea of who they are – where they have been, where they are now and where they are going – they are much more capable of overcoming the fear of taking risks and risking failure.

By becoming more aware of their strengths and 'areas for development', young people are able to undertake a journey of self-actualisation and personal growth that places them firmly in the driving seat. When a child knows that their life goal might involve an element of public speaking, for example, they begin to embrace opportunities to practise public speaking rather than shying away from them. Vernon Howard (1975) expressed this idea admirably:

> *Awareness of your weakness and confusion makes you strong because conscious awareness is the bright light that destroys the darkness of negativity... Detection of inner negativity is not a negative act, but a courageously positive act that makes you a new person.*[12]

CLOSING THE GAP

Sometimes, it feels like the problem of social disadvantage and inequality has been dumped at education's door – that it is somehow the job of teachers to create a fairer and more equal society, on top of everything else. To be fair, when we look at the problem on a global scale, there is a strong case to be made for the idea that education can create a fairer and more equal world, since many children in developing countries do not have access to school-based education.[13]

Domestically, however, this feels like a tall order. The causes of social and economic disadvantage are many and varied, and teachers do not dictate social and economic policy. Likewise, the consequences of social and economic disadvantage are many and varied, including poorer educational attainment, lower wages and reduced life expectancy.

Nevertheless, if there is anything that teachers and school leaders can do to close the disadvantage gap in terms of educational outcomes, then clearly this is something we should pursue. Qualifications are like keys – they open doors and opportunities and are associated with higher earnings, on average. As John Tomsett (2015) suggests, 'a good set of examination results is the best pastoral care for students from socio-economically deprived backgrounds'.[14]

In the UK, between 2011 and 2019 the attainment gap between disadvantaged pupils and their peers narrowed slightly, both at primary and secondary level. As Becky Francis wrote recently, 'this progress was testament to the enormous efforts of teachers and school leaders across

England, as well as policies such as the pupil premium, which provided funding and focus.'[15] As we discussed in *Chapter 7*, however, recently this trend has unfortunately reversed – a pattern that will likely be exacerbated by the period of school closures due to COVID-19.[16]

As we saw in *Chapter 2: A brief history of Learning to Learn*, there is a wealth of evidence that educational initiatives that focus on developing metacognition, self-regulation and oracy skills are especially beneficial for children from disadvantaged backgrounds. As we have seen, *Learning Skills* is no different in this regard. There is therefore a strong imperative for school leaders to seriously consider implementing a *Learning Skills* curriculum to boost the attainment of all pupils, with accelerated progress among children from disadvantaged backgrounds.

COURAGEOUS LEADERSHIP

Fundamentally, the extent to which students and teachers feel emboldened to confront and overcome the kinds of fears we outlined above boils down to courageous leadership: having the courage to make bold decisions, guided by a strong sense of moral purpose; having the courage to distribute leadership to those who can shoulder it; and having the courage to question long-held beliefs in the light of new evidence.

More than anything, it's about having the courage to take risks, to make mistakes and to learn from them as a method for getting even better at what we do. We tell our students all the time that they need to learn from their mistakes. It's important that as teachers we afford ourselves the same luxury. As Paul Meredith suggested in the excerpt above, 'true confidence comes not from getting things right, but from being prepared to be wrong'. When schools are led in courageous ways, many of the fears described above can be systematically confronted and overcome. And just as the 'litany against fear' describes, where the fear has gone, good things appear in its place.

When we set out on this journey ten years ago, Sea View had recently been placed in 'special measures'. It would have been really easy to play it safe, and to allocate those five lessons a week to English and maths. In establishing the *Learning Skills* curriculum, Stuart McLaughlin exemplified courageous leadership, and it is no small thing to be courageous when your neck is on the line. In turn, Stuart's bold leadership inspired the *Learning Skills* team to have the courage of our convictions, too.

When we set out on this journey, in all honesty we didn't really know what we were letting ourselves in for. But we believed in the moral purpose of what we were trying to achieve, and we were driven as much by this as by research evidence. We soon found that having the courage of your convictions doesn't half help when the people with clipboards come around to judge you, as they inevitably do from time to time. When they say nice things, that's great. And when they criticise you, you either think, *Hmmm, you have a good point there, thanks for the feedback*, or, *Sorry, but you don't really know what you're talking about.*

But either way, you don't crumble or retreat, because you know this stuff better than they do – you live and breathe it every day. Being driven by a sense of moral purpose, taking risks and allowing yourself to learn from your mistakes – these things make you fearless in the face of such judgements. And fearlessness is the most liberating thing in the world.

LAST WORDS

We have spent too much time in the wonderful world of EduTwitter to think that by writing this book we will have convinced everyone on the planet to stop what they're doing and start implementing a *Learning Skills* curriculum. Happily, we also know enough about change management to understand that this is actually a good thing, because it wouldn't be desirable to go from a standing start to widespread implementation. However, we do hope to have persuaded at least some readers that Learning to Learn might not be a busted flush after all, and that actually there is a strong case for adapting and implementing the *Learning Skills* approach in new and different contexts. Some readers may even share our belief that there is a moral imperative to do so.

We started this book by asking, 'What's the one thing you would change about your pupils?', and we shared some examples of the replies we receive whenever we ask this question. However, there is another category of responses that we occasionally hear that we didn't mention in the Introduction. We might call this the 'heartbreaking' category:

> '*I wish people would pay them more attention.*'
> '*Poverty/opportunities.*'
> '*Their parents.*'
> '*Opportunities.*'

As individual teachers, we are limited in our ability to change structural inequality, generational poverty or family circumstances. We are also limited in our ability to influence national education policy. However, we are uniquely positioned to change the life trajectory of every young person we teach, and that makes us incredibly privileged and powerful.

There are exceptions – school-based teachers can't easily influence the lives of homeschoolers and school refusers – but, for the vast majority of children, we have an almost daily window into their lives for 12 years. Over the course of a school career, a child will take part in over ten thousand lessons. That's over ten thousand opportunities to help them develop the knowledge, skills, habits and dispositions that will shape and serve them for the rest of their lives.

How best should we spend this precious window of time? This is the question that drives almost every aspect of the education debate. The education system has a boilerplate answer to this question: teach them well, as the song goes, and try to ensure that they leave school with an armful of good qualifications. It's hard to argue with that, and we wouldn't want to; after all, this book is about an approach to teaching and learning that improves examination results. The question is: are qualifications enough? We would suggest that they are not. Qualifications might open doors, but they don't teach you how to thrive and survive on the other side.

If, like us, you believe that all children are able to get better at learning stuff – and if you set about making it happen – there is every reason to believe that you will make huge strides toward achieving this goal. This does not have to be done at the expense of gaining qualifications. The evidence we have outlined in this book suggests that it is possible to do both: that we can help children gain qualifications while simultaneously helping them become more confident, articulate, proactive, independent, curious, resilient, able to solve problems, think critically and creatively and get along with one another. And if we are able to replicate and improve on these findings in more schools, then we will know for sure.

This is where you come in, reader. Whether you work in the mainstream, independent or alternative sector; whether you're UK-based or international; and whether you're a parent, student or concerned citizen – we would love to hear from you. Let us know what you think of the book, and if there's anything we can do to help you along your way, we'll be happy to help. Drop us a line at rethinking-ed.org/contact. And if you're a Twitter type, please share your thoughts using the hashtag #FITMK.

We look forward to continuing the journey with you.

ACKNOWLEDGEMENTS

Heartfelt thanks are owed to many people who have helped us along this journey of 15 years and counting. Firstly, we owe an enormous debt of gratitude to Stuart McLaughlin, the courageous and visionary headteacher who gave us the freedom to do something bold and different when it would have been so much easier not to. Likewise, to all the colleagues and students it has been our privilege to work with along the way. Thanks in particular go to our fellow travellers on the *Learning Skills* bus: Paul Meredith, Sophie Mills, Rosa Ferrer-Verduch and Ravinder Shari, to name just a few – your enthusiasm, creativity and dedication shaped this thing into what it has become.

We would also like to express our gratitude to the many friends and colleagues who have read parts or all of the manuscript and provided us with invaluable critique and/or encouragement. Namely: Phil Beadle, Jackie Beere OBE, Alex Black, Christian Bokhove, Becky Carlzon, Chris Chivers, Guy Claxton, Amy Cooper, Mark Enser, Peter Ford, Sue Gerrard, Ian Gilbert, Scherto Gill, Polly Glegg, Jo Gurvidi, Alan Howe, Jennifer Joint, Simon Lancaster, Tony Mannion, Laura McInerney, Neil Mercer, Peps McCrea, Stuart McLaughlin, Mary Myatt, Tom Sherrington, Karen Spence-Thomas, Martyn Steiner, Roo Stenning, Andy Threadgould, John Tomsett, James Tucker, Steve Turnbull, Patrick Whibley and Dylan Wiliam. Special thanks go to Ollie Lovell, teacher and host of the *Education Research Reading Room* podcast, whose boundless energy, knowledge and support have made him an invaluable critical friend and contributor of ideas – albeit from the other side of the planet. The generosity and insight of all our reviewers is greatly appreciated, while any remaining errors are ours alone.

Huge thanks to Jonathan Barnes, Grainne Treanor and Emma Aldous at John Catt for doing such a spectacular job in making our ideas look readable and presentable. Also to Alex Sharratt, for his unfailing patience as self-imposed deadline after self-imposed deadline whizzed silently by. Perhaps the main thing we have learned is that we are spectacularly bad at predicting how long it takes to write books.

Finally, to Ruth, Thomas, Harry and Matilda. For all the times we have been absent, or merely absent-minded – we are sorry, but it really was ever so important to us.

NOTES

Introduction

1. Isbell, L. (2017) Can't or won't: The culture of helplessness, *Inside Higher Education*, 14 March, original emphasis. Available at: https://www.insidehighered.com/advice/2017/03/14/professor-examines-why-her-students-seem-act-so-helpless-essay.
2. Walker, P. (2015) Depression and self-harm soar among private school pupils, poll suggests, *the Observer*, 4 October. Available at: https://www.theguardian.com/education/2015/oct/04/depression-self-harm-eating-disorders-private-school-pupils-headteachers-poll.
3. Mannion, J. (2018) Metacognition, self-regulation, oracy: A mixed methods case study of a complex, whole-school Learning to Learn intervention. PhD thesis, Hughes Hall, University of Cambridge. Available at: https://www.repository.cam.ac.uk/handle/1810/289131.
4. Mannion, J. & Mercer, N. (2016) Learning to learn: improving attainment, closing the gap at key stage 3, *Curriculum Journal*, 27(2), pp. 246–271.
5. Mannion, J., McAllister, K. & Mercer, N. (2018) The *Learning Skills* curriculum: raising the bar, closing the gap at GCSE, *Impact, the Journal of the Chartered College of Teaching*, Sept 2018.
6. Education Endowment Foundation (2020) *The Teaching and Learning Toolkit*. Available at: https://educationendowmentfoundation.org.uk/evidence-summaries/teaching-learning-toolkit/meta-cognition-and-self-regulation.
7. Sinek, S. (2011) *Start with Why: How Great Leaders Inspire Everyone to Take Action*. London: Penguin.
8. Education Endowment Foundation (2018) *Metacognition and self-regulated learning: Guidance report*. London: EEF, p. 8.
9. Flavell, J.H. (1979) Metacognition and cognitive monitoring: A new area of cognitive–developmental inquiry, *American Psychologist*, 34(10), p. 910.

Chapter 1

1. Santayana, G. (1905) *The Life of Reason: Reason in Common Sense*. New York: Scribner's, p284.
2. DfE (2010) *New endowment fund to turn around weakest schools and raise standards for disadvantaged pupils*. London, Department for Education, Press Notice 2010/0115. Available at: https://www.gov.uk/government/news/new-endowment-fund-to-turn-around-weakest-schools-and-raise-standards-for-disadvantaged-pupils.
3. EEF (2018) Our mission. Available at: https://educationendowmentfoundation.org.uk/about/history.
4. Higgins, S., Kokotsaki, D. & Coe, R.J. (2011) *Toolkit of Strategies to Improve Learning: Summary for Schools Spending the Pupil Premium*. Sutton Trust. Available at: https://educationendowmentfoundation.org.uk/evidence-summaries/teaching-learning-toolkit.
5. 'The EEF at 5: We've done a lot. There's a lot left to do', by EEF Chairman Sir Peter Lampl. Available at: https://educationendowmentfoundation.org.uk/news/the-eef-at-5.
6. https://educationendowmentfoundation.org.uk/evidence-summaries/teaching-learning-toolkit; accessed June 20, 2020.

7   If you're interested, there's a fascinating interview with Professor Adrian Simpson on *The Education Research Reading Room* podcast that deals with this issue comprehensively. Available at: ollielovell.com/errr/adriansimpson.

8   Mannion, J. (2017) Evidence-informed practice: the importance of professional judgment, *Impact, the Journal of the Chartered College of Teachers*. Interim edition, pp. 38–40. Available at: https://impact.chartered.college/article/mannion-evidence-informed-practice-professional-judgement.

9   Kluger, A.N. & DeNisi, A. (1996) The effects of feedback interventions on performance: A historical review, a meta-analysis, and a preliminary feedback intervention theory, *Psychological Bulletin*, 119(2), pp. 254–284.

10 Education Endowment Foundation (2020) Teaching and Learning Toolkit entry for metacognition and self-regulation. Available at: https://educationendowmentfoundation.org.uk/evidence-summaries/teaching-learning-toolkit/meta-cognition-and-self-regulation.

11 Schwartz, J. (2017) Learning to Learn: You, too, can rewire Your brain, *New York Times*, 4 August. Available at: https://www.nytimes.com/2017/08/04/education/edlife/learning-how-to-learn-barbara-oakley.html.

12 Oakley, B., Sejnowski, T. & McConville, A. (2018) *Learning How to Learn: How to Succeed in School Without Spending All Your Time Studying*. New York, NY: Tarcher Perigee.

13 Christodoulou, D. (2018) Book review: *Learning How to Learn*. *Times Education Supplement*, 7 September. Available at: https://www.tes.com/news/book-review-learning-how-learn.

14 Education Endowment Foundation (2020) *Teaching and Learning Toolkit* entry for metacognition and self-regulation. Available at: https://educationendowmentfoundation.org.uk/evidence-summaries/teaching-learning-toolkit/meta-cognition-and-self-regulation.

15 Gove, M. (2013) Speech on the white paper 'The importance of teaching'. Available at: https://www.gov.uk/government/speeches/michael-gove-speaks-about-the-importance-of-teaching.

16 Mance, H. (2016) Britain has had enough of experts, says Gove. *Financial Times*, 3 June. Available at: https://www.ft.com/content/3be49734-29cb-11e6-83e4-abc22d5d108c.

17 Littleton, K. & Mercer, N. (2013) *Interthinking: Putting Talk to Work*. Abingdon, UK: Routledge, p. 15.

18 Education Endowment Foundation (2020) *The Teaching and Learning Toolkit*. Available at: https://educationendowmentfoundation.org.uk/evidence-summaries/teaching-learning-toolkit/meta-cognition-and-self-regulation.

19 Engelmann, S., Becker, W.C., Carnine, D. & Gersten, R. (1988) The Direct Instruction follow through model: Design and outcomes, *Education and Treatment of Children*, 11(4), pp. 303–317.

20 Bennett, T. (2013) *Teacher proof: Why Research in education doesn't always mean what it claims, and what you can do about it*. London: Routledge, pp. 160–170.

21 Tricot, A. & Sweller, J. (2014) Domain-specific knowledge and why teaching generic skills does not work, *Educational Psychology Review*, 26(2), pp. 265–283.

22 Christodoulou, D. (2013) *Seven Myths About Education*. London: Routledge.

23 Counsell, C. (2011) Disciplinary knowledge for all, the secondary history curriculum and history teachers' achievement, *The Curriculum Journal*, 22(2), pp. 201–225.

24 Hayes, D. (2012) Education is bad for you, *Huffington Post*, 3 February. Available at: https://www.huffingtonpost.co.uk/dennis-hayes/education-is-bad-for-you_b_1249900.html.

25 Ecclestone, K. & Hayes, D. (2008) *The Dangerous Rise of Therapeutic Education*. London: Routledge, p. 47.

26 Hayes, D. (2005) Learning's too good for 'em, *Times Educational Supplement*, 19 August. Available at: https://www.tes.com/news/learnings-too-good-em.

Chapter 2

1   Comenius, J.A. (1632) *Didactica magna* ('The Great Didactic'; translation by M.W. Keatinge). New York, NY: Russell & Russell, reprinted 1967.

2   Watkins, C. (2001) *Learning about Learning Enhances Performance.* London: Institute of Education National School Improvement Network (Research Matters Series No. 13).

3   Watkins, C. (2010) *Learning, Performance and Improvement.* London: Institute of Education, International Network for School Improvement (Research Matters series).

4   e.g. see Hall, D., James, D. & Marsden, N. (2012) Marginal gains: Olympic lessons in high performance for organisations, *HR Bulletin: Research and Practice*, 7(2), pp. 9–13.

5   Slater, M. (2012) Olympic cycling: Marginal gains underpin Team GB dominance. *BBC Sport.* Available at: https://www.bbc.co.uk/sport/olympics/19174302.

6   James, W. (1890) *The Principles of Psychology*, Vol. 1. New York, NY: Henry Holt and Co., pp. 272–273.

7   Fox, E. & Riconscente, M. (2008) Metacognition and Self-Regulation in James, Piaget, and Vygotsky, *Educational Psychology Review*, 20(4), p. 373.

8   Miel, A. (1959) Learning more about learning: A key to curriculum development. In A. Frazier (ed.), *Learning More About Learning*, (pp. 1–4). Washington DC: Association for Supervision and Curriculum Development, p. 3, original emphases.

9   Bruner, J. (ed.) (1966) Learning About Learning: A Conference Report. U.S. Department of Health, Education and Welfare: Bureau of Research.

10 Number of hits yielded on the eric.ed.gov educational research database, using the search term <pubyear:XXXX AND ('learning to learn' OR 'learn to learn' OR 'learning how to learn' OR 'learn how to learn' OR 'learning about learning' OR 'learning-centred' OR 'learning-centered' OR 'campaign for learning' OR 'learning orientation' OR 'competency-based' OR 'meta-learning' OR 'metacognition' OR 'self-regulation' OR 'self-regulated learning')>. Search conducted March 2020.

11 Flavell, J.H. (1976) Metacognitive aspects of problem-solving. In L.B. Resnick (ed.), *The Nature of Intelligence.* Hillsdale NJ: Erlbaum.

12 Brown, A.L. (1978) Knowing when, where, and how to remember: A problem of metacognition. In R. Glaser (ed.), *Advances in Instructional Psychology* (Vol. 1). Hillsdale, NJ: Lawrence Erlbaum Associates.

13 Flavell, J.H. (1979) Metacognition and cognitive monitoring, *American Psychologist*, 34, pp. 906–911.

14 Claxton, G. (2006) *Learning to learn, the fourth generation: making sense of personalised learning.* Bristol: TLO Ltd, p. 1.

15 Adapted from Claxton, G. (2006) *Learning to learn, the fourth generation: making sense of personalised learning.* Bristol: TLO Ltd.

16 Hattie, J., Biggs, J. & Purdie, N. (1996) Effects of learning skills interventions on student learning: a meta-analysis, *Review of Educational Research*, 66(2), pp. 99–136.

17 Gardner, H. (1983) *Multiple Intelligences: The Theory in Practice.* New York, NY: Basic Books.

18 Goleman, D. (1995) *Emotional Intelligence: Why it can matter more than IQ.* New York, NY: Bantam.

19 Hargreaves, D. (2004) *Personalised Learning: Next steps in Working Laterally.* London: Specialist Schools and Academies Trust.

20 Department for Children, Schools and Families (2007) *Social and Emotional Aspects of Learning for Secondary Schools.* Nottingham: DCSF Publications.

21 Qualifications and Curriculum Authority (2007) *Personal, Learning and Thinking Skills Framework.* London: QCA.

22 Claxton, G. (2006) *Learning to Learn, the Fourth Generation: Making Sense of Personalised Learning.* Bristol: TLO Ltd, p. 3.

23 Smith, R. (2002) Self-esteem: the kindly apocalypse, *Journal of Philosophy of Education*, 36(1), pp. 87–100.

24 Ecclestone, K. (2004) Developing Self-esteem and Emotional Well-being – Inclusion or Intrusion?, *Adults Learning*, 16(3), p. 11.

25 e.g. Smith, R. (2002) Self-esteem: the kindly apocalypse, *Journal of Philosophy of Education*, 36(1), pp. 87–100.

26 Cigman, R. (2004) Situated self-esteem, *Journal of Philosophy of Education*, 38(1), pp. 91–105.

27 Kristjansson, K. (2007) Justified self-esteem, *Journal of Philosophy of Education*, 41(2), pp. 247–261.

28 Goldacre, B. (2006) *Brain Gym, anyone? I need teachers*. Available at https://www.badscience.net/2006/02/brain-gym-anyone-i-need-teachers/.

29 Goldacre, B. (2006) Brain Gym exercises do pupils no favours, *the Guardian*, 18 March. Available at: www.theguardian.com/commentisfree/2006/mar/18/comment.badscience.

30 Claxton, G. (2006) *Learning to Learn, The Fourth Generation: Making Sense of Personalised Learning*. Bristol: TLO Ltd, p. 4-7.

31 Reiner, C. & Willingham, D. (2010) The myth of learning styles, *Change: The Magazine of Higher Learning*, 42(5), pp. 32–35.

32 Coffield, F. (2004) Revealing figures behind the styles, *Times Higher Educational Supplement*, 2 January.

33 Claxton (2006) p. 8, original emphasis.

34 Claxton G (2018) *The Learning Power Approach: Teaching Learners to Teach Themselves*. Carmarthen: Crown House, p. 10.

35 e.g. see Brandt, R. (1990) On knowledge and cognitive skills: A conversation with David Perkins, *Educational Leadership*, 47(5), pp. 50–53.

36 Ritchhart, R. (2002) *Intellectual Character: What It Is, Why It Matters And How To Get It*. San Francisco, CA: Jossey-Bass.

37 Ritchhart, R. (2015) *Creating Cultures of Thinking*. San Francisco, CA: Jossey-Bass.

38 Hetland, L., Winner, E., Veenema, S. & Kimberley, S. (2007) *Studio Thinking: The Real Benefits of Visual Arts Education*. New York, NY: Teachers College Press.

39 Berger, R. (2003) *An Ethic of Excellence: Building a Culture of Craftmanship with Students*. Portsmouth, NH: Heinemann.

40 Berger, R., Woodfin, L. & Vilen, A. (2016) *Learning That Lasts: Challenging, Engaging, and Empowering Students with Deeper Instruction*. San Francisco, CA: Jossey-Bass.

41 Costa, A. & Kallick, B. (eds) (2009) *Learning and Leading with Habits of Mind: 16 Essential Characteristics for Success*. Alexandria, VA, Association for Supervision & Curriculum Development.

42 Claxton, G. (2018) *The Learning Power Approach: Teaching Learners to Teach Themselves*. Carmarthen: Crown House, pp. 6–7.

43 Watkins, C. (2006) Explorations in metalearning from a narrative stance. Paper presented at the European Association for Research on Learning and Instruction Special Interest Group 16: Metacognition, University of Cambridge, 19–21 July. Available at https://www.chriswatkins.net/download/109.

44 Shayer, M. & Adey, P. (2002) *Learning Intelligence: Cognitive Acceleration Across the Curriculum*. Maidenhead: Open University Press.

45 Baird, J. & Northfield, J. (1992) *Learning from the PEEL Experience*. Melbourne: Monash University Press.

46 Edwards, C. & Gandina, L. (2011) *The Hundred Languages of Children: The Reggio Emilia Experience in Transformation*. Santa Barbara, CA: Greenwood Press.

47 Veevers, N. & Allison, P. (2011) *Kurt Hahn: Inspirational, Visionary, Outdoor and Experiential Educator*. Boston, MA: Sense Publishers.

48 Peterson, A. (1972) *International Baccalaureate*. London: Harrap.

49 Claxton, G. (2018) *The Learning Power Approach: Teaching Learners to Teach Themselves*. Carmarthen: Crown House, p. 201.

50 Claxton, G. (2018) *The Learning Power Approach: Teaching Learners to Teach Themselves*. Carmarthen: Crown House, pp. 201–202.

51 This section is based on Mannion, J. (2020) Metacognition, self-regulation and self-regulated learning: What's the difference?, *Impact, the Journal of the Chartered College of Teaching*, 8 (Spring), pp. 66–69.

52 Higgins, S., Kokotsaki, D. & Coe, R.J. (2011) *Toolkit of Strategies to Improve Learning: Summary for Schools Spending the Pupil Premium*. Sutton Trust. Available at: https://educationendowmentfoundation.org.uk/evidence-summaries/teaching-learning-toolkit.

53 Dinsmore, D.L., Alexander, P.A. & Loughlin, S.M. (2008) Focusing the conceptual lens on metacognition, self-regulation, and self-regulated learning, *Educational Psychology Review*, 20(4), p. 392.

54 Schunk, D.H. (2008) Metacognition, self-regulation, and self-regulated learning: Research recommendations, *Educational Psychology Review*, 20(4), p. 465.

55 Education Endowment Foundation (2018) *Metacognition and Self-regulated Learning: Guidance report*. London: EEF.

56 Education Endowment Foundation (2018) *Metacognition and Self-regulated Learning: Guidance report*. London: EEF, p. 9.

57 Muijs, D. & Bokhove, C. (2020) *Metacognition and Self-Regulation: Evidence Review*. London: Education Endowment Foundation.

58 The EEF's definition was used by Schraw et al. (2006) – however, this is an exception, rather than the norm. See Schraw, G., Crippen, K.J. & Hartley, K. (2006) Promoting self-regulation in science education: metacognition as part of a broader perspective on learning, *Research in Science Education*, 36, pp. 111–139.

59 Alexander, P. (2008) Why this and why now? Introduction to the special issue on metacognition, self-regulation, and self-regulated learning, *Educational Psychology Review*, 20(4), p. 370.

60 See also 'Learning to learn to learn to learn'.

61 Flavell, J.H. (1976) Metacognitive aspects of problem solving. In L.B. Resnick (ed.), *The nature of intelligence* (pp. 231–235). Hillsdale, NJ: Lawrence Erlbaum, p. 232.

62 Flavell, J.H. (1979) Metacognition and cognitive monitoring: A new area of cognitive–developmental inquiry, *American Psychologist*, 34(10), pp. 906–911.

63 To peruse Chris's phenomenal output on Learning to Learn and other topics over the years, visit http://chriswatkins.net/publications.

64 Watkins, C. (2001) *Learning about Learning Enhances Performance*. London, Institute of Education National School Improvement Network (Research Matters Series No. 13), p. 1.

65 Bandura, A. (1991) Social cognitive theory of self-regulation, *Organizational Behavior and Human Decision Processes*, 50, pp. 248–287.

66 Dinsmore, D.L., Alexander, P.A. & Loughlin, S.M. (2008) Focusing the conceptual lens on metacognition, self-regulation, and self-regulated learning, *Educational Psychology Review*, 20(4), p. 405.

67 van Merriënboer, J.J.G. & Kirschner, P.A. (2018) *Ten Steps to Complex Learning*(3rd edn). New York, NY: Routledge.

68 Fox, E. & Riconscente, M. (2008) Metacognition and self-regulation in James, Piaget, and Vygotsky, *Educational Psychology Review*, 20(4), p. 374.

69 Bandura, A. (1986) *Social Foundations of Thought and Action: A Social Cognitive Theory*. Englewood Cliffs, NJ: Prentice-Hall.

70 Schunk, D.H. (2008) Metacognition, self-regulation, and self-regulated learning: Research recommendations, *Educational Psychology Review*, 20(4), p. 465.

71 Whitebread D. & Basilio M. (2012) The emergence and early development of self-regulation in young children, *Profesorado: Revista de Curriculum y Formacion del Profesorado*,16, pp. 16–33.

72 It is worth noting that this is not typical in some countries. It is, however, very much the case in the UK – especially within the state secondary sector, and especially in years 10 and 11.

73 Bruner, J.S. (1978) The role of dialogue in language acquisition. In A. Sinclair, R.J. Jarvelle & W.J.M. Levelt (eds), *The Child's Concept of Language*. New York, NY: Springer-Verlag.

74 Claxton, G. (2012) Virtues of uncertainty, *Aeon* magazine, 17 September. Available at: https://aeon.co/essays/a-life-of-tests-is-no-preparation-for-the-tests-of-life.

75 Zimmerman, B.J. (2002) Becoming a self-regulated learner: An overview, *Theory into Practice*, 41(2), pp. 64–72 (p. 65).

76 van Merriënboer, J.J.G. & Kirschner, P.A. (2018) *Ten Steps to Complex Learning* (3rd edn). New York, NY: Routledge.

77 Mercer, N. (2016) Education and the social brain: linking language, thinking, teaching and learning, *Éducation & Didactique*, 10(2), pp. 9–23.

78 Lyn Dawes has published several excellent books exploring the use of talking points as a tool for stimulating classroom dialogue. See, for example, Dawes, L. (2012) *Talking Points: Discussion Activities in the Primary Classroom*. Abingdon: Routledge.

79 Coe, R. (2002) *It's the Effect Size, Stupid*. Paper presented at the annual conference of the British Educational Research Association, University of Exeter, 12–14 September. Available at: https://www.leeds.ac.uk/educol/documents/00002182.htm.

80 **(a)** Chiu, C.W.T. (1998) *Synthesizing Metacognitive Interventions: What Training Characteristics Can Improve Reading Performance?* Paper presented at the Annual Meeting of the American Educational Research Association San Diego, CA, 13–17 April;
(b) Dignath, C. & Büttner, G. (2008) Components of fostering self-regulated learning among students. A meta-analysis on intervention studies at primary and secondary school level, *Metacognition and Learning*, 3, pp. 231–264;
(c) Donker, A.S., de Boer, H., Kostons, D., Dignath, C. & Van der Werf, M.P.C. (2014) Effectiveness of learning strategy instruction on academic performance: A meta-analysis, *Educational Research Review*, 11, pp. 1–26;
(d) Dignath, C., Büttner, G. & Langfeldt, H.P. (2008) How can primary school students learn self-regulated strategies most effectively? A meta-analysis on self-regulation training programmes, *Educational Research Review*, 3(2), pp. 101–129;
(e) Haller, E., Child, D. & Walberg, H.J. (1988) Can comprehension be taught? A quantitative synthesis, *Educational Researcher*, 17(9), pp. 5–8;
(f) Hattie, J., Biggs, J. & Purdie, N. (1996) Effects of learning skills interventions on student learning: a meta-analysis, *Review of Educational Research*, 66(2), pp. 99–136;
(g) Higgins, S., Hall, E., Baumfield, V. & Moseley, D. (2005) A meta-analysis of the impact of the implementation of thinking skills approaches on pupils. In: *Research Evidence in Education Library*. EPPI-Centre, Social Science Research Unit, Institute of Education, University of London.
(h) Klauer, K.J. & Phye, G.D. (2008). Inductive Reasoning: A Training Approach. *Review of Educational Research*, 78.1 pp 85-123.

81 Perry, V., Albeg, L. & Tung, C. (2012) Meta-analysis of single-case design research on self-regulatory interventions for academic performance, *Journal of Behavioral Education*, 21(3), p. 225.

82 Torgerson, D., Torgerson, C., Ainsworth, H., Buckley, H.M., Heaps, C., Hewitt, C. & Mitchell, N. (2014) *Improving Writing Quality: Evaluation Report and Executive Summary*. May 2014. London: EEF, p. 2.

83 Hanley, P., Slavin, R. & Elliott, L. (2015) *Thinking, Doing, Talking Science. Evaluation Report and Executive Summary*. London: Education Endowment Foundation, p. 3.

84 Wiliam, D. (2011) *Embedded Formative Assessment*. Bloomingdale, IN: Solution Tree Press.

85 Speckesser, S., Runge, J., Foliano, F., Bursnall, M., Hudson-Sharp, N., Rolfe, H. & Anders, J. (2018) *Embedding Formative Assessment: Evaluation Report*. Education Endowment Foundation, NIESR, p. 4.

86 Speckesser, S., Runge, J., Foliano, F., Bursnall, M., Hudson-Sharp, N., Rolfe, H. & Anders, J. (2018) *Embedding Formative Assessment: Evaluation Report*. Education Endowment Foundation, NIESR, p. 4.

87 Paris, S. & Winograd, P. (2003) *The Role of Self-regulated Learning in Contextual Teaching: Principles and Practices for Teacher Preparation*. A commissioned paper for the U.S. Department of Education Project. Available at: http://www.ciera.org/library/archive/2001-04/0104prwn.pdf.

88 e.g. Bandura, A. (2006) Guide for constructing self-efficacy scales. In F. Pajares & T. Urdan (eds), *Self-Efficacy Beliefs of Adolescents* (Vol. 5., pp. 307–337). Greenwich, CT: Information Age Publishing.

89 Bandura, A. (1991) Social cognitive theory of self-regulation, *Organizational Behavior and Human Decision Processes*, 50, pp. 248–287.

90 Wolters, C.A., Yu, S.L. & Pintrich, P.R. (1996) The relation between goal orientation and students' motivational beliefs and self-regulated learning, *Learning and Individual Differences*, 8, pp. 211–238.

91 Wolters, C.A. & Pintrich, P.R. (1998) Contextual differences in student motivation and self-regulated learning in maths, English, and social studies classrooms, *Instructional Science*, 26, p. 27.

92 Veenman, M.V.J., Van Hout-Wolters, H.A.M. & Afflerbach, P. (2006) Metacognition and learning: conceptual and methodological considerations, *Metacognition and Learning*, 1(1), p. 6.

93 Husbands, C. (2015) *Can (and should) research and practice shape schooling?* Presentation to the Institute of Education Research and Development Network, June 2015.

94 RSA (2011) *Opening Minds Competence Framework*. Available at: http://www.rsaopeningminds.org.uk.

95 Higgins, S., Wall, K., Baumfield, V., Hall, E., Leat, D., Moseley, D. & Woolner, P. (2007) *Learning to Learn in Schools Phase 3 Evaluation: Final Report*. London: Campaign for Learning.

96 Claxton, G., Chambers, M., Powell, G. & Lucas, B. (2011) *The Learning Powered School: Pioneering 21st Century Education*. Bristol: TLO Ltd.

97 James, M., Black, P., McCormick, R., Pedder, D. & Wiliam, D. (2006) Learning How to Learn, in classrooms, schools and networks: Aims, design and analysis, *Research Papers in Education*, 21(2), pp. 101–118.

98 http://www.rsaopeningminds.org.uk/about-rsa-openingminds.

99 NTRP (National Teacher Research Panel) (2006) *Opening Minds: A Competency-based Curriculum for the Twenty First Century*. Available at: http://enlearn.pbworks.com/f/Opening+Minds.pdf.

100 Aynsley, S., Brown, C. & Sebba, J. (2012) *RSA Opening Minds: An Evaluative Review*. London: RSA, p. 2.

101 Higgins, S., Wall, K., Baumfield, V., Hall, E., Leat, D., Moseley, D. & Woolner, P. (2007) *Learning to Learn in Schools Phase 3 Evaluation: Final Report*. London: Campaign for Learning.

102 Higgins, S., Wall, K., Baumfield, V., Hall, E., Leat, D., Moseley, D. & Woolner, P. (2007) *Learning to Learn in Schools Phase 3 Evaluation: Final Report*. London: Campaign for Learning., p. 46.

103 Higgins, S. et al (2007) *Learning to Learn in Schools Phase 3 Evaluation: Final Report*. London: Campaign for Learning., p. 46.

104 Claxton, G., Chambers, M., Powell, G. & Lucas, B. (2011) *The Learning Powered School: Pioneering 21st Century Education*. Bristol: TLO Ltd, p. 42.

105 Claxton, G. (2002) *Building Learning Power*. Bristol: TLO Ltd.

106 Claxton, G., Chambers, M., Powell, G. & Lucas, B. (2011) *The Learning Powered School: Pioneering 21st Century Education*. Bristol: TLO Ltd, p. 4.

107 Claxton, G., Chambers, M., Powell, G. & Lucas, B. (2011) *The Learning Powered School: Pioneering 21st Century Education*. Bristol: TLO Ltd, p. 246.

108 James, M., Black, P., McCormick, R., Pedder, D. & Wiliam, D. (2006) Learning How to Learn, in classrooms, schools and networks: Aims, design and analysis, *Research Papers in Education*, 21(2), pp. 101–118.

109 James, M. (2006) *Learning How to Learn – In Classrooms, schools and networks*, Teaching and Learning Research Briefing (17), p. 3. Available at: http://www.leeds.ac.uk/educol/documents/176239.doc.

110 Higgins, S. (2009) *Learning to Learn*. Durham: Beyond Current Horizons Project, p. 4.

111 James, M., Black, P., Carmichael, P., Conner, C., Dudley, P., Fox, A., Frost, D., Honour, L., MacBeath, J., McCormick, R., Marshall, B., Pedder, D., Procter, R., Swaffield, S. & Wiliam, D. (2006) *Learning How to Learn: Tools for Schools*. London, UK: Routledge, p. 104.

112 Slavin, R. & Smith, D. (2009) The relationship between sample sizes and effect sizes in systematic reviews in education, *Educational Evaluation and Policy Analysis*, 31(4), pp. 500–506.

113 Claxton, G., Chambers, M., Powell, G. & Lucas, B. (2011) *The Learning Powered School: Pioneering 21st Century Education*. Bristol: TLO Ltd, p. 245.

114 Hautamäki, J., Arinen, P., Eronen, S., Hautamäki, A., Kupianien, S., Lindblom, B., Niemivirta, M., Pakaslahti, L., Rantanen, P. & Scheinin, P. (2002) *Assessing Learning-to-Learn: A Framework*. Helsinki: Centre for Educational Assessment, Helsinki University/National Board of Education.

115 Deakin-Crick. R., Broadfoot, P. & Claxton, G. (2004) Developing an effective lifelong learning inventory: the ELLI Project, *Assessment in Education*, 11(3), November 2004, pp. 247–272.

116 Elshout-Mohr, M., Meijer, J., Oostdam, R. & van Gelderen, A. (2004) *CCST: A Test for Cross-Curricular Skills*. Amsterdam: SCO – Kohnstamm Institution, University of Amsterdam.

117 James, M. (2006) *Learning how to learn – in classrooms, schools and networks*, Teaching and Learning Research Programme: Teaching and Learning Research Briefing (17). July 2006, p. 3.

118 Higgins, S., Wall, K., Baumfield, V., Hall, E., Leat, D., Moseley, D. & Woolner, P. (2007a) *Learning to Learn in Schools Phase 3 Evaluation: Final Report*. London: Campaign for Learning, p. 46.

119 Claxton, G., Chambers, M., Powell, G. & Lucas, B. (2011) *The Learning Powered School: Pioneering 21st Century Education*. Bristol: TLO Ltd, p. 6.

120 James, M., Black, P., McCormick, R., Pedder, D. & Wiliam, D. (2006) Learning How to Learn, in Classrooms, Schools and Networks: Aims, design and analysis, *Research Papers in Education*, 21(2), p. 104.

Chapter 3

1 Feynman, R. (2007) *What Do You Care What Other People Think? Further Adventures of a Curious Character*. London: Penguin, pp. 117–118.

2 Gibb, N. (2017) *The importance of vibrant and open debate in education*. Speech at the researchED National Conference, London, 9 September. Available at: https://www.nickgibb.org.uk/news/nick-gibb-importance-vibrant-and-open-debate-education.

3 Hargreaves, D. (2006) *Personalising Learning 6: The final gateway: school design and organisation*. London: Specialist Schools and Academies Trust.

4 Qualifications and Curriculum Authority (2007) *Personal, Learning and Thinking Skills Framework*. London: QCA.

5 Department for Children, Schools and Families (2007) *Social and emotional aspects of learning for secondary schools*. Nottingham: DCSF Publications.

6 Tyre, P. (2014) 'I've Been a Pariah for So Long'. *Politico Magazine*. Available at: https://www.politico.com/magazine/politico50/2014/ive-been-a-pariah-for-so-long.html#.WfseNhOONcA. See also the #leftytrad hashtag on Twitter.

7 Hirsch, E.D. (1987) *Cultural Literacy: What Every American Needs to Know*. Boston, MA: Houghton Mifflin.

8   Hirsch, E.D. (1987) *Cultural Literacy: What Every American Needs to Know*. Boston, MA: Houghton Mifflin.

9   Oakeshott, M. (1959) *The Voice of Poetry in the Conversation of Mankind*. London: Bowes and Bowes.

10 Hirsch, E.D. (2007) *The Knowledge Deficit: Closing the Shocking Education Gap for American Children*. New York, NY: Houghton Mifflin, pp. xi–22.

11 Willingham, D. (2009) *Why Don't Students Like School?* San Francisco, CA: Jossey-Bass, p. 19.

12 Gove, M. (2012) Secretary of State for Education Michael Gove gives speech to IAA, 14 November. Available at: https://www.gov.uk/government/speeches/secretary-of-state-for-education-michael-gove-gives-speech-to-iaa.

13 *Should We Fill 21st Century Learners' Heads with Pure Facts?* Debate from the 2017 Global Schools and Education Forum. Available at: https://vimeo.com/209041563.

14 Hirsch, E.D. (2000) 'You can always look it up' ... or can you?, *American Educator*, (Spring), pp. 4–9.

15 Wiliam, D. (2017) 'I've come to the conclusion Sweller's Cognitive Load Theory is the single most important thing for teachers to know.' Twitter, 26 January. Available at: https://twitter.com/dylanwiliam/status/824682504602943489.

16 Atkinson, R. C., & Shiffrin, R. M. (1968). Chapter: Human memory: A proposed system and its control processes. In Spence, K. W., & Spence, J. T. *The psychology of learning and motivation* (Volume 2). New York: Academic Press. pp. 89–195.

17 Willingham, D. (2009) *Why Don't Students Like School?* San Francisco, CA: Jossey-Bass, p. 11.

18 From Willingham, D. (2009) *Why Don't Students Like School?* San Francisco, CA: Jossey-Bass, p. 42.

19 Miller, G.A. (1956) The magical number seven, plus or minus two: Some limits on our capacity for processing information, *Psychological Review*, 63, pp. 81–97, p. 81.

20 Cowan, N. (2001) The magical number 4 in short-term memory: A reconsideration of mental storage capacity, *Behavioral and Brain Sciences*, 24, pp. 87–114.

21 Sweller, J. (2009) What human cognitive architecture tells us about constructivism. In S. Tobias & T.M. Duffy (eds), *Constructivist Instruction: Success or Failure?*, pp. 127–143. New York, NY: Routledge/Taylor & Francis Group.

22 Larkin, J., McDermott, J., Simon, D.P. & Simon, H.A. (1980) Expert and novice performance in solving physics problems, *Science*, 208(4450), p. 1342.

23 Tricot, A. & Sweller, J. (2014) Domain-specific knowledge and why teaching generic skills does not work, *Educational Psychology Review*, 26(2), pp. 265–283.

24 Geary, D.C. (2008) An evolutionarily informed education science, *Educational Psychologist*, 43, pp. 279–295.

25 Geary, D.C. (2012) Evolutionary educational psychology. In K.R. Harris, S. Graham & T. Urdan (editors-in-chief), *Educational Psychology Handbook: Vol. 1. Theories, Constructs, and Critical Issues*, pp. 595–620. Washington DC: American Psychological Association.

26 Tricot, A. & Sweller, J. (2014) Domain-specific knowledge and why teaching generic skills does not work, *Educational Psychology Review*, 26(2), pp. 265–283.

27 Tricot, A. & Sweller, J. (2014) Domain-specific knowledge and why teaching generic skills does not work, *Educational Psychology Review*, 26(2), pp. 265–283, p. 269.

28 Tricot, A. & Sweller, J. (2014) Domain-specific knowledge and why teaching generic skills does not work, *Educational Psychology Review*, 26(2), pp. 265–283, p. 269.

29 Tricot, A. & Sweller, J. (2014) Domain-specific knowledge and why teaching generic skills does not work, *Educational Psychology Review*, 26(2), pp. 265–283, p. 268.

30 Tricot, A. & Sweller, J. (2014) Domain-specific knowledge and why teaching generic skills does not work, *Educational Psychology Review*, 26(2), pp. 265–283, p. 265.

31 Sweller, J. (2016) Story of a research program. In S. Tobias, J.D. Fletcher & D.C. Berliner (series eds), Acquired Wisdom Series, *Education Review*, 23, 10 February, p. 12.

32 https://ourworldindata.org/literacy.

33 Anderson, J.R., Reder, L.M & Simon, H.A. (1996) Situated learning and education, *Educational Researcher*, 25(4), pp. 5–11.

34 Kaufman, J.C. & Baer, J. (2002) Could Steven Spielberg manage the Yankees?: Creative thinking in different domains, *Korean Journal of Thinking & Problem Solving*, 12, pp. 5–14, p. 12.

35 Gove, M. (2012) Secretary of State for Education Michael Gove gives speech to IAA, 14 November. Available at: https://www.gov.uk/government/speeches/secretary-of-state-for-education-michael-gove-gives-speech-to-iaa.

36 *Should we fill 21st Century Learners' Heads with Pure Facts?* Debate from the 2017 Global Schools and Education Forum. Available at: https://vimeo.com/209041563.

37 Willingham, D. (2009) *Why Don't Students Like School?* San Francisco, CA: Jossey-Bass, pp. 20–38; emphases added.

38 Willingham, D. (2009) *Why Don't Students Like School?* San Francisco, CA: Jossey-Bass, p. 20.

39 Willingham, D. (2009) *Why Don't Students Like School?* San Francisco, CA: Jossey-Bass, p. 20.

40 https://www.merriam-webster.com/dictionary/knowledge.

41 https://www.merriam-webster.com/dictionary/skill.

42 Sherrington, T. (2017) *The Learning Rainforest: Great Teaching in Real Classrooms.* Woodbridge: John Catt Educational Ltd, p. 143.

43 Sherrington, T. (2017) *The Learning Rainforest: Great Teaching in Real Classrooms.* Woodbridge: John Catt Educational Ltd, p. 268.

44 Waeytens, K., Lens, W. & Vandenberghe, R. (2002) 'Learning to learn': teachers' conceptions of their supporting role, *Learning and Instruction*, 12, p. 313.

45 Waeytens, K., Lens, W. & Vandenberghe, R. (2002) 'Learning to learn': teachers' conceptions of their supporting role, *Learning and Instruction*, 12, p. 316.

46 Waeytens, K., Lens, W. & Vandenberghe, R. (2002) 'Learning to learn': teachers' conceptions of their supporting role, *Learning and Instruction*, 12, p. 314.

47 Waeytens, K., Lens, W. & Vandenberghe, R. (2002) 'Learning to learn': teachers' conceptions of their supporting role, *Learning and Instruction*, 12, p. 316.

48 Bjork, R.A., Dunlosky, J. & Kornell, N. (2013) Self-regulated learning: beliefs, techniques, and illusions, *Annual Review of Psychology*, 64, pp. 417–444.

49 de Bruin, A.B.H. & van Merriënboer, J.J.G. (2017) Bridging cognitive load and self-regulated learning research: a complementary approach to contemporary issues in educational research, *Learning and Instruction*, 51, pp. 1–9.

50 Kirschner, P.A., Sweller, J., Kirschner, F. & Zambrano R.J. (2018) From Cognitive Load Theory to Collaborative Cognitive Load Theory, *International Journal of Computer-Supported Collaborative Learning*, 13, pp. 213–233.

51 Retnowati, E., Ayres, P. & Sweller, J. (2017) Can collaborative learning improve the effectiveness of worked examples in learning mathematics?, *Journal of Educational Psychology*, 109(5), pp. 666–679.

52 Sweller, J., van Merrienboer, J.J.G. & Paas, F. (2019) Cognitive Architecture and Instructional Design: 20 Years Later, *Educational Psychology Review*, 31(2), pp. 261–292.

53 Sweller, J., van Merrienboer, J.J.G. & Paas, F. (2019) Cognitive Architecture and Instructional Design: 20 Years Later, *Educational Psychology Review*, 31(2), pp. 261–292, p. 284.

54 van Merriënboer, J.J.G. & Kirschner, P.A. (2018) *Ten Steps to Complex Learning* (3rd edn). New York, NY: Routledge, p, 277.

55 Sweller, J. (2016) Story of a Research Program. In S. Tobias, J.D. Fletcher & D.C. Berliner (Series eds), Acquired Wisdom Series, *Education Review*, 23, 10 February, p. 12.

56 Burgess, K. (2013) Speaking in public is worse than death for most, *The Times*, 30 October. Available at: https://www.thetimes.co.uk/article/speaking-in-public-is-worse-than-death-for-most-5l2bvqlmbnt.

57 Stanford, P. (2015) Who needs a designer debating hall?, *the Telegraph*, 13 June. Available at: https://www.telegraph.co.uk/education/educationopinion/11670225/Who-needs-a-designer-debating-hall.html.

58 Romeo, R.R., Leonard, J.A., Robinson, S.T., West, M.R., Mackey, A.P., Rowe, M.L. & Gabrieli, J.D.E. (2018) Beyond the 30-million-word gap: Children's conversational exposure is associated with language-related brain function, *Psychological Science*, 29(5), pp. 700–710.

59 Mannion, J. & Mercer, N. (2018) *Oracy across the Welsh curriculum: A research-based review: key principles and recommendations for teachers*. Oracy Cambridge report for the Welsh Government. Available at https://oracycambridge.org/wp-content/uploads/2018/07/Oracy-across-the-Welsh-curriculum-July-2018.pdf.

60 Tricot, A. & Sweller, J. (2014) Domain-specific knowledge and why teaching generic skills does not work, *Educational Psychology Review*, 26(2), p. 268.

61 Law, J., McBean, K. & Rush, R. (2011) Communication skills in a population of primary school-aged children raised in an area of pronounced social disadvantage, *International Journal of Language & Communication Disorders*, 46, pp. 657–664.

62 Abrami, P.C., Bernard, R.M., Borokhovski, E., Waddington, D.I., Wade, C.A. & Persson, T. (2015) Strategies for teaching students to think critically: A meta-analysis, *Review of Educational Research*, 85(2), pp. 275–314.

63 Hitchcock, D. (2004) The effectiveness of computer-assisted instruction in critical thinking, *Informal Logic*, 24(3), pp. 183–218.

64 Reed, J.H. & Kromrey, J.D. (2001) Teaching critical thinking in a community college history course: Empirical evidence from infusing Paul's model, *College Student Journal*, 35(2), pp. 201–215.

65 Rimiene, V. (2002) Assessing and developing students' critical thinking, *Psychology Learning & Teaching*, 2(1), pp. 17–22.

66 Solon, T. (2007) Generic critical thinking infusion and course content learning in Introductory Psychology, *Journal of Instructional Psychology*, 34(2), pp. 95–109.

67 Tricot, A. & Sweller, J. (2014) Domain-specific knowledge and why teaching generic skills does not work, *Educational Psychology Review*, 26(2), p. 265.

68 van Merriënboer, J.J.G. & Kirschner, P.A. (2018) *Ten steps to complex learning* (3rd edn). New York, NY: Routledge, pp. 293–294.

69 Anderson, J.R., Reder, L.M. & Simon, H.A. (1996) Situated learning and education, *Educational Researcher*, 25(4), p. 7.

70 Anderson, J.R., Reder, L.M. & Simon, H.A. (1996) Situated learning and education, *Educational Researcher*, 25(4), p. 10.

71 Bregman, R. (2017) *Poverty Isn't a Lack of Character; It's a Lack of Cash*. Presentation at TED 2017. Available at: https://www.ted.com/talks/rutger_bregman_poverty_isn_t_a_lack_of_character_it_s_a_lack_of_cash.

72 Higgins, S. (2009) *Learning to Learn*. Durham: Beyond Current Horizons Project, p. 3.

73 Qualifications and Curriculum Authority (2007) *Personal, Learning and Thinking Skills Framework*. London: QCA.

74 Sherrington, T. (2017) *The Learning Rainforest: Great Teaching in Real Classrooms*. Woodbridge: John Catt Educational Ltd, p. 55.

75 If you have an idle moment, visit tinyurl.com/funnyflight to see some hilarious silent footage of early attempts at aviation.

76 This chapter was written before the COVID-19 lockdown happened, but you get the point; see https://www.quora.com/How-many-people-are-in-the-air-flying-at-any-given-time.

77 Rogers, E.M. (1995) *Diffusion of Innovations*. New York, NY: Free Press. Available at: https://web.stanford.edu/class/symbsys205/Diffusion%20of%20Innovations.htm.

78 Black, P. & Wiliam, D. (1998) Inside the Black Box: Raising standards through classroom assessment, *Phi Delta Kappan*, 80(2), p. 140.

79 Black, P. & Wiliam, D. (1998) Inside the Black Box: Raising standards through classroom assessment, *Phi Delta Kappan*, 80(2), p. 147.

80 Coe, R. (2013) *Improving Education: A Triumph of Hope over Experience*. Inaugural Lecture of Professor Robert Coe, Durham University, 18 June 2013.

81 Black, P. & Wiliam, D. (1998) Inside the Black Box: Raising standards through classroom assessment, *Phi Delta Kappan*, 80(2), p. 140.

82 Christodoulou, D. (2016) *Why did Assessment for Learning fail?* Presentation at the Wellington Festival of Education. Available at: https://www.youtube.com/watch?v=qLpAalDaqQY.

83 Wiliam, D. (2020) Personal correspondence.

84 Speckesser, S., Runge, J., Foliano, F., Bursnall, M., Hudson-Sharp, N., Rolfe, H. & Anders, J. (2018) *Embedding Formative Assessment: Evaluation report*. Education Endowment Foundation, NIESR.

85 Wiliam, D. (2016) *Leadership for Teacher Learning: Creating a Culture Where All Teachers Improve So That All Students Succeed*. West Palm Beach, FL: Learning Sciences International, p. 208.

86 Kelly, B. (2012) Implementation science for psychology in education. In: B. Kelly & D.F. Perkins (eds), *Handbook of Implementation Science for Psychology in Education*. Cambridge: Cambridge University Press, p. 3.

87 As well as this being the focus of James's next book, we now run an online version of the 'Implementing School Improvement' programme - visit rethinking-ed.org for details.

88 Kelly, B. & Perkins, D.F. (2012) *Handbook of Implementation Science for Psychology in Education*. Cambridge: Cambridge University Press.

89 Gibb, N. (2015) *The Importance of the Teaching Profession*. Speech at the researchED conference. Available at: https://www.gov.uk/government/speeches/nick-gibb-the-importance-of-the-teaching-profession.

90 Gibb, N. (2015) *The importance of the teaching profession*. Speech at the researchED conference. Available at: https://www.gov.uk/government/speeches/nick-gibb-the-importance-of-the-teaching-profession.

91 Education Endowment Foundation (2020). *The Teaching and Learning Toolkit*. Available at: https://educationendowmentfoundation.org.uk/evidence-summaries/teaching-learning-toolkit/meta-cognition-and-self-regulation.

92 Hayes, D. (2012) Education is bad for you, *Huffington Post*, 3 February. Available at: https://www.huffingtonpost.co.uk/dennis-hayes/education-is-bad-for-you_b_1249900.html.

93 Bennett, T. (2013) *Teacher proof: Why Research in Education Doesn't Always Mean What It Claims, and What You Can So About It*. London: Routledge.

94 Ecclestone, K. & Hayes, D. (2008) *The Dangerous Rise of Therapeutic Education*. London: Routledge.

Chapter 4

1 A favoured saying of the former head teacher of Sea View, although the phrase has a distinguished lineage: https://quoteinvestigator.com/2016/04/25/get.

2 That's an overhead projector, for any Gen Z readers.

3 Gutman, L.M. & Schoon, I. (2013) *The Impact of Non-cognitive Skills on Outcomes for Young People. Literature Review*. An Institute of Education report for the Department for Education. Available at https://helmtraining.co.uk/wp-content/uploads/2017/03/Gutman-and-Schoon-Impact-of-non-cognitive-skills-on-outcomes-for-young-people-1.pdf.

4 ASCL (2019) *The Forgotten Third: Final Report of the Commission of Inquiry*. Available at: https://www.ascl.org.uk/ASCL/media/ASCL/Our%20view/Campaigns/The-Forgotten-Third_full-report.pdf.

5 Covington, M. & Beery, R. (1976) *Self-worth and school learning*. New York, NY: Holt, Rinehart and Winston.

6   Joshi, G.P. (2005) Multimodal analgesia techniques and postoperative rehabilitation, *Anesthesiology Clinics of North America*, 23(1), pp. 185–202.

7   Kehlet H. & Dahl J.B. (1993) The value of 'multimodal' or 'balanced analgesia' in postoperative pain treatment, *Anesthesia & Analgesia*, 77(5), pp. 1048–1056.

8   Mathiesen, O., Dahl, B., Thomsen, B.A., Kitter, B., Sonne, N., Dahl, J.B. & Kehlet, H. (2013) A comprehensive multimodal pain treatment reduces opioid consumption after multilevel spine surgery, *European Spine Journal*, 22, pp. 2089–2096.

9   Craig, P., Dieppe, P., Macintyre, S., Michie, S., Nazareth, I. & Petticrew, M. (2008b) *Developing and Evaluating Complex Interventions: New Guidance*. London: Medical Research Council, p. 6.

10 Hall, D., James, D. & Marsden, N. (2012) Marginal gains: Olympic lessons in high performance for organisations, *HR Bulletin: Research and Practice*, 7(2), pp. 9–13.

11 Craig, P., Dieppe, P., Macintyre, S., Michie, S., Nazareth, I. & Petticrew, M. (2008a) Developing and evaluating complex interventions: the new Medical Research Council guidance, *British Medical Journal*, 337, pp. 979–983.

12 Mannion, J. (2018) Metacognition, self-regulation, oracy: A mixed methods case study of a complex, whole-school Learning to Learn intervention. PhD thesis, Hughes Hall, University of Cambridge. Available at: https://www.repository.cam.ac.uk/handle/1810/289131.

13 Allen, R. (2017) Stop shooting silver bullets and learn to trust our teachers again, *the Guardian*, 7 November. Available at: https://www.theguardian.com/education/2017/nov/07/trust-teachers-auditing-performance.

14 EEF (Education Endowment Foundation) (2017c) Projects. Available at: http://educationendowmentfoundation.org.uk/our-work/projects.

15 English, M.C. & Kitsantas, A. (2013) Supporting Student Self-Regulated Learning in Problem- and Project-Based Learning, *Interdisciplinary Journal of Problem-Based Learning*, 7(2), pp. 127–150.

16 Stefanou, C., Stolk, J.D., Prince, M., Chen, J.C. & Lord, S. M. (2013) Self-regulation and autonomy in problem- and project-based learning environments, *Active Learning in Higher Education*, 14(2), pp. 109–122.

17 e.g. see Condliffe, B., Quint, J., Visher, M.G., Bangser, M.R., Drohojowska, S., Saco, L. & Nelson, E. (2017) *Project-Based Learning – a Literature Review*. New York, NY: MDRC. Available at: https://www.mdrc.org/sites/default/files/Project-Based_Learning-LitRev_Final.pdf.

18 Claxton, G. (2006) *Learning to learn, the fourth generation: making sense of personalised learning*. Bristol: TLO Ltd.

19 Hattie, J. (2009) *Visible Learning: A Synthesis of over 800 Meta-Analyses relating to Achievement*. London: Routledge.

20 Petty, G. (2006) *Evidence based teaching*. Cheltenham: Nelson Thornes.

21 Trickey S. & Topping, K.J. (2004) 'Philosophy for Children: A systematic review', *Research Papers in Education*, 19(3), pp. 363–278.

22 Mercer, N. (1995) *The Guided Construction of Knowledge: talk amongst teachers and learners*. Clevedon: Multilingual Matters.

23 Mercer, N. & Littleton, K. (2007) *Dialogue and the Development of Children's Thinking*. London: Routledge.

24 Slavin, R.E. (2008) Cooperative Learning, Success for All, and Evidence-based Reform in education, *Éducation et didactique*, 2(2), pp. 149–157.

25 According to one study, in order to achieve a high level of reliability, a teacher would have to be observed six times, by five different observers. See Ho, A.D. & Kane, T.J. (2013) *The Reliability of Classroom Observations by School Personnel*. Harvard Graduate School of Education. A Measures of Effective Teaching (MET) report for the Bill and Melinda Gates Foundation. Available at: https://files.eric.ed.gov/fulltext/ED540957.pdf.

26 See movingmountainstrust.org for details.

27 Ofsted (2015) *Key Stage 3: The Wasted Years?* Department for Education. Available at: https://assets.publishing.service.gov.uk/government/uploads/system/uploads/attachment_data/file/459830/Key_Stage_3_the_wasted_years.pdf.

28 McInerney, L. (2018) Education ministers need to stop arguing about skills, *SchoolsWeek*, 26 January. Available at: https://schoolsweek.co.uk/education-ministers-need-to-stop-arguing-about-skills.

Chapter 5

1 Sir David Brailsford, quoted in Harrell, E. (2015) How 1% performance improvements led to Olympic gold, *Harvard Business Review*. Available at: https://hbr.org/2015/10/how-1-performance-improvements-led-to-olympic-gold.

2 Rogers, C. (1961) *On Becoming a Person: A therapist's view of psychotherapy.* London: Constable, p. 276.

3 An extensive body of research literature sits behind each of these points. If you'd like to explore this in more detail, see Mannion, J. (2018) Metacognition, self-regulation, oracy: A mixed methods case study of a complex, whole-school Learning to Learn intervention. PhD thesis, Hughes Hall, University of Cambridge, pp. 51–54. Available at https://www.repository.cam.ac.uk/handle/1810/289131.

4 Recommended viewing – available online at bbc.co.uk/programmes/m000772n.

5 A note to primary and tertiary colleagues. The *Learning Skills* curriculum was developed in a secondary school, and while there are many elements that are applicable at the primary and tertiary levels, this section describes how the approach can be implemented in a secondary school. If you would like to explore how these ideas can be adapted to other settings, drop us a line rethinking-ed.org/contact – we'll be happy to help.

6 Downey, C., Byrne, J. & Souza, A. (2013) Leading and managing the competence-based curriculum: Conscripts, volunteers and champions at work within the departmentalised environment of the secondary school, *The Curriculum Journal*, 23(4), p. 378.

7 Human Resources? Is that really all we are?

8 Jaycox, L., McCaffrey, D., Ocampo, B., Shelley, G., Blake, S., Peterson, D... & Cuby, J. (2006) Challenges in the evaluation and implementation of school-based prevention and intervention programs on sensitive topics, *American Journal of Evaluation*, 27(3), p. 338.

9 Dignath, C., Buettner, G. & Langfeldt, H.P. (2008) How can primary school students learn self-regulated learning strategies most effectively? A meta-analysis of self-regulation training programmes, *Educational Research Review*, 3, pp. 101–129.

10 The 'dreaming it' thing we mean quite literally. At an early planning session, one member of the team, Millsy, revealed that she had had a dream where she envisaged how we could structure a weekly cycle of lessons. We all stared incredulously at the projected screen on the lounge wall as she translated her dream into a weekly lesson planning pro forma. That document was saved as 'Millsy's dream', and this became the basis for lesson planning in the first year.

11 Banerjee, R., Weare, K. & Farr, W. (2013) Working with 'social and emotional aspects of learning' (SEAL): associations with school ethos, pupil social experiences, attendance and attainment, *British Education Research Journal*, 40, p. 718.

12 Durlak, J.A., Weissberg, R.P., Dymnicki, A.B., Taylor, R.D. & Schellinger, K.B. (2011) The impact of enhancing students' social and emotional learning: a meta-analysis of school-based universal interventions, *Child Development*, 82(1), pp. 405–432.

13 Thorndike E.L. & Woodworth R.S. (1901) The influence of improvement in one mental function upon the efficiency of other functions (I), *Psychological Review*, 8, pp. 247–261.

14 Gentner, D. & Toupin, C. (1986) Systematicity and surface similarity in the development of analogy, *Cognitive Science*, 10(3), pp. 277–300.

15 Holyoak, K., Junn, E. & Billman, D. (1984) Development of analogical problem solving skills, *Child Development*, 55, pp. 2042–2055.

16 Willingham, D. (2002) Inflexible knowledge: The first step to expertise, *American Educator*, Winter Issue, pp. 8–19.

17 Adey, P. & Shayer, M. (1993) An exploration of long-term far-transfer effects following an extended intervention programme in the high school science curriculum, *Cognition and Instruction*, 11(1), pp. 1–29.

18 Webb, P., Whitlow, J.W. & Venter, D. (2017) From Exploratory Talk to Abstract Reasoning: a Case for Far Transfer?, *Educational Psychology Review*, 29, pp. 565–581.

19 Scherer, R., Siddiq, F. & Sánchez Viveros, B. (2019) The cognitive benefits of learning computer programming: A meta-analysis of transfer effects, *Journal of Educational Psychology*, 111(5), pp. 764–792.

20 Hipkins, R. & Cowie, B. (2014) Learning to learn, lifewide and lifelong learning: Reflections on the New Zealand experience. In R. Deakin-Crick, C. Stringher & K. Ren (eds), *Learning to learn: International perspectives from theory and practice*, (pp. 297–298). London: Routledge.

21 **(a)** Baker, C. (2006) *Foundations of bilingual education and bilingualism*. Clevedon: Multilingual Matters; Littleton, K. & Mercer, N. (2013) *Interthinking: putting talk to work*. Abingdon, UK: Routledge;
    (b) Engle, R.A. (2006) Framing interactions to foster generative learning: A situative explanation of transfer in a community of learners classroom, *Journal of the Learning Sciences*, 15(4), pp. 451–498;
    (c) Claxton, G. (2006) *Learning to Learn, The Fourth Generation*. Bristol: TLO Ltd;
    (d) Pellegrino, J. & Hilton, M. (2012) *Education for life and work: Developing transferable knowledge and skills in the 21st century*. Washington, DC: National Research Academy;
    (e) Goldstone, R.L & Day, S.B. (2012) Introduction to 'New Conceptualizations of Transfer of Learning', *Educational Psychologist*, 47(3), pp. 149–152;
    (f) Engle, R.A., Lam, D.P., Meyer, X.S. & Nix, S. (2012) How does expansive framing promote transfer? Several proposed explanations, *Educational Psychologist*, 47, pp. 215–231;
    (g) Perkins, D.N. & Salomon, G. (2012) Knowledge to go: A motivational and dispositional view of transfer, *Educational Psychologist*, 47(3), pp. 248–258;
    (h) Reed, S.K. (2012) Learning by mapping across situations, *The Journal of the Learning Sciences*, 21, pp. 354–398;
    (i) Pintrich, P. & de Groot, E. (1990) Motivational and self-regulated learning components of classroom academic performance, *Journal of Educational Psychology*, 82, pp. 33–40;
    (j) Lobato, J., Rhodehamel, B. & Hohensee, C. (2012) 'Noticing' as an alternative transfer of learning process, *The Journal of the Learning Sciences*, 21, pp. 433–482.

22 Wiliam, D. (2016) *Leadership for Teacher Learning*. West Palm Beach, FL: Learning Sciences International.

23 Wilkinson, A. (1965) The Concept of Oracy, *Educational Review*, 17(4), p. 13.

24 Wilkinson, A. (1965) *Spoken English*. Birmingham, University of Birmingham Press.

25 Walker, M. (2017) *Monkeys lie to one another*. BBC Earth, 18 February. Available at: http://www.bbc.com/earth/story/20170210-monkeys-lie-to-one-another.

26 Lancaster, S. (2016) *Speak Like a Leader*. Presentation at TEDxVerona. Available at: youtube.com/watch?v=bGBamfWasNQ.

27 Barnes, D., Britton, J. & Rosen, H. (1971) *Language, the learner and the school: a research report*. Harmondsworth: Penguin.

28 Barnes, D. (1976) *From Communication to Curriculum*. Harmondsworth: Penguin.

29 Bullock, A. (1975) *A Language for Life: Report of the Committee of Inquiry appointed by the Secretary of State for Education and Science*. London: Her Majesty's Stationery Office.

30 Johnson, J. (1994) The National Oracy Project. In S. Brindley (ed), (pp. 33–42). *Teaching English*. London: Routledge.

31 Vasagar, J. (2012) Thousands of vocational qualifications to be stripped out of GCSE league tables, *the Guardian*, 31 January. Available at: https://www.theguardian.com/education/2012/jan/31/vocational-qualifications-stripped-league-tables.

32 Stacey, G. (2013) Our announcement on speaking and listening assessments, *The Ofqual Blog*. Available at: https://ofqual.blog.gov.uk/2013/09/04/our-announcement-on-speaking-and-listening-assessments.

33 Millard, W. & Menzies, L. (2016) *Oracy: The State of Speaking in Our Schools*. London: Voice 21.

34 Lee, D. & Hatesohi, D. (1993) *Listening: Our Most Used Communications Skill*. University of Missouri. Available at: https://extension2.missouri.edu/cm150.

35 van Oers, B., Elbers, E., Wardekker, W. & van der Veer, R. (eds) (2008) *The transformation of learning: advances in cultural-historical activity theory*. Cambridge and New York, NY: Cambridge University Press.

36 Whitebread, D., Mercer, N., Howe, C. & Tolmie, A. (eds) (2013) Self-regulation and dialogue in primary classrooms, *British Journal of Educational Psychology Monograph Series II: Psychological Aspects of Education – Current Trends*, 10. Leicester: BPS.

37 Vygotsky, L. (1962) *Thought and Language*. Cambridge, MA: MIT Press.

38 Vygotsky, L. (1978) *Mind in Society: The development of higher psychological processes*. Cambridge, MA, Harvard University Press.

39 Vass, E. & Littleton, K (2010) Peer collaboration and learning in the classroom. In: K. Littleton, C. Wood & J. Kleine Staarman (eds), (pp. 105–136). *International Handbook of Psychology in Education*. Leeds: Emerald, p. 107.

40 Hart, B. & Risley, T. (1995) *Meaningful Differences in the Everyday Experiences of Young American Children*. Baltimore, MD: Paul Brookes.

41 Goswami, U. & Bryant, P. (2007) *Children's Cognitive Development and Learning* (Primary Review Research Survey). Cambridge: University of Cambridge Faculty of Education.

42 Dawes, L. (2008) *The Essential Speaking and Listening: Talk for learning at KS2*. London: Routledge.

43 Mercer, N. & Littleton, K. (2007) *Dialogue and the Development of Children's Thinking*. London: Routledge.

44 Romeo, R., Leonard, J.A., Robinson, S.T., West, M.R., Mackey, A.P., Rowe, M.L. & Gabrieli, J.D.E. (2018) Beyond the 30 million word gap: children's conversational exposure is associated with language-related brain function, *Psychological Science*, 29, pp. 700–710.

45 Trafton, A. (2018) Back-and-forth exchanges boost children's brain response to language, *MIT News Office*. Available at: http://news.mit.edu/2018/conversation-boost-childrens-brain-response-language-0214.

46 Mercer, N. & Mannion, J. (2018) *Oracy across the Welsh curriculum: A research-based review: key principles and recommendations for teachers*. Oracy Cambridge report for the Welsh Government. Available at: https://oracycambridge.org/wp-content/uploads/2018/07/Oracy-across-the-Welsh-curriculum-July-2018.pdf. Happily, the Welsh government has since acted on many of the recommendations in this report; we look forward to seeing how this plays out across the Welsh education system in the years to come.

47 **(a)** Adey, P. & Shayer, M. (1994) *Really Raising Standards: Cognitive intervention and academic achievement*. London: Routledge; O'Connor, C., Michaels, S. & Chaplin, S. (2015) 'Scaling Down' to explore the role of talk in learning: from district intervention to controlled classroom study. In L.B. Resnick, C.S.C. Asterhan and S.N. Clarke (eds), *Socializing Intelligence Through Academic Talk and Dialogue*. Washington DC: American Educational Research Association; Wilkinson, I.A.G., Murphy, P.K. & Binici, S. (2015) Dialogue-intensive pedagogies for promoting reading comprehension: What we know, what we need to know. In L.B. Resnick, C.S.C. Asterhan and S.N. Clarke (eds), *Socializing Intelligence Through Academic Talk and Dialogue*. Washington DC: American Educational Research Association;

(b) Dunsmuir, S. & Blatchford, P. (2004) Predictors of writing competence in 4- to 7-year old children, *British Journal of Educational Psychology*, 74(3), pp. 461–483; Dockrell, J.E. & Connelly, V. (2009) The impact of oral language skills on the production of written text, *BJEP Monograph Series II, Number 6 – Teaching and Learning Writing*, 1(1), pp. 45–62; Maxwell, B., Burnett, C., Reidy, J., Willis, B. & Demack, S. (2015) *Oracy Curriculum, Culture and Assessment Toolkit: Evaluation Report and Executive Summary*. London: Education Endowment Foundation;

(c) Alexander, R. (2008) *Towards Dialogic Teaching: Rethinking Classroom Talk* (4th edn). York: Dialogos UK; Goswami, U. (2015) *Children's Cognitive Development and Learning*. York: Cambridge Primary Review Trust; Mercer, N., Wegerif, R. & Dawes, L. (1999) Children's talk and the development of reasoning in the classroom, *British Educational Research Journal*, 25, pp. 95–111;

(d) Sheehy, K., Rix, J. with Collins, J., Hall, K., Nind, M. & Wearmouth, J. (2009) A systematic review of whole class, subject-based pedagogies with reported outcomes for the academic and social inclusion of pupils with special educational needs. In: *Research Evidence in Education Library*. London: EPPI-Centre, Social Science Research Unit, Institute of Education, University of London; The Communication Trust (2013) *A Generation Adrift*. London: The Communication Trust; Maxwell, B., Burnett, C., Reidy, J., Willis, B. & Demack, S. (2015) *Oracy Curriculum, Culture and Assessment Toolkit: Evaluation Report and Executive Summary*. London: Education Endowment Foundation;

(e) Bialystok, E. & Feng, X. (2010) Language proficiency and its implications for monolingual and bilingual children. In: A.Y. Durgunoglu & C. Goldenberg (eds), (pp. 121–138). *Dual Language Learners: The development and assessment of oral and written language*. New York, NY: Guilford Press; Sorge, G.B., Toplak, M.E. & Bialystok, E. (2017) Interactions between levels of attention ability and levels of bilingualism in children's executive functioning, *Developmental Science*, 20(1), pp. 1–16; Grundy, J. & Timmer, K. (2017) Bilingualism and working memory capacity: A comprehensive meta-analysis, *Second Language Research*, 33(3), pp. 325–340;

(f) Adey, P. & Shayer, M. (2015) The effects of cognitive acceleration. In L.B. Resnick, C.S.C. Asterhan & S.N. Clarke (eds), *Socializing Intelligence Through Academic Talk and Dialogue*. Washington DC: American Educational Research Association; Zohar, A. & Nemet, F. (2002) Fostering students' knowledge and argumentation skills through dilemmas in human genetics, *Journal of Research in Science Teaching*, 39(1), pp. 35–62;

(g) Ofsted (2010) *Learning: Creative Approaches That Raise Standards*. Manchester: Ofsted; Trickey, S. & Topping, K.J. (2006) Collaborative philosophical enquiry for school children: Socio-emotional effects at 10–12 years, *School Psychology International*, 27(5), pp. 599–614;

(h) Chiu, C.W.T. (1998) *Synthesizing Metacognitive Interventions: What training characteristics can improve reading performance?* Paper presented at the Annual Meeting of the American Educational Research Association, San Diego, CA, 13–17 April 1998; Kutnik, P. & Berdondini, L. (2009) Can the enhancement of group working in classrooms provide a basis for effective communication in support of school-based cognitive achievement in classrooms of young learners?, *Cambridge Journal of Education*, 39(1), pp. 71–94; Webb, N.M., Franke, M.L., Turrou, A.C. and Ing, M. (2015) An exploration of teacher practices in relation to profiles of small-group dialogue. In L.B. Resnick, C.S.C. Asterhan and S.N. Clarke (eds), (pp. 87–98). *Socializing Intelligence Through Academic Talk and Dialogue*. Washington DC: American Educational Research Association;

(i) Howe, C. & Mercer, N. (2007) *Children's Social Development, Peer Interaction and Classroom Learning* (Primary Review Research Survey). Cambridge: University of Cambridge Faculty of Education;

(j) Alexander, R. (2008) *Towards Dialogic Teaching: Rethinking Classroom Talk* (4th edn). York: Dialogos UK; Ofsted (2003) *The Education of Six Year Olds in England,*

Denmark and Finland: An International Comparative Study. London: Ofsted; Qualifications and Curriculum Authority (QCA) (2008) *Curriculum Evidence Probe 2 Report: Dialogue and Curriculum Development.* Available at: curee.co.uk/files/publication/1234197541/FINAL_Building_the_Evidence_ Base_Probe_2_full_report1.pdf;

(k) Jensen, J. (2008) Developing historical empathy through debate: An action research study, *Social Studies Research and Practice,* 3(1), pp. 55–67;

(l) Akerman, R. & Neale, I. (2011) *Debating the Evidence: An International Review of Current Situation and Perceptions.* Reading: CfBT Education Trust;

(m) The Communication Trust (2013) *A Generation Adrift.* London: The Communication Trust; Hart, B. & Risley, T. (1995) *Meaningful Differences in the Everyday Experiences of Young American Children.* Baltimore, MD: Paul Brookes; Locke, A., Ginsborg, J. & Peers, I. (2002) Development and disadvantage: Implications for the early years and beyond, *International Journal of Language and Communication Disorders,* 37(1), pp. 3–15; Roulstone, S., Law, J., Rush., R., Clegg, J. & Peters, T. (2011) *Investigating the Role of Language in Children's Early Educational Outcomes,* Research Report DFE-RR134; Waldfogel, J. & Washbrook, E. (2010) *Low Income and Early Cognitive Development in the UK.* London: Sutton Trust;

(n) Bryan, K., Freer, J. & Furlong, C. (2007) Language and communication difficulties in juvenile offenders, *International Journal of Language and Communication Disorders,* 42(5), pp. 505–520; Clegg, J. (2004) Language and Behaviour: An Exploratory Study of Pupils in an Exclusion Unit, *Proceedings of the British Psychological Society Developmental Section Annual Conference,* Leeds, September;

(o) Ashley, L., Duberley, J., Sommerlad, H. & Scholarios, D. (2015) *A Qualitative Evaluation of Non-Educational Barriers to the Elite Professions.* London: Social Mobility and Child Poverty Commission; de Vries, R. & Rentfrow, J. (2016) *A Winning Personality: The Effects of Background on Personality and Earnings.* London: The Sutton Trust.

48 Mercer, N., Phillips, T. & Somekh, B. (2008) Research note, spoken language and new technology (SLANT), *Journal of Computer Assisted Learning,* 7, pp. 195–202.

49 Mercer, N. (1994) The quality of talk in children's joint activity at the computer, *Journal of Computer Assisted Learning,* 10, p. 24.

50 Mercer, N. (1994) The quality of talk in children's joint activity at the computer, *Journal of Computer Assisted Learning,* 10, p. 24.

51 Mercer, N. (1995) *The Guided Construction of Knowledge: Talk amongst teachers and learners.* Clevedon: Multilingual Matters, p. 104.

52 e.g. see Michaels, S., O'Connor, C. & Resnick, L. (2008) Deliberative discourse idealized and realized: Accountable talk in the classroom and in civic life, *Studies in Philosophy and Education,* 27(4), pp. 283–297.

53 Mercer, N. (2008) *Three Kinds of Talk.* University of Cambridge: Thinking Together, p. 1. Available at: thinkingtogether.educ.cam.ac.uk/resources/5_examples_of_talk_ in_groups.pdf.

54 Janis, I.L. (1972). *Victims of groupthink; a psychological study of foreign-policy decisions and fiascos.* Boston, MA: Houghton, Mifflin.

55 This, of course, is very different from the specious argument that schools and universities should be 'safe spaces' where young people have the right to be protected from information they find challenging, or from views that differ from their own.

56 thinkingtogether.educ.cam.ac.uk/resources.

57 Thinking Together (2019) *Ground Rules for Exploratory Talk.* Available at: https://thinkingtogether.educ.cam.ac.uk/resources/Ground_rules_for_Exploratory_Talk.pdf.

58 Cleghorn, P. (2002) *Thinking through Philosophy.* Blackburn: Educational Printing Services Ltd.

59 You can build an entire state school with £18m; see http://news.bbc.co.uk/1/hi/education/4952004.stm.

60 https://www.harrowschool.org.uk/The-Super-Curriculum.

61 harrowschool.org.uk/Debating-in-Calcutta.

62 https://www.westminster.org.uk/co-curriculum/societies/.

63 Gardiner-Hill, C. (2009) Debating Society: F Block Balloon Debate. Posted 25 November. Available at: https://www.etoncollege.com/newsarticle?id=230.

64 To see just how consistent this pattern has been, spend a few seconds scrolling down this web page: https://en.m.wikipedia.org/wiki/List_of_Prime_Ministers_of_the_United_Kingdom_by_education.

65 See esu.org/resources.

66 Tsaousides, T. (2017) Why Are We Afraid of Speaking in Public?, *Psychology Today*, 27 November. Available at: https://www.psychologytoday.com/gb/blog/smashing-the-brainblocks/201711/why-are-we-scared-public-speaking.

67 Lake, R. (2015) *Fear of Public Speaking Statistics and How to Overcome Glossophobia*. Available at: https://www.creditdonkey.com/fear-of-public-speaking-statistics.html.

68 Dwyer, K. & Davidson, M. (2012) Is public speaking really more feared than death?, *Communication Research Reports*, 29, pp. 99–107. In one study, the rank order of fears reported is as follows: speaking before a group, 40.6%; heights, 32.0%; insects and bugs, 22.0%; financial problems, 22.0%; deep water, 21.5%; sickness, 18.8%; death, 18.7%; flying, 18.3%: loneliness, 13.6%; dogs, 11.2%; driving or riding in a car, 8.8%; darkness, 7.9%; elevators, 7.6%; escalators, 4.8%.

69 Burgess, K. (2013) Speaking in public is worse than death for most, *The Times*, 30 October. Available at: https://www.thetimes.co.uk/article/speaking-in-public-is-worse-than-death-for-most-5l2bvqlmbnt.

70 Howe, A. (2018) Upgrading oracy: placing 'spoken delivery and response' at the heart of the curriculum. *Oracy Cambridge*. Available at: https://www.oracycambridge.org/2018/12/02/upgrading-oracy.

71 Chambless, D.L. & Ollendick, T.H. (2001) Empirically supported psychological interventions: Controversies and evidence, *Annual Review of Psychology*, 52(1), pp. 685–716.

72 Nash, G., Crimmins, G. & Oprescu, F. (2016) If first-year students are afraid of public speaking assessments what can teachers do to alleviate such anxiety?, *Assessment & Evaluation in Higher Education*, 41(4), pp. 586–600.

73 Malouff, J.M. & Emmerton, A.J. (2014) Students can give psychology away: Oral presentations on YouTube, *Psychology Learning & Teaching*, 13(1), pp. 38–42.

74 Andolina, M.W. & Conklin, H.G. (2018) Speaking with confidence and listening with empathy: The impact of *Project Soapbox* on high school students, *Theory & Research in Social Education*, 46(3), pp. 374--409.

75 Finn, A.N., Sawyer, C.R. & Schrodt, P. (2009) Examining the effect of exposure therapy on public speaking state anxiety, *Communication Education*, 58(1), pp. 92–109.

76 Lancaster, S. (2016) *Speak like a leader*. Presentation at TEDxVerona. Available at: https://www.youtube.com/watch?v=bGBamfWasNQ.

77 Cited in Chance, P. (1986) *Thinking in the classroom: A survey of programs*. New York, NY: Teachers College, Columbia University, p. 41.

78 Lipman, M. (1973) *Philosophy for Children*. Montclair, NJ: Institute for the Advancement of Philosophy for Children, p. 3.

79 Lipman, M. (1973) *Philosophy for Children*. Montclair, NJ: Institute for the Advancement of Philosophy for Children, p. 20.

80 Karras, R. (1979) Final evaluation of the pilot programme in philosophical reasoning in Lexington elementary schools, *Thinking*, 1(3/4), pp. 26–32.

81 Shipman, V. (1983) Evaluation replication of the Philosophy for Children program – Final report, *Thinking*, 5(1), pp. 45–57.

82 Iorio, J., Weinstein, M. & Martin, J. (1984) A review of District 24's Philosophy for Children program, *Thinking* 5(2), pp. 28–35.

83 Educational testing service (New Jersey) (1978) Pompton Lakes and Newark 1976–78. A complete abstract. In M. Lipman (1988), *Philosophy Goes to School*, pp. 219–224. Philadelphia, PA: Temple University Press.

84 Trickey S. & Topping, K.J. (2004) Philosophy for Children: A systematic review, *Research Papers in Education*, 19(3), pp. 363–278.

85 Gorard, S, Siddiqui, N. & See, B.H. (2015) *Philosophy for Children: SAPERE, Evaluation Report and Executive Summary*. London: Education Endowment Foundation.

86 Topping, K.J. & Trickey, S. (2007) Collaborative philosophical enquiry for school children: Cognitive gains at two-year follow-up, *British Journal of Educational Psychology*, 77(4), pp. 787–796.

87 Topping, K.J. & Trickey, S. (2007) Impact of philosophical enquiry on school students' interactive behaviour, *Thinking Skills and Creativity*, 2, pp. 73–84.

88 Trickey, S. & Topping, K.J. (2006) Collaborative philosophical enquiry for school children: Socio-emotional effects at 10–12 years, *School Psychology International*, 27(5), pp. 599–614.

89 Trickey, S. & Topping, K.J. (2006) Collaborative philosophical enquiry for school children: Socio-emotional effects at 10–12 years, *School Psychology International*, 27(5), pp. 599–614.

90 Gregson, M., Spedding, P., Moseley, D. & Baumfield, V. (2008) *Evaluation of the Northumberland Raising Aspirations in Society (NRAIS) Project. Project Report.* Sunderland: University of Sunderland Press.

91 See also https://www.sapere.org.uk/about-us/p4c-videos.aspx.

92 Fisher, R. (1990) *Teaching Children to Think*. England: Nelson Thornes.

93 e.g. see Buckley, J. (2012) *Pocket P4C: Getting Started with Philosophy for Children*. Chelmsford: One Slice Books.

94 In case you're interested, the NASA website has an excellent, child friendly explanation of why the sky is blue. See https://spaceplace.nasa.gov/blue-sky/en/.

95 For an extended version of a 10-step procedure similar to this one, see Nottingham, J. (2016) *Encouraging Learning: A P4C guide for parents*. Available at: https://p4c.com/philosophize-with-your-children/2/.

96 Fisher, R. (1990) *Teaching Children to Think*. England: Nelson Thornes.

97 SAPERE (2009) *Information Pack: An Explanation of Philosophy for Children with Examples of Practice, Evaluations and Research*. SAPERE: Charity no. 1037019.

98 Lane, N.R. & Lane, S.A. (1986) Rationality, Self-esteem and autonomy through collaborative enquiry, *Oxford Review of Education*, 12(3), pp. 263–275.

99 Spoiler: it is, but some people think it isn't.

100 See, for example, https://www.teachthought.com/critical-thinking/metacognition-50-questions-help-students-think-think. We also heartily recommend Sutcliffe, R., Bigglestone, T. & Buckley, J. (2019) *Thinking Moves, A to Z: Metacognition made simple*. London: Dialogue Works.

101 Hübner, S., Nückles, M. & Renkla, A. (2010) Writing learning journals: Instructional support to overcome learning-strategy deficits, *Learning and Instruction*, 20(1), pp. 18–29.

102 Wäschle, K., Gebhardt, A., Oberbusch, E.M. & Nückles, M. (2015) Journal writing in science: Effects on comprehension, interest, and critical reflection, *Journal of Writing Research*, 7(1), pp. 41–64.

103 Glogger, I., Schwonke, R., Holzäpfel, L., Nückles, M. & Renkl, A. (2012) Learning strategies assessed by journal writing: Prediction of learning outcomes by quantity, quality, and combinations of learning strategies, *Journal of Educational Psychology*, 104(2), pp. 452–468 (p. 464).

104 Lang, G. (2018) Using Learning journals to increase metacognition, motivation, and learning in computer information systems education, *Information Systems Education Journal*, 16(6), pp. 39–47.

105 Coles, A. & Banfield, G. (2012) Creativity and mathematics: Using learning journals, *Mathematics Teaching*, 228, pp. 6–11.

106 Denton, A.W. (2018) The Use of a learning journal in an introductory statistics course, *Psychology Learning & Teaching*, 17(1), pp. 84–93.

107 Kupeli, N., Chatzitheodorou, G., Troop, N.A., McInnerney, D., Stone, P. & Candy, B. (2019) Expressive writing as a therapeutic intervention for people with advanced

disease: A systematic review, *BMC Palliative Care*, 18(1), p. 65. Available at https://bmcpalliatcare.biomedcentral.com/track/pdf/10.1186/s12904-019-0449-y.

108 Schippers, M., Scheepers, A. & Peterson, J. (2015) A scalable goal-setting intervention closes both the gender and ethnic minority achievement gap, *Palgrave Communications*, 1, pp. 1–13. Available at https://www.researchgate.net/publication/279224047_A_scalable_goal-setting_intervention_closes_both_the_gender_and_ethnic_minority_achievement_gap.

109 Schippers, M., Scheepers, A. & Peterson, J. (2015) A scalable goal-setting intervention closes both the gender and ethnic minority achievement gap, *Palgrave Communications*, 1, pp. 1–13. Available at https://www.researchgate.net/publication/279224047_A_scalable_goal-setting_intervention_closes_both_the_gender_and_ethnic_minority_achievement_gap., p. 3.

110 Because they contained information that may have been deemed sensitive, learning journals were locked away by the teacher after each session.

111 Puff, R. (2013) An overview of meditation: its origins and traditions, *Psychology Today*, 7 July. Available at: https://www.psychologytoday.com/gb/blog/meditation-modern-life/201307/overview-meditation-its-origins-and-traditions.

112 From van Dam, N.T., van Vugt, M.K., Vago, D.R., Schmalzl, L., Saron, C.D., Olendzki, A.... & Meyer, D.E. (2018) Mind the hype: A critical evaluation and prescriptive agenda for research on mindfulness and meditation, *Perspectives on Psychological Science*, 13(1), pp. 36–61.

113 A search of the PUBMED medical research database for <meditation AND (meta-analysis OR systematic review)> yielded 315 hits; the same search of the ERIC education research database yielded just 6 hits.

114 Gathright, E.C., Salmoirago-Blotcher, E., DeCosta, J., Balletto, B.L., Donahue, M.L.... & Scott-Sheldon, L. (2019) The impact of transcendental meditation on depressive symptoms and blood pressure in adults with cardiovascular disease: A systematic review and meta-analysis, *Complementary Therapies in Medicine*, 46, pp. 172–179.

115 Garland, E.L., Brintz, C.E., Hanley, A.W., Roseen, E.J., Atchley, R.M.... & Keefe, F.J. (2019) Mind-Body Therapies for Opioid-Treated Pain: A systematic review and meta-analysis, *JAMA Internal Medicine*. doi.org/10.1001/jamainternmed.2019.4917.

116 Sabe, M., Sentissi, O. & Kaiser, S. (2019) Meditation-based mind-body therapies for negative symptoms of schizophrenia: Systematic review of randomized controlled trials and meta-analysis, *Schizophrenia Research*, 212, pp. 15–25.

117 Wang, X., Li, P., Pan, C., Dai, L., Wu, Y. & Deng, Y. (2019) The Effect of mind–body therapies on insomnia: A systematic review and meta-analysis, *Evidence-Based Complementary and Alternative Medicine*, 2019, Article ID 9359807. doi.org/10.1155/2019/9359807.

118 Chan, J., Deng, K., Wu, J. & Yan, J.H. (2019) Effects of meditation and mind–body exercises on older adults' cognitive performance: A meta-analysis, *The Gerontologist*. gnz022. doi.org/10.1093/geront/gnz022.

119 Mitchell, J.T., Zylowska, L. & Kollins, S.H. (2015) mindfulness meditation training for attention-deficit/hyperactivity disorder in adulthood: Current empirical support, treatment overview, and future directions, *Cognitive and Behavioral Practice*, 22(2), pp. 172–191.

120 Witt, K., Boland, A., Lamblin, M., McGorry, P.D., Veness, B.... & Robinson, J. (2019) Effectiveness of universal programmes for the prevention of suicidal ideation, behaviour and mental ill health in medical students: a systematic review and meta-analysis, *Evidence-Based Mental Health*, 22, pp. 84–90.

121 Semple, R.J., Lee, J., Rosa, D., Miller, L.F. (2010) A randomized trial of mindfulness-based cognitive therapy for children: Promoting mindful attention to enhance social-emotional resiliency in children, *Journal of Child and Family Studies*, 19(2), pp. 218–229.

122 Semple, R.J., Lee, J., Rosa, D., Miller, L.F. (2010) A randomized trial of mindfulness-based cognitive therapy for children: Promoting mindful attention to enhance

social-emotional resiliency in children, *Journal of Child and Family Studies*, 19(2), pp. 218–229, p. 218.

123 Lazar, S.W., Kerr, C.E., Wasserman, R.H., Gray, J.R., Greve, D.N., Treadway, M.T.... Fischl, B. (2005) Meditation experience is associated with increased cortical thickness, *Neuroreport*, 16(17), pp. 1893–1897.

124 Hölzel, B.K., Carmody, J., Vangel, M., Congleton, C., Yerramsetti, S.M., Gard, T. & Lazar, S.W. (2011) Mindfulness practice leads to increases in regional brain gray matter density, *Psychiatry Research*, 191(1), pp. 36–43.

125 Walton, A. (2016) Science shows meditation benefits children's brains and behaviour, *Forbes*, 18 October. Available at: https://www.forbes.com/sites/alicegwalton/2016/10/18/the-many-benefits-of-meditation-for-children.

126 Waters, L., Barsky, A., Ridd, A. & Allen, K. (2014) Contemplative education: A systematic, evidence-based review of the effect of meditation interventions in schools, *Educational Psychology Review*, 27, pp. 103–134.

127 Waters, L., Barsky, A., Ridd, A. & Allen, K. (2014) Contemplative education: a systematic, evidence-based review of the effect of meditation interventions in schools, *Educational Psychology Review*, 27, pp. 103–134, p. 129.

128 Waters, L., Barsky, A., Ridd, A. & Allen, K. (2014) Contemplative education: a systematic, evidence-based review of the effect of meditation interventions in schools, *Educational Psychology Review*, 27, pp. 103–134, p. 129.

129 Waters, L., Barsky, A., Ridd, A. & Allen, K. (2014) Contemplative education: a systematic, evidence-based review of the effect of meditation interventions in schools, *Educational Psychology Review*, 27, pp. 103–134, pp. 129–130.

130 Mrazek, M.D., Franklin, M.S., Phillips, D.T., Baird, B. & Schooler, J.W. (2013) Mindfulness training improves working memory capacity and GRE performance while reducing mind wandering, *Psychological Science*, 24(5), pp. 776–781.

131 Mrazek, M.D., Franklin, M.S., Phillips, D.T., Baird, B. & Schooler, J.W. (2013) Mindfulness training improves working memory capacity and GRE performance while reducing mind wandering, *Psychological Science*, 24(5), pp. 776–781, p. 776.

132 Erbe, R. & Lohrmann, D. (2015) Mindfulness meditation for adolescent stress and well-being: A systematic review of the literature with implications for school health programs, *Health Educator*, 47(2), pp. 12–19.

133 Erbe, R. & Lohrmann, D. (2015) Mindfulness meditation for adolescent stress and well-being: A systematic review of the literature with implications for school health programs, *Health Educator*, 47(2), pp. 12–19, p. 15.

134 Goyal, M., Singh, S., Sibinga, E.M.S., Gould, N.F., Rowland-Seymour, A.... & Haythornthwaite, J.A. (2014) Meditation programs for psychological stress and well-being: A systematic review and meta-analysis, *JAMA Internal Medicine*, 174(3), pp. 357–368.

135 van Dam, N.T., van Vugt, M.K., Vago, D.R., Schmalzl, L., Saron, C.D., Olendzki, A.... & Meyer, D.E. (2018) Mind the hype: A critical evaluation and prescriptive agenda for research on mindfulness and meditation, *Perspectives on Psychological Science*, 13(1), pp. 36–61.

136 Robinson, M. (2013) *Trivium 21c: Preparing Young People for the Future with Lessons from the Past*. Carmarthen: Independent Thinking Press, p. 18.

137 Costa, A. (2008) Habits of mind: Learnings that last. In A. Costa (ed.), *The School as a Home for the Mind*, (pp. 29–48). Thousand Oaks, CA: Corwin.

138 If you do this, you might want to create a 'vertical slice team' comprising a range of different job roles and a range of different subject specialisms – e.g. a senior leader, a middle leader, a teaching assistant, the Special Needs Coordinator, an early years teacher, an experienced teacher...whatever makes the most sense in your setting. You may need to meet together several times until you arrive at a language of learning that everyone agrees on. This should then be sent out to the wider school – students and staff – for consultation and feedback, which again should be acted upon until consensus is reached.

139 Claxton, G., Chambers, M., Powell, G. & Lucas, B. (2011) *The Learning Powered School: Pioneering 21st century education*. Bristol: TLO Ltd.

140 Trafton, A. (2018) Back-and-forth exchanges boost children's brain response to language, *MIT News Office*. Available at: http://news.mit.edu/2018/conversation-boost-childrens-brain-response-language-0214.

141 Willingham, D. (2007). Critical thinking: Why is it so hard to teach?, *American Educator*, Summer, pp. 8–19.

142 Willingham, D. (2019) *How To Teach Critical Thinking*. New South Wales (NSW) Department of Education.

143 For a fascinating introduction to the 'rationalists', a group of people who try to overcome human cognitive biases in order to be 'Less Wrong' about stuff, see Chivers, T. (2019) *The AI Does Not Hate You: Superintelligence, rationality and the race to save the world*. London: Weidenfeld & Nicolson.

144 Willingham, D. (2009) *Why Don't Students Like School?* San Francisco, CA: Jossey-Bass, p. 22, emphasis added.

145 e.g. see https://etonx.com/courses/critical-thinking or https://www.dulwich.org.uk/senior-school/free-learning/critical-thinking.

146 OCR (2011) *Level 2 Thinking and Reasoning Skills Specification*. OCR.

147 Some of this section originally appeared in Mannion, J. (2020) *Promoting independence through project-based learning*. Education Exchange: Chartered College of Teaching.

148 Hattie, J. (2012) *Visible Learning for Teachers: Maximizing impact on learning*. London: Routledge, p. 96.

149 Boekaerts, M. (2002) Bringing about change in the classroom: Strengths and weaknesses of the self-regulated learning approach, *Learning and Instruction*, 12(6), p. 594.

150 Schunk D. & Ertmer, P. (2000) Self-regulation and academic learning: Self-efficacy enhancing interventions. In M. Boekaerts, P. Pintrich & M. Zeidner (eds), *Handbook of Self-Regulation*, (pp. 631–649). San Diego, CA: Academic Press, p. 631, emphases added.

151 Schunk D. & Ertmer, P. (2000) Self-regulation and academic learning: Self-efficacy enhancing interventions. In M. Boekaerts, P. Pintrich & M. Zeidner (eds), *Handbook of Self-Regulation*, (pp. 631–649). San Diego, CA: Academic Press, p. 631.

152 HMG (2004) Every Child Matters: Change for children London: Her Majesty's Government. Available at: http://www.educationengland.org.uk/documents/pdfs/2004-ecm-change-for-children.pdf.

153 Humphrey, N., Lendrum, A. & Wigelsworth, M. (2010) Social and Emotional Aspects of Learning (SEAL) Programme in Secondary Schools: National evaluation. London: Department for Education. Available at: https://assets.publishing.service.gov.uk/government/uploads/system/uploads/attachment_data/file/181718/DFE-RR049.pdf.

154 Ofsted/Audit Commission (2003) *School Place Planning: The influence of school place planning on school standards and social inclusion*. London: Ofsted/Audit Commission. Available at: http://www.educationengland.org.uk/documents/pdfs/2003-school-place-planning.pdf.

155 e.g. see Banerjee, R., Watling, D. & Caputi, M. (2011) Peer relations and the understanding of *faux pas*: Longitudinal evidence for bidirectional associations, *Child Development*, 82(6), pp. 1887–1905.

156 For example, see Mosley, J. & Tew, M. (2013) *Quality Circle Time in the Secondary School*. London: David Fulton Publishers, Taylor and Francis.

157 The phrase 'ground rules', often traced back to sport (and specifically baseball), means 'local rules' in that sporting context. For example, at Wrigley Field, where the Chicago Cubs play, there is a wall covered in ivy. So at Wrigley Field, in addition to the usual rules of baseball, teams also agree to a local ground rule: if the ball gets stuck in the ivy, the player moves forward two bases; if it falls out of the ivy, the ball remains in play.

158 For a gripping account of the power of games, see McGonigal, J. (2015) *SuperBetter: A revolutionary approach to getting stronger, happier, braver and more resilient – powered by the science of games*. London: Harper Collins.

159 English, M.C. & Kitsantas, A. (2013) Supporting student self-regulated learning in problem- and project-based learning, *Interdisciplinary Journal of Problem-Based Learning*, 7(2), pp. 127–150.

160 Stefanou, C., Stolk, J.D., Prince, M., Chen, J.C. & Lord, S.M. (2013) Self-regulation and autonomy in problem- and project-based learning environments, *Active Learning in Higher Education*, 14(2), pp. 109–122.

161 Menzies, V., Hewitt, C., Kokotsaki, D., Collyer, C. & Wiggins, A. (2016) *Project Based Learning: Evaluation report and executive summary*. School of Education. Education Endowment Foundation.

162 Menzies, V., Hewitt, C., Kokotsaki, D., Collyer, C. & Wiggins, A. (2016) *Project Based Learning: Evaluation report and executive summary*. School of Education. Education Endowment Foundation, p. 4.

163 Menzies, V., Hewitt, C., Kokotsaki, D., Collyer, C. & Wiggins, A. (2016) *Project Based Learning: Evaluation report and executive summary*. School of Education. Education Endowment Foundation, p. 4.

164 Balemen, N. & Özer Keskin, M. (2018) The effectiveness of project-based learning on science education: A meta-analysis search, *International Online Journal of Education and Teaching*, 5(4), pp. 849–865.

165 Strobel, J., & van Barneveld, A. (2009) When is PBL more effective? A meta-synthesis of meta-analyses comparing pbl to conventional classrooms, *Interdisciplinary Journal of Problem-Based Learning*, 3(1), pp. 44–58.

166 Walker, A. & Leary, H. (2009) A problem based learning meta analysis: Differences across problem types, implementation types, disciplines, and assessment levels, *Interdisciplinary Journal of Problem-Based Learning*, 3(1), pp. 12–43.

167 Duckworth, C., Akerman, R., MacGregor, A., Salter, E. & Vorhaus, J. (2009) *Self-Regulated Learning: A literature review*. Centre for Research on wider benefits of learning: Research Reports 33, p. i.

168 Duckworth, C., Akerman, R., MacGregor, A., Salter, E. & Vorhaus, J. (2009) *Self-Regulated Learning: A literature review*. Centre for Research on wider benefits of learning: Research Reports 33, p. ii.

169 Barron, B. & Darling-Hammond, L. (2008) *Teaching for meaningful learning: A review of research on inquiry-based and cooperative learning. Powerful Learning: What We Know About Teaching for Understanding*, (pp. 11–70). San Francisco, CA: Jossey-Bass.

170 Condliffe, B., Quint, J., Visher, M.G., Bangser, M.R., Drohojowska, S., Saco, L. & Nelson, E. (2017) *Project-Based Learning – A literature review*. New York, NY: MDRC, p.iii. Available at: https://www.mdrc.org/sites/default/files/Project-Based_Learning-LitRev_Final.pdf.

171 Condliffe, B., Quint, J., Visher, M.G., Bangser, M.R., Drohojowska, S., Saco, L. & Nelson, E. (2017) *Project-Based Learning – A literature review*. New York, NY: MDRC, pp. 50–51. Available at: https://www.mdrc.org/sites/default/files/Project-Based_Learning-LitRev_Final.pdf.

172 This was really quite amazing. See here: https://dengarden.com/landscaping/How-to-Build-a-Greenhouse-Made-From-Plastic-Bottles.

173 e.g. James, M. & McCormick, R. (2009) Teachers learning how to learn, *Teaching and Teacher Education*, 25(7), pp. 973–982.

174 See, for example, Blossom, Y., Yung-Kai, L., Cheng-Chieh, L. & Tien-Tse, L. (2013) Job autonomy, its predispositions and its relation to work outcomes in community health centers in Taiwan, *Health Promotion International*, 28(2), pp. 166–177.

175 Watkins, C. (2001) *Learning about learning enhances performance*. London: Institute of Education National School Improvement Network (Research Matters series No 13), p. 7.

176 e.g. see Fortier, M.S., Vallerand, R.J. & Guay, F. (1995) Academic motivation and school performance: Toward a structural model, *Contemporary Educational Psychology*, 20, pp. 257–274.

177 Kirschner, P. & van Merriënboer, J.G. (2013) Do learners really know best? Urban legends in education, *Educational Psychologist*, 48(3), p. 178.

178 Deci, E. & Ryan, R. (1985) *Intrinsic Motivation and Self-determination in Human Behaviour*. New York, NY: Plenum Press.

179 For example, see Harris, S. (2011) Government to crackdown on the 'Mickey Mouse' GCSEs introduced by Labour. *Daily Mail*, 7 May. Available at: http://www.dailymail.co.uk/news/article-1384470/Crackdown-soft-GCSEs-introduced-Labour.html.

180 Gove, M. (2012) *Secretary of State for Education Michael Gove gives speech to IAA.* 14 November. Available at: https://www.gov.uk/government/speeches/secretary-of-state-for-education-michael-gove-gives-speech-to-iaa.

181 Harrison, N., James, D. & Last, K. (2012) *The impact of the pursuit of ASDAN's Certificate of Personal Effectiveness (CoPE) on GCSE attainment. Project Report.* UWE/ASDAN. Available at: http://eprints.uwe.ac.uk/16808.

182 ASDAN (2018) *ASDAN Level 2 Award of Personal Effectiveness Specification.* Available at: https://www.asdan.org.uk/courses/qualifications/award-of-personal-effectiveness.

183 Peters, S. (2012) *The Chimp Paradox: The mind management program to help you achieve success, confidence, and happiness*. London: Vermilion.

184 Andrew Weil 4–7–8 Breathing Technique: https://www.youtube.com/watch?v=_-C_VNM1Vd0.

185 Other energy drinks are available.

186 Scutt, C. (2019) Using Cognitive Science in Education: Selected reading, *Chartered College of Teaching Research Reviews*. Available at: https://my.chartered.college/2019/12/using-cognitive-science-in-education-selected-reading.

187 https://www.learningscientists.org/.

188 https://cogscisci.wordpress.com/.

189 https://sites.google.com/view/developingminds.

190 A recent episode of the *Education Research Reading Room* podcast with Catherine Scott makes the case for meta-memory brilliantly, and is well worth an hour of your time. Available at: http://www.ollielovell.com/errr/catherinescott.

191 Dunlosky, J. & Bjork, R. (2008) The integrated nature of metamemory and memory. In J. Dunlosky, R. Bjork, (eds), *Handbook of Memory and Metamemory*, (pp. 11–28). Psychology Press, p. 11.

192 Flavell, J. (1971) First discussant's comments: What is memory development the development of?, *Human Development*, 14, pp. 272–278.

193 Flavell, J. (1971) First discussant's comments: What is memory development the development of?, *Human Development*, 14, pp. p. 277.

194 Karably, K. & Zabrucky, K.M. (2009) Children's metamemory: A review of the literature and implications for the classroom, *International Electronic Journal of Elementary Education*, 2(1), pp. 32–52.

195 Kirschner, P.A., Sweller. J. & Clark, R.E. (2006) Why minimal guidance during instruction does not work: An analysis of the failure of constructivist, discovery, problem-based, experiential, and inquiry-based teaching, *Educational Psychologist*, 41(2), p. 75–77.

196 Mannion, J. (2016) *A Glossary of Learning Terms*. Available at: https://rethinking-ed.org/a-glossary-of-learning-terms.

197 Mannion, J. (2016) *Learning is Multidimensional: Embrace the complexity!* Guest blog for the Learning Scientists: 6 December. Available at: http://www.learningscientists.org/blog/2016/12/6-1.

198 Watkins, C. (2001) *Learning about learning enhances performance*. London, Institute of Education National School Improvement Network (Research Matters series No 13), p. 1.

199 Graham, S., McKeown, D., Kiuhara, S. & Harris, K.R. (2012) A meta-analysis of writing instruction for students in the elementary grades, *Journal of Educational Psychology*, 104, pp. 879–896.

200 Goldberg, A., Russell, M., Cook, A. & Russell, E.M. (2003) The effect of computers on student writing: A meta-analysis of studies from 1992 to 2002, *The Journal of Technology, Learning, and Assessment*, 2, pp. 2–51.

201 Poole, D.M. & Preciado, M.K. (2016) Touch typing instruction: Elementary teachers' beliefs and practices, *Computers and Education*, 102, pp. 1–14.

202 van Weerdenburg, M., Tesselhof, M. & van der Meijden, H. (2019) Touch-typing for better spelling and narrative-writing skills on the computer, *Journal of Computer Assisted Learning*, 35, pp. 143–152.

203 https://www.typingclub.com.

204 https://www.typingclub.com.

205 McGrew, S., Breakstone, J., Ortega, T., Smith, M. & Wineburg, S. (2018) Can students evaluate online sources? Learning from assessments of civic online reasoning, *Theory & Research in Social Education*, 46, pp. 1–29.

206 Wineburg, S. & McGrew, S. (2017) Lateral reading: Reading less and learning more when evaluating digital information (Stanford History Education Group Working Paper No. 2017-A1). Available at: https://papers.ssrn.com/sol3/papers.cfm?abstract_id=3048994 or http://dx.doi.org/10.2139/ssrn.3048994.

207 Wineburg, S. & McGrew, S. (2017) Lateral reading: Reading less and learning more when evaluating digital information (Stanford History Education Group Working Paper No. 2017-A1). Available at: https://papers.ssrn.com/sol3/papers.cfm?abstract_id=3048994 or http://dx.doi.org/10.2139/ssrn.3048994, p. 1.

208 Willingham, D. (2017) *Here's a 21st century skill – and how to teach it!* Available at: http://www.danielwillingham.com/daniel-willingham-science-and-education-blog/heres-a-21st-century-skill-and-how-to-teach-it .

209 Horn, S. & Veermans, K. (2019) Critical thinking efficacy and transfer skills defend against 'fake news' at an international school in Finland, *Journal of Research in International Education*, 18(1), pp. 23–41.

210 Morisano, D., Hirsh, J., Peterson, J., Pihl, R. & Shore, B. (2010) Setting, elaborating, and reflecting on personal goals improves academic performance, *The Journal of Applied Psychology*, 95, pp. 255–264.

211 Schippers, M., Scheepers, A. & Peterson, J. (2015) A scalable goal-setting intervention closes both the gender and ethnic minority achievement gap, *Palgrave Commun*, 1, 15014.

212 Finnie, R., Poirier, W., Bozkurt, E., Peterson, J.B., Fricker, T. & Pratt, M. (2017) *Using Future Authoring to Improve Student Outcomes*. Toronto: Higher Education Quality Council of Ontario. Available at: http://www.heqco.ca/SiteCollectionDocuments/HEQCO%20Formatted_EPRI-Mohawk.pdf.

213 Sutcliffe, R., Bigglestone, T. & Buckley, J. (2019) *Thinking Moves, A to Z: Metacognition made simple*. London: Dialogue Works.

214 https://oracycambridge.org/wp-content/uploads/2020/06/The-Oracy-Skills-Framework-and-Glossary.pdf.

215 Maxwell, B., Burnett, C., Reidy, J., Willis, B. & Demack, S. (2015) Oracy Curriculum, Culture and Assessment Toolkit Evaluation report and Executive summary. Education Endowment Foundation. Available at: https://educationendowmentfoundation.org.uk/projects-and-evaluation/projects/voice-21-pilot.

216 https://educationendowmentfoundation.org.uk/projects-and-evaluation/projects/voice-21-pilot.

217 Voice 21 (2019) *The Oracy Benchmarks*. Voice 21. Available at https://voice21.org/wp-content/uploads/2019/11/Benchmarks-report.pdf.

218 Lancaster, S. (2016) *Speak Like a Leader*. Presentation at TEDxVerona. Available at: https://www.youtube.com/watch?v=bGBamfWasNQ.

219 This extract is available from many sources, including: Winston Churchill's inspiring wartime speeches in Parliament, *BBC News*, 8 May 2020. Available at: https://www.bbc.com/news/uk-politics-52588148.

220 Lancaster, S. (2018) *You Are Not Human: How words kill.* London: Biteback.

221 Quoted in Chomsky & Krauss: An Origins Project Dialogue (OFFICIAL) – (Part 1/2). Available at: https://youtu.be/MI1G919Bts0?t=620.

222 Lancaster, S. (2016) *The Rule of Three: A top speechwriter explains....* Available at: https://www.youtube.com/watch?v=Dd2yd1qOtng.

223 Crawford, C., Macmillan, L. & Vignoles, A. (2014) *Progress made by high-attaining children from disadvantaged backgrounds: research report.* Social Mobility Commission. Available at: http://dera.ioe.ac.uk/20433/1/High_attainers_progress_report_final.pdf.

224 Oakes, S. & Griffin, M. (2016) *The A Level Mindset: 40 activities for transforming student commitment, motivation and productivity.* Carmarthen: Crown House.

225 Gutman, L.M. & Schoon, I. (2013) *The impact of non-cognitive skills on outcomes for young people. Literature review.* An Institute of Education report for the Department for Education. Available at https://helmtraining.co.uk/wp-content/uploads/2017/03/Gutman-and-Schoon-Impact-of-non-cognitive-skills-on-outcomes-for-young-people-1.pdf.

226 Oakes, S. & Griffin, M. (2018) *The Student Mindset: A 30-item toolkit for anyone learning anything.* Carmarthen: Crown House.

Chapter 6

1 It is very deep indeed.

2 Downey, C., Byrne, J. & Souza, A. (2013) Leading and managing the competence-based curriculum: Conscripts, volunteers and champions at work within the departmentalised environment of the secondary school, *The Curriculum Journal*, 23(4), p. 378.

3 Education Policy Institute (2019) *Education in England: Annual Report 2019.* Available at https://epi.org.uk/publications-and-research/annual-report-2019/.

4 Education Policy Institute (2019) *Education in England: Annual Report 2019.* Available at https://epi.org.uk/publications-and-research/annual-report-2019, p. 18.

5 Education Policy Institute (2019) *Education in England: Annual Report 2019.* Available at https://epi.org.uk/publications-and-research/annual-report-2019, p. 18. (And this was before COVID-19.)

6 Rock, L. (2012) Thousands of pupils shamed out of free school meals, *the Guardian*, 23 Sept. Available at https://www.theguardian.com/education/2012/sep/23/free-school-meals-stigma.

7 For a detailed account of all data strands, see Mannion, J. (2018) Metacognition, self-regulation, oracy: A mixed methods case study of a complex, whole-school Learning to Learn intervention. PhD thesis, Hughes Hall, University of Cambridge. Available at: https://www.repository.cam.ac.uk/handle/1810/289131.

8 To explore the baseline analysis in more detail, see Mannion, J. (2018) Metacognition, self-regulation, oracy: A mixed methods case study of a complex, whole-school Learning to Learn intervention. PhD thesis, Hughes Hall, University of Cambridge. Available at: https://www.repository.cam.ac.uk/handle/1810/289131.

9 This is a simplified explanation of statistical significance testing, and it's actually a hotly contested area, with some people saying we should stop using it altogether. See, for example, Amrhein, V., Greenland, S. & McShane, B. (2019) Scientists rise up against statistical significance, *Nature*, 567(7748), pp. 305–307.

10 Wiliam, D. (1998) *The validity of teacher assessments.* Paper presented at the 22nd annual conference of the International Group for the Psychology of Mathematics Education, Stellenbosch, South Africa.

11 Tymms, P., Merrell, C. & Bailey, K. (2017) The long-term impact of effective teaching, *School Effectiveness and School Improvement*, 29(2), pp. 242–261.
12 Because only headline figures were available, it was not possible to carry out statistical significance testing on the ATL data.
13 Braun, V. & Clarke V. (2006) Using thematic analysis in psychology, *Qualitative Research in Psychology*, 3(2), pp. 77–101.
14 Because we are interested in the content of the journal entries and not the students' literacy skills, in some instances spellings have been corrected in the excerpts included here.
15 Watkins, C. (2001) Learning about Learning Enhances Performance, *London: Institute of Education School Improvement Network*, Research Matters series No. 13.
16 Watkins, C. (2010). Learning, Performance and Improvement, *London, Institute of Education, International Network for School Improvement*, Research Matters Series No 34.

Chapter 7

1 Peacock, A. (2016) *Learning without limits*. Presentation at TEDxNorwich. Available at: https://www.youtube.com/watch?v=8oxxPi6c-Nw.
2 Dobelli, R. (2013) *The Art of Thinking Clearly*. London: Hodder & Stoughton.
3 Dobelli, R. (2013) *The Art of Thinking Clearly*. London: Hodder & Stoughton., p. 23.
4 Dobelli, R. (2013) *The Art of Thinking Clearly*. London: Hodder & Stoughton, p. 18.
5 Simpson makes this point forcefully in a fascinating episode of the *Education Research Reading Room* podcast called 'Critiquing the meta-analysis', available at ollielovell.com/errr/adriansimpson.
6 To explore this in more detail, please see Mannion, J. (2018) Metacognition, self-regulation, oracy: A mixed methods case study of a complex, whole-school Learning to Learn intervention. PhD thesis, Hughes Hall, University of Cambridge. Available at: https://www.repository.cam.ac.uk/handle/1810/289131.
7 Mannion, J. (2018) Metacognition, self-regulation, oracy: A mixed methods case study of a complex, whole-school Learning to Learn intervention. PhD thesis, Hughes Hall, University of Cambridge. Available at: https://www.repository.cam.ac.uk/handle/1810/289131.
8 Mannion, J. (2019) *Teacher talk: the beating heart of effective professional learning and development*. Oracy Cambridge. Available at: https://oracycambridge.org/2019/06/13/teacher-talk.

Chapter 8

1 Kelly, B. (2014) *Science, Change and Accountability: Making Use of Implementation Science*. Keynote presentation at the 'Implementing Implementation Science' conference, University of Cambridge, 28 July.
2 Flavell, J.H. (1979) Metacognition and cognitive monitoring: A new area of cognitive–developmental inquiry. *American Psychologist*, 34(10), p. 910.
3 Thompson, M. & Wiliam, D. (2008) Tight but loose: a conceptual framework for scaling up school reforms. In E.C. Wylie (ed.), *Tight but loose: scaling up teacher professional development in diverse contexts* (RR-08-29, pp. 1–44). Princeton, NJ: Educational Testing Service, p. 35.
4 Gawande, A. (2009) *The Checklist Manifesto: How to Get Things Right*. New York, NY: Metropolitan Books.

5 Allen, D. (2001) *Getting Things Done: The Art of Stress-Free Productivity*. London: Penguin Books Ltd.
6 Kelly B (2012) Implementation Science for Psychology in Education. In: B. Kelly and D.F. Perkins (eds), *Handbook of Implementation Science for Psychology in Education*. Cambridge: Cambridge University Press.
7. Some people don't like the phrase 'vertical slice' because it implies hierarchy; they prefer to describe the team as cross-sectional, or representative, or simply a 'change team'. But the name doesn't really matter – it's the principle of having an implementation team comprising a range of stakeholders that's the thing.
8. Claxton, G., Chambers, M., Powell, G. & Lucas, B. (2011) *The Learning Powered School: Pioneering 21st Century Education*. Bristol: TLO Ltd, p4.

Chapter 9

1 Gendler, R. (1988) *The Book of Qualities*. New York, NY: Harper Perennial.
2 Rowling, J.K. (2008) From a speech given at a Harvard commencement. Available at: https://news.harvard.edu/gazette/story/2008/06/text-of-j-k-rowling-speech/.
3 Cited in Canfield, J., Hansen, M. & Hewitt, L. (2001) *The Power of Focus*. London: Vermilion, p. 168.
4 Education Endowment Foundation (2020) *The Teaching and Learning Toolkit*. Available at: https://educationendowmentfoundation.org.uk/evidence-summaries/teaching-learning-toolkit/meta-cognition-and-self-regulation.
5 Herbert, F. (1965) *Dune*. Philadelphia, PA: Chilton Books.
6 Marks, I. (1979) Exposure therapy for phobias and obsessive-compulsive disorders, *Hospital Practice*, 14(2), pp. 101–108.
7 de Silva, P. & Rachman, S. (1981) Is exposure a necessary condition for fear-reduction?, *Behaviour Research and Therapy*, 19(3), pp. 227–232.
8 Milad, M.R. & Quirk, G.J. (2012) Fear extinction as a model for translational neuroscience: ten years of progress, *Annual Review of Psychology*, 63, pp. 129–151.
9 Worth, J. (2018) Latest teacher retention statistics paint a bleak picture for teacher supply in England, *National Foundation for Educational Research*. Available at: https://www.nfer.ac.uk/news-events/nfer-blogs/latest-teacher-retention-statistics-paint-a-bleak-picture-for-teacher-supply-in-england.
10 Ball, S.J. (2003) The teacher's soul and the terrors of performativity, *Journal of Education Policy*, 18(2), pp. 215–228.
11 Emerson, R.W. (1870) Society and Solitude. In R.A. Bosco and D.E. Wilson (eds), *The Collected Works of Ralph Waldo Emerson, VII* (2007). Cambridge, MA: Harvard University Press, p. 132.
12 Howard, V. (1975) *The Power of Your Supermind*. Camarillo, CA: DeVorss & Company, pp. 37–38.
13 OXFAM (2019) *The Power of Education to Fight inequality: How increasing educational inequality and quality is crucial to fighting economic and gender inequality*. Oxfam Briefing Paper – September 2019. Oxfam International.
14 Tomsett, J. (2015) *This much I know about love over fear... Creating a culture for truly great teaching*. Camarthen: Crown House, p. 40.
15 Francis, B. (2020) The disadvantage gap has grown – here's how we fix it. *Times Educational Supplement*, 3 June. Available at: https://www.tes.com/news/disadvantage-gap-has-grown-heres-how-we-fix-it.
16 Francis, B. (2020) The disadvantage gap has grown – here's how we fix it. *Times Educational Supplement*, 3 June. Available at: https://www.tes.com/news/disadvantage-gap-has-grown-heres-how-we-fix-it.

INDEX